GIRL GENIUS ®

AGATHA HETERODYNE
& THE
CHAPEL OF BONES

A Gaslamp Fantasy
with
ADVENTURE, ROMANCE & MAD SCIENCE

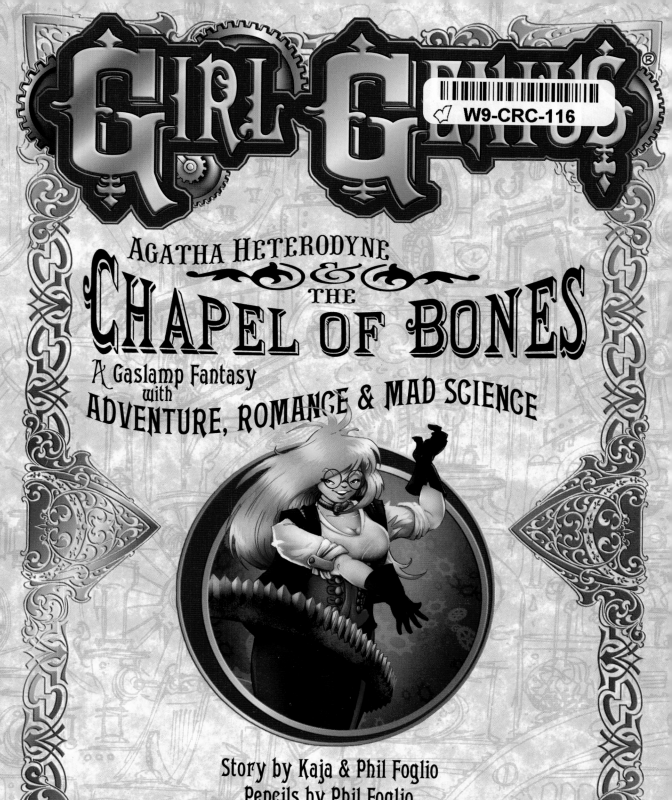

Story by Kaja & Phil Foglio
Pencils by Phil Foglio
Colors by Cheyenne Wright

AIRSHIP
ENTERTAINMENT

OTHER BOOKS FROM AIRSHIP ENTERTAINMENT AND STUDIO FOGLIO

Girl Genius® Graphic Novels

Girl Genius Volume One:
Agatha Heterodyne and the Beetleburg Clank

Girl Genius Volume Two:
Agatha Heterodyne and the Airship City

Girl Genius Volume Three:
Agatha Heterodyne and the Monster Engine

Girl Genius Volume Four:
Agatha Heterodyne and the Circus of Dreams

Girl Genius Volume Five:
Agatha Heterodyne and the Clockwork Princess

Girl Genius Volume Six:
Agatha Heterodyne and the Golden Trilobite

Girl Genius Volume Seven:
Agatha Heterodyne and the Voice of the Castle

Girl Genius Volume Eight:
Agatha Heterodyne and the Chapel of Bones

Other Graphic Novels

What's New with Phil & Dixie Collection

Robert Asprin's MythAdventures®

Buck Godot, zap gun for hire:
• *Three Short Stories*
• *PSmIth*
• *The Gallimaufry*

Girl Genius® is published by:
Airship Entertainment™: a happy part of Studio Foglio, LLC
2400 NW 80th St #129 Seattle WA 98117-4449, USA

Please visit our Web sites at www.airshipbooks.com and www.girlgenius.net

Story by Phil & Kaja Foglio. Pencils by Phil Foglio. Main story colors by Cheyenne Wright. Selected spot illustrations colored by Kaja Foglio and/or Cheyenne Wright. Logos, Lettering, Artist Bullying & Book Design by Kaja. Fonts mostly by Comicraft– www.comicbookfonts.com.

This material originally appeared from February 2008-November 2008 at www.girlgenius.net.

Published simultaneously in Hardcover (ISBN 978-1-890856-48-9) and Softcover (ISBN 978-1-890856-47-2) editions.

First Printing: May 2009   PRINTED IN THE USA

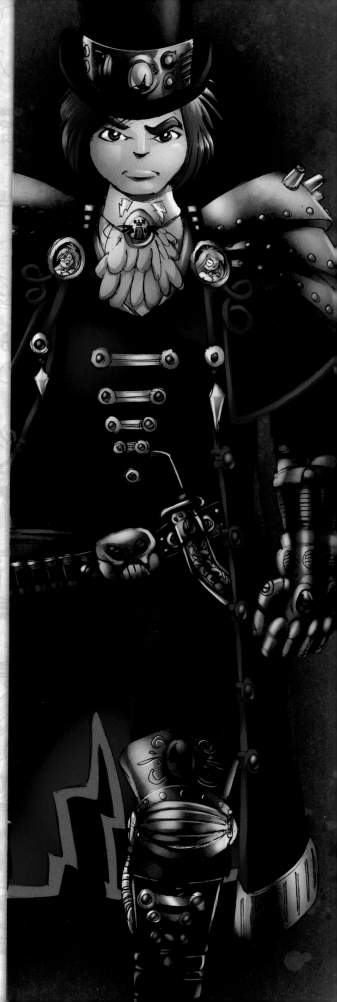

Special thanks to Russ Tarleton, who once summed it up like this: "It's my job to assume that everyone in the World is insane and wants to hurt you." We've been so glad to have you holding our hands through all those contracts—what *would* we do without you?

KAJA FOGLIO

Before she was ignominiously transferred to the Department of Creative History, Professor Foglio occupied the Anna Russell Chair of Operatic Appreciation & Extreme Patience at Transylvania Polygnostic University's own College of Music and Harmonious Animal Noises. It was there that she made her breakthroughs in atonal musical notation that allowed scholars to faithfully reproduce the sounds of jackhammers, howler monkeys, and even the snores of other professors who happened to share the same office as she, (and yet had the nerve to swear that they themselves did not snore.) In the spirit of academic goodwill, these professors shall, at this time, go unnamed. *Dear.*

PHIL FOGLIO

Before he was lured to the ivory-covered ivy towers of T.P.U., Professor Foglio prepared himself for his future life of academic adventure by raising porcupines for their pelts. From these simple creatures, he learned many valuable life skills, the most important being: "If You Are Weird And Dangerous, People Won't Eat You…Unless They Are *Extremely Hungry.*" A lesson he has taken care to remember. Eventually, this idyllic period of his life came to an end when a freak tornado swept away his entire porcupine herd and deposited them upon the superstructure of the giant airship *Castle Wulfenbach.* To everyone's surprise, they have thrived in their new aerial home, and, to this day, remain a serious threat to The Empire. Professor Foglio does *not snore.*

CHEYENNE WRIGHT

Once a year, Professor Wright leaves the hermetically sealed vault where he stores his chromatic engines and indulges in field research in the great Wieliczka Salt Mine near Krakow. There, hundreds of meters beneath the ground, he attempts to explain color theory to a tribe of blind mole-men he discovered while on vacation. It is, he grudgingly admits, a "tough room." While they have yet to be able to color-coordinate, the grateful subter-restrials have declared him a god, which places him in an unusual tax bracket. They also insist on supplying him with regular tributes of salt, cave crickets, and sodium chloride. He worries about his blood pressure, but affirms that the crickets taste "disturbingly delicious." Recipes can be found at: *www.arcanetimes.com.*

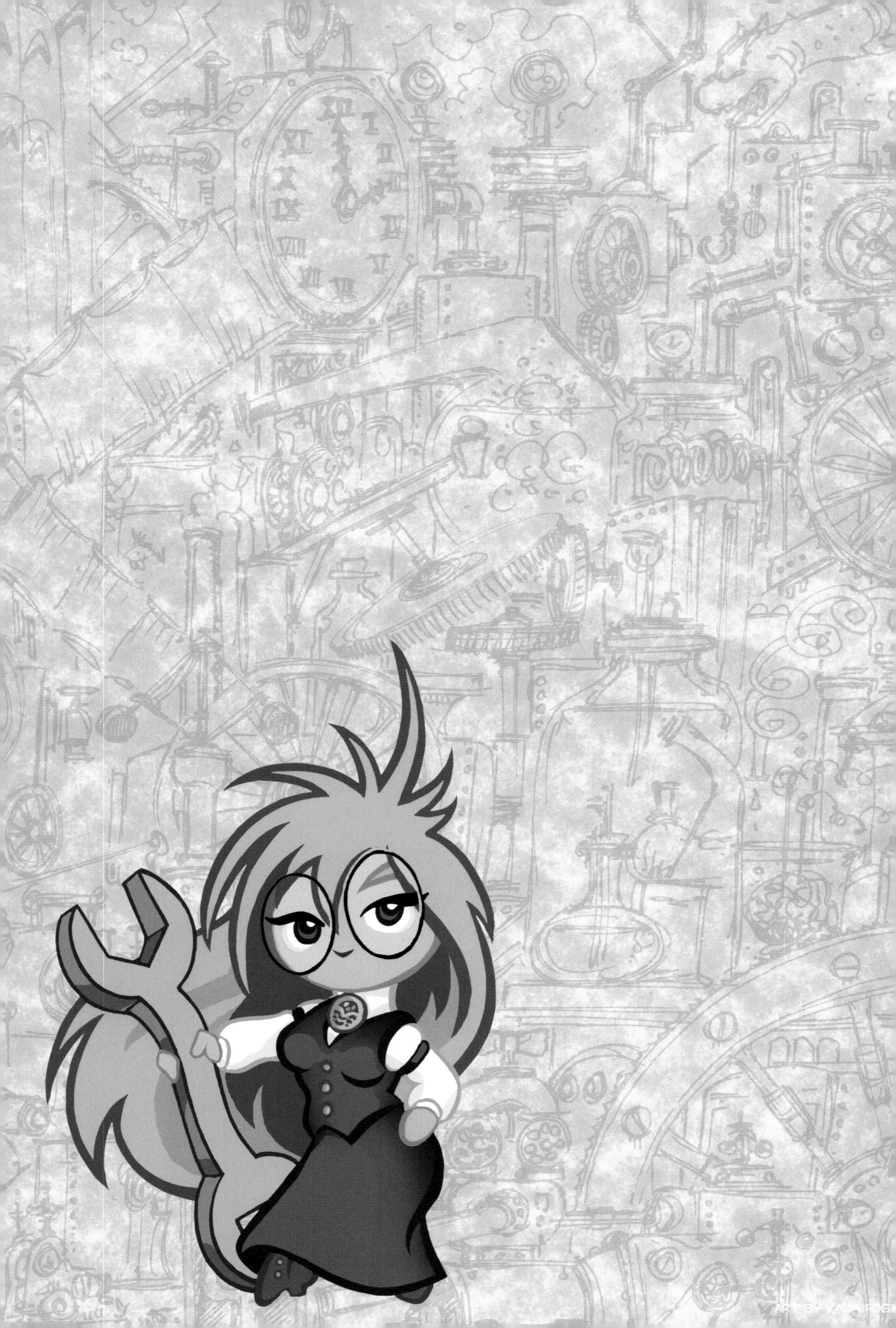
ART BY KAJA FOG

· THE STORY SO FAR ·

Agatha Clay was an unlucky student at Transylvania Polygnostic University, until an accident revealed her hidden "spark:" a capacity for mad science beyond the reach of all but the most gifted. This alone would have been enough to bring her to the attention of Baron Wulfenbach, the powerful Spark who held the fractious ruling houses of Europa under his thumb, but Agatha was *also* the last of the famous Heterodyne family–beloved folk heroes who disappeared many years ago. This troubled the Baron. The return of a Heterodyne would have a destabilizing effect upon the peace he had spent the last two decades building. The Baron was also displeased because his only son, Gilgamesh, had fallen in love with Agatha. While uniting the houses of Wulfenbach and Heterodyne would have solved many political problems, The Baron had excellent reasons to believe that Agatha was actually a malevolent entity known as "The Other," who almost destroyed Europa twenty years before.

Agatha made her way across Europa to Mechanicsburg, the ancestral home of the Heterodyne family. Along the way, she was befriended by Zeetha, the lost princess of the lost city of Skifander; Krosp, a construct engineered to be the Emperor of all Cats; and the players of *Master Payne's Traveling Circus of Adventure!* She also won the loyalty of the Jägermonsters: a group of construct soldiers who served the Heterodyne family in darker days when the Heterodynes were not heroes, but a bloodthirsty scourge upon the neighboring lands.

In the town of Sturmhalten, Agatha ran afoul of the Knights of Jove: a secret society whose agenda is still unclear, but seems to involve the downfall of the Baron, and *either* the return of the diabolical "Other" *or* the legendary "Storm King" who once united Europa in a brief golden age. There, Agatha met Tarvek Sturmvoraus, a descendant of the original Storm King. Agatha was briefly possessed by the mind of the "Other," and a bid for power within the order left Sturmhalten crawling with monsters and surrounded by Wulfenbach troops. Tarvek was captured, but Agatha fought her way to freedom, badly injuring the Baron in the process.

Now, Agatha is in Mechanicsburg. The Baron is also in the town, recovering from his injuries in Mechanicsburg's famous hospital. A faction of the Knights of Jove has already made an attempt to take the town and capture the Baron, but their army of war clanks was single-handedly wiped out by Gilgamesh Wulfenbach. Another faction has just flown in a charismatic girl claiming to be Agatha. This imposter has already entered Castle Heterodyne.

The Castle is a self-aware mechanical fortress which was badly damaged in the war with the "Other." Ongoing repairs are made by the Baron's worst convicts. Agatha has disguised herself as one of these. Her only hope of survival is to repair the castle and activate the town's defenses, before the Baron's peace is shattered and hostile forces overwhelm her town.

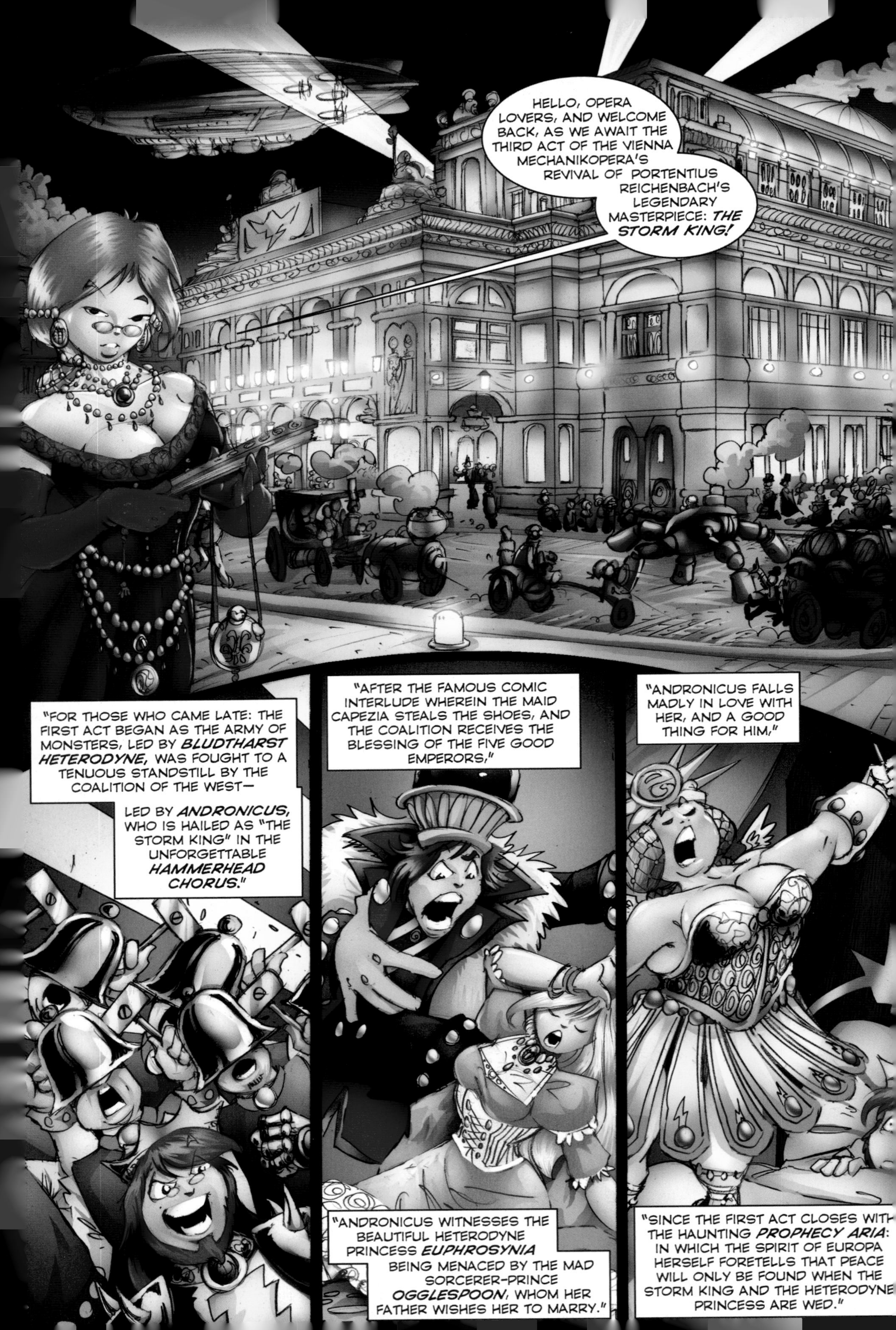
HELLO, OPERA LOVERS, AND WELCOME BACK, AS WE AWAIT THE THIRD ACT OF THE VIENNA MECHANIKOPERA'S REVIVAL OF PORTENTIUS REICHENBACH'S LEGENDARY MASTERPIECE: THE STORM KING!
"FOR THOSE WHO CAME LATE: THE FIRST ACT BEGAN AS THE ARMY OF MONSTERS, LED BY BLUDTHARST HETERODYNE, WAS FOUGHT TO A TENUOUS STANDSTILL BY THE COALITION OF THE WEST—
LED BY ANDRONICUS, WHO IS HAILED AS "THE STORM KING" IN THE UNFORGETTABLE HAMMERHEAD CHORUS."
"AFTER THE FAMOUS COMIC INTERLUDE WHEREIN THE MAID CAPEZIA STEALS THE SHOES, AND THE COALITION RECEIVES THE BLESSING OF THE FIVE GOOD EMPERORS,"
"ANDRONICUS WITNESSES THE BEAUTIFUL HETERODYNE PRINCESS EUPHROSYNIA
BEING MENACED BY THE MAD SORCERER-PRINCE OGGLESPOON, WHOM HER FATHER WISHES HER TO MARRY."
"ANDRONICUS FALLS MADLY IN LOVE WITH HER, AND A GOOD THING FOR HIM,"
"SINCE THE FIRST ACT CLOSES WITH THE HAUNTING PROPHECY ARIA: IN WHICH THE SPIRIT OF EUROPA HERSELF FORETELLS THAT PEACE WILL ONLY BE FOUND WHEN THE STORM KING AND THE HETERODYNE PRINCESS ARE WED."

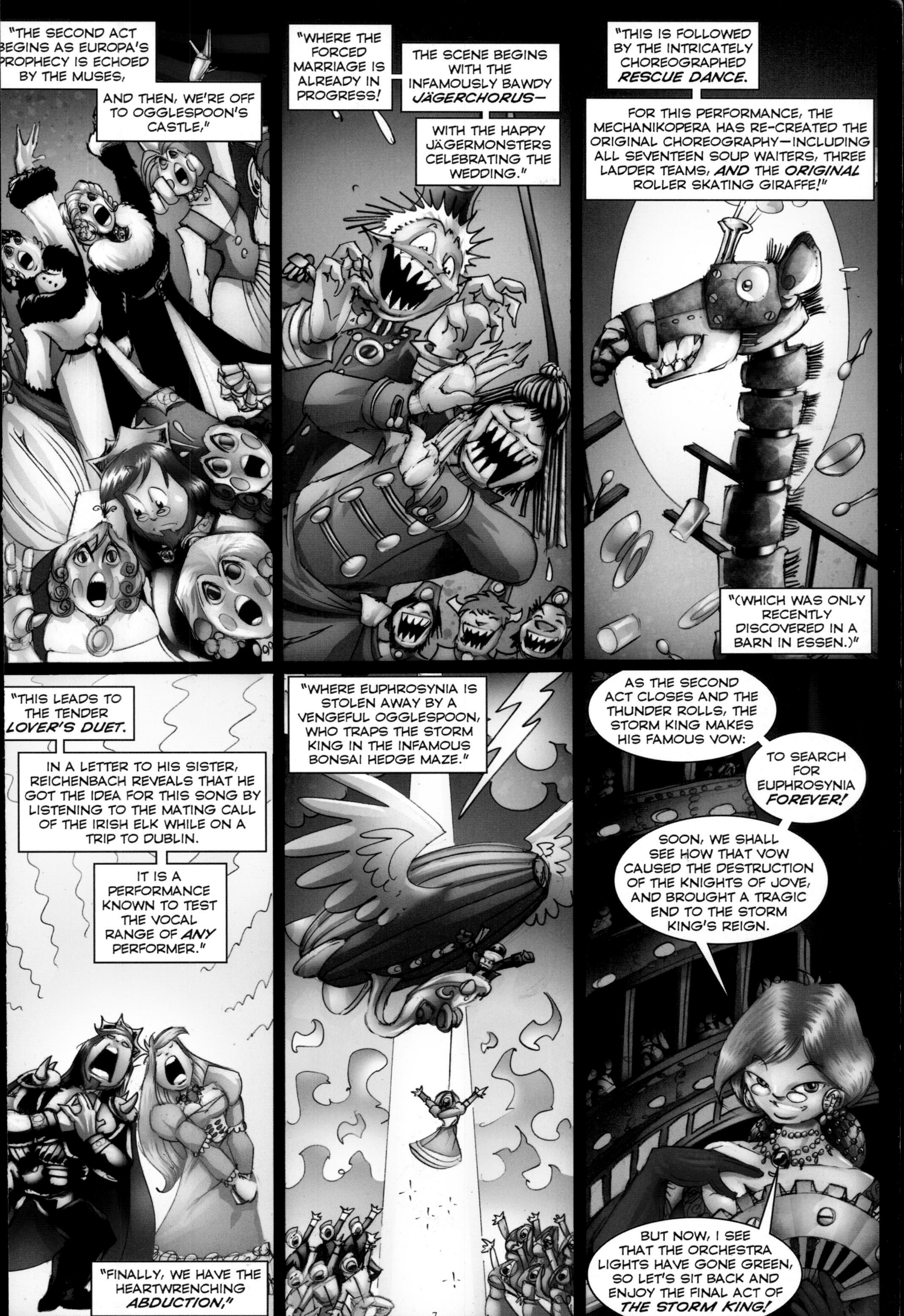
"THE SECOND ACT BEGINS AS EUROPA'S PROPHECY IS ECHOED BY THE MUSES,
AND THEN, WE'RE OFF TO OGGLESPOON'S CASTLE,"
"WHERE THE FORCED MARRIAGE IS ALREADY IN PROGRESS!
THE SCENE BEGINS WITH THE INFAMOUSLY BAWDY *JÄGERCHORUS*—
WITH THE HAPPY JÄGERMONSTERS CELEBRATING THE WEDDING."
"THIS IS FOLLOWED BY THE INTRICATELY CHOREOGRAPHED *RESCUE DANCE*.
FOR THIS PERFORMANCE, THE MECHANIKOPERA HAS RE-CREATED THE ORIGINAL CHOREOGRAPHY—INCLUDING ALL SEVENTEEN SOUP WAITERS, THREE LADDER TEAMS, *AND* THE *ORIGINAL* ROLLER SKATING GIRAFFE!"
"(WHICH WAS ONLY RECENTLY DISCOVERED IN A BARN IN ESSEN.)"
"THIS LEADS TO THE TENDER *LOVER'S DUET*.
IN A LETTER TO HIS SISTER, REICHENBACH REVEALS THAT HE GOT THE IDEA FOR THIS SONG BY LISTENING TO THE MATING CALL OF THE IRISH ELK WHILE ON A TRIP TO DUBLIN.
IT IS A PERFORMANCE KNOWN TO TEST THE VOCAL RANGE OF *ANY* PERFORMER."
"FINALLY, WE HAVE THE HEARTWRENCHING *ABDUCTION*,"
"WHERE EUPHROSYNIA IS STOLEN AWAY BY A VENGEFUL OGGLESPOON, WHO TRAPS THE STORM KING IN THE INFAMOUS BONSAI HEDGE MAZE."
AS THE SECOND ACT CLOSES AND THE THUNDER ROLLS, THE STORM KING MAKES HIS FAMOUS VOW:
TO SEARCH FOR EUPHROSYNIA *FOREVER!*
SOON, WE SHALL SEE HOW THAT VOW CAUSED THE DESTRUCTION OF THE KNIGHTS OF JOVE, AND BROUGHT A TRAGIC END TO THE STORM KING'S REIGN.
BUT NOW, I SEE THAT THE ORCHESTRA LIGHTS HAVE GONE GREEN, SO LET'S SIT BACK AND ENJOY THE FINAL ACT OF *THE STORM KING!*

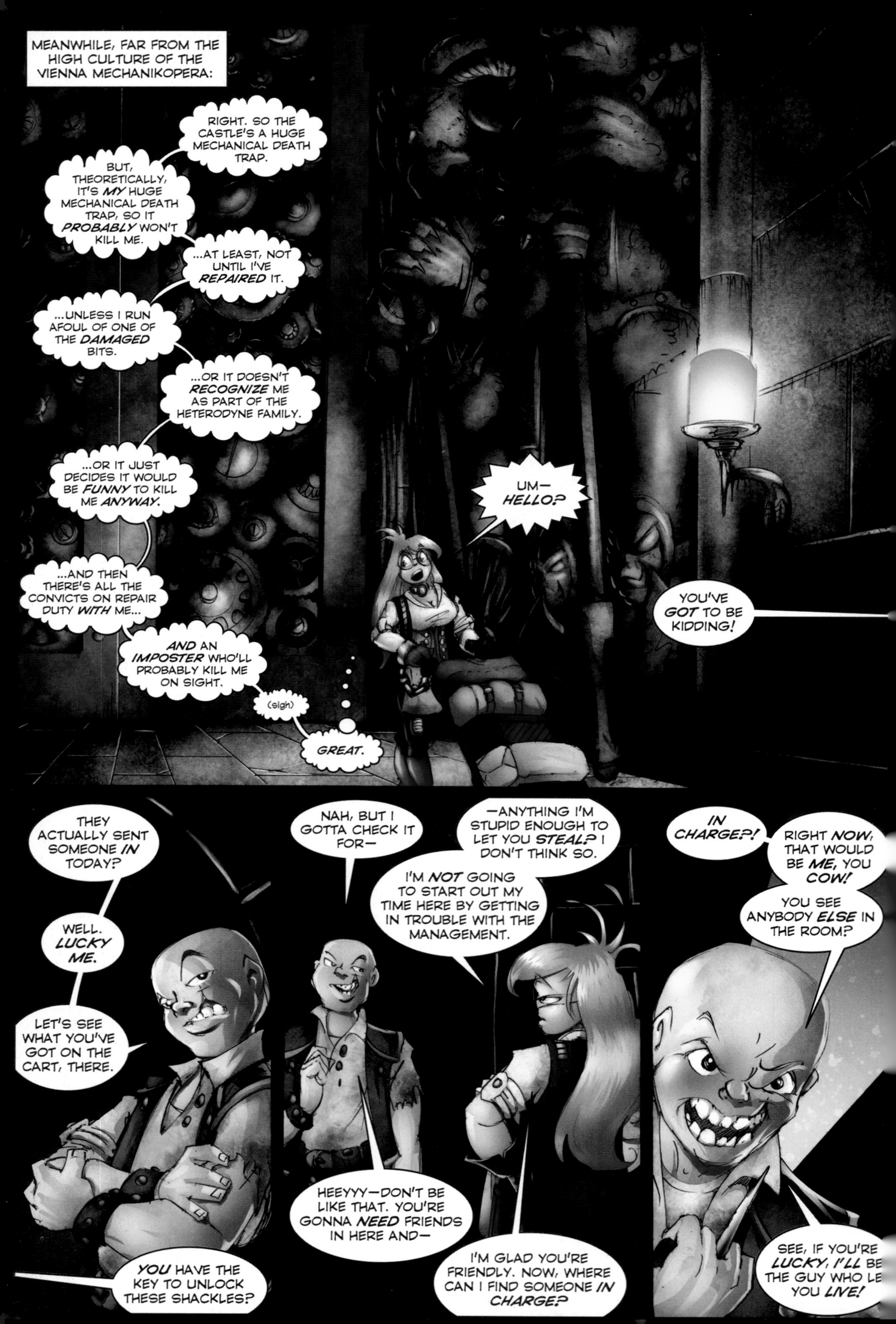
MEANWHILE, FAR FROM THE HIGH CULTURE OF THE VIENNA MECHANIKOPERA:
RIGHT. SO THE CASTLE'S A HUGE MECHANICAL DEATH TRAP.
BUT, THEORETICALLY, IT'S MY HUGE MECHANICAL DEATH TRAP, SO IT PROBABLY WON'T KILL ME.
...AT LEAST, NOT UNTIL I'VE REPAIRED IT.
...UNLESS I RUN AFOUL OF ONE OF THE DAMAGED BITS.
...OR IT DOESN'T RECOGNIZE ME AS PART OF THE HETERODYNE FAMILY.
...OR IT JUST DECIDES IT WOULD BE FUNNY TO KILL ME ANYWAY.
...AND THEN THERE'S ALL THE CONVICTS ON REPAIR DUTY WITH ME...
AND AN IMPOSTER WHO'LL PROBABLY KILL ME ON SIGHT.
(sigh)
GREAT.
UM— HELLO?
YOU'VE GOT TO BE KIDDING!
THEY ACTUALLY SENT SOMEONE IN TODAY?
WELL. LUCKY ME.
LET'S SEE WHAT YOU'VE GOT ON THE CART, THERE.
YOU HAVE THE KEY TO UNLOCK THESE SHACKLES?
NAH, BUT I GOTTA CHECK IT FOR—
—ANYTHING I'M STUPID ENOUGH TO LET YOU STEAL? I DON'T THINK SO.
I'M NOT GOING TO START OUT MY TIME HERE BY GETTING IN TROUBLE WITH THE MANAGEMENT.
HEEYYY—DON'T BE LIKE THAT. YOU'RE GONNA NEED FRIENDS IN HERE AND—
I'M GLAD YOU'RE FRIENDLY. NOW, WHERE CAN I FIND SOMEONE IN CHARGE?
IN CHARGE?!
RIGHT NOW, THAT WOULD BE ME, YOU COW!
YOU SEE ANYBODY ELSE IN THE ROOM?
SEE, IF YOU'RE LUCKY, I'LL BE THE GUY WHO LE YOU LIVE!

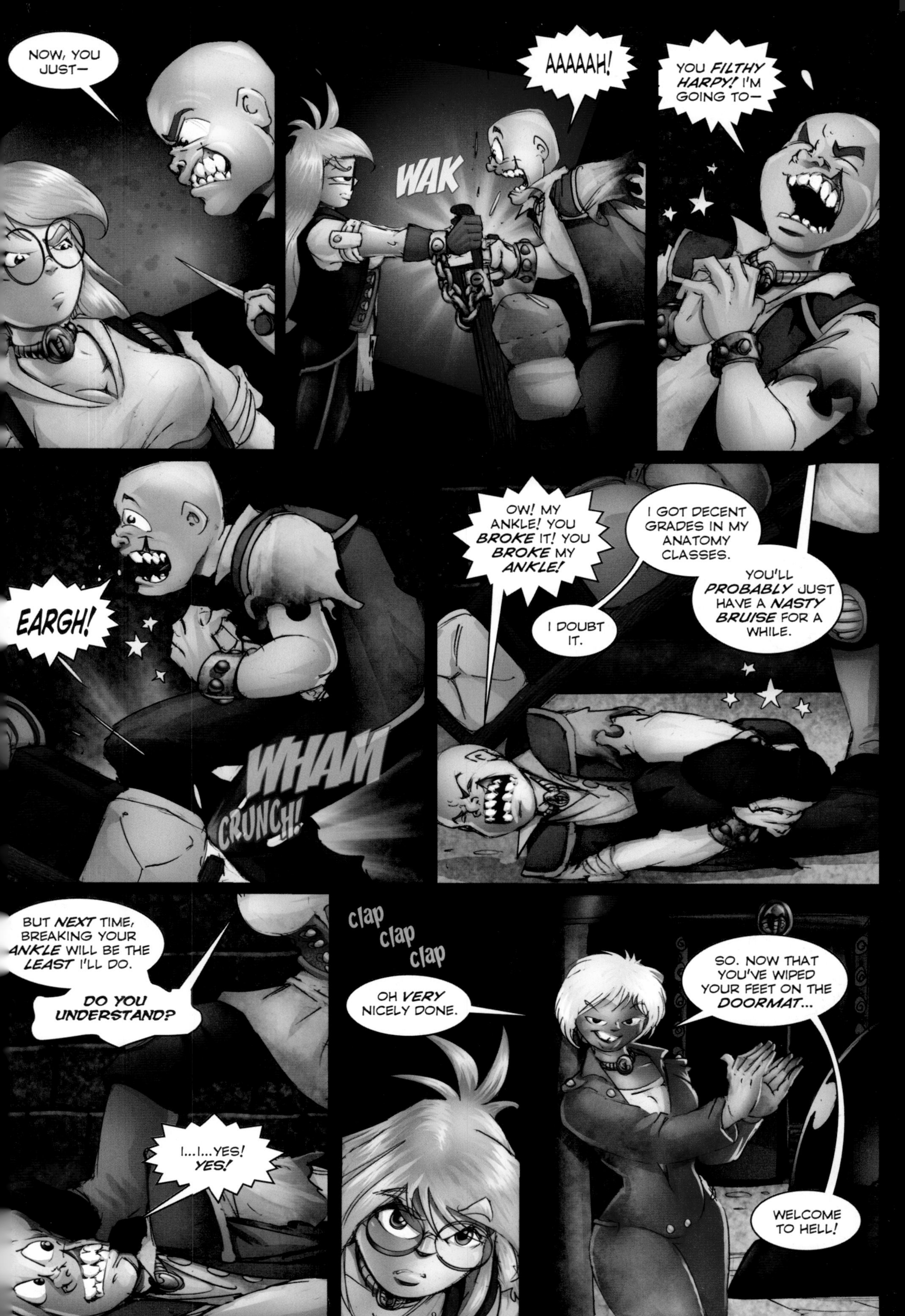

NOW, YOU JUST—
AAAAAH!
WAK
YOU *FILTHY HARPY!* I'M GOING TO—
EARGH!
WHAM
CRUNCH!
OW! MY *ANKLE!* YOU *BROKE* IT! YOU *BROKE* MY *ANKLE!*
I DOUBT IT.
I GOT DECENT GRADES IN MY ANATOMY CLASSES.
YOU'LL *PROBABLY* JUST HAVE A *NASTY BRUISE* FOR A WHILE.
BUT *NEXT* TIME, BREAKING YOUR *ANKLE* WILL BE THE *LEAST* I'LL DO.
DO YOU UNDERSTAND?
I...I...YES! ***YES!***
clap clap clap
OH *VERY* NICELY DONE.
SO. NOW THAT YOU'VE WIPED YOUR FEET ON THE *DOORMAT...*
WELCOME TO HELL!

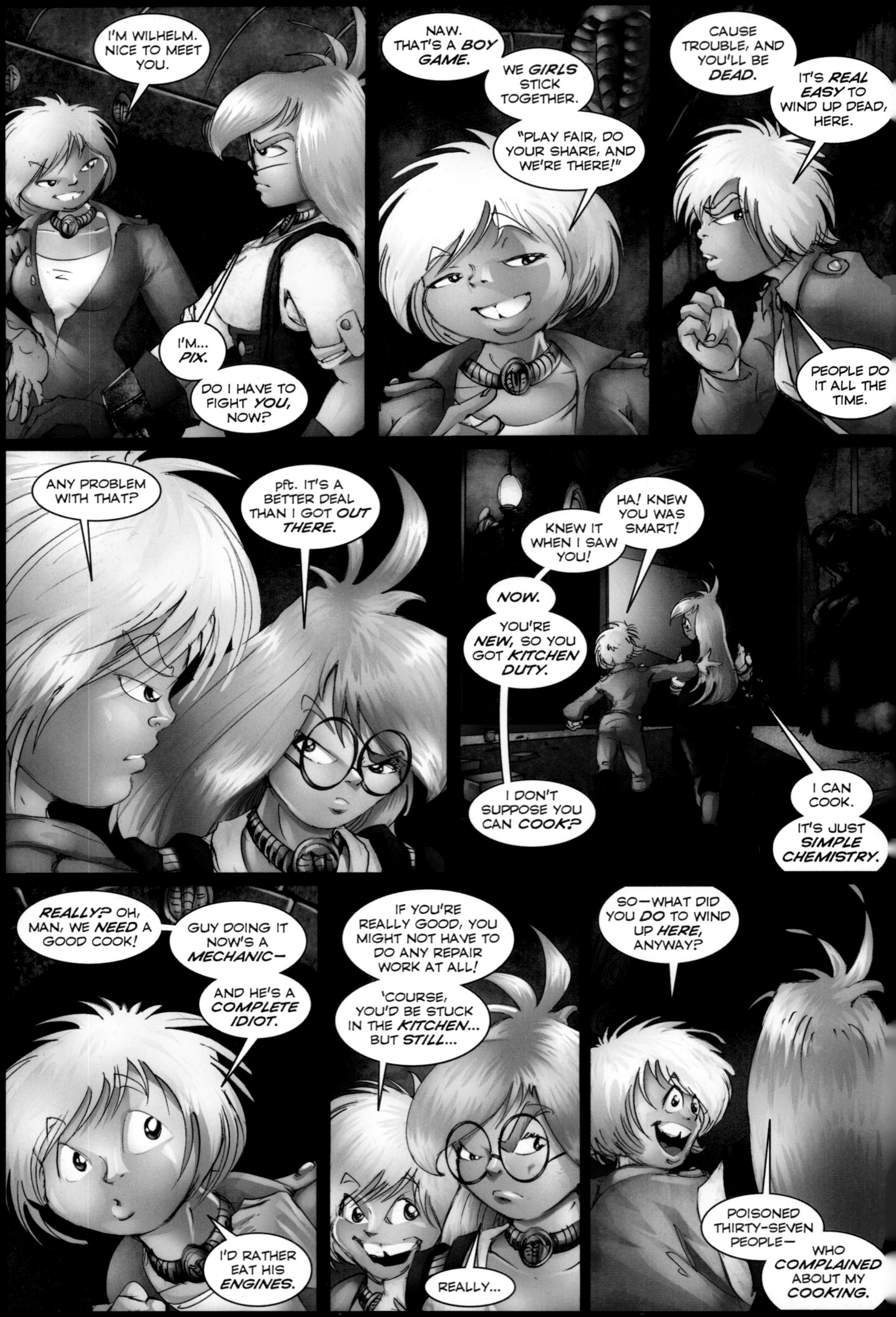

I'M WILHELM. NICE TO MEET YOU.
I'M... *PIX.*
DO I HAVE TO FIGHT *YOU,* NOW?
NAW. THAT'S A *BOY GAME.*
WE *GIRLS* STICK TOGETHER.
"PLAY FAIR, DO YOUR SHARE, AND WE'RE THERE!"
CAUSE TROUBLE, AND YOU'LL BE *DEAD.*
IT'S *REAL EASY* TO WIND UP DEAD, HERE.
PEOPLE DO IT ALL THE TIME.
ANY PROBLEM WITH THAT?
pft. IT'S A BETTER DEAL THAN I GOT *OUT THERE.*
HA! KNEW YOU WAS SMART!
KNEW IT WHEN I SAW YOU!
NOW.
YOU'RE *NEW,* SO YOU GOT *KITCHEN DUTY.*
I DON'T SUPPOSE YOU CAN *COOK?*
I CAN COOK.
IT'S JUST *SIMPLE CHEMISTRY.*
REALLY? OH, MAN, WE *NEED* A GOOD COOK!
GUY DOING IT NOW'S A *MECHANIC—*
AND HE'S A *COMPLETE IDIOT.*
I'D RATHER EAT HIS *ENGINES.*
IF YOU'RE REALLY GOOD, YOU MIGHT NOT HAVE TO DO ANY REPAIR WORK AT ALL!
'COURSE, YOU'D BE STUCK IN THE *KITCHEN*... BUT *STILL*...
REALLY...
SO—WHAT DID YOU *DO* TO WIND UP *HERE,* ANYWAY?
POISONED THIRTY-SEVEN PEOPLE—
WHO *COMPLAINED* ABOUT MY *COOKING.*

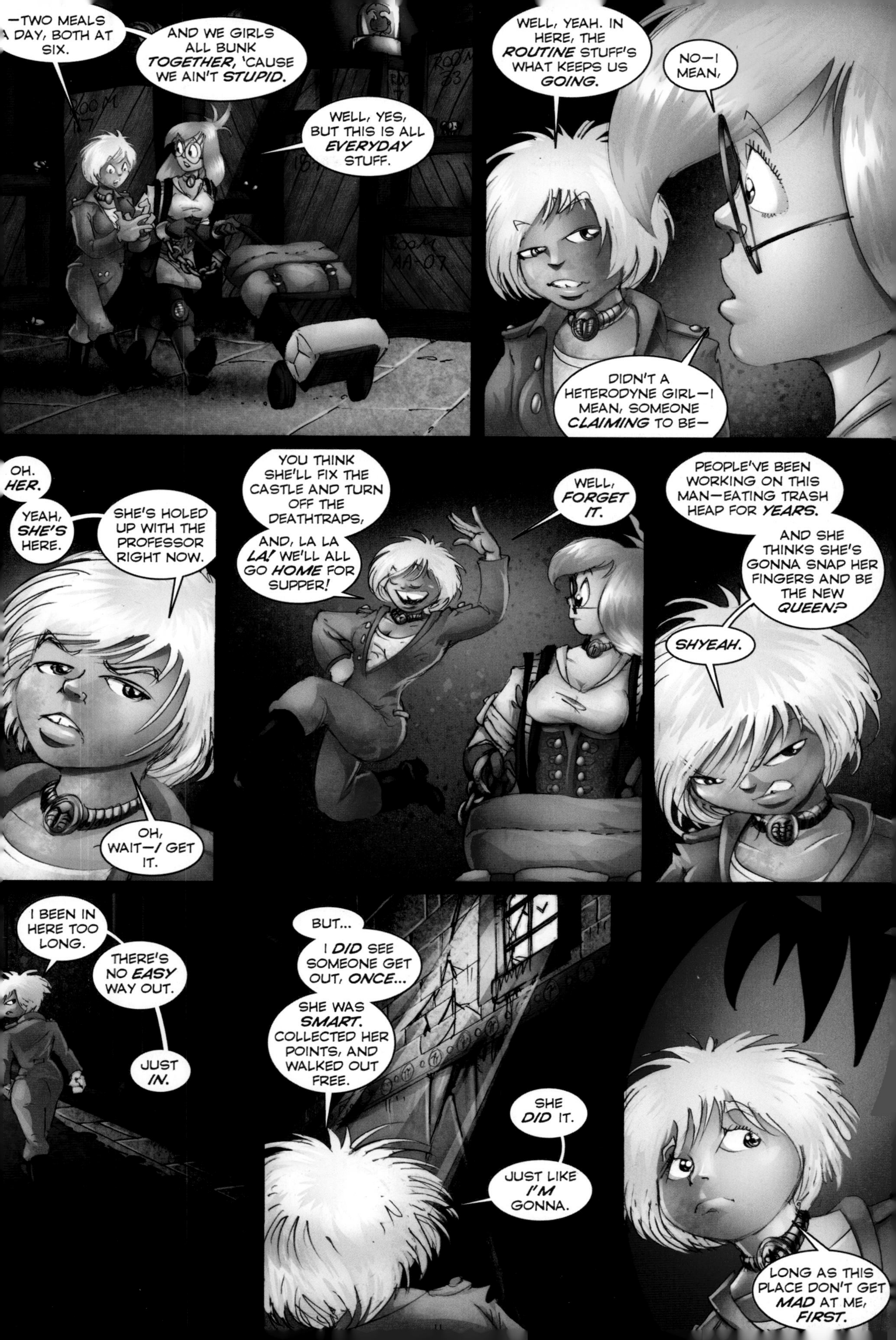

—TWO MEALS A DAY, BOTH AT SIX.
AND WE GIRLS ALL BUNK TOGETHER, 'CAUSE WE AIN'T STUPID.
WELL, YES, BUT THIS IS ALL EVERYDAY STUFF.
WELL, YEAH. IN HERE, THE ROUTINE STUFF'S WHAT KEEPS US GOING.
NO—I MEAN,
DIDN'T A HETERODYNE GIRL—I MEAN, SOMEONE CLAIMING TO BE—
OH. HER.
YEAH, SHE'S HERE.
SHE'S HOLED UP WITH THE PROFESSOR RIGHT NOW.
OH, WAIT—I GET IT.
YOU THINK SHE'LL FIX THE CASTLE AND TURN OFF THE DEATHTRAPS,
AND, LA LA LA! WE'LL ALL GO HOME FOR SUPPER!
WELL, FORGET IT.
PEOPLE'VE BEEN WORKING ON THIS MAN-EATING TRASH HEAP FOR YEARS.
AND SHE THINKS SHE'S GONNA SNAP HER FINGERS AND BE THE NEW QUEEN?
SHYEAH.
I BEEN IN HERE TOO LONG.
THERE'S NO EASY WAY OUT.
JUST IN.
BUT...
I DID SEE SOMEONE GET OUT, ONCE...
SHE WAS SMART. COLLECTED HER POINTS, AND WALKED OUT FREE.
SHE DID IT.
JUST LIKE I'M GONNA.
LONG AS THIS PLACE DON'T GET MAD AT ME, FIRST.

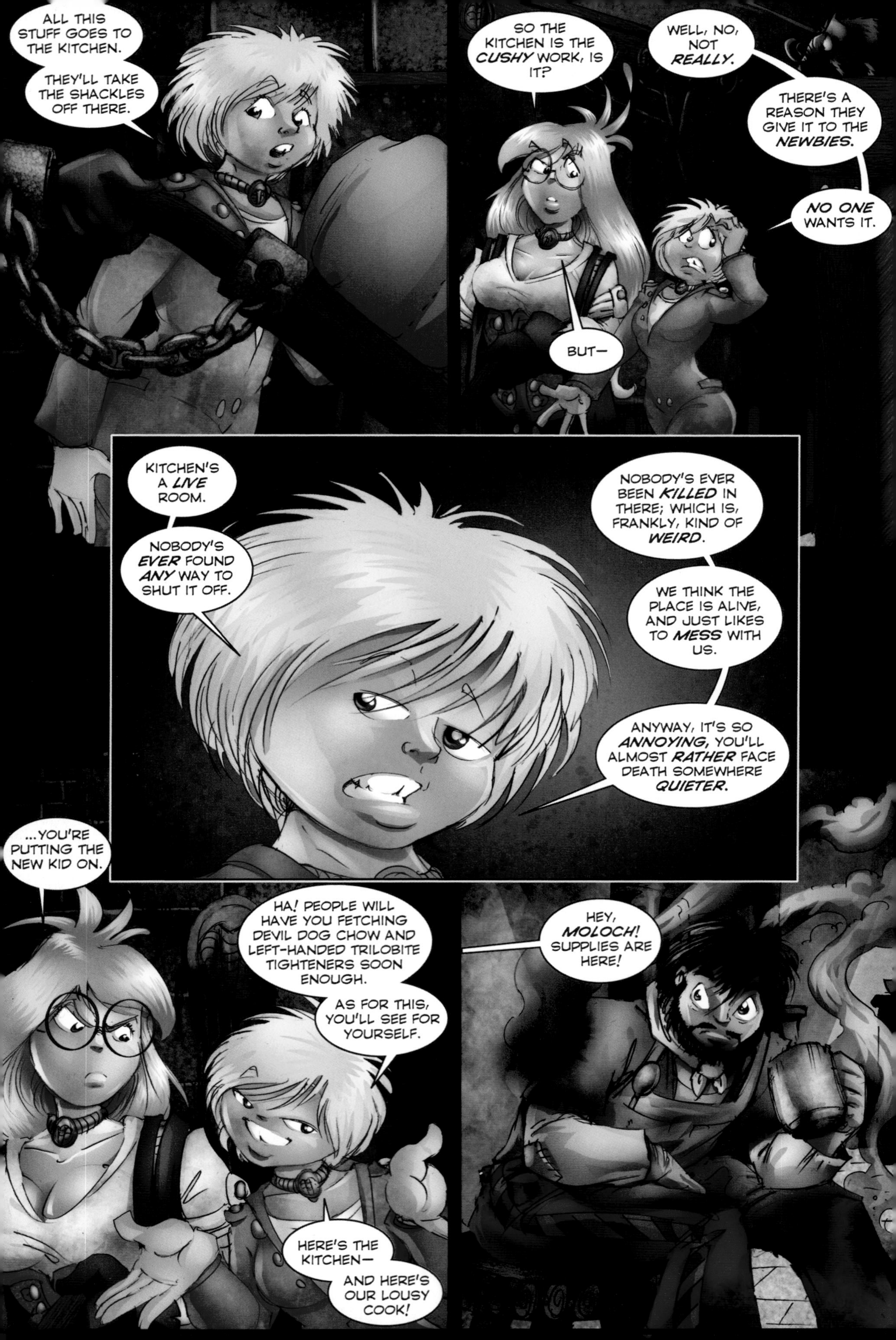
ALL THIS STUFF GOES TO THE KITCHEN.
THEY'LL TAKE THE SHACKLES OFF THERE.
SO THE KITCHEN IS THE CUSHY WORK, IS IT?
WELL, NO, NOT REALLY.
THERE'S A REASON THEY GIVE IT TO THE NEWBIES.
NO ONE WANTS IT.
BUT—
KITCHEN'S A LIVE ROOM.
NOBODY'S EVER FOUND ANY WAY TO SHUT IT OFF.
NOBODY'S EVER BEEN KILLED IN THERE; WHICH IS, FRANKLY, KIND OF WEIRD.
WE THINK THE PLACE IS ALIVE, AND JUST LIKES TO MESS WITH US.
ANYWAY, IT'S SO ANNOYING, YOU'LL ALMOST RATHER FACE DEATH SOMEWHERE QUIETER.
...YOU'RE PUTTING THE NEW KID ON.
HA! PEOPLE WILL HAVE YOU FETCHING DEVIL DOG CHOW AND LEFT-HANDED TRILOBITE TIGHTENERS SOON ENOUGH.
AS FOR THIS, YOU'LL SEE FOR YOURSELF.
HERE'S THE KITCHEN—
AND HERE'S OUR LOUSY COOK!
HEY, MOLOCH! SUPPLIES ARE HERE!

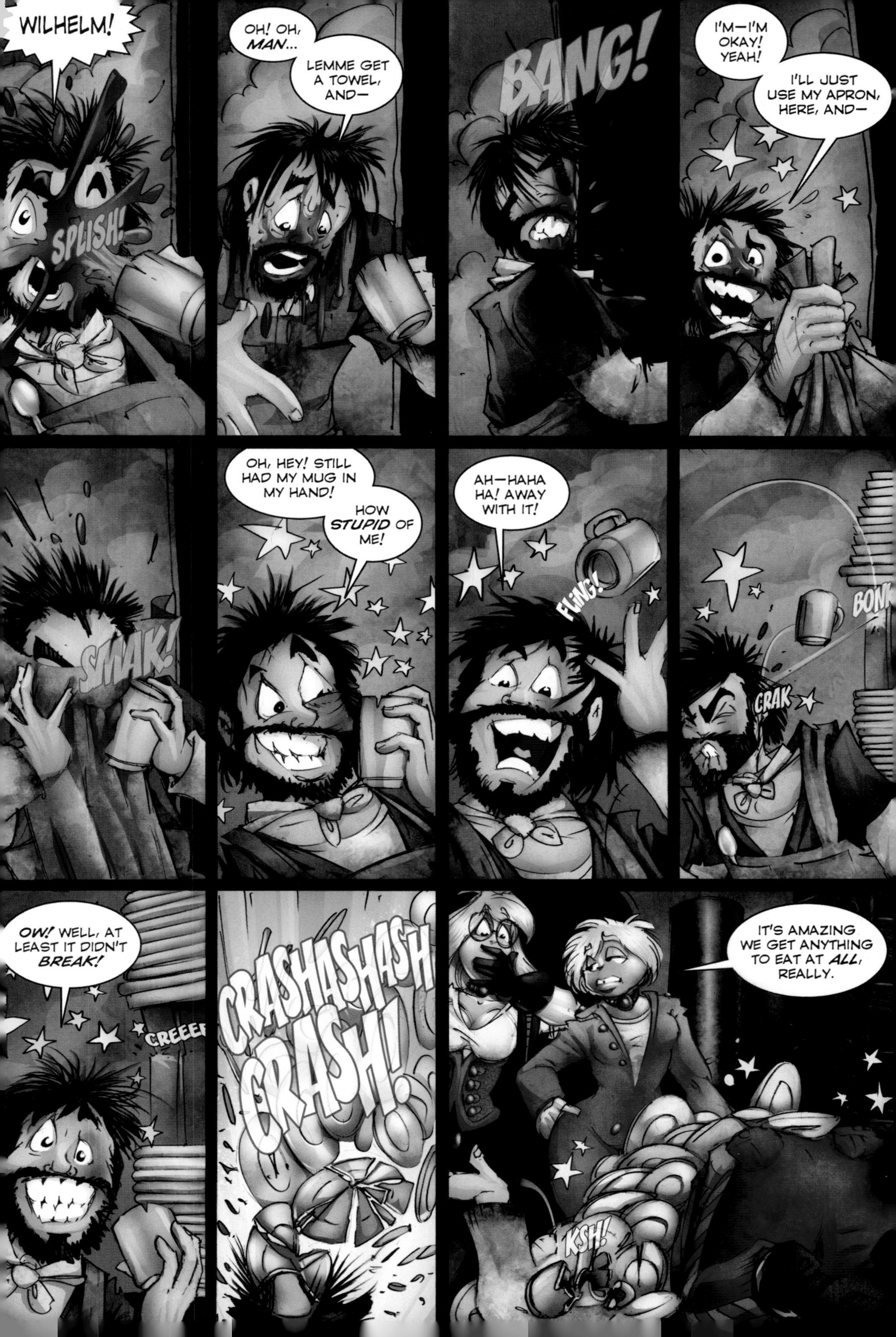
WILHELM!
SPLISH!
OH! OH, MAN...
LEMME GET A TOWEL, AND—
BANG!
I'M—I'M OKAY! YEAH!
I'LL JUST USE MY APRON, HERE, AND—
SMAK!
OH, HEY! STILL HAD MY MUG IN MY HAND!
HOW STUPID OF ME!
AH—HAHA HA! AWAY WITH IT!
FLING!
BONK
CRAK
OW! WELL, AT LEAST IT DIDN'T BREAK!
CREEEE
CRASHASHASH CRASH!
IT'S AMAZING WE GET ANYTHING TO EAT AT ALL, REALLY.
KSH!

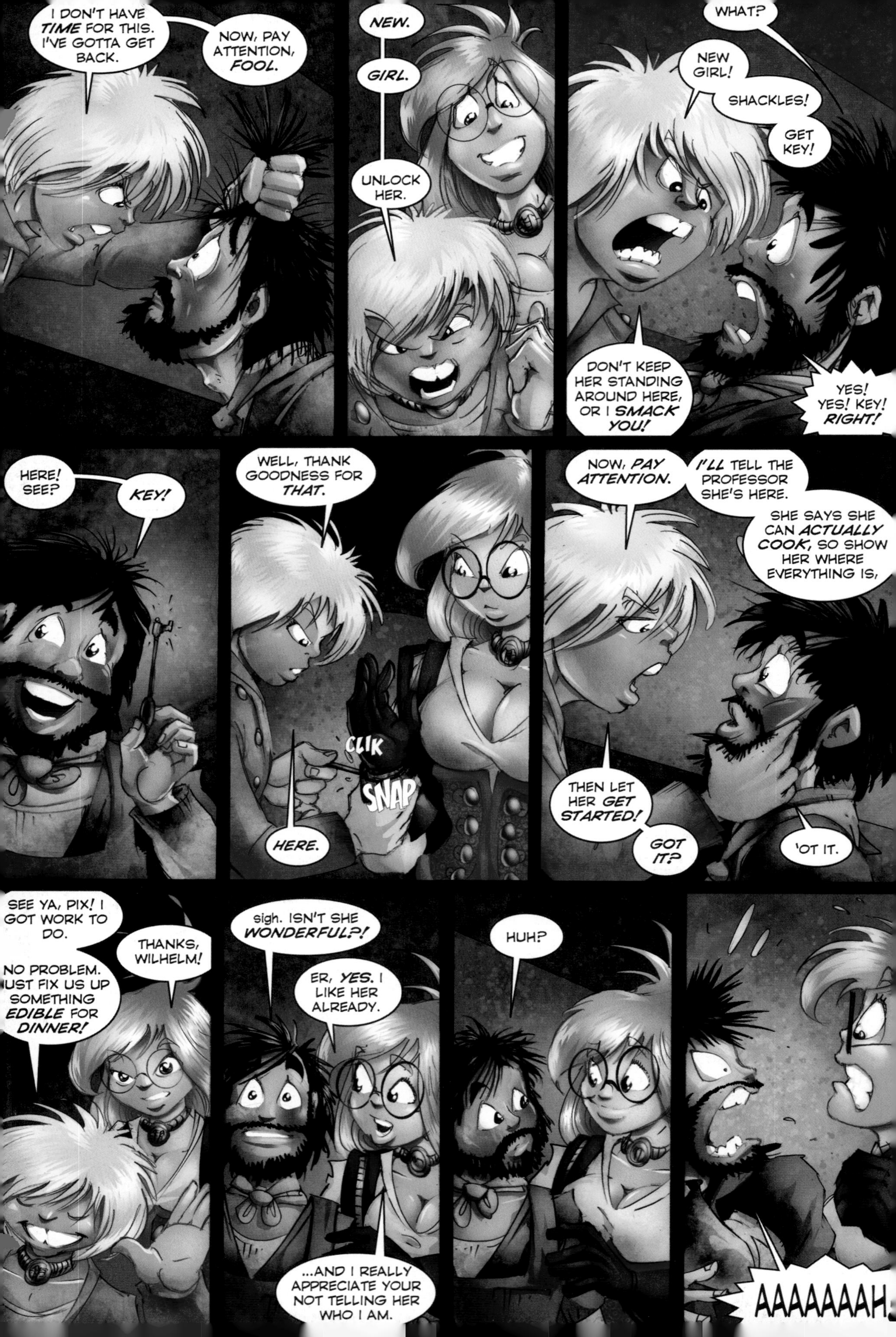
I DON'T HAVE *TIME* FOR THIS. I'VE GOTTA GET BACK.
NOW, PAY ATTENTION, *FOOL.*
NEW.
GIRL.
UNLOCK HER.
WHAT?
NEW GIRL!
SHACKLES!
GET KEY!
DON'T KEEP HER STANDING AROUND HERE, OR I *SMACK YOU!*
YES! YES! KEY! *RIGHT!*
HERE! SEE?
KEY!
WELL, THANK GOODNESS FOR *THAT.*
CLIK
SNAP
HERE.
NOW, *PAY ATTENTION.*
I'LL TELL THE PROFESSOR SHE'S HERE.
SHE SAYS SHE CAN *ACTUALLY COOK,* SO SHOW HER WHERE EVERYTHING IS,
THEN LET HER *GET STARTED!*
GOT IT?
'OT IT.
SEE YA, PIX! I GOT WORK TO DO.
THANKS, WILHELM!
NO PROBLEM. JUST FIX US UP SOMETHING *EDIBLE* FOR *DINNER!*
sigh. ISN'T SHE *WONDERFUL?!*
ER, *YES.* I LIKE HER ALREADY.
...AND I REALLY APPRECIATE YOUR NOT TELLING HER WHO I AM.
HUH?
AAAAAAAH.

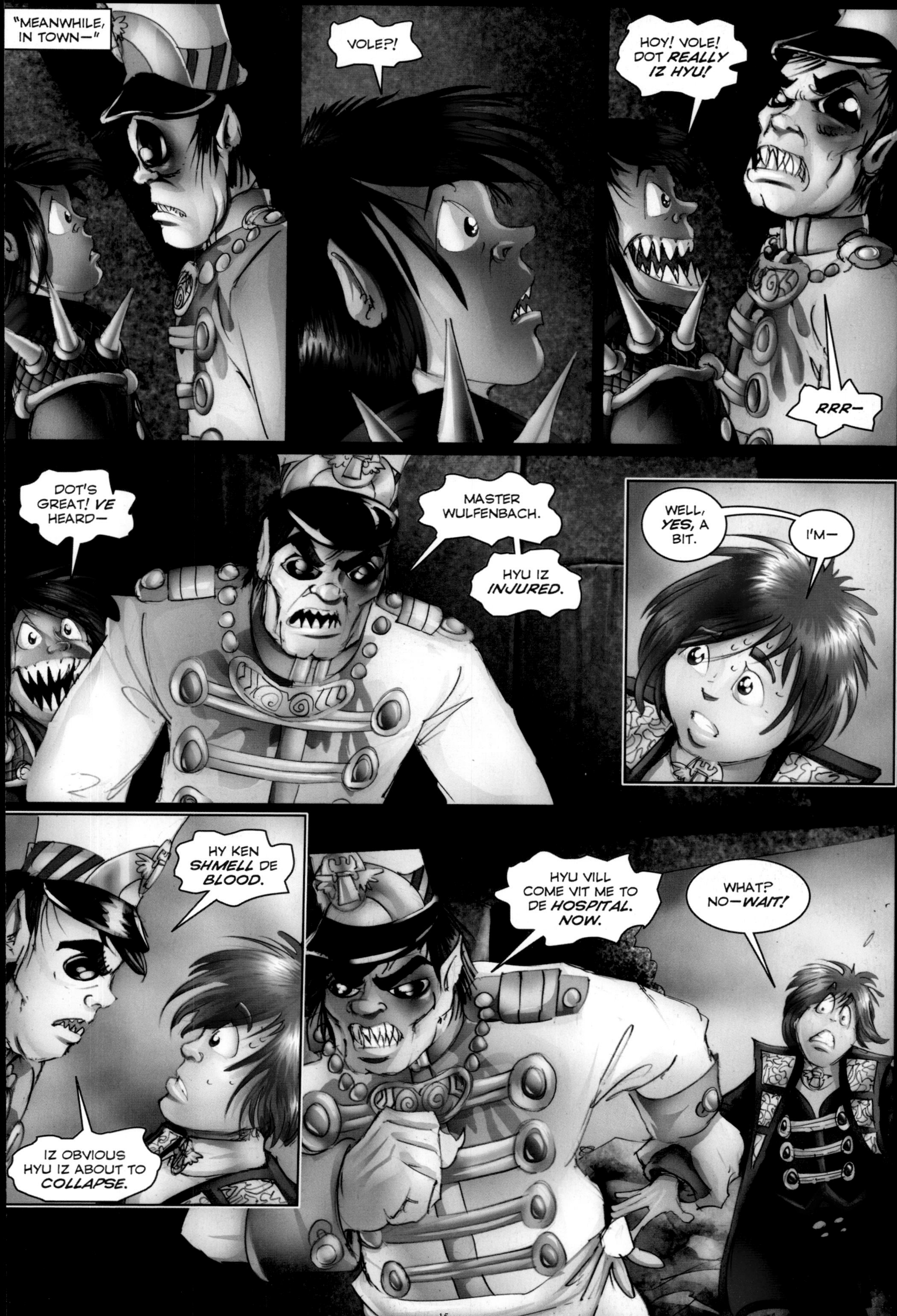
"MEANWHILE, IN TOWN—"
VOLE?!
HOY! VOLE! DOT REALLY IZ HYU!
RRR—
DOT'S GREAT! VE HEARD—
MASTER WULFENBACH.
HYU IZ INJURED.
WELL, YES, A BIT.
I'M—
HY KEN SHMELL DE BLOOD.
IZ OBVIOUS HYU IZ ABOUT TO COLLAPSE.
HYU VILL COME VIT ME TO DE HOSPITAL. NOW.
WHAT? NO—WAIT!

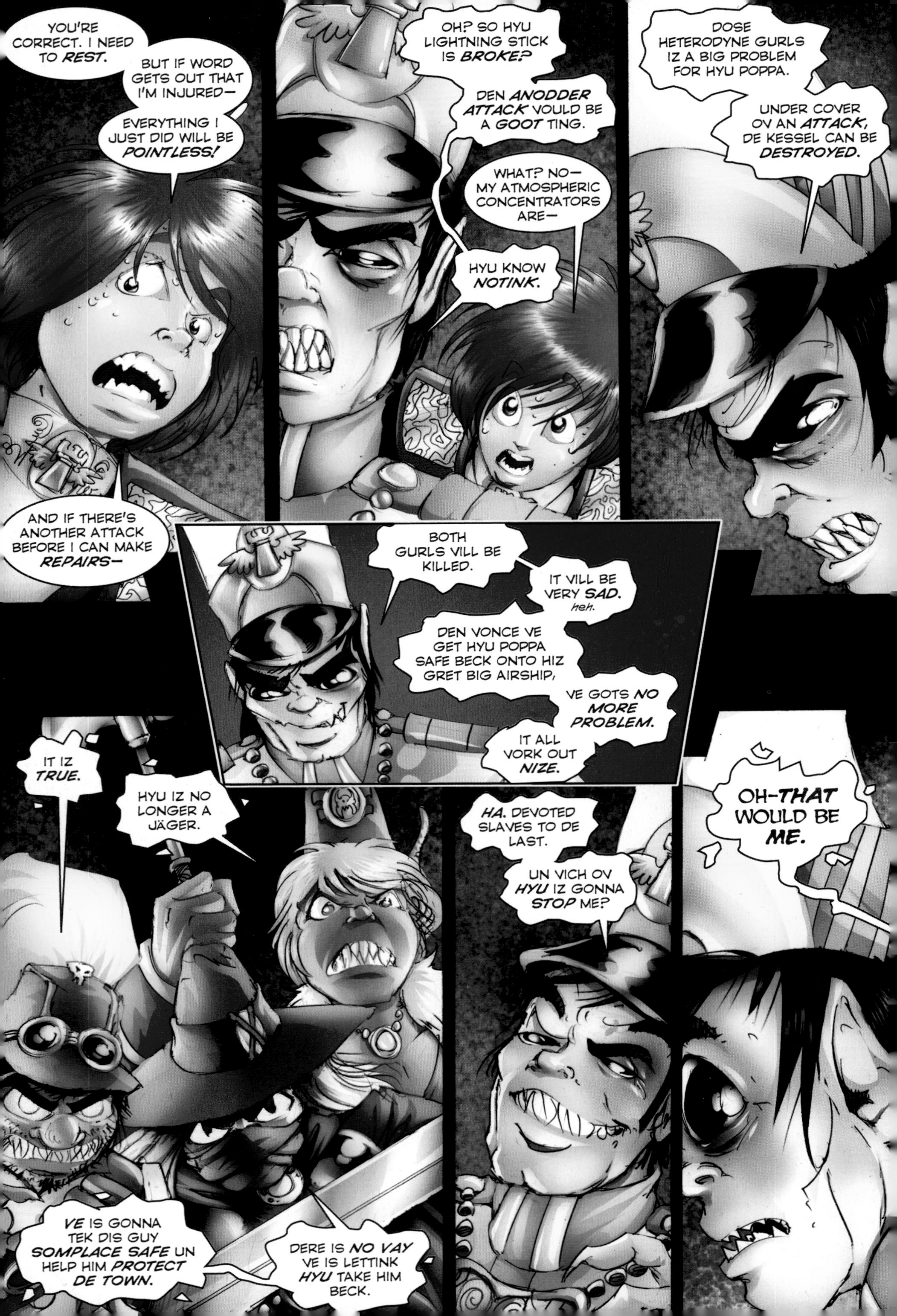

YOU'RE CORRECT. I NEED TO *REST*.
BUT IF WORD GETS OUT THAT I'M INJURED—
EVERYTHING I JUST DID WILL BE *POINTLESS!*
OH? SO HYU LIGHTNING STICK IS *BROKE?*
DEN *ANODDER ATTACK* VOULD BE A *GOOT* TING.
WHAT? NO— MY ATMOSPHERIC CONCENTRATORS ARE—
HYU KNOW *NOTINK*.
DOSE HETERODYNE GURLS IZ A BIG PROBLEM FOR HYU POPPA.
UNDER COVER OV AN *ATTACK*, DE KESSEL CAN BE *DESTROYED*.
AND IF THERE'S ANOTHER ATTACK BEFORE I CAN MAKE *REPAIRS*—
BOTH GURLS VILL BE KILLED.
IT VILL BE VERY *SAD*. *heh.*
DEN VONCE VE GET HYU POPPA SAFE BECK ONTO HIZ GRET BIG AIRSHIP,
VE GOTS *NO MORE PROBLEM*.
IT ALL VORK OUT *NIZE*.
IT IZ *TRUE*.
HYU IZ NO LONGER A JÄGER.
VE IS GONNA TEK DIS GUY *SOMPLACE SAFE* UN HELP HIM *PROTECT DE TOWN*.
DERE IS *NO VAY* VE IS LETTINK *HYU* TAKE HIM BECK.
HA. DEVOTED SLAVES TO DE LAST.
UN VICH OV *HYU* IZ GONNA *STOP* ME?
OH-*THAT* WOULD BE *ME*.

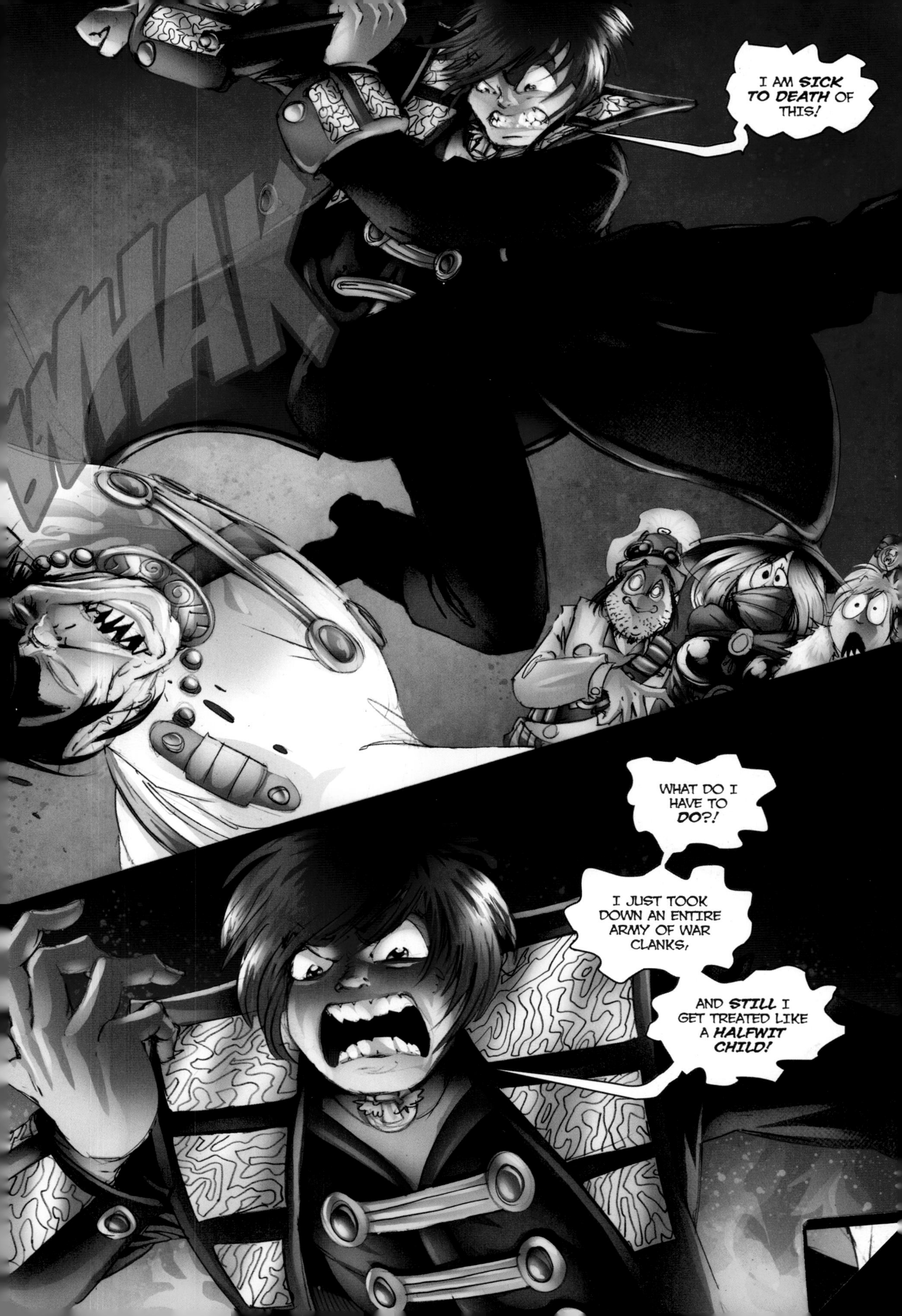

WHAK
I AM SICK TO DEATH OF THIS!
WHAT DO I HAVE TO DO?!
I JUST TOOK DOWN AN ENTIRE ARMY OF WAR CLANKS,
AND STILL I GET TREATED LIKE A HALFWIT CHILD!

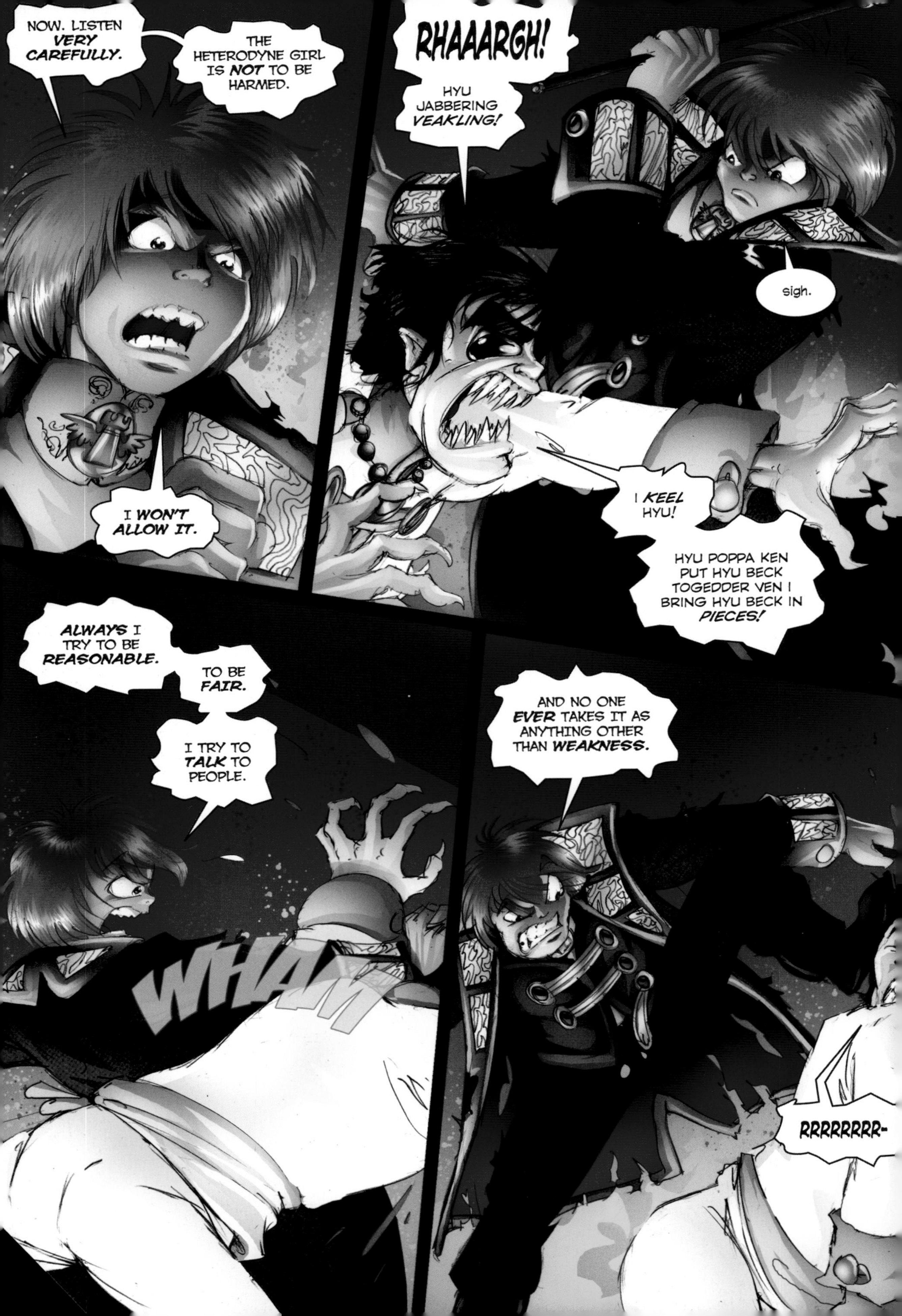
NOW. LISTEN VERY CAREFULLY.
THE HETERODYNE GIRL IS NOT TO BE HARMED.
I WON'T ALLOW IT.
RHAAARGH!
HYU JABBERING VEAKLING!
sigh.
I KEEL HYU!
HYU POPPA KEN PUT HYU BECK TOGEDDER VEN I BRING HYU BECK IN PIECES!
ALWAYS I TRY TO BE REASONABLE.
TO BE FAIR.
I TRY TO TALK TO PEOPLE.
WHAM
AND NO ONE EVER TAKES IT AS ANYTHING OTHER THAN WEAKNESS.
RRRRRRRR-

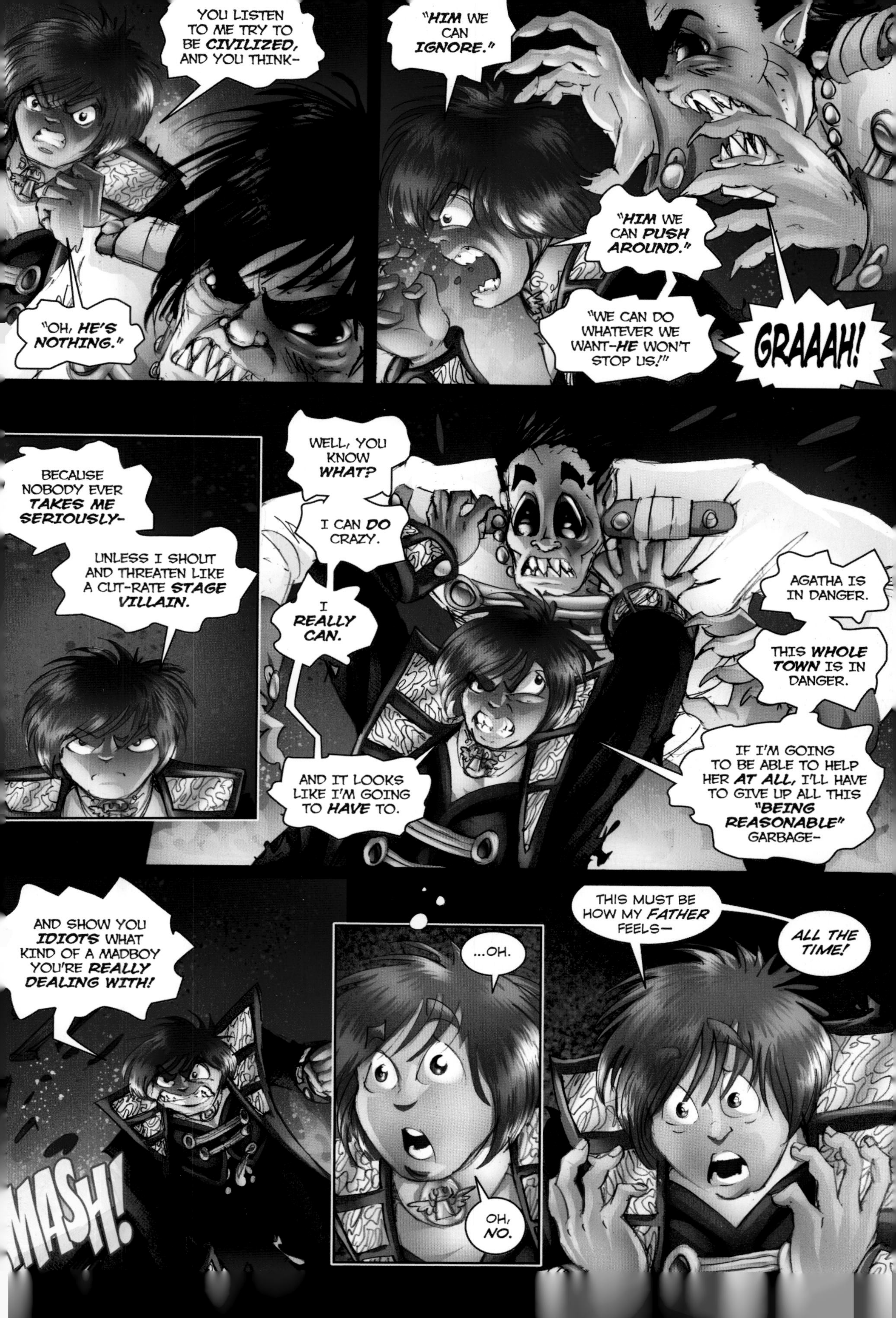
YOU LISTEN TO ME TRY TO BE CIVILIZED, AND YOU THINK-
"OH, HE'S NOTHING."
"HIM WE CAN IGNORE."
"HIM WE CAN PUSH AROUND."
"WE CAN DO WHATEVER WE WANT-HE WON'T STOP US!"
GRAAAH!
BECAUSE NOBODY EVER TAKES ME SERIOUSLY-
UNLESS I SHOUT AND THREATEN LIKE A CUT-RATE STAGE VILLAIN.
WELL, YOU KNOW WHAT?
I CAN DO CRAZY.
I REALLY CAN.
AND IT LOOKS LIKE I'M GOING TO HAVE TO.
AGATHA IS IN DANGER.
THIS WHOLE TOWN IS IN DANGER.
IF I'M GOING TO BE ABLE TO HELP HER AT ALL, I'LL HAVE TO GIVE UP ALL THIS "BEING REASONABLE" GARBAGE-
AND SHOW YOU IDIOTS WHAT KIND OF A MADBOY YOU'RE REALLY DEALING WITH!
MASH!
...OH.
OH, NO.
THIS MUST BE HOW MY FATHER FEELS—
ALL THE TIME!

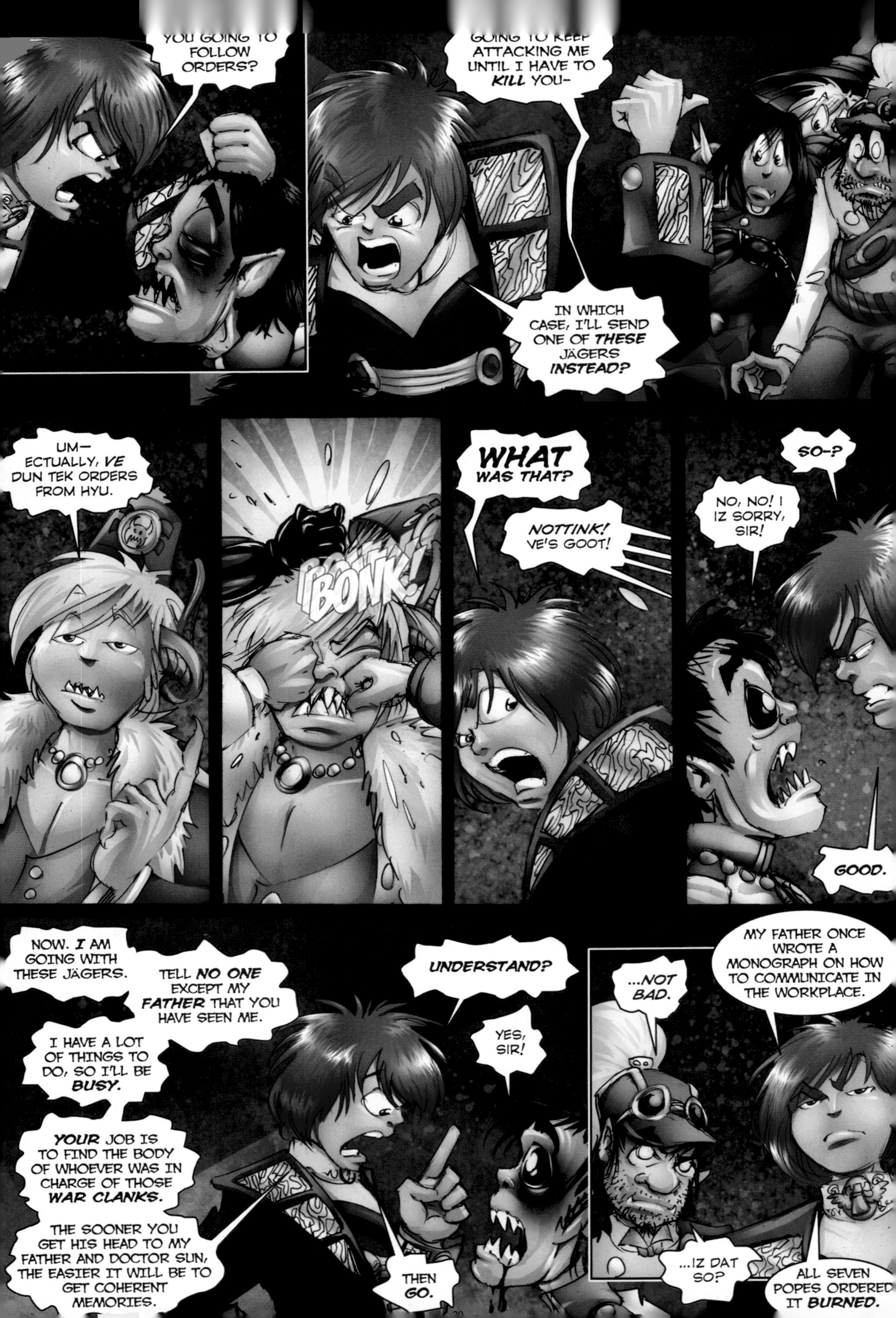
YOU GOING TO FOLLOW ORDERS?
GOING TO KEEP ATTACKING ME UNTIL I HAVE TO KILL YOU-
IN WHICH CASE, I'LL SEND ONE OF THESE JÄGERS INSTEAD?
UM— ECTUALLY, VE DUN TEK ORDERS FROM HYU.
BONK!
WHAT WAS THAT?
NOTTINK! VE'S GOOT!
SO-?
NO, NO! I IZ SORRY, SIR!
GOOD.
NOW. I AM GOING WITH THESE JÄGERS.
TELL NO ONE EXCEPT MY FATHER THAT YOU HAVE SEEN ME.
I HAVE A LOT OF THINGS TO DO, SO I'LL BE BUSY.
YOUR JOB IS TO FIND THE BODY OF WHOEVER WAS IN CHARGE OF THOSE WAR CLANKS.
THE SOONER YOU GET HIS HEAD TO MY FATHER AND DOCTOR SUN, THE EASIER IT WILL BE TO GET COHERENT MEMORIES.
UNDERSTAND?
YES, SIR!
THEN GO.
...NOT BAD.
MY FATHER ONCE WROTE A MONOGRAPH ON HOW TO COMMUNICATE IN THE WORKPLACE.
...IZ DAT SO?
ALL SEVEN POPES ORDERED IT BURNED.

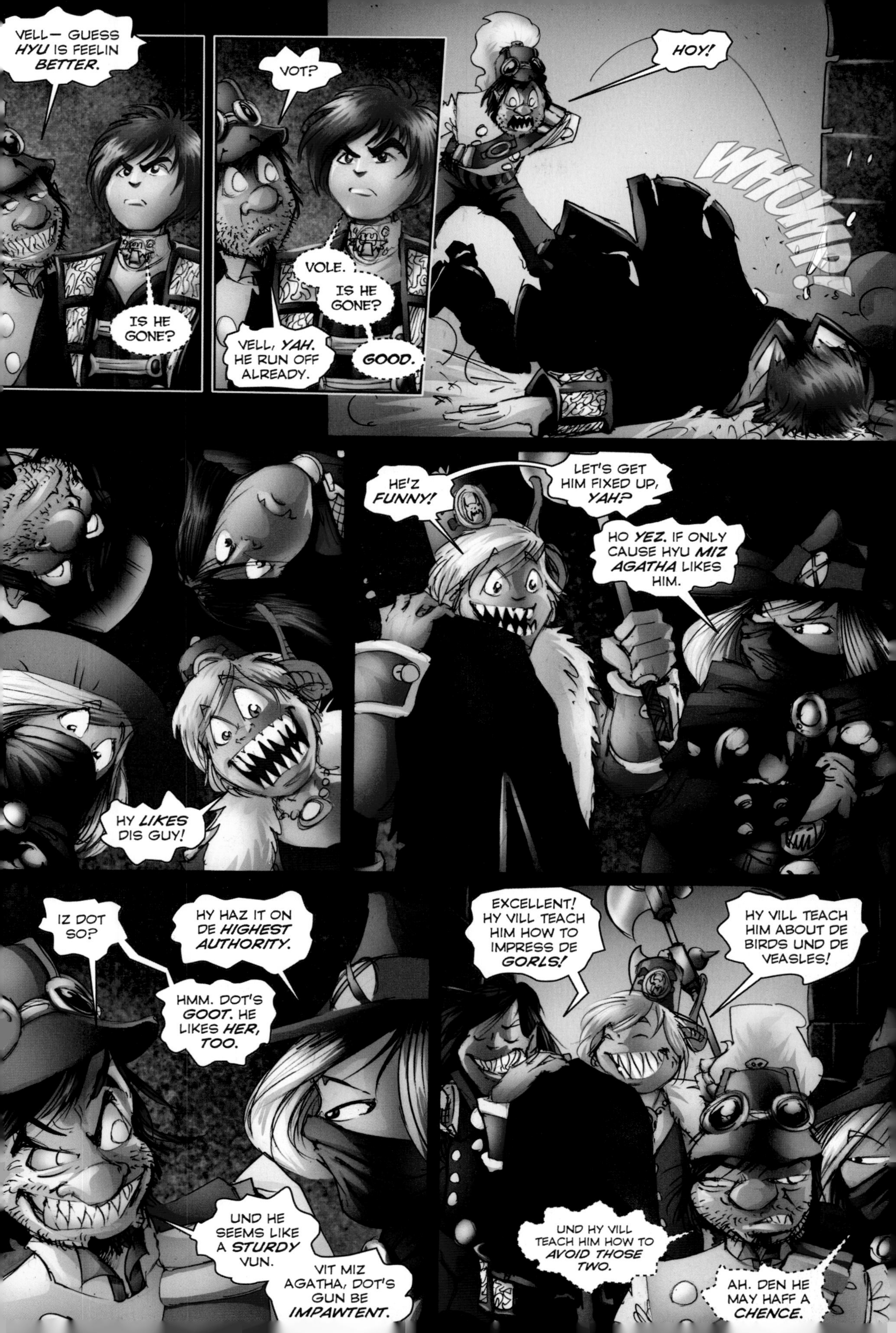

VELL— GUESS HYU IS FEELIN BETTER.
IS HE GONE?
VOT?
VOLE.
IS HE GONE?
VELL, YAH. HE RUN OFF ALREADY.
GOOD.
HOY!
WHUMP!
HY LIKES DIS GUY!
HE'Z FUNNY!
LET'S GET HIM FIXED UP, YAH?
HO YEZ. IF ONLY CAUSE HYU MIZ AGATHA LIKES HIM.
IZ DOT SO?
HY HAZ IT ON DE HIGHEST AUTHORITY.
HMM. DOT'S GOOT. HE LIKES HER, TOO.
UND HE SEEMS LIKE A STURDY VUN.
VIT MIZ AGATHA, DOT'S GUN BE IMPAWTENT.
EXCELLENT! HY VILL TEACH HIM HOW TO IMPRESS DE GORLS!
HY VILL TEACH HIM ABOUT DE BIRDS UND DE VEASLES!
UND HY VILL TEACH HIM HOW TO AVOID THOSE TWO.
AH. DEN HE MAY HAFF A CHENCE.

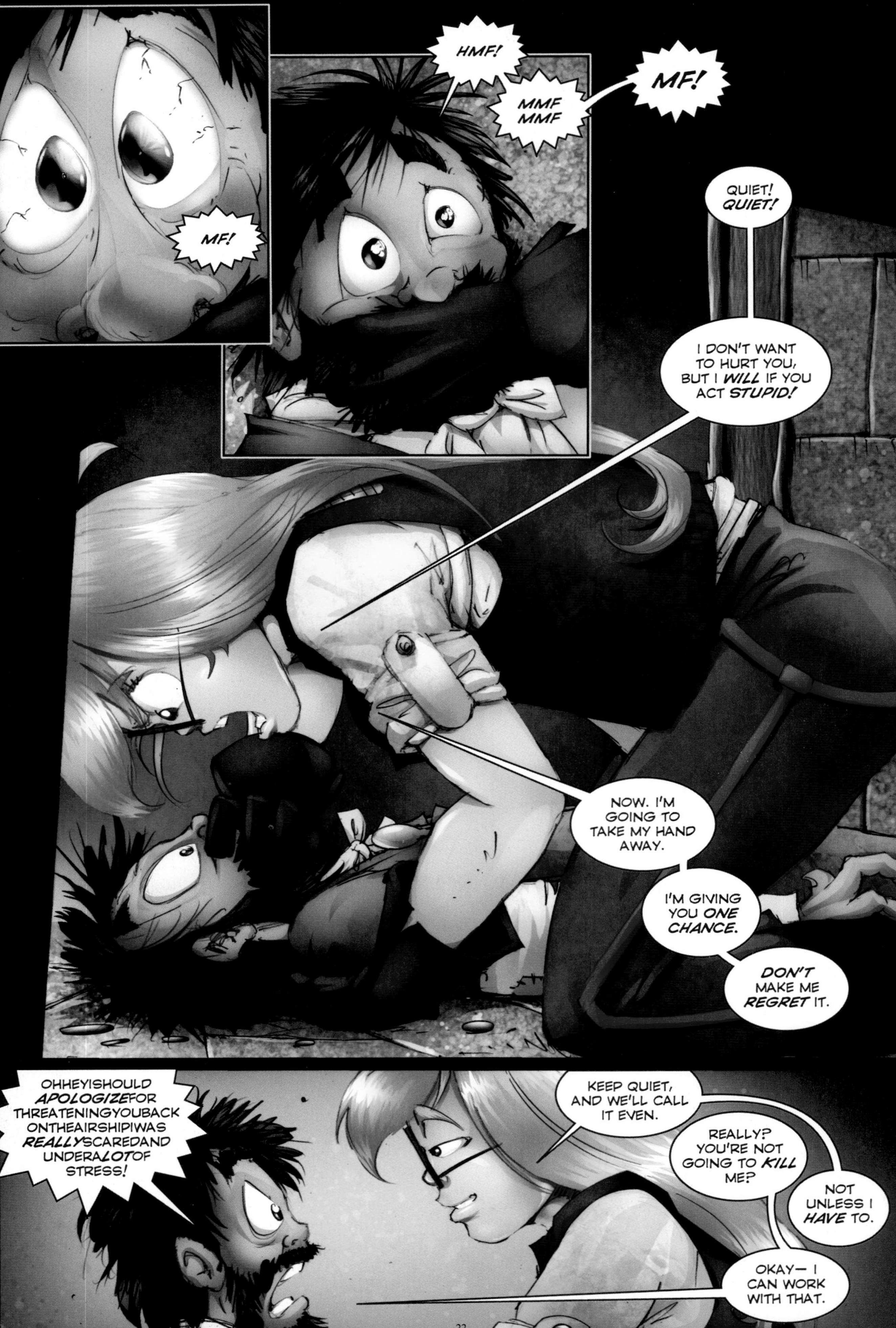
HMF!
MMF MMF
MF!
MF!
QUIET! QUIET!
I DON'T WANT TO HURT YOU, BUT I WILL IF YOU ACT STUPID!
NOW. I'M GOING TO TAKE MY HAND AWAY.
I'M GIVING YOU ONE CHANCE.
DON'T MAKE ME REGRET IT.
OHHEYISHOULD APOLOGIZEFOR THREATENINGYOUBACK ONTHEAIRSHIPIWAS REALLYSCAREDAND UNDERALOTOF STRESS!
KEEP QUIET, AND WE'LL CALL IT EVEN.
REALLY? YOU'RE NOT GOING TO KILL ME?
NOT UNLESS I HAVE TO.
OKAY— I CAN WORK WITH THAT.

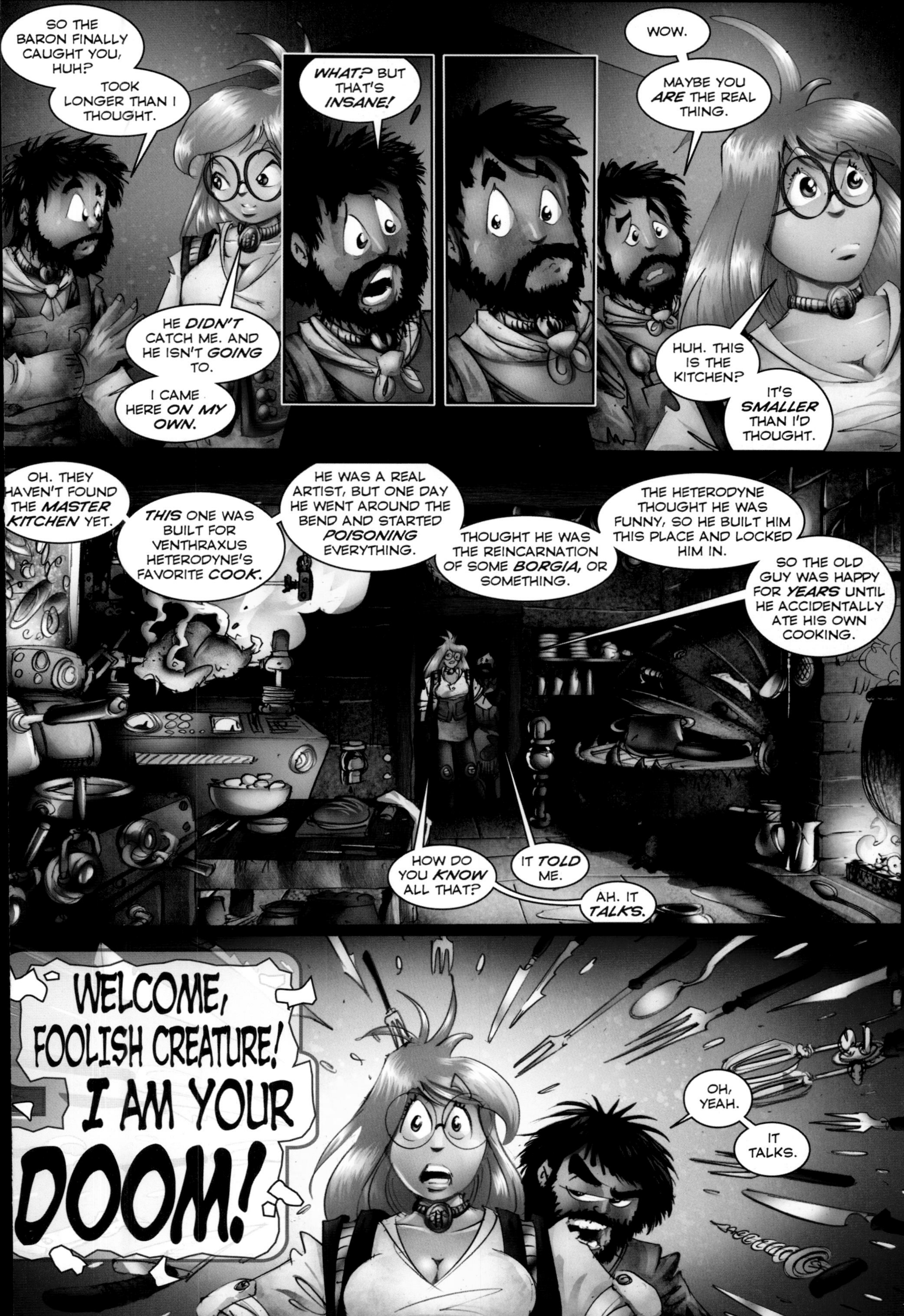

SO THE BARON FINALLY CAUGHT YOU, HUH?
TOOK LONGER THAN I THOUGHT.
HE *DIDN'T* CATCH ME. AND HE ISN'T *GOING* TO.
I CAME HERE **ON MY OWN.**
WHAT? BUT THAT'S ***INSANE!***
WOW.
MAYBE YOU ***ARE*** THE REAL THING.
HUH. THIS IS THE KITCHEN?
IT'S ***SMALLER*** THAN I'D THOUGHT.
OH. THEY HAVEN'T FOUND THE ***MASTER KITCHEN*** YET.
THIS ONE WAS BUILT FOR VENTHRAXUS HETERODYNE'S FAVORITE ***COOK.***
HE WAS A REAL ARTIST, BUT ONE DAY HE WENT AROUND THE BEND AND STARTED ***POISONING*** EVERYTHING.
THOUGHT HE WAS THE REINCARNATION OF SOME ***BORGIA,*** OR SOMETHING.
THE HETERODYNE THOUGHT HE WAS FUNNY, SO HE BUILT HIM THIS PLACE AND LOCKED HIM IN.
SO THE OLD GUY WAS HAPPY FOR ***YEARS*** UNTIL HE ACCIDENTALLY ATE HIS OWN COOKING.
HOW DO YOU ***KNOW*** ALL THAT?
IT ***TOLD*** ME.
AH. IT ***TALKS.***
WELCOME, FOOLISH CREATURE! I AM YOUR DOOM!
OH, YEAH.
IT TALKS.

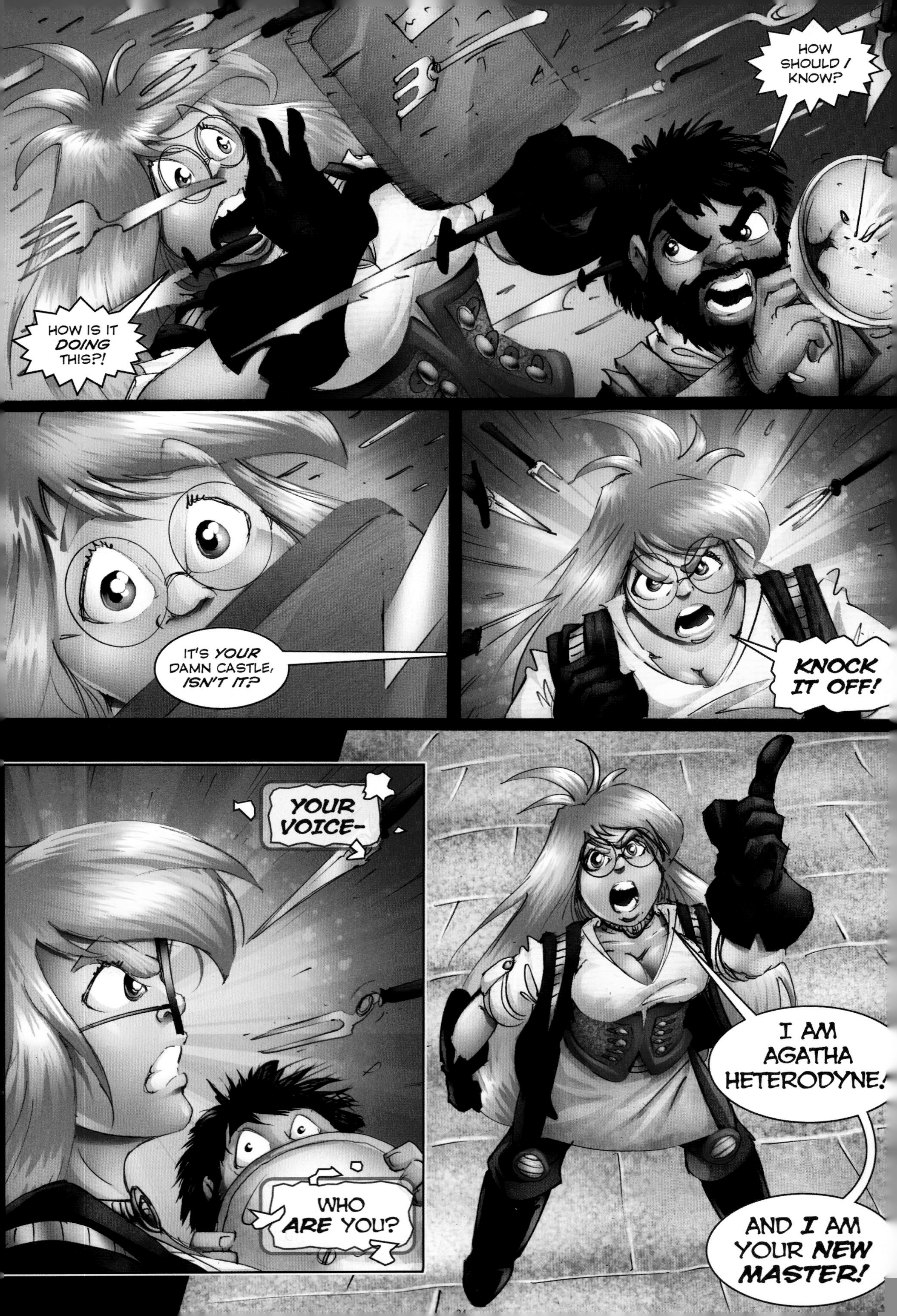
HOW IS IT *DOING* THIS?!
HOW SHOULD *I* KNOW?
IT'S *YOUR* DAMN CASTLE, *ISN'T IT?*
KNOCK IT OFF!
YOUR VOICE-
WHO *ARE* YOU?
I AM AGATHA HETERODYNE!
AND *I* AM YOUR *NEW MASTER!*

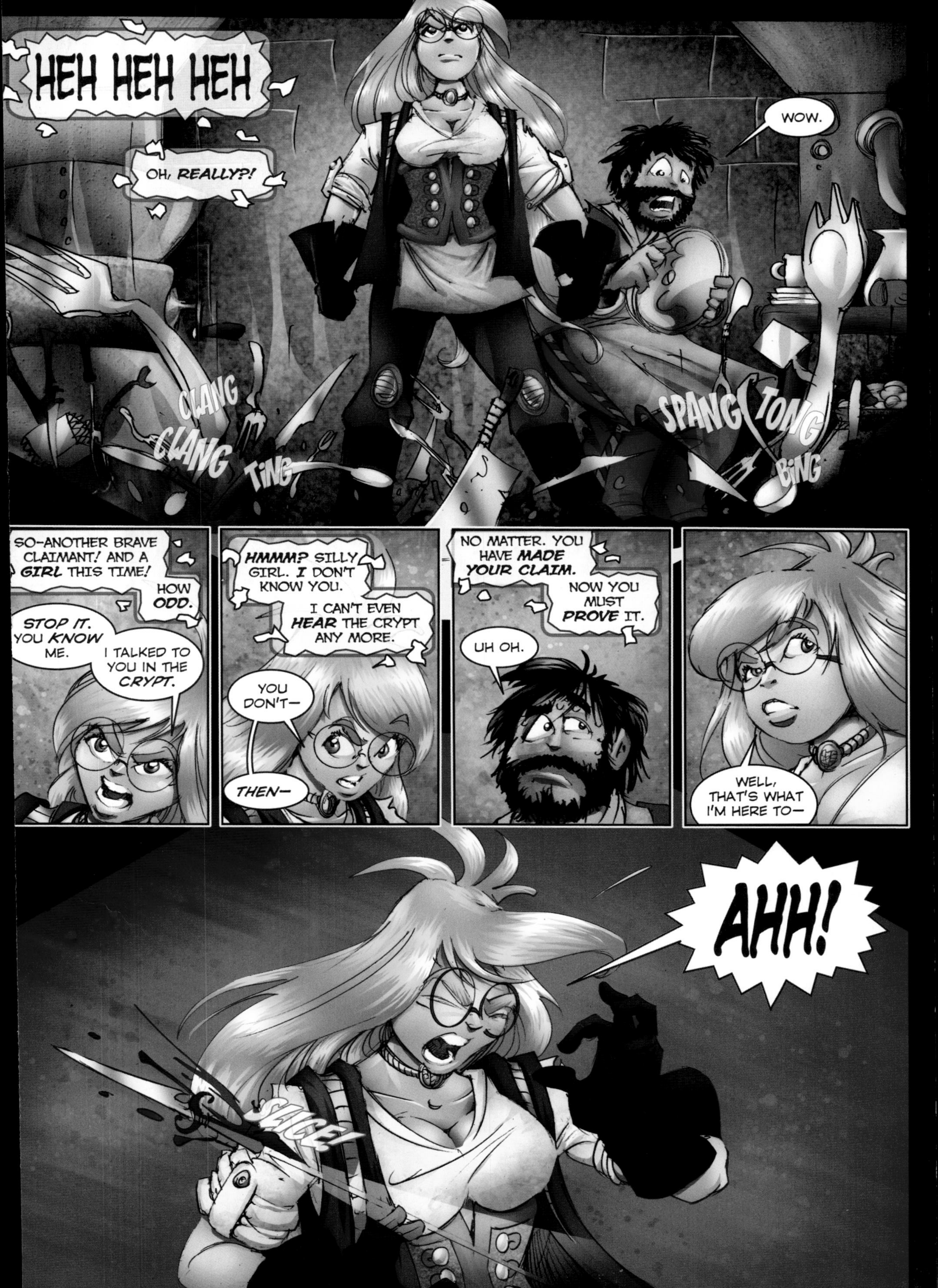

HEH HEH HEH
OH, REALLY?!
WOW.
CLANG
CLANG
TING
SPANG
TONG
BING
SO-ANOTHER BRAVE CLAIMANT! AND A GIRL THIS TIME!
HOW ODD.
STOP IT. YOU KNOW ME.
I TALKED TO YOU IN THE CRYPT.
HMMM? SILLY GIRL. I DON'T KNOW YOU.
I CAN'T EVEN HEAR THE CRYPT ANY MORE.
YOU DON'T—
THEN—
NO MATTER. YOU HAVE MADE YOUR CLAIM.
NOW YOU MUST PROVE IT.
UH OH.
WELL, THAT'S WHAT I'M HERE TO—
AHH!
SLICE!

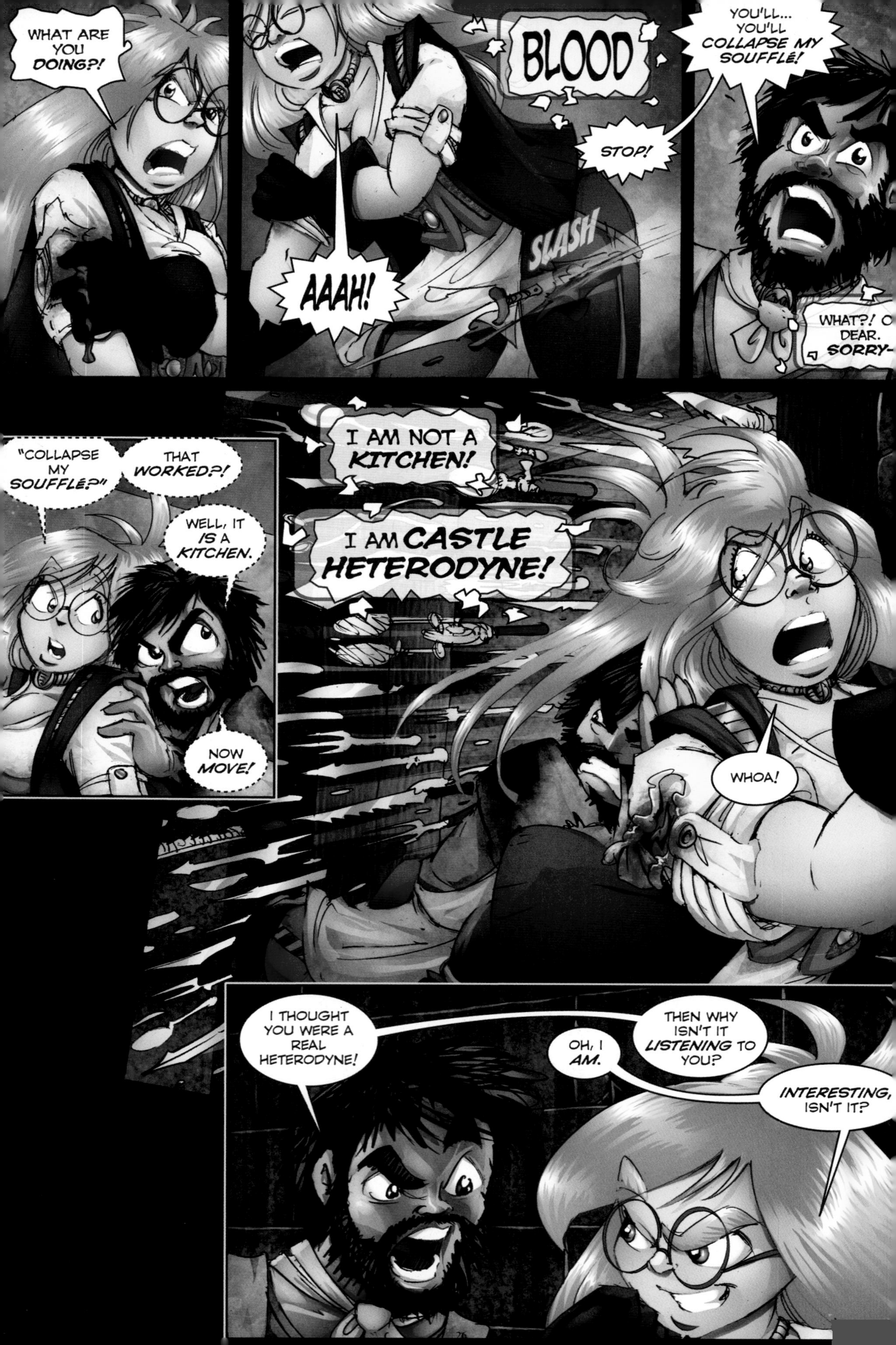
WHAT ARE YOU DOING?!
AAAH!
BLOOD
SLASH
STOP!
YOU'LL... YOU'LL COLLAPSE MY SOUFFLÉ!
WHAT?! O DEAR. SORRY-
I AM NOT A KITCHEN!
I AM CASTLE HETERODYNE!
"COLLAPSE MY SOUFFLÉ?"
THAT WORKED?!
WELL, IT IS A KITCHEN.
NOW MOVE!
WHOA!
I THOUGHT YOU WERE A REAL HETERODYNE!
THEN WHY ISN'T IT LISTENING TO YOU?
OH, I AM.
INTERESTING, ISN'T IT?

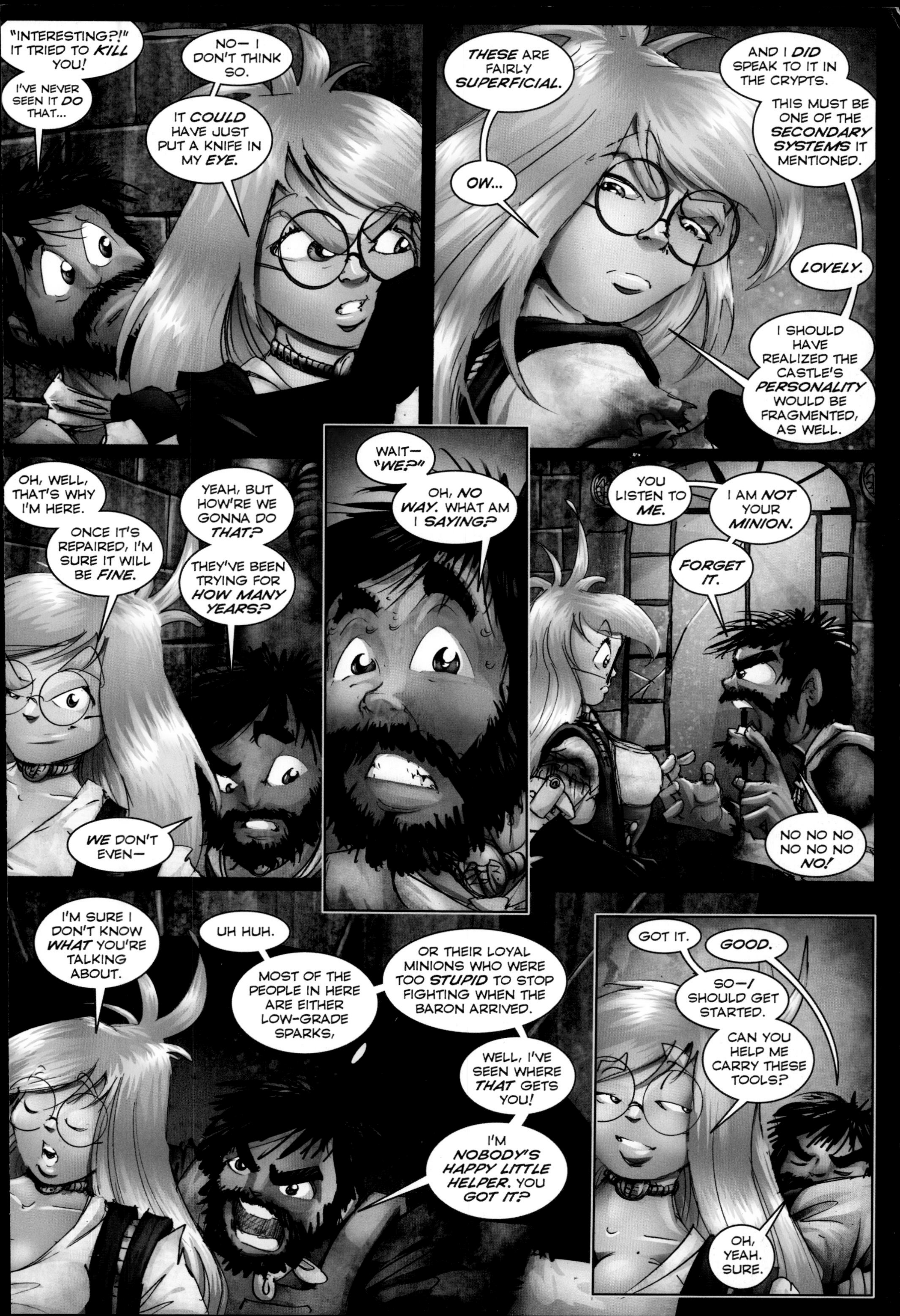
"INTERESTING?!" IT TRIED TO KILL YOU!
I'VE NEVER SEEN IT DO THAT...
NO— I DON'T THINK SO.
IT COULD HAVE JUST PUT A KNIFE IN MY EYE.
THESE ARE FAIRLY SUPERFICIAL.
OW...
AND I DID SPEAK TO IT IN THE CRYPTS.
THIS MUST BE ONE OF THE SECONDARY SYSTEMS IT MENTIONED.
LOVELY.
I SHOULD HAVE REALIZED THE CASTLE'S PERSONALITY WOULD BE FRAGMENTED, AS WELL.
OH, WELL, THAT'S WHY I'M HERE.
ONCE IT'S REPAIRED, I'M SURE IT WILL BE FINE.
YEAH, BUT HOW'RE WE GONNA DO THAT?
THEY'VE BEEN TRYING FOR HOW MANY YEARS?
WE DON'T EVEN—
WAIT— "WE?"
OH, NO WAY. WHAT AM I SAYING?
YOU LISTEN TO ME.
I AM NOT YOUR MINION.
FORGET IT.
NO NO NO NO NO NO NO!
I'M SURE I DON'T KNOW WHAT YOU'RE TALKING ABOUT.
UH HUH.
MOST OF THE PEOPLE IN HERE ARE EITHER LOW-GRADE SPARKS,
OR THEIR LOYAL MINIONS WHO WERE TOO STUPID TO STOP FIGHTING WHEN THE BARON ARRIVED.
WELL, I'VE SEEN WHERE THAT GETS YOU!
I'M NOBODY'S HAPPY LITTLE HELPER. YOU GOT IT?
GOT IT.
GOOD.
SO—I SHOULD GET STARTED.
CAN YOU HELP ME CARRY THESE TOOLS?
OH, YEAH. SURE.

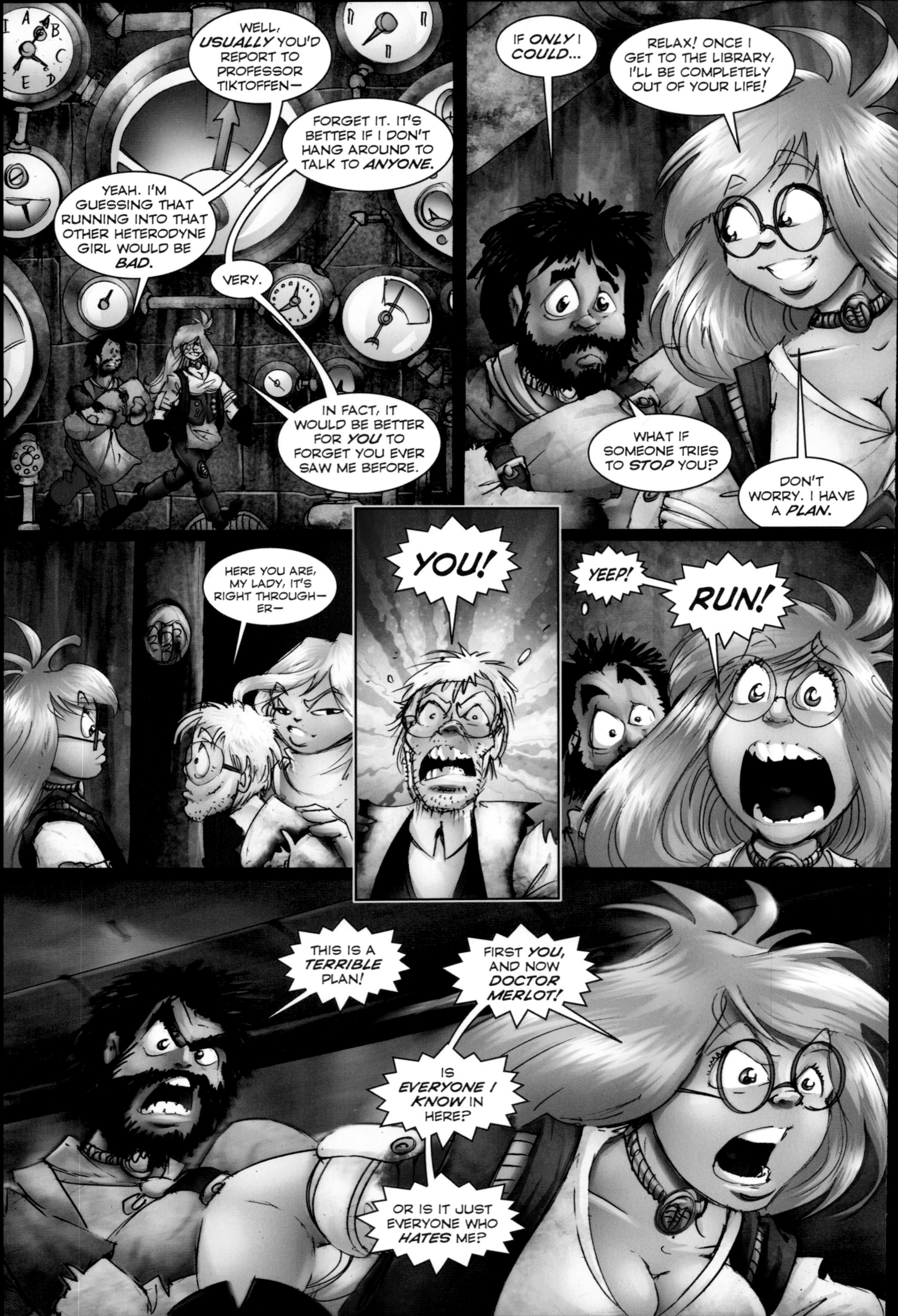
WELL, USUALLY YOU'D REPORT TO PROFESSOR TIKTOFFEN—
YEAH. I'M GUESSING THAT RUNNING INTO THAT OTHER HETERODYNE GIRL WOULD BE BAD.
FORGET IT. IT'S BETTER IF I DON'T HANG AROUND TO TALK TO ANYONE.
VERY.
IN FACT, IT WOULD BE BETTER FOR YOU TO FORGET YOU EVER SAW ME BEFORE.
IF ONLY I COULD...
RELAX! ONCE I GET TO THE LIBRARY, I'LL BE COMPLETELY OUT OF YOUR LIFE!
WHAT IF SOMEONE TRIES TO STOP YOU?
DON'T WORRY. I HAVE A PLAN.
HERE YOU ARE, MY LADY, IT'S RIGHT THROUGH—ER—
YOU!
YEEP!
RUN!
THIS IS A TERRIBLE PLAN!
FIRST YOU, AND NOW DOCTOR MERLOT!
IS EVERYONE I KNOW IN HERE?
OR IS IT JUST EVERYONE WHO HATES ME?

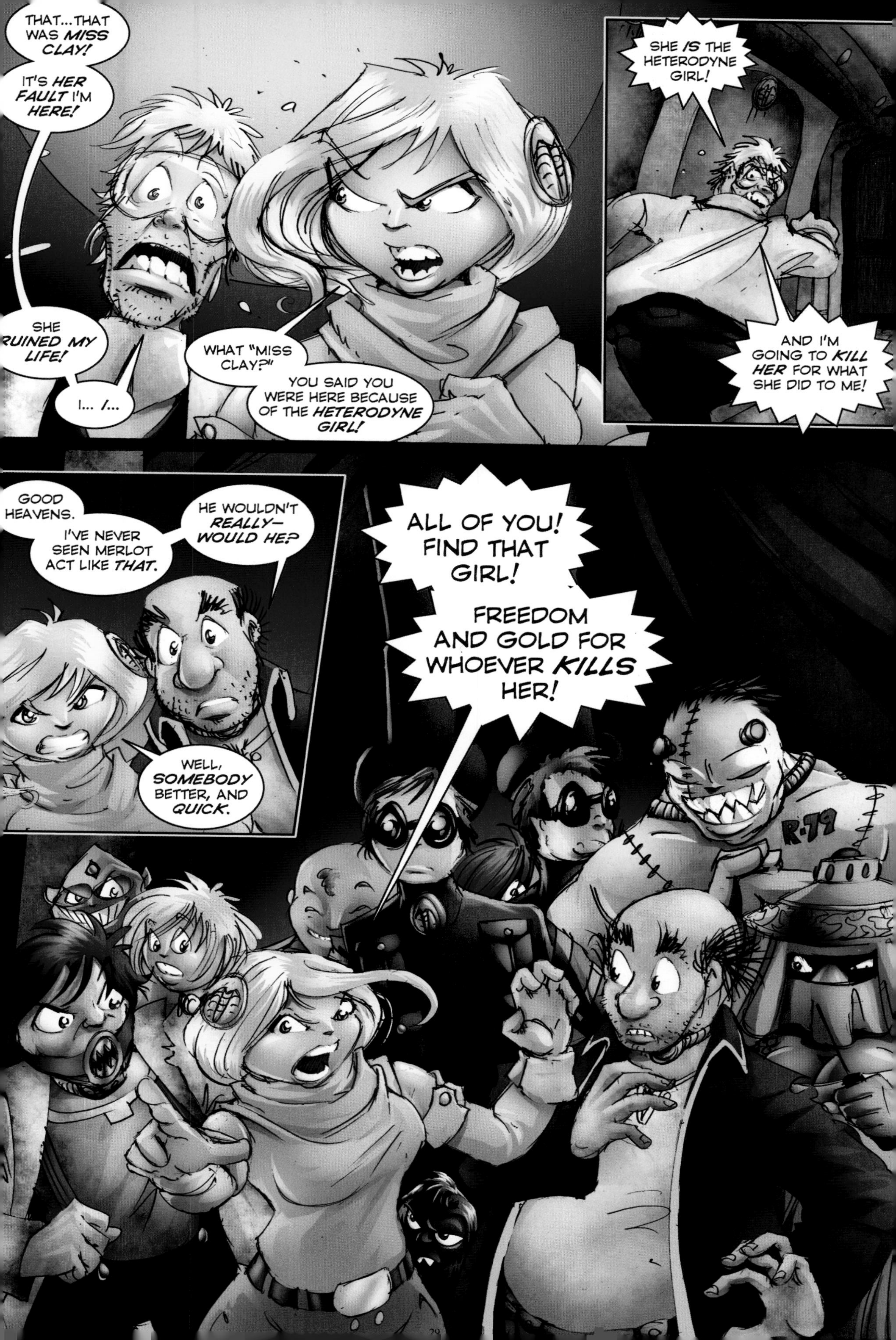
THAT... THAT WAS MISS CLAY!
IT'S HER FAULT I'M HERE!
SHE RUINED MY LIFE!
I... I...
WHAT "MISS CLAY?"
YOU SAID YOU WERE HERE BECAUSE OF THE HETERODYNE GIRL!
SHE IS THE HETERODYNE GIRL!
AND I'M GOING TO KILL HER FOR WHAT SHE DID TO ME!
GOOD HEAVENS.
I'VE NEVER SEEN MERLOT ACT LIKE THAT.
HE WOULDN'T REALLY— WOULD HE?
WELL, SOMEBODY BETTER, AND QUICK.
ALL OF YOU! FIND THAT GIRL!
FREEDOM AND GOLD FOR WHOEVER KILLS HER!
R-79

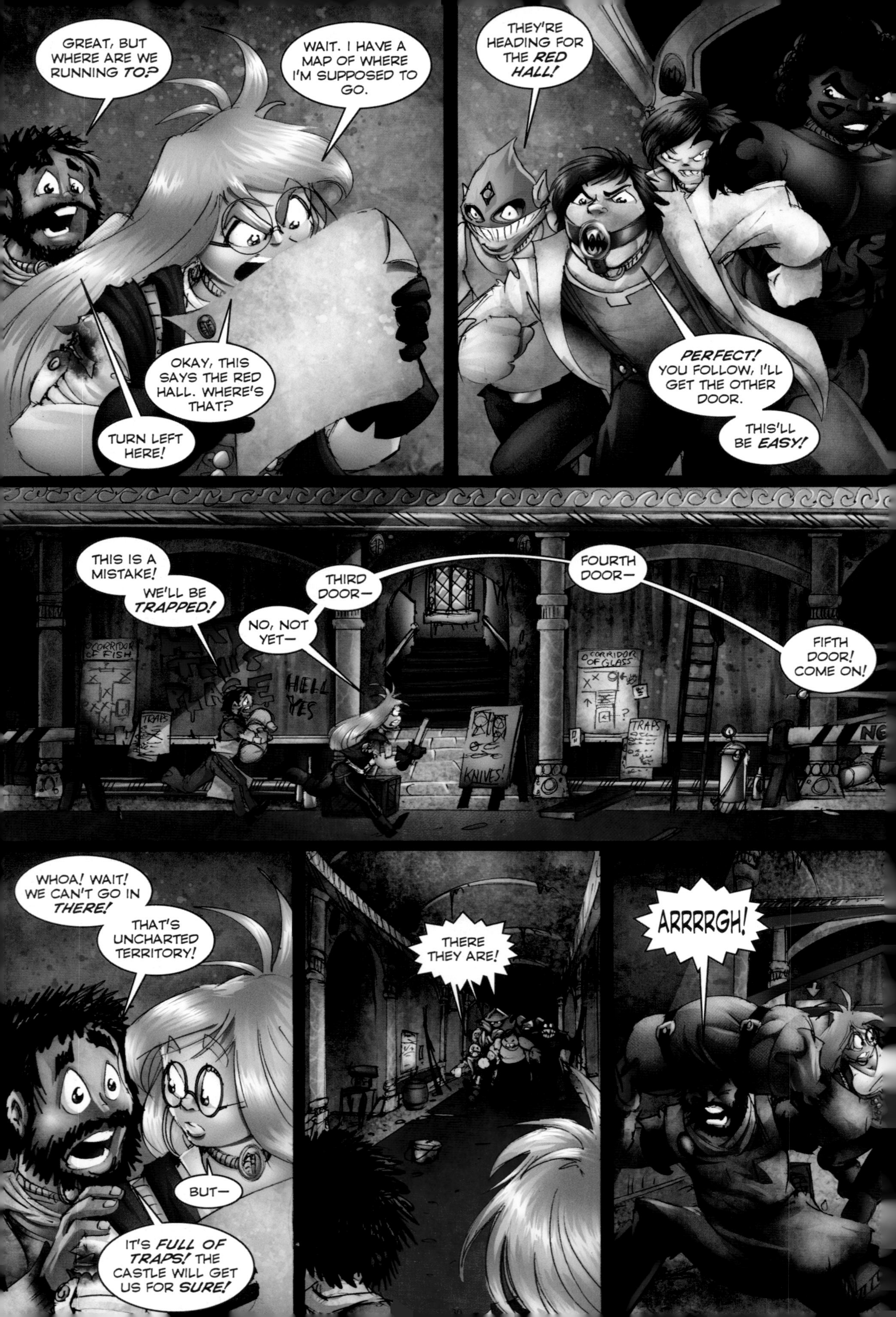
GREAT, BUT WHERE ARE WE RUNNING TO?
WAIT. I HAVE A MAP OF WHERE I'M SUPPOSED TO GO.
OKAY, THIS SAYS THE RED HALL. WHERE'S THAT?
TURN LEFT HERE!
THEY'RE HEADING FOR THE RED HALL!
PERFECT! YOU FOLLOW, I'LL GET THE OTHER DOOR.
THIS'LL BE EASY!
THIS IS A MISTAKE!
WE'LL BE TRAPPED!
NO, NOT YET—
THIRD DOOR—
FOURTH DOOR—
FIFTH DOOR! COME ON!
CORRIDOR OF FISH
HELL YES
TRAPS
KNIVES!
CORRIDOR OF GLASS
TRAPS
WHOA! WAIT! WE CAN'T GO IN THERE!
THAT'S UNCHARTED TERRITORY!
BUT—
IT'S FULL OF TRAPS! THE CASTLE WILL GET US FOR SURE!
THERE THEY ARE!
ARRRRGH!

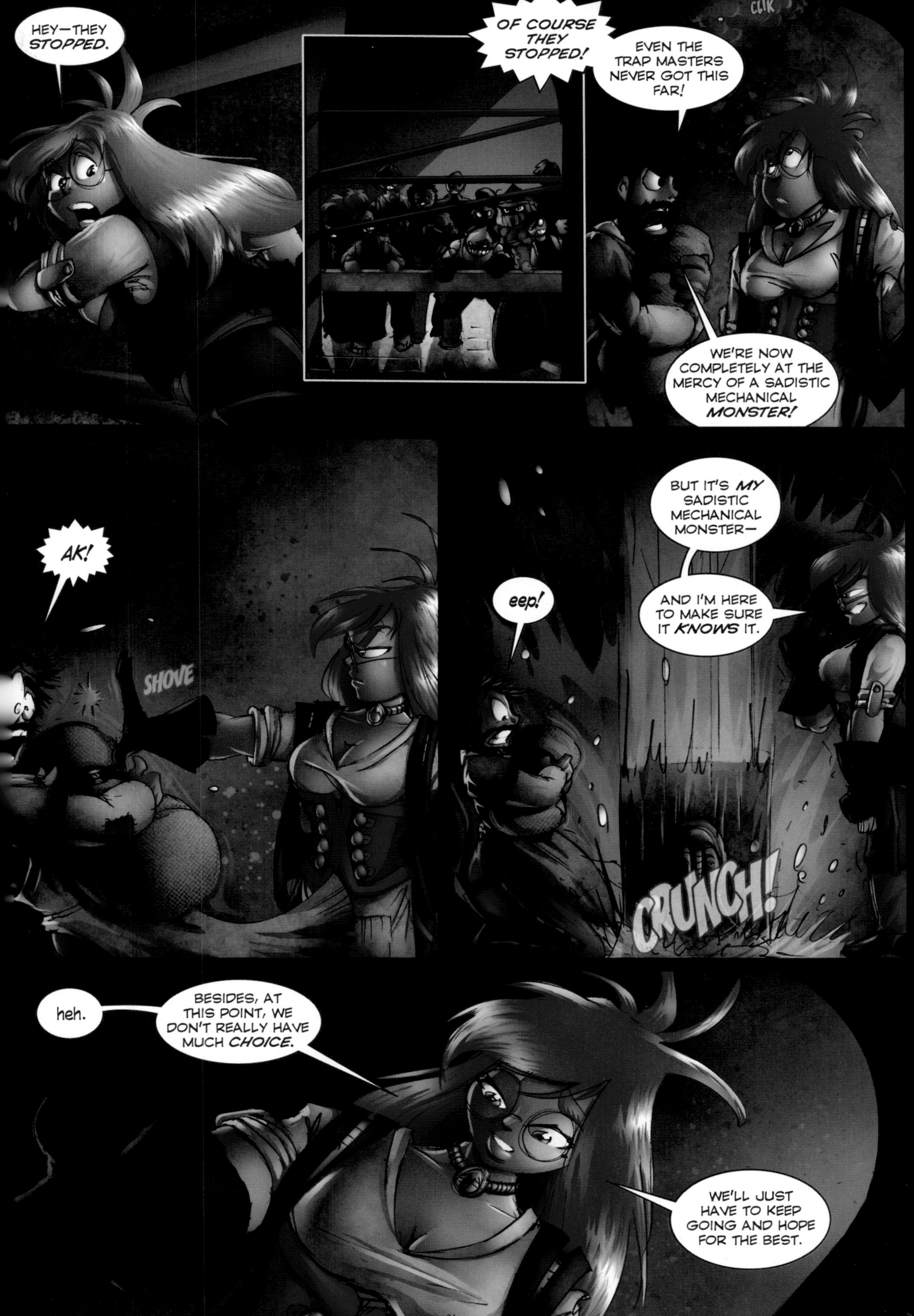
HEY—THEY STOPPED.
OF COURSE THEY STOPPED!
CLIK
EVEN THE TRAP MASTERS NEVER GOT THIS FAR!
WE'RE NOW COMPLETELY AT THE MERCY OF A SADISTIC MECHANICAL MONSTER!
AK!
SHOVE
eep!
BUT IT'S MY SADISTIC MECHANICAL MONSTER—
AND I'M HERE TO MAKE SURE IT KNOWS IT.
CRUNCH!
heh.
BESIDES, AT THIS POINT, WE DON'T REALLY HAVE MUCH CHOICE.
WE'LL JUST HAVE TO KEEP GOING AND HOPE FOR THE BEST.

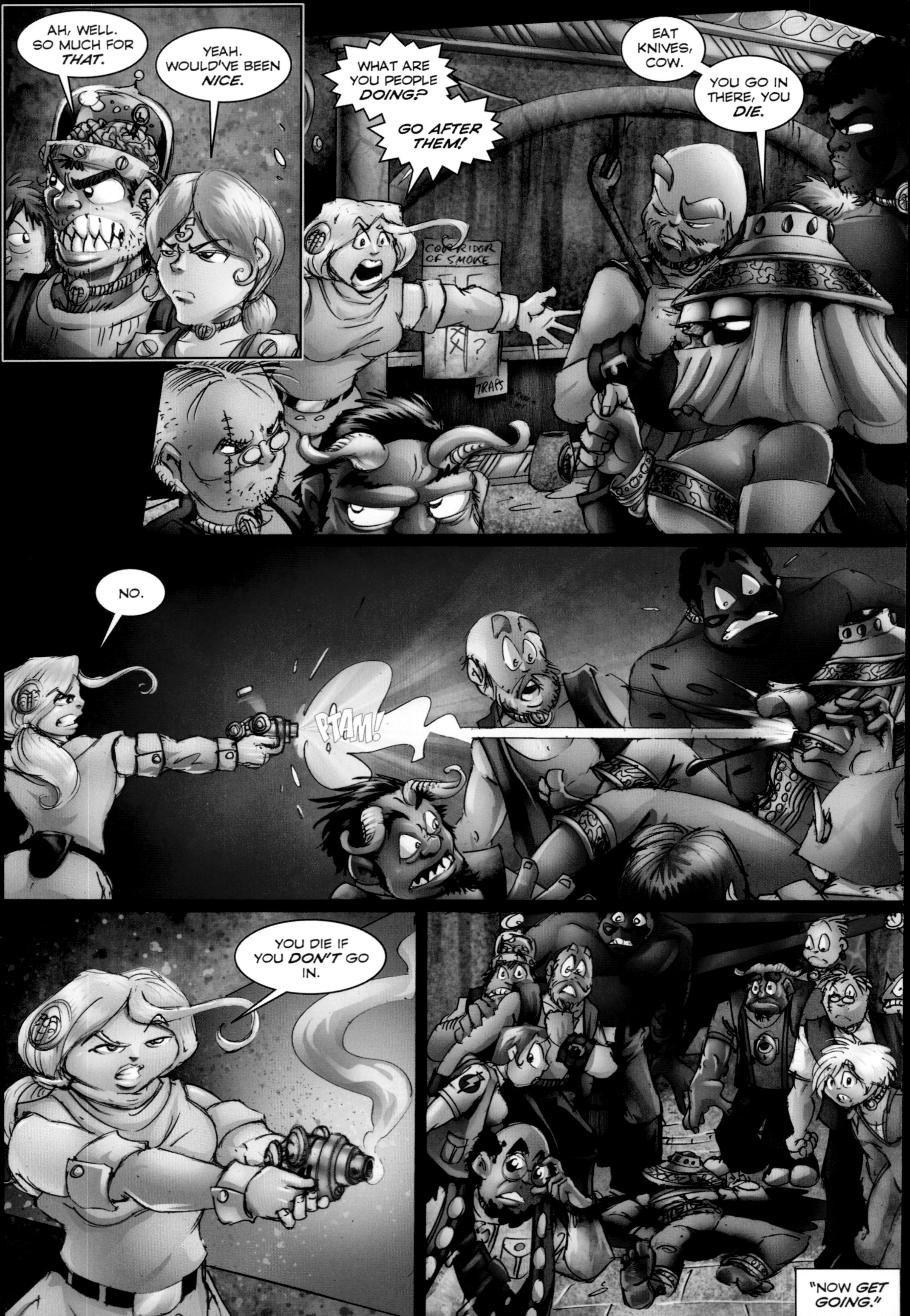
AH, WELL. SO MUCH FOR *THAT*.
YEAH. WOULD'VE BEEN *NICE*.
WHAT ARE YOU PEOPLE *DOING?*
GO AFTER THEM!
CORRIDOR OF SMOKE
TRAPS
EAT KNIVES, COW.
YOU GO IN THERE, YOU *DIE*.
NO.
PTAM!
YOU DIE IF YOU *DON'T* GO IN.
"NOW *GET GOING*."

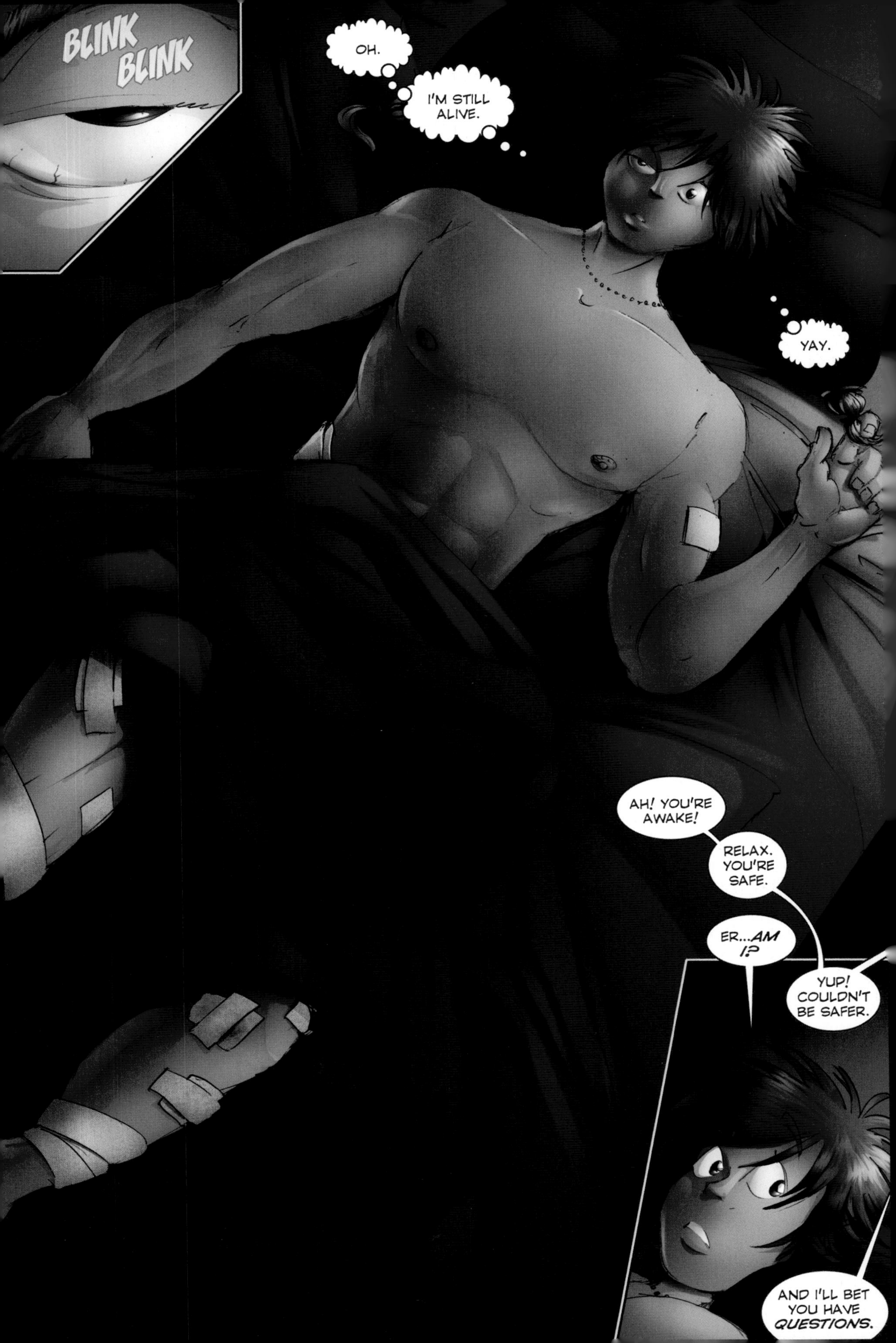
BLINK BLINK
OH.
I'M STILL ALIVE.
YAY.
AH! YOU'RE AWAKE!
RELAX. YOU'RE SAFE.
ER...*AM I?*
YUP! COULDN'T BE SAFER.
AND I'LL BET YOU HAVE *QUESTIONS.*

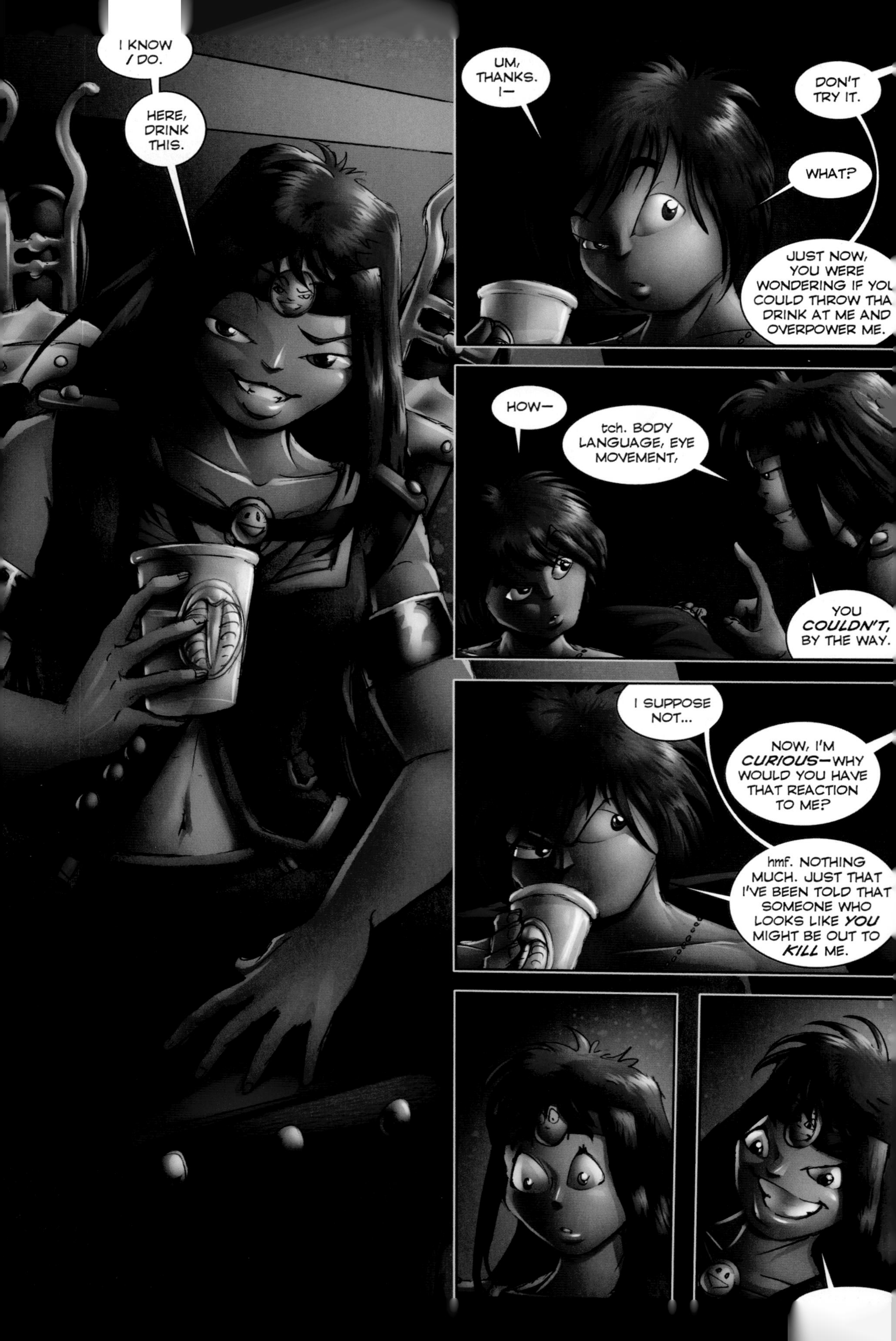
I KNOW *I* DO.
HERE, DRINK THIS.
UM, THANKS. I—
DON'T TRY IT.
WHAT?
JUST NOW, YOU WERE WONDERING IF YOU COULD THROW THAT DRINK AT ME AND OVERPOWER ME.
HOW—
tch. BODY LANGUAGE, EYE MOVEMENT,
YOU *COULDN'T,* BY THE WAY.
I SUPPOSE NOT...
NOW, I'M *CURIOUS*—WHY WOULD YOU HAVE THAT REACTION TO ME?
hmf. NOTHING MUCH. JUST THAT I'VE BEEN TOLD THAT SOMEONE WHO LOOKS LIKE *YOU* MIGHT BE OUT TO *KILL* ME.

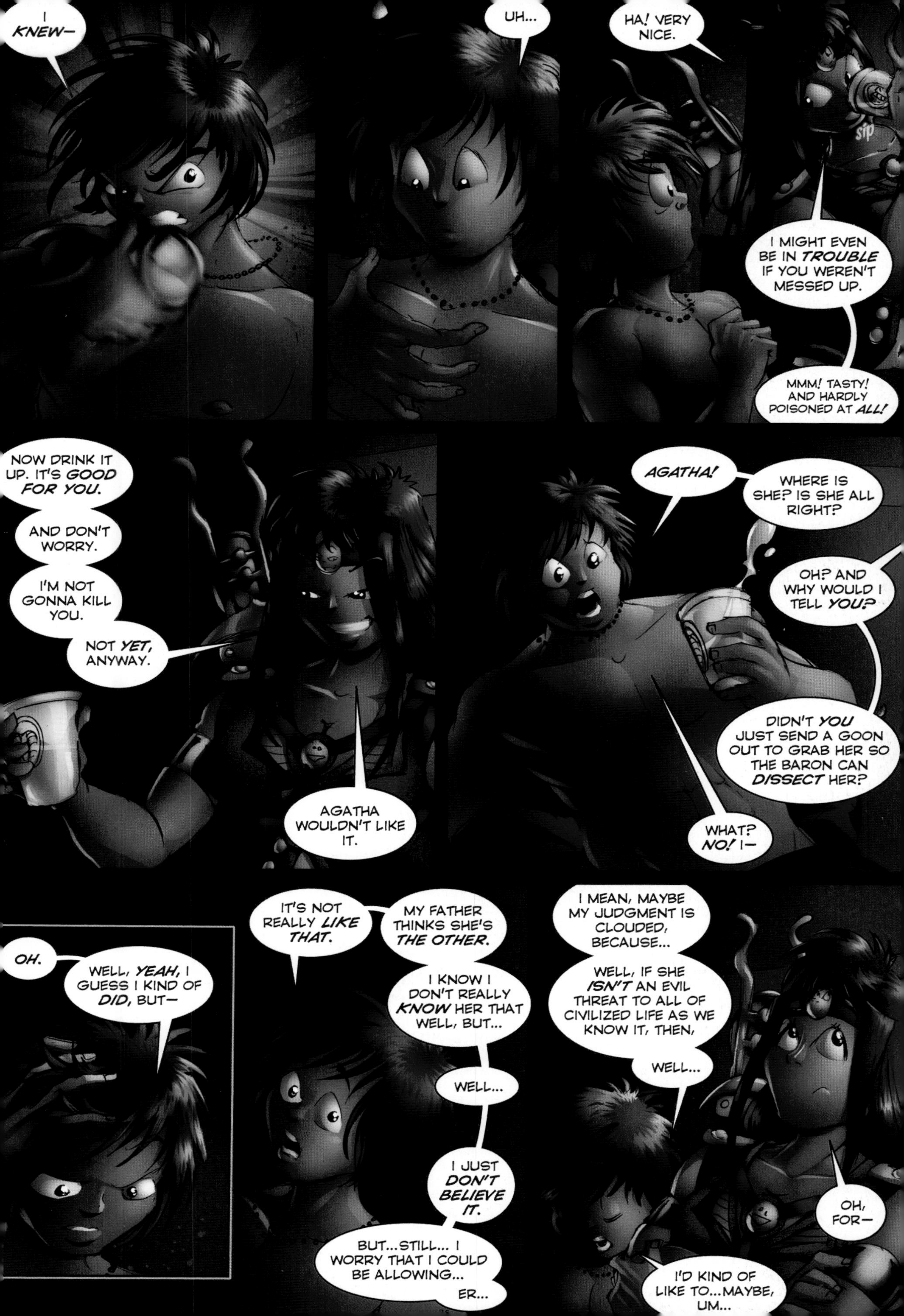
I KNEW—
UH...
HA! VERY NICE.
sip
I MIGHT EVEN BE IN TROUBLE IF YOU WEREN'T MESSED UP.
MMM! TASTY! AND HARDLY POISONED AT ALL!
NOW DRINK IT UP. IT'S GOOD FOR YOU.
AND DON'T WORRY.
I'M NOT GONNA KILL YOU.
NOT YET, ANYWAY.
AGATHA WOULDN'T LIKE IT.
AGATHA!
WHERE IS SHE? IS SHE ALL RIGHT?
OH? AND WHY WOULD I TELL YOU?
DIDN'T YOU JUST SEND A GOON OUT TO GRAB HER SO THE BARON CAN DISSECT HER?
WHAT? NO! I—
OH.
WELL, YEAH, I GUESS I KIND OF DID, BUT—
IT'S NOT REALLY LIKE THAT.
MY FATHER THINKS SHE'S THE OTHER.
I KNOW I DON'T REALLY KNOW HER THAT WELL, BUT...
WELL...
I JUST DON'T BELIEVE IT.
BUT...STILL... I WORRY THAT I COULD BE ALLOWING...
ER...
I MEAN, MAYBE MY JUDGMENT IS CLOUDED, BECAUSE...
WELL, IF SHE ISN'T AN EVIL THREAT TO ALL OF CIVILIZED LIFE AS WE KNOW IT, THEN,
WELL...
OH, FOR—
I'D KIND OF LIKE TO...MAYBE, UM...

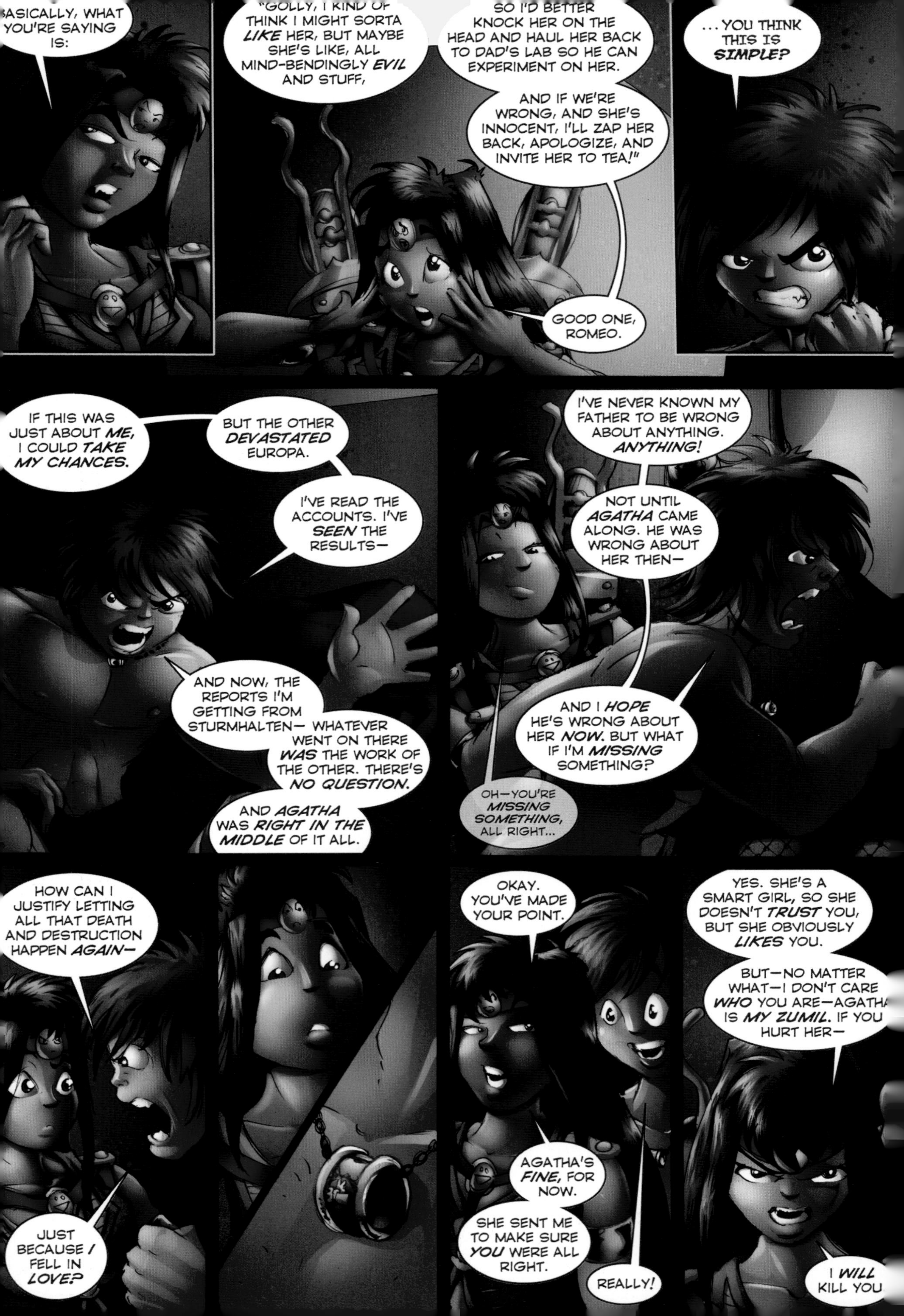

BASICALLY, WHAT YOU'RE SAYING IS:
"GOLLY, I KIND OF THINK I MIGHT SORTA *LIKE* HER, BUT MAYBE SHE'S LIKE, ALL MIND-BENDINGLY *EVIL* AND STUFF,
SO I'D BETTER KNOCK HER ON THE HEAD AND HAUL HER BACK TO DAD'S LAB SO HE CAN EXPERIMENT ON HER.
AND IF WE'RE WRONG, AND SHE'S INNOCENT, I'LL ZAP HER BACK, APOLOGIZE, AND INVITE HER TO TEA!"
GOOD ONE, ROMEO.
...YOU THINK THIS IS *SIMPLE?*
IF THIS WAS JUST ABOUT *ME,* I COULD *TAKE MY CHANCES.*
BUT THE OTHER *DEVASTATED* EUROPA.
I'VE READ THE ACCOUNTS. I'VE *SEEN* THE RESULTS—
AND NOW, THE REPORTS I'M GETTING FROM STURMHALTEN— WHATEVER WENT ON THERE *WAS* THE WORK OF THE OTHER. THERE'S *NO QUESTION.*
AND *AGATHA* WAS *RIGHT IN THE MIDDLE* OF IT ALL.
I'VE NEVER KNOWN MY FATHER TO BE WRONG ABOUT ANYTHING. *ANYTHING!*
NOT UNTIL *AGATHA* CAME ALONG. HE WAS WRONG ABOUT HER THEN—
AND I *HOPE* HE'S WRONG ABOUT HER *NOW.* BUT WHAT IF I'M *MISSING* SOMETHING?
OH—YOU'RE *MISSING SOMETHING,* ALL RIGHT...
HOW CAN I JUSTIFY LETTING ALL THAT DEATH AND DESTRUCTION HAPPEN *AGAIN*—
JUST BECAUSE *I* FELL IN *LOVE?*
OKAY. YOU'VE MADE YOUR POINT.
AGATHA'S *FINE,* FOR NOW.
SHE SENT ME TO MAKE SURE *YOU* WERE ALL RIGHT.
REALLY!
YES. SHE'S A SMART GIRL, SO SHE DOESN'T *TRUST* YOU, BUT SHE OBVIOUSLY *LIKES* YOU.
BUT—NO MATTER WHAT—I DON'T CARE *WHO* YOU ARE—AGATHA IS *MY ZUMIL.* IF YOU HURT HER—
I *WILL* KILL YOU.

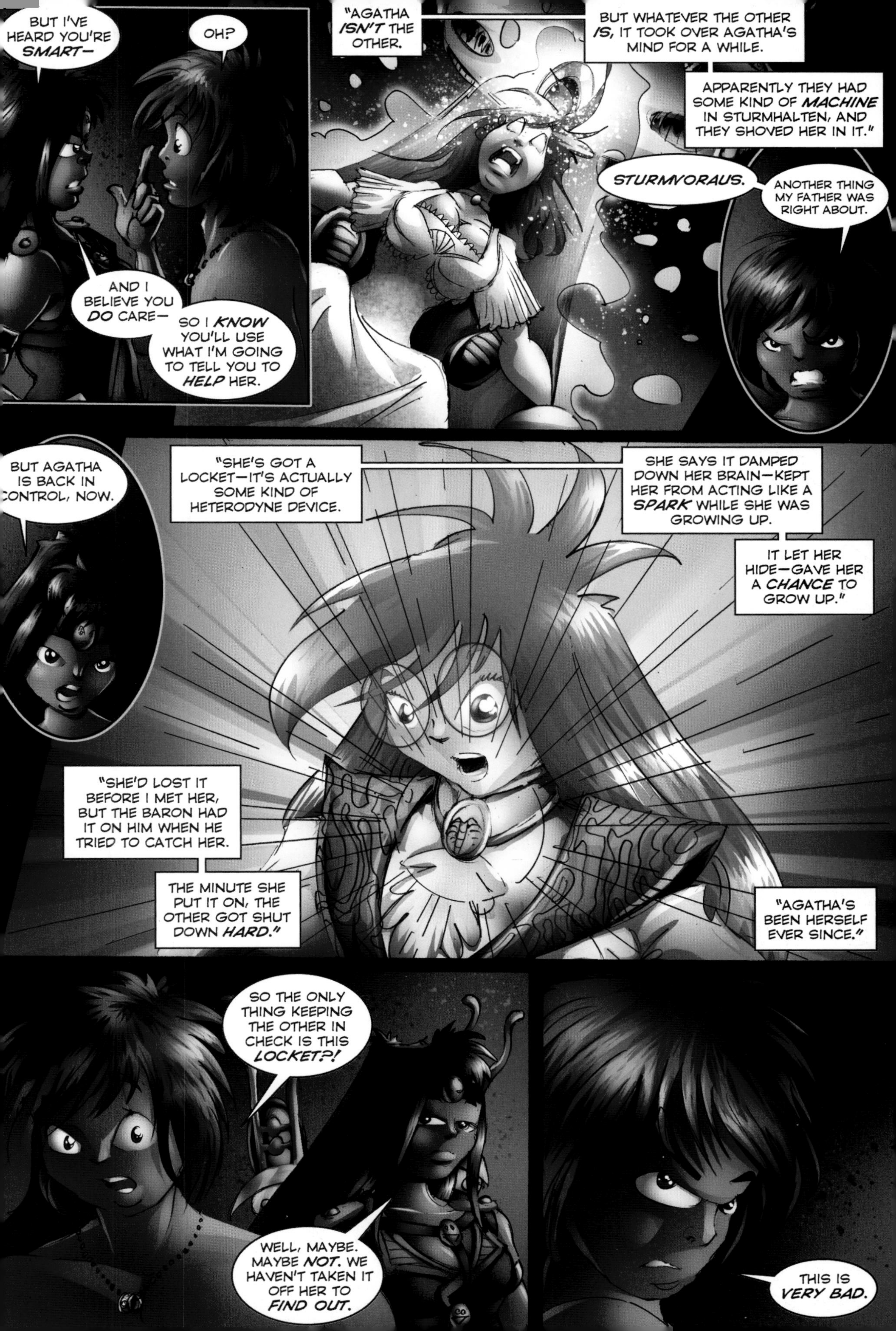
BUT I'VE HEARD YOU'RE SMART—
OH?
AND I BELIEVE YOU DO CARE—
SO I KNOW YOU'LL USE WHAT I'M GOING TO TELL YOU TO HELP HER.
"AGATHA ISN'T THE OTHER.
BUT WHATEVER THE OTHER IS, IT TOOK OVER AGATHA'S MIND FOR A WHILE.
APPARENTLY THEY HAD SOME KIND OF MACHINE IN STURMHALTEN, AND THEY SHOVED HER IN IT."
STURMVORAUS.
ANOTHER THING MY FATHER WAS RIGHT ABOUT.
BUT AGATHA IS BACK IN CONTROL, NOW.
"SHE'S GOT A LOCKET—IT'S ACTUALLY SOME KIND OF HETERODYNE DEVICE.
SHE SAYS IT DAMPED DOWN HER BRAIN—KEPT HER FROM ACTING LIKE A SPARK WHILE SHE WAS GROWING UP.
IT LET HER HIDE—GAVE HER A CHANCE TO GROW UP."
"SHE'D LOST IT BEFORE I MET HER, BUT THE BARON HAD IT ON HIM WHEN HE TRIED TO CATCH HER.
THE MINUTE SHE PUT IT ON, THE OTHER GOT SHUT DOWN HARD."
"AGATHA'S BEEN HERSELF EVER SINCE."
SO THE ONLY THING KEEPING THE OTHER IN CHECK IS THIS LOCKET?!
WELL, MAYBE. MAYBE NOT. WE HAVEN'T TAKEN IT OFF HER TO FIND OUT.
THIS IS VERY BAD.

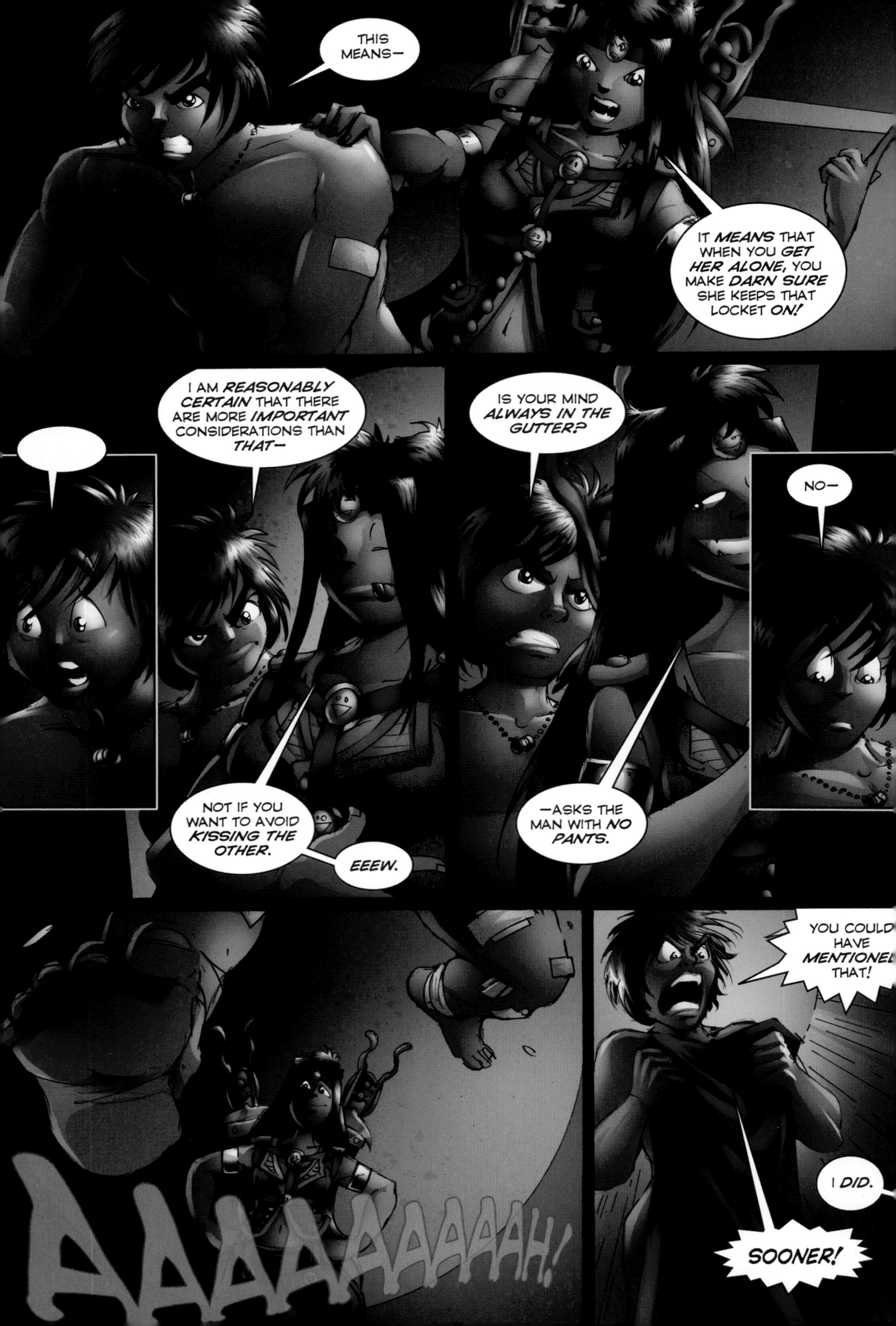
THIS MEANS—
IT MEANS THAT WHEN YOU GET HER ALONE, YOU MAKE DARN SURE SHE KEEPS THAT LOCKET ON!
I AM REASONABLY CERTAIN THAT THERE ARE MORE IMPORTANT CONSIDERATIONS THAN THAT—
NOT IF YOU WANT TO AVOID KISSING THE OTHER.
EEEW.
IS YOUR MIND ALWAYS IN THE GUTTER?
—ASKS THE MAN WITH NO PANTS.
NO—
AAAAAAAAAAH!
YOU COULD HAVE MENTIONED THAT!
I DID.
SOONER!

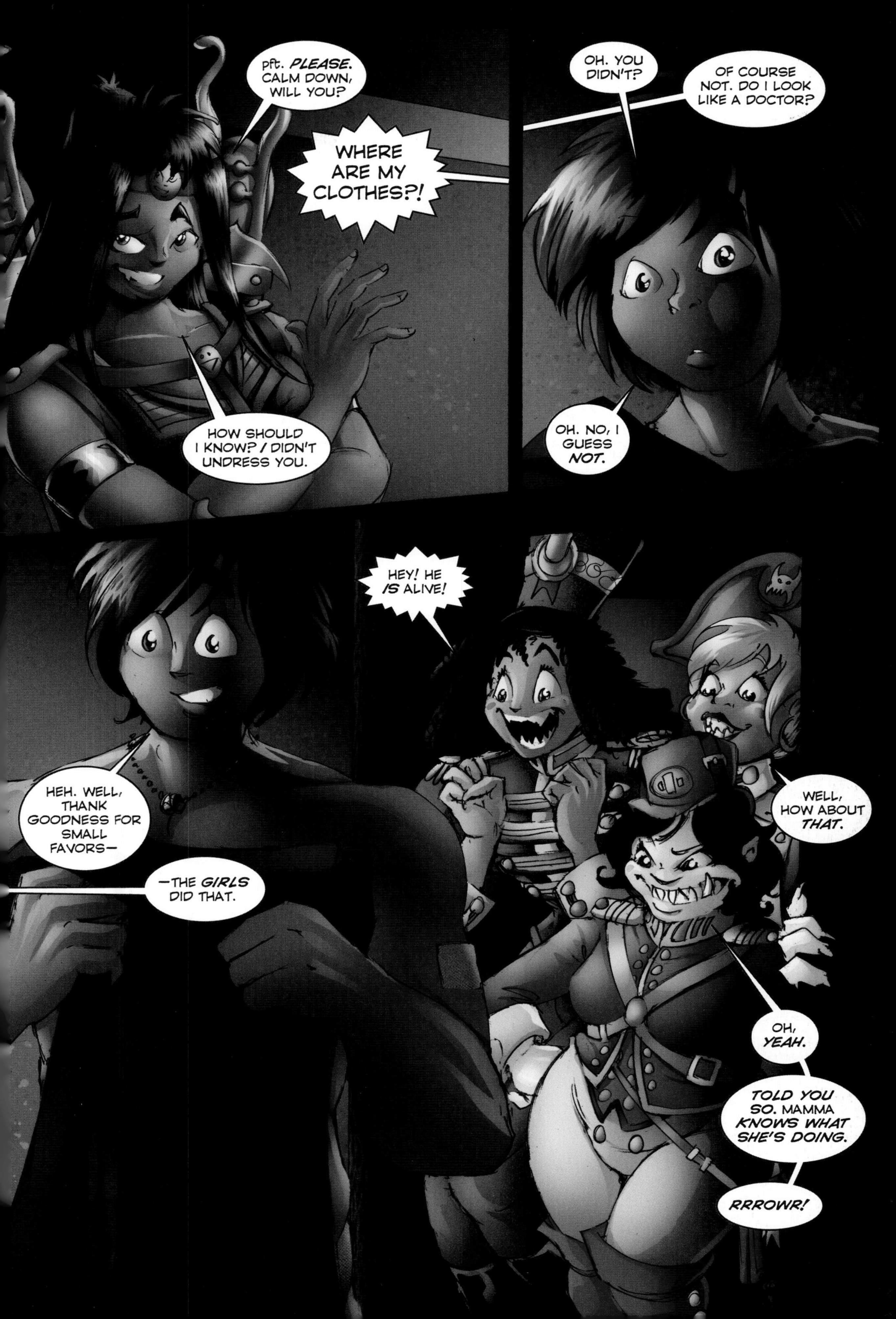

pft. PLEASE. CALM DOWN, WILL YOU?
WHERE ARE MY CLOTHES?!
HOW SHOULD I KNOW? I DIDN'T UNDRESS YOU.
OH. YOU DIDN'T?
OF COURSE NOT. DO I LOOK LIKE A DOCTOR?
OH. NO, I GUESS NOT.
HEY! HE IS ALIVE!
HEH. WELL, THANK GOODNESS FOR SMALL FAVORS—
—THE GIRLS DID THAT.
WELL, HOW ABOUT THAT.
OH, YEAH.
TOLD YOU SO. MAMMA KNOWS WHAT SHE'S DOING.
RRROWR!

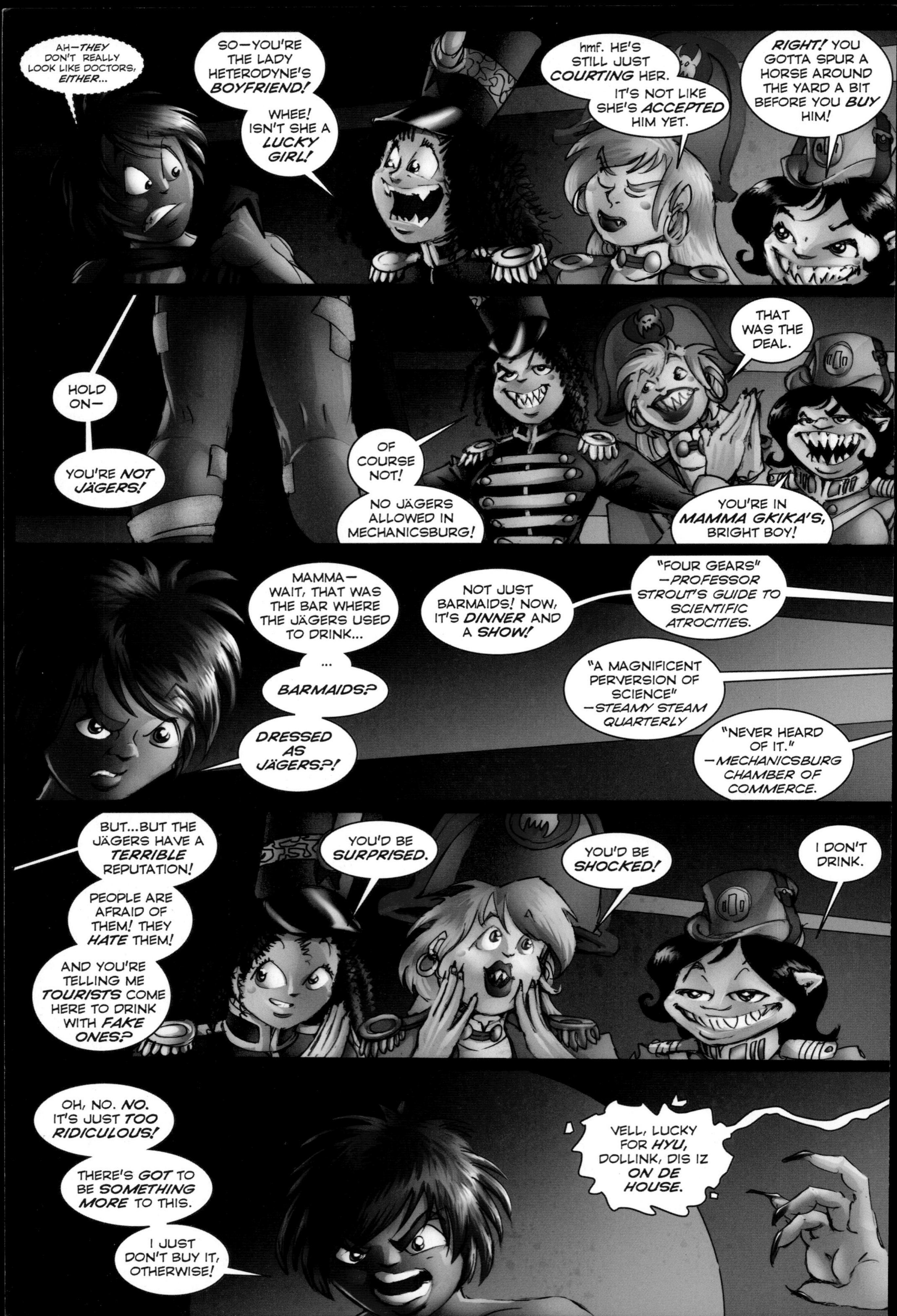
AH—THEY DON'T REALLY LOOK LIKE DOCTORS, EITHER...
SO—YOU'RE THE LADY HETERODYNE'S BOYFRIEND!
WHEE! ISN'T SHE A LUCKY GIRL!
hmf. HE'S STILL JUST COURTING HER.
IT'S NOT LIKE SHE'S ACCEPTED HIM YET.
RIGHT! YOU GOTTA SPUR A HORSE AROUND THE YARD A BIT BEFORE YOU BUY HIM!
HOLD ON—
YOU'RE NOT JÄGERS!
THAT WAS THE DEAL.
OF COURSE NOT!
NO JÄGERS ALLOWED IN MECHANICSBURG!
YOU'RE IN MAMMA GKIKA'S, BRIGHT BOY!
MAMMA— WAIT, THAT WAS THE BAR WHERE THE JÄGERS USED TO DRINK...
...
BARMAIDS?
DRESSED AS JÄGERS?!
NOT JUST BARMAIDS! NOW, IT'S DINNER AND A SHOW!
"FOUR GEARS" —PROFESSOR STROUT'S GUIDE TO SCIENTIFIC ATROCITIES.
"A MAGNIFICENT PERVERSION OF SCIENCE" —STEAMY STEAM QUARTERLY
"NEVER HEARD OF IT." —MECHANICSBURG CHAMBER OF COMMERCE.
BUT...BUT THE JÄGERS HAVE A TERRIBLE REPUTATION!
PEOPLE ARE AFRAID OF THEM! THEY HATE THEM!
AND YOU'RE TELLING ME TOURISTS COME HERE TO DRINK WITH FAKE ONES?
YOU'D BE SURPRISED.
YOU'D BE SHOCKED!
I DON'T DRINK.
OH, NO. NO. IT'S JUST TOO RIDICULOUS!
THERE'S GOT TO BE SOMETHING MORE TO THIS.
I JUST DON'T BUY IT, OTHERWISE!
VELL, LUCKY FOR HYU, DOLLINK, DIS IZ ON DE HOUSE.

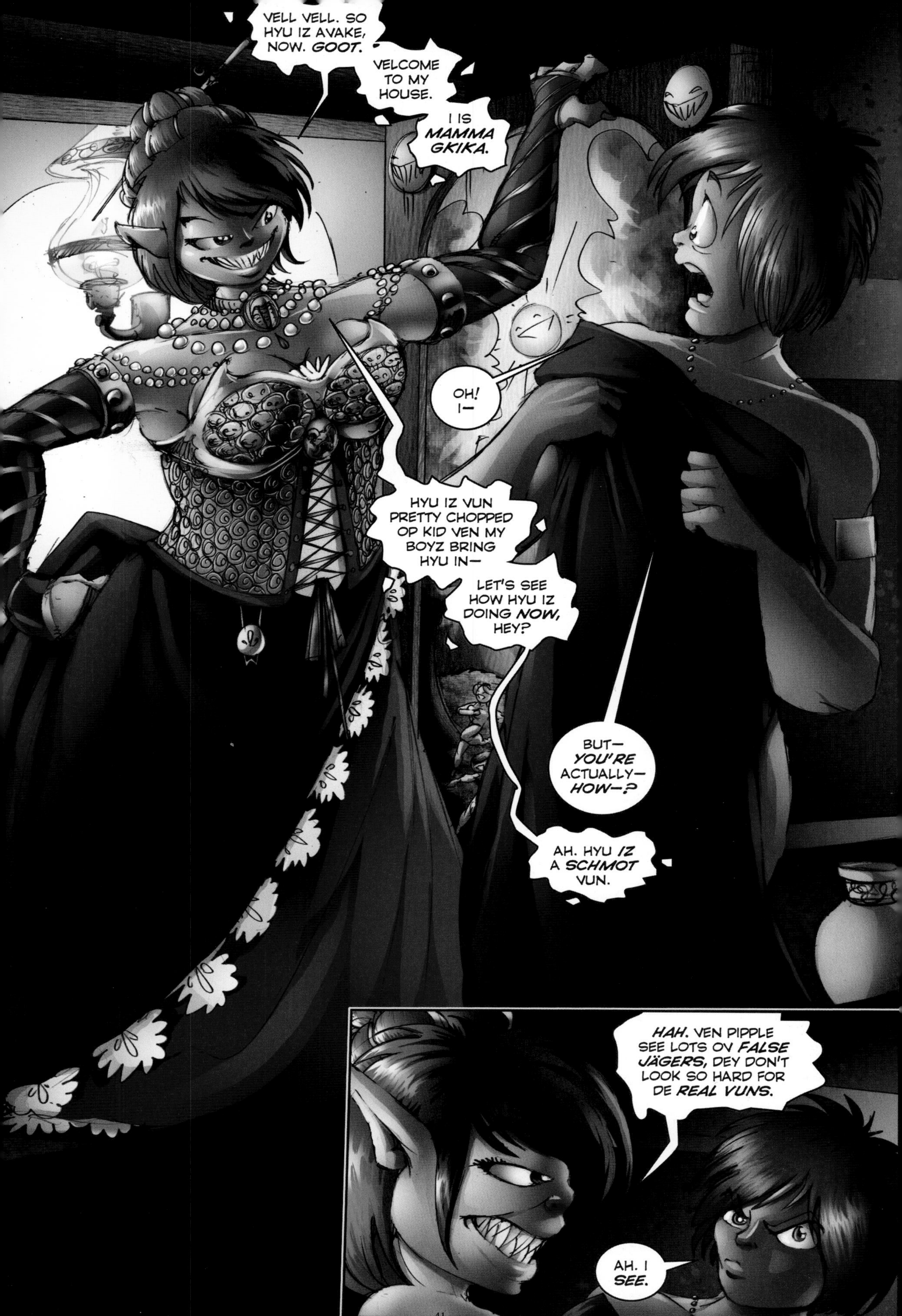
VELL VELL. SO HYU IZ AVAKE, NOW. GOOT.
VELCOME TO MY HOUSE.
I IS MAMMA GKIKA.
OH! I—
HYU IZ VUN PRETTY CHOPPED OP KID VEN MY BOYZ BRING HYU IN—
LET'S SEE HOW HYU IZ DOING NOW, HEY?
BUT— YOU'RE ACTUALLY— HOW—?
AH. HYU IZ A SCHMOT VUN.
HAH. VEN PIPPLE SEE LOTS OV FALSE JÄGERS, DEY DON'T LOOK SO HARD FOR DE REAL VUNS.
AH. I SEE.

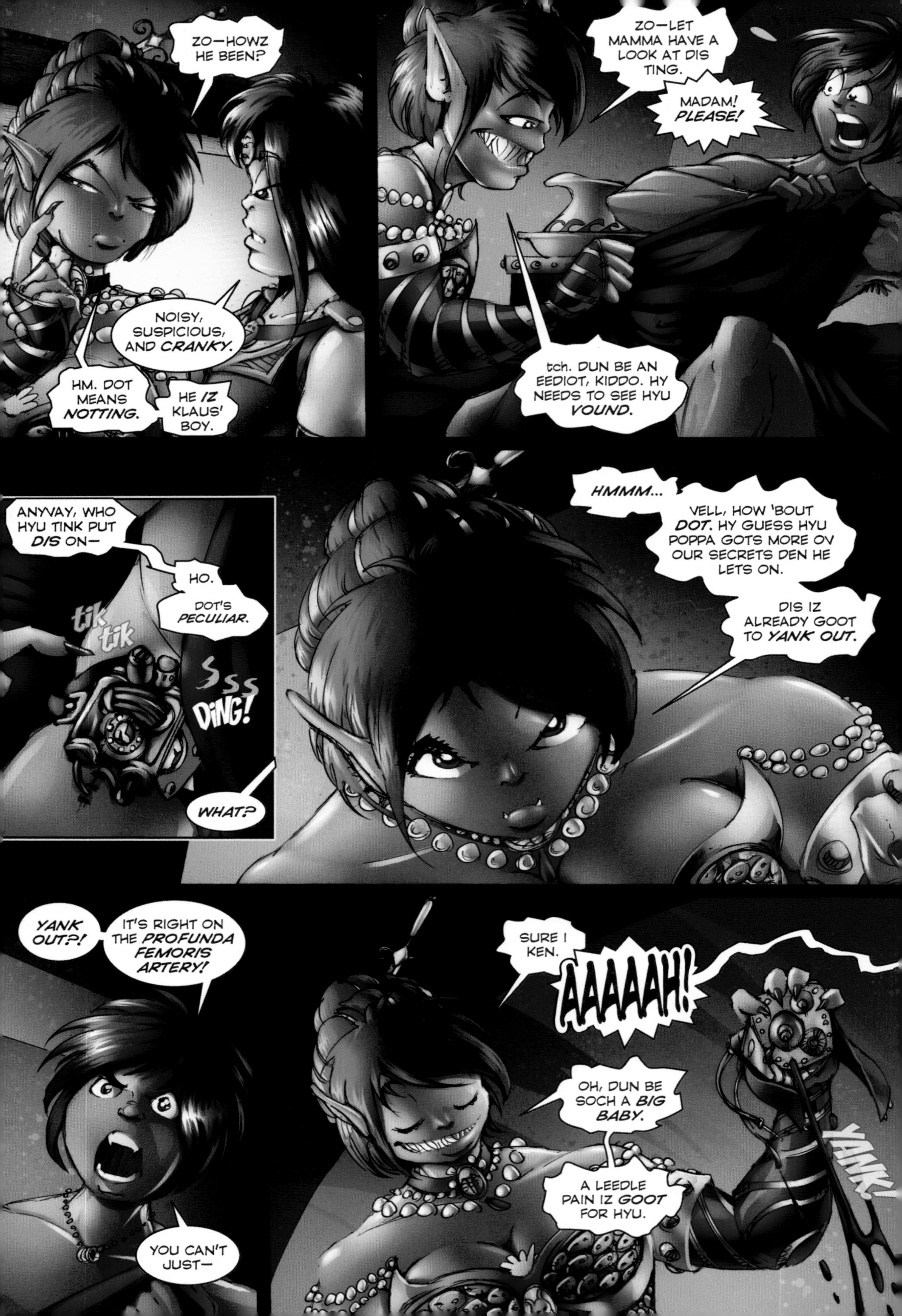
ZO—HOWZ HE BEEN?
NOISY, SUSPICIOUS, AND *CRANKY.*
HM. DOT MEANS *NOTTING.*
HE *IZ* KLAUS' BOY.
ZO—LET MAMMA HAVE A LOOK AT DIS TING.
MADAM! *PLEASE!*
tch. DUN BE AN EEDIOT, KIDDO. HY NEEDS TO SEE HYU *VOUND.*
ANYVAY, WHO HYU TINK PUT *DIS* ON—
HO.
DOT'S *PECULIAR.*
tik tik
Sss
DiNG!
WHAT?
HMMM...
VELL, HOW 'BOUT *DOT.* HY GUESS HYU POPPA GOTS MORE OV OUR SECRETS DEN HE LETS ON.
DIS IZ ALREADY GOOT TO *YANK OUT.*
YANK OUT?!
IT'S RIGHT ON THE *PROFUNDA FEMORIS ARTERY!*
YOU CAN'T JUST—
SURE I KEN.
AAAAAH!
OH, DUN BE SOCH A *BIG BABY.*
A LEEDLE PAIN IZ *GOOT* FOR HYU.
YANK!

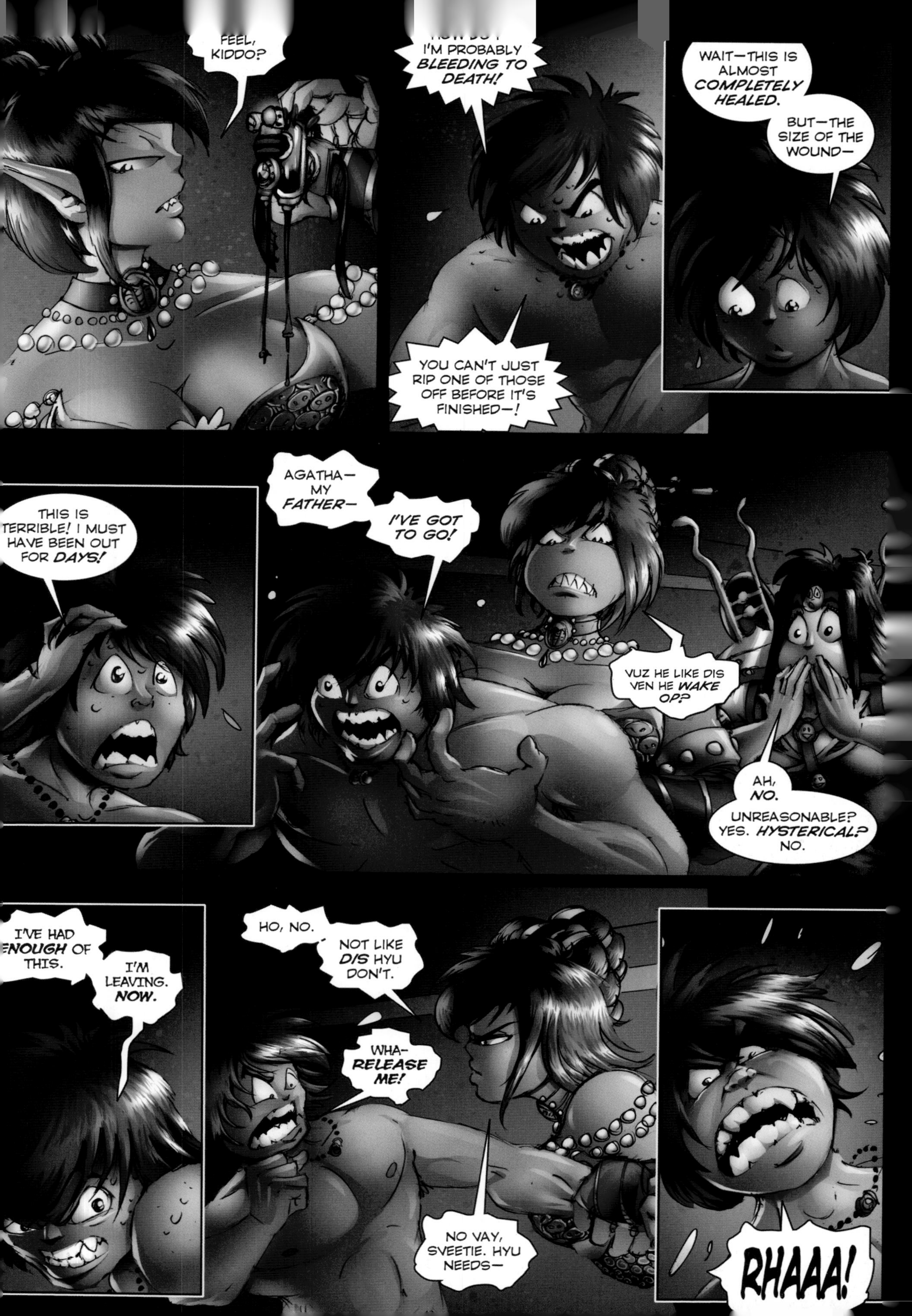

FEEL, KIDDO?
I'M PROBABLY *BLEEDING TO DEATH!*
YOU CAN'T JUST RIP ONE OF THOSE OFF BEFORE IT'S FINISHED—!
WAIT—THIS IS ALMOST *COMPLETELY HEALED.*
BUT—THE SIZE OF THE WOUND—
THIS IS TERRIBLE! I MUST HAVE BEEN OUT FOR *DAYS!*
AGATHA— MY *FATHER—*
I'VE GOT TO GO!
VUZ HE LIKE DIS VEN HE *WAKE OP?*
AH, **NO.** UNREASONABLE? YES. *HYSTERICAL?* NO.
I'VE HAD **ENOUGH** OF THIS.
I'M LEAVING. **NOW.**
HO, NO.
NOT LIKE *DIS* HYU DON'T.
WHA- **RELEASE ME!**
NO VAY, SVEETIE. HYU NEEDS—
RHAAA!

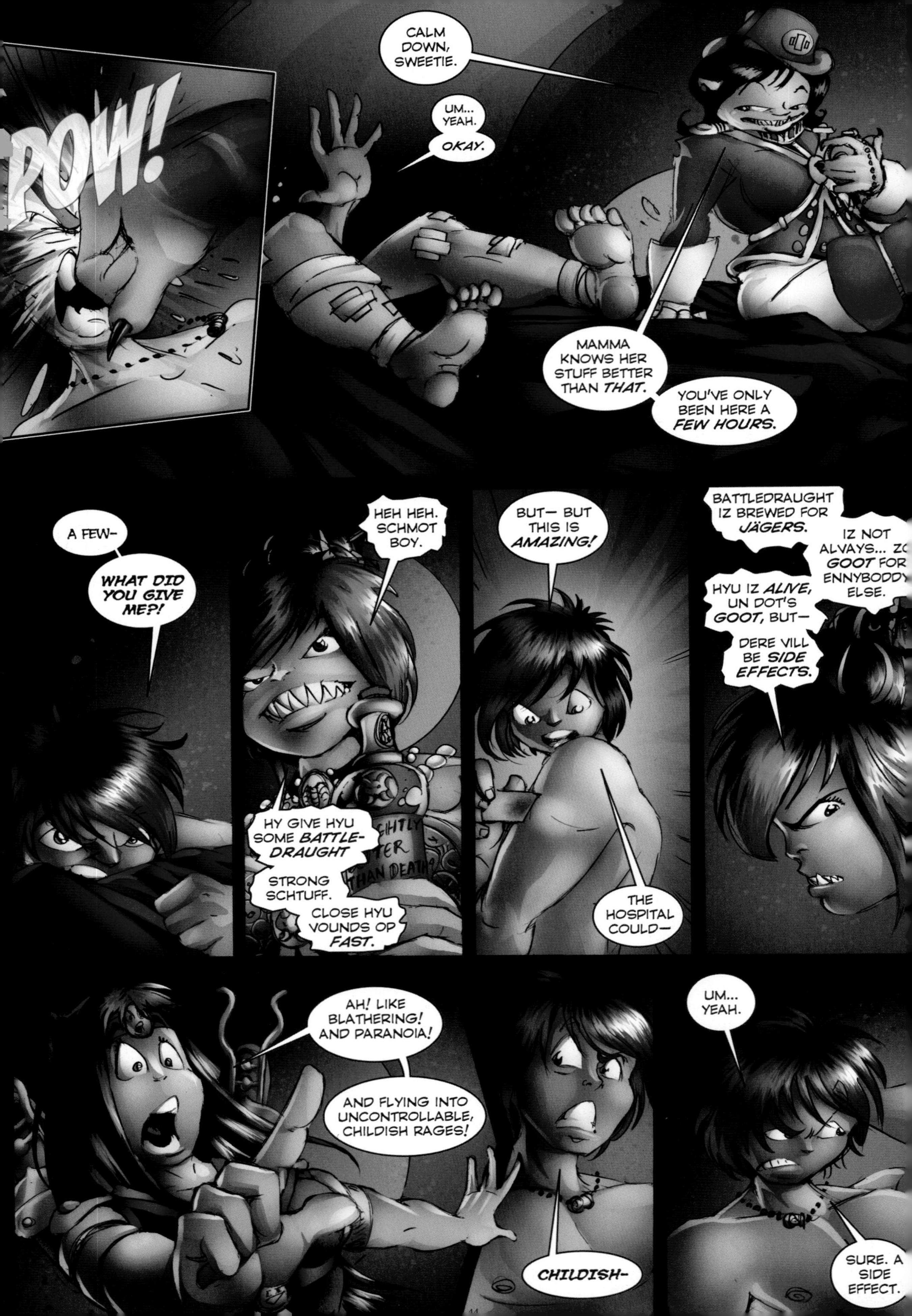
POW!
CALM DOWN, SWEETIE.
UM... YEAH.
OKAY.
MAMMA KNOWS HER STUFF BETTER THAN THAT.
YOU'VE ONLY BEEN HERE A FEW HOURS.
A FEW-
WHAT DID YOU GIVE ME?!
HEH HEH. SCHMOT BOY.
HY GIVE HYU SOME BATTLE-DRAUGHT
STRONG SCHTUFF.
CLOSE HYU VOUNDS OP FAST.
BUT— BUT THIS IS AMAZING!
THE HOSPITAL COULD—
BATTLEDRAUGHT IZ BREWED FOR JÄGERS.
HYU IZ ALIVE, UN DOT'S GOOT, BUT—
DERE VILL BE SIDE EFFECTS.
IZ NOT ALVAYS... ZO GOOT FOR ENNYBODDY ELSE.
AH! LIKE BLATHERING! AND PARANOIA!
AND FLYING INTO UNCONTROLLABLE, CHILDISH RAGES!
CHILDISH-
UM... YEAH.
SURE. A SIDE EFFECT.

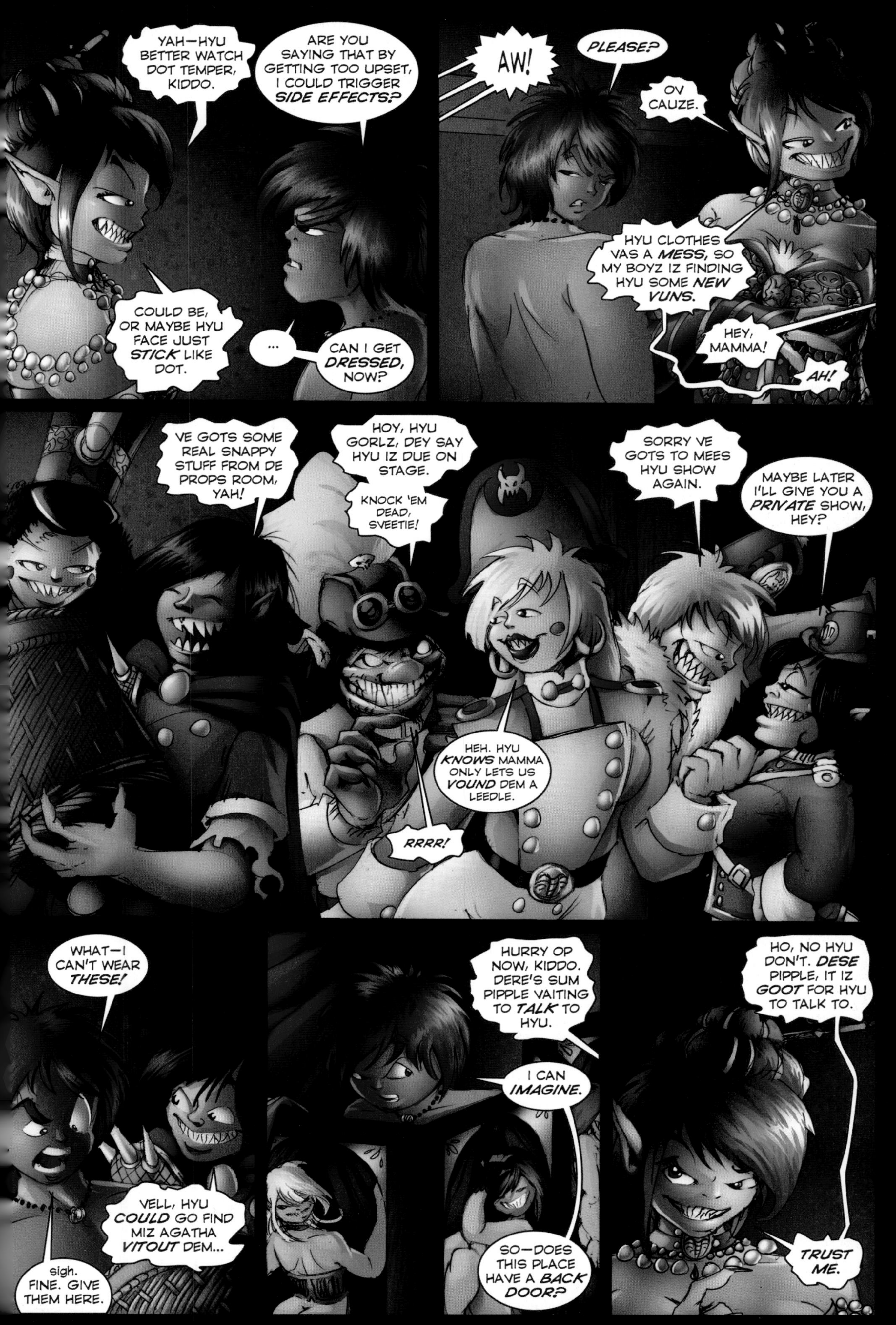
YAH—HYU BETTER WATCH DOT TEMPER, KIDDO.
ARE YOU SAYING THAT BY GETTING TOO UPSET, I COULD TRIGGER SIDE EFFECTS?
COULD BE, OR MAYBE HYU FACE JUST STICK LIKE DOT.
...
CAN I GET DRESSED, NOW?
AW!
PLEASE?
OV CAUZE.
HYU CLOTHES VAS A MESS, SO MY BOYZ IZ FINDING HYU SOME NEW VUNS.
HEY, MAMMA!
AH!
VE GOTS SOME REAL SNAPPY STUFF FROM DE PROPS ROOM, YAH!
HOY, HYU GORLZ, DEY SAY HYU IZ DUE ON STAGE.
KNOCK 'EM DEAD, SVEETIE!
SORRY VE GOTS TO MEES HYU SHOW AGAIN.
MAYBE LATER I'LL GIVE YOU A PRIVATE SHOW, HEY?
HEH. HYU KNOWS MAMMA ONLY LETS US VOUND DEM A LEEDLE.
RRRR!
WHAT—I CAN'T WEAR THESE!
VELL, HYU COULD GO FIND MIZ AGATHA VITOUT DEM...
sigh. FINE. GIVE THEM HERE.
HURRY OP NOW, KIDDO. DERE'S SUM PIPPLE VAITING TO TALK TO HYU.
I CAN IMAGINE.
SO—DOES THIS PLACE HAVE A BACK DOOR?
HO, NO HYU DON'T. DESE PIPPLE, IT IZ GOOT FOR HYU TO TALK TO.
TRUST ME.

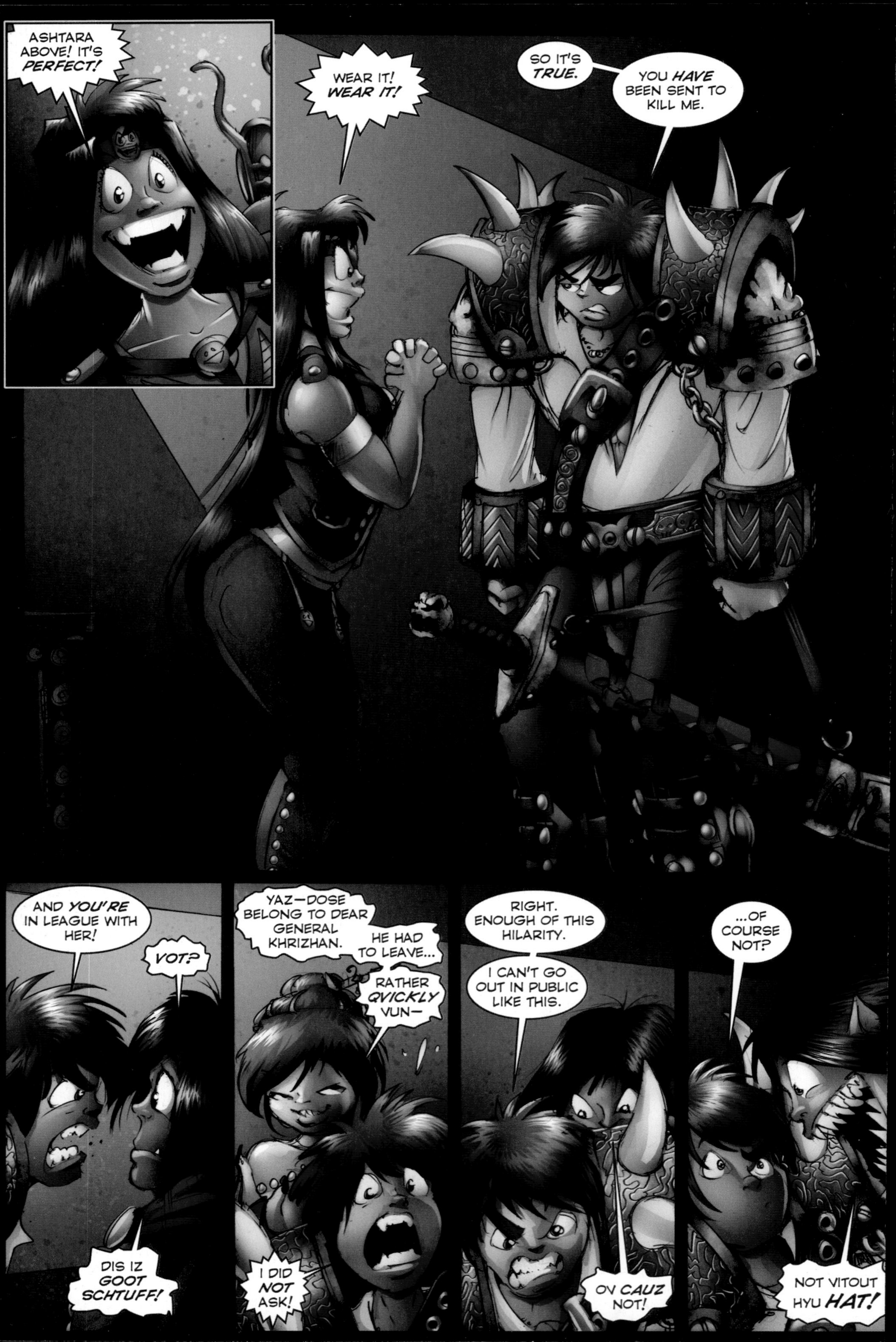
ASHTARA ABOVE! IT'S *PERFECT!*
WEAR IT! *WEAR IT!*
SO IT'S *TRUE*.
YOU *HAVE* BEEN SENT TO KILL ME.
AND *YOU'RE* IN LEAGUE WITH HER!
VOT?
DIS IZ *GOOT* *SCHTUFF!*
YAZ—DOSE BELONG TO DEAR GENERAL KHRIZHAN.
HE HAD TO LEAVE...
RATHER *QVICKLY* VUN—
I DID *NOT* ASK!
RIGHT. ENOUGH OF THIS HILARITY.
I CAN'T GO OUT IN PUBLIC LIKE THIS.
OV *CAUZ* NOT!
...OF COURSE NOT?
NOT VITOUT HYU *HAT!*

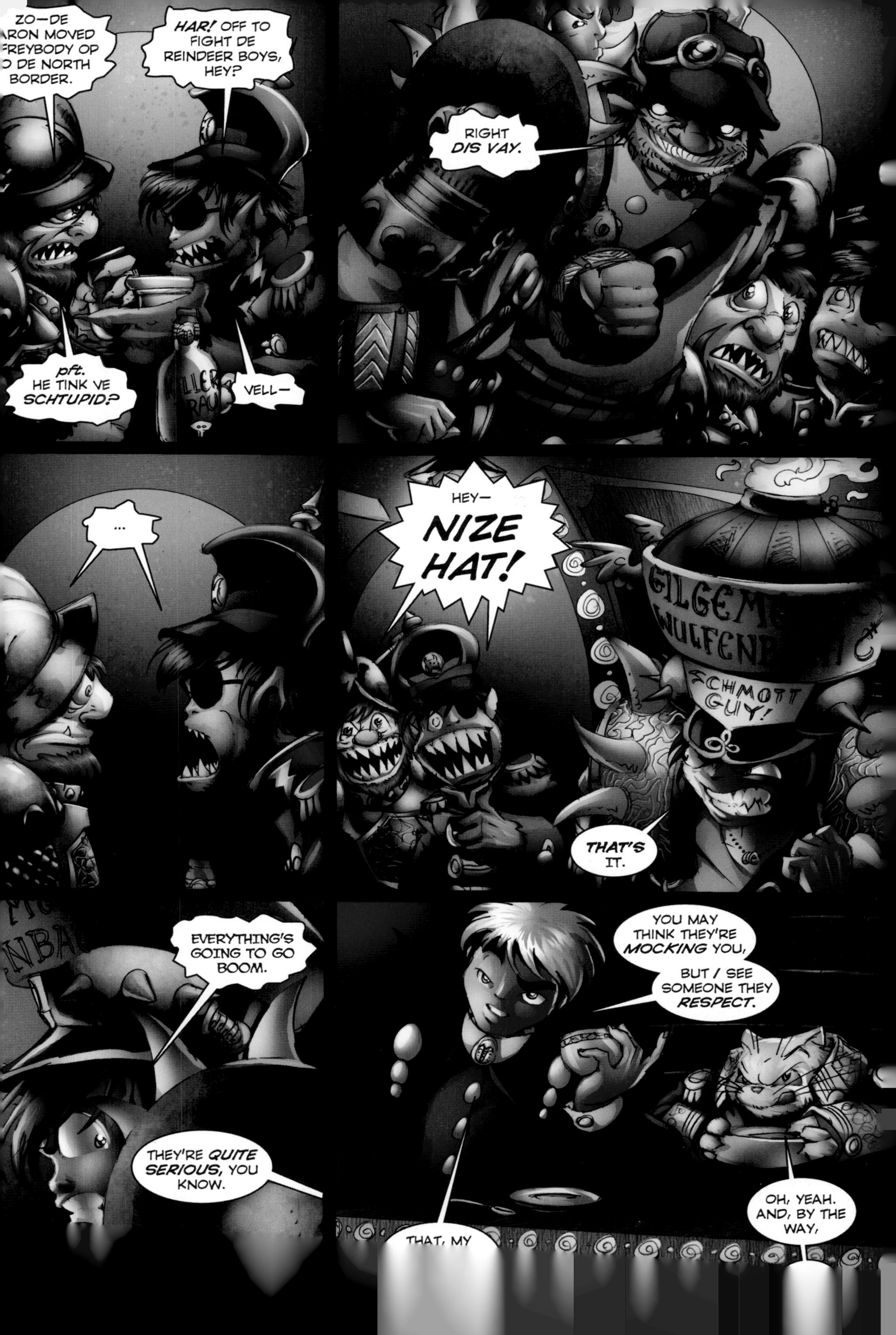

ZO—DE
ARON MOVED
EVERYBODY OP
O DE NORTH
BORDER.
HAR! OFF TO FIGHT DE REINDEER BOYS, HEY?
pft. HE TINK VE SCHTUPID?
VELL—
RIGHT DIS VAY.
...
HEY— NIZE HAT!
GILGEM
WULFEN
SCHMOTT GUY!
THAT'S IT.
EVERYTHING'S GOING TO GO BOOM.
THEY'RE QUITE SERIOUS, YOU KNOW.
YOU MAY THINK THEY'RE MOCKING YOU,
BUT I SEE SOMEONE THEY RESPECT.
THAT, MY
OH, YEAH. AND, BY THE WAY,

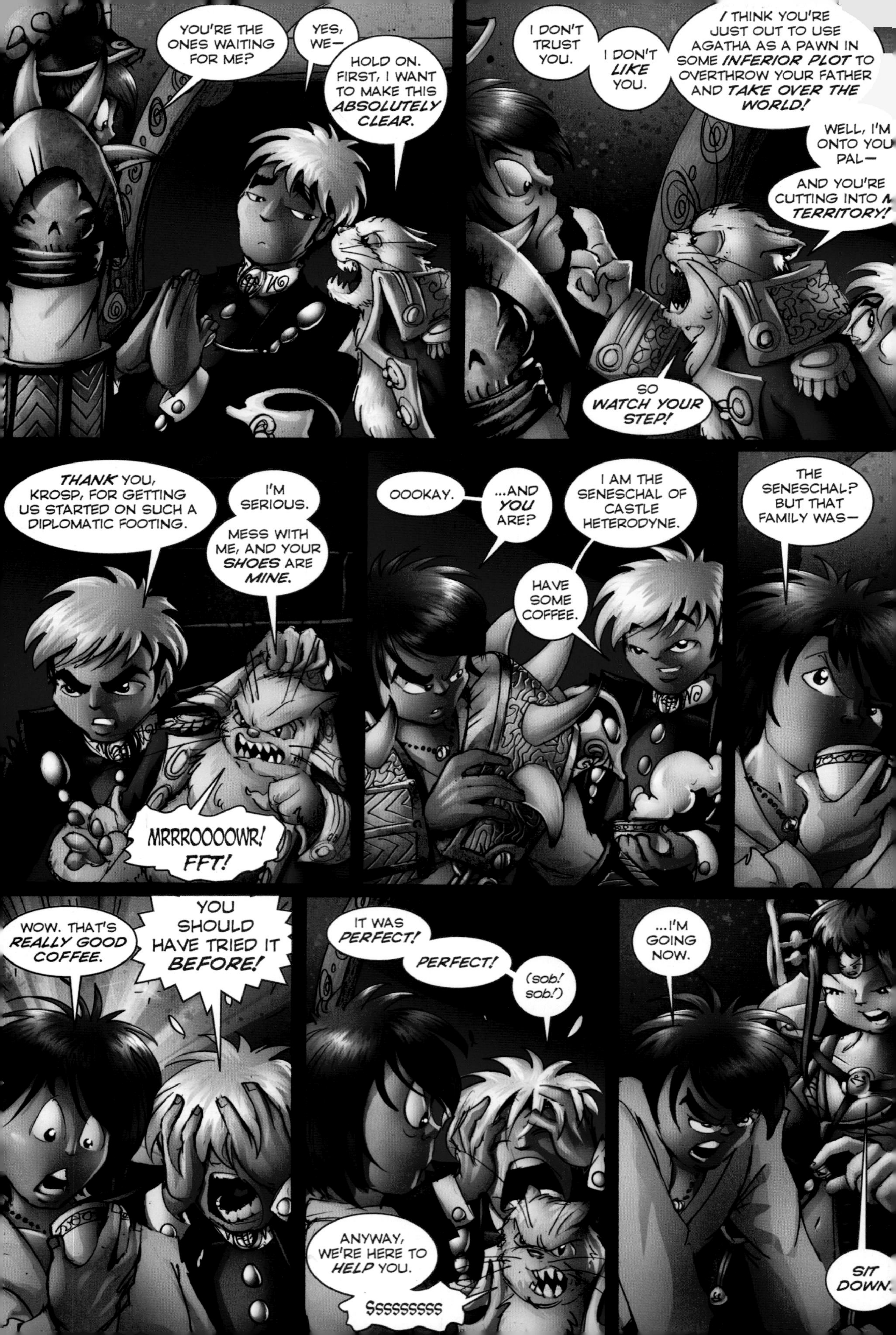

YOU'RE THE ONES WAITING FOR ME?
YES, WE—
HOLD ON. FIRST, I WANT TO MAKE THIS ABSOLUTELY CLEAR.
I DON'T TRUST YOU.
I DON'T LIKE YOU.
I THINK YOU'RE JUST OUT TO USE AGATHA AS A PAWN IN SOME INFERIOR PLOT TO OVERTHROW YOUR FATHER AND TAKE OVER THE WORLD!
WELL, I'M ONTO YOU PAL—
AND YOU'RE CUTTING INTO TERRITORY!
SO WATCH YOUR STEP!
THANK YOU, KROSP, FOR GETTING US STARTED ON SUCH A DIPLOMATIC FOOTING.
I'M SERIOUS.
MESS WITH ME, AND YOUR SHOES ARE MINE.
MRRROOOOWR! FFT!
OOOKAY.
...AND YOU ARE?
I AM THE SENESCHAL OF CASTLE HETERODYNE.
HAVE SOME COFFEE.
THE SENESCHAL? BUT THAT FAMILY WAS—
WOW. THAT'S REALLY GOOD COFFEE.
YOU SHOULD HAVE TRIED IT BEFORE!
IT WAS PERFECT!
PERFECT!
(sob! sob!)
ANYWAY, WE'RE HERE TO HELP YOU.
SSSSSSSSS
...I'M GOING NOW.
SIT DOWN.

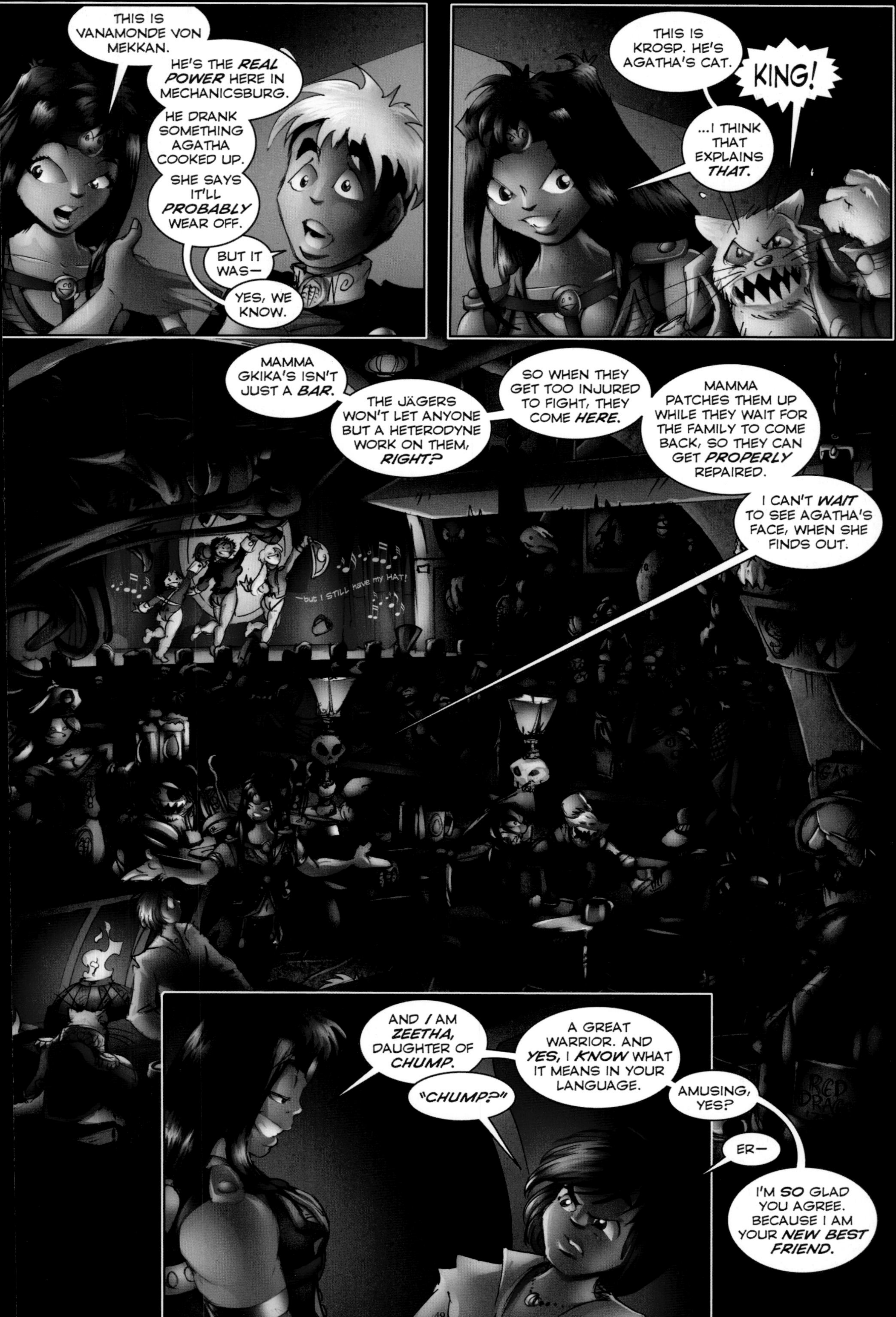
THIS IS VANAMONDE VON MEKKAN.
HE'S THE *REAL POWER* HERE IN MECHANICSBURG.
HE DRANK SOMETHING AGATHA COOKED UP.
SHE SAYS IT'LL *PROBABLY* WEAR OFF.
BUT IT WAS—
YES, WE KNOW.
THIS IS KROSP. HE'S AGATHA'S CAT.
...I THINK THAT EXPLAINS *THAT*.
KING!
MAMMA GKIKA'S ISN'T JUST A *BAR*.
THE JÄGERS WON'T LET ANYONE BUT A HETERODYNE WORK ON THEM, *RIGHT?*
SO WHEN THEY GET TOO INJURED TO FIGHT, THEY COME *HERE*.
MAMMA PATCHES THEM UP WHILE THEY WAIT FOR THE FAMILY TO COME BACK, SO THEY CAN GET *PROPERLY* REPAIRED.
I CAN'T *WAIT* TO SEE AGATHA'S FACE, WHEN SHE FINDS OUT.
—but I STILL have my HAT!
GAS
AND *I* AM *ZEETHA*, DAUGHTER OF *CHUMP*.
"CHUMP?"
A GREAT WARRIOR. AND *YES*, I *KNOW* WHAT IT MEANS IN YOUR LANGUAGE.
AMUSING, YES?
ER—
I'M *SO* GLAD YOU AGREE. BECAUSE I AM YOUR *NEW BEST FRIEND*.
RED DRA

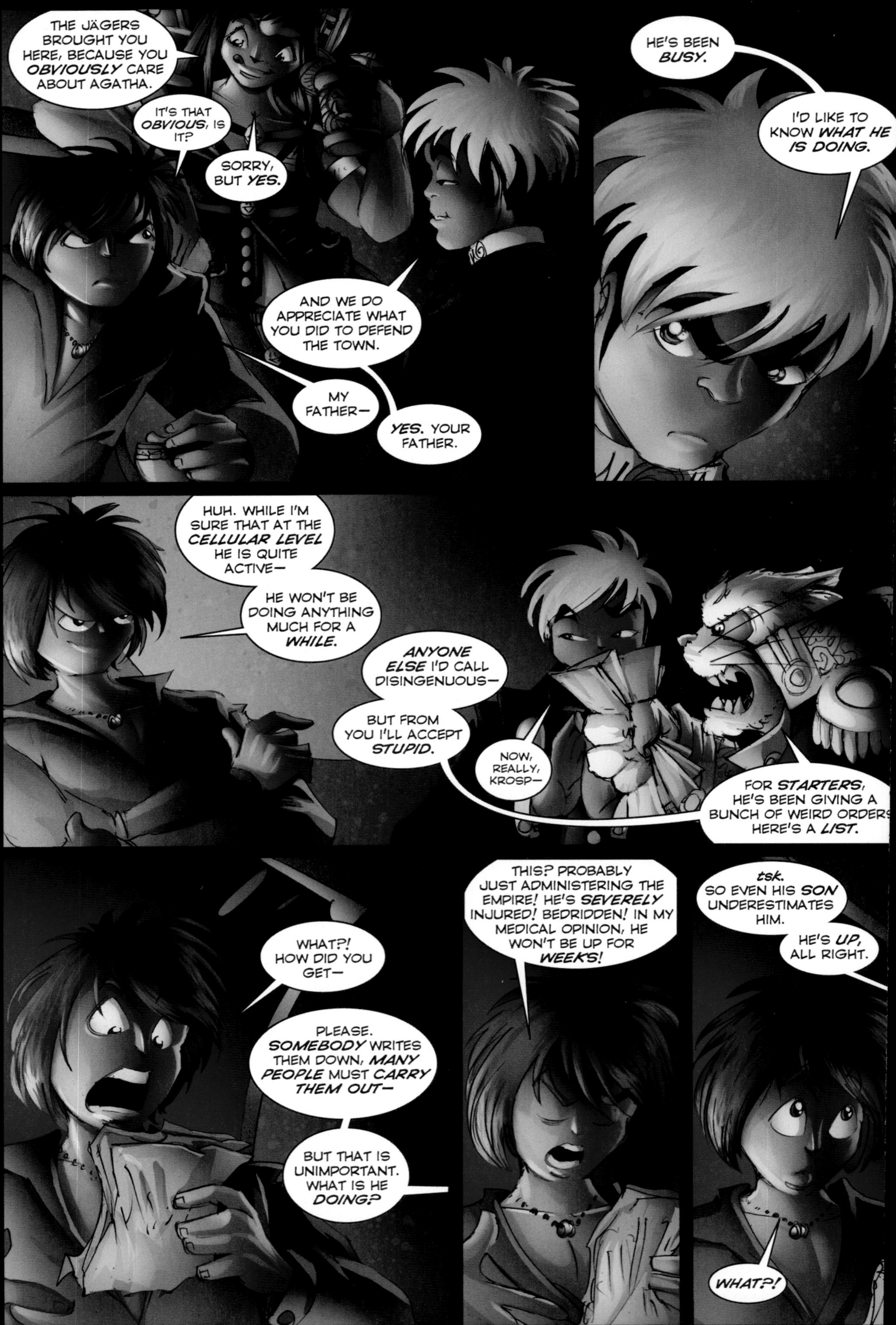
THE JÄGERS BROUGHT YOU HERE, BECAUSE YOU OBVIOUSLY CARE ABOUT AGATHA.
IT'S THAT OBVIOUS, IS IT?
SORRY, BUT YES.
AND WE DO APPRECIATE WHAT YOU DID TO DEFEND THE TOWN.
MY FATHER—
YES. YOUR FATHER.
HE'S BEEN BUSY.
I'D LIKE TO KNOW WHAT HE IS DOING.
HUH. WHILE I'M SURE THAT AT THE CELLULAR LEVEL HE IS QUITE ACTIVE—
HE WON'T BE DOING ANYTHING MUCH FOR A WHILE.
ANYONE ELSE I'D CALL DISINGENUOUS—
BUT FROM YOU I'LL ACCEPT STUPID.
NOW, REALLY, KROSP—
FOR STARTERS, HE'S BEEN GIVING A BUNCH OF WEIRD ORDERS HERE'S A LIST.
WHAT?! HOW DID YOU GET—
PLEASE. SOMEBODY WRITES THEM DOWN, MANY PEOPLE MUST CARRY THEM OUT—
BUT THAT IS UNIMPORTANT. WHAT IS HE DOING?
THIS? PROBABLY JUST ADMINISTERING THE EMPIRE! HE'S SEVERELY INJURED! BEDRIDDEN! IN MY MEDICAL OPINION, HE WON'T BE UP FOR WEEKS!
tsk. SO EVEN HIS SON UNDERESTIMATES HIM.
HE'S UP, ALL RIGHT.
WHAT?!

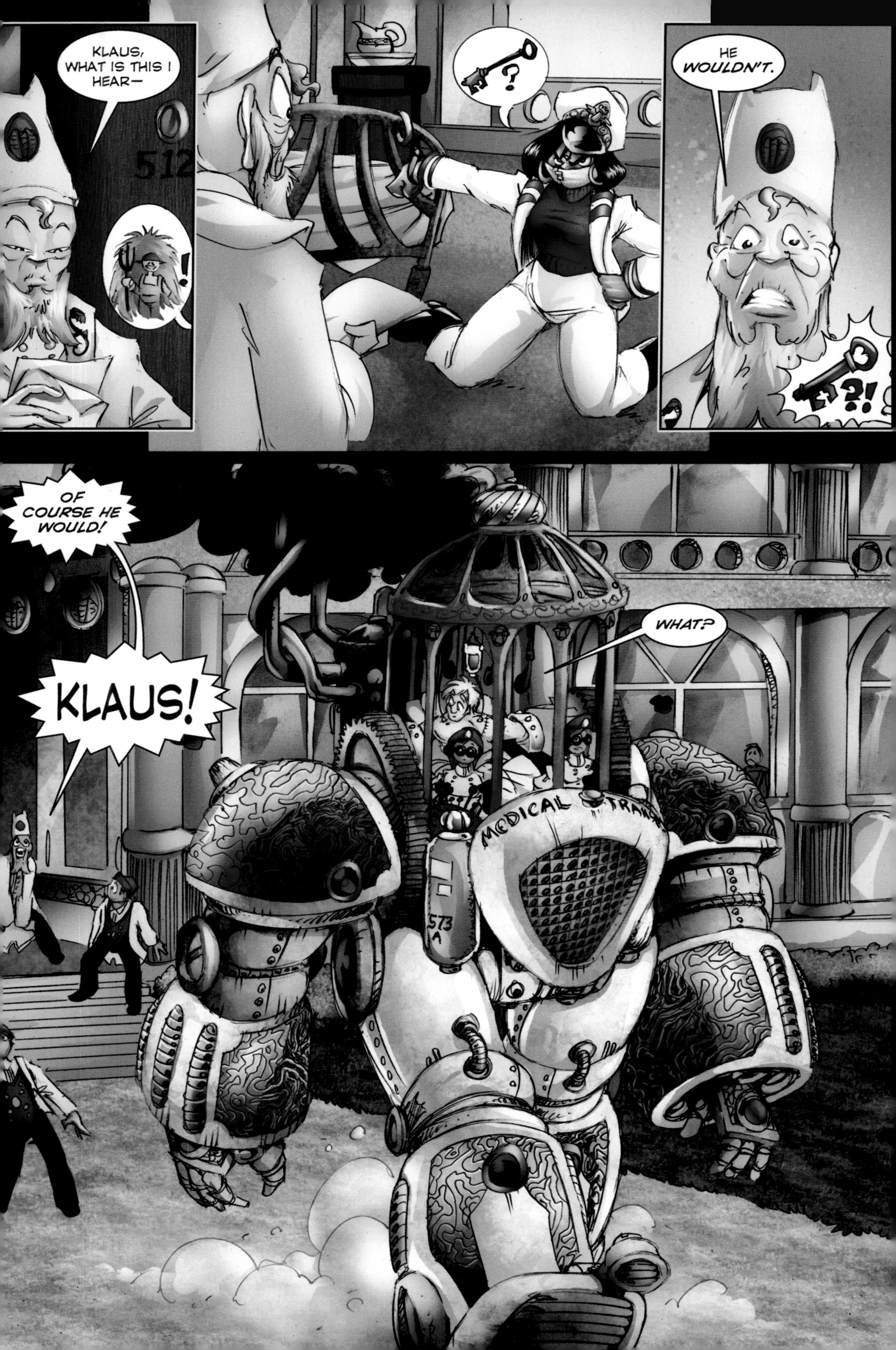
KLAUS, WHAT IS THIS I HEAR—
512
!
?
HE WOULDN'T.
?!
OF COURSE HE WOULD!
KLAUS!
WHAT?
MEDICAL TRANS
573 A

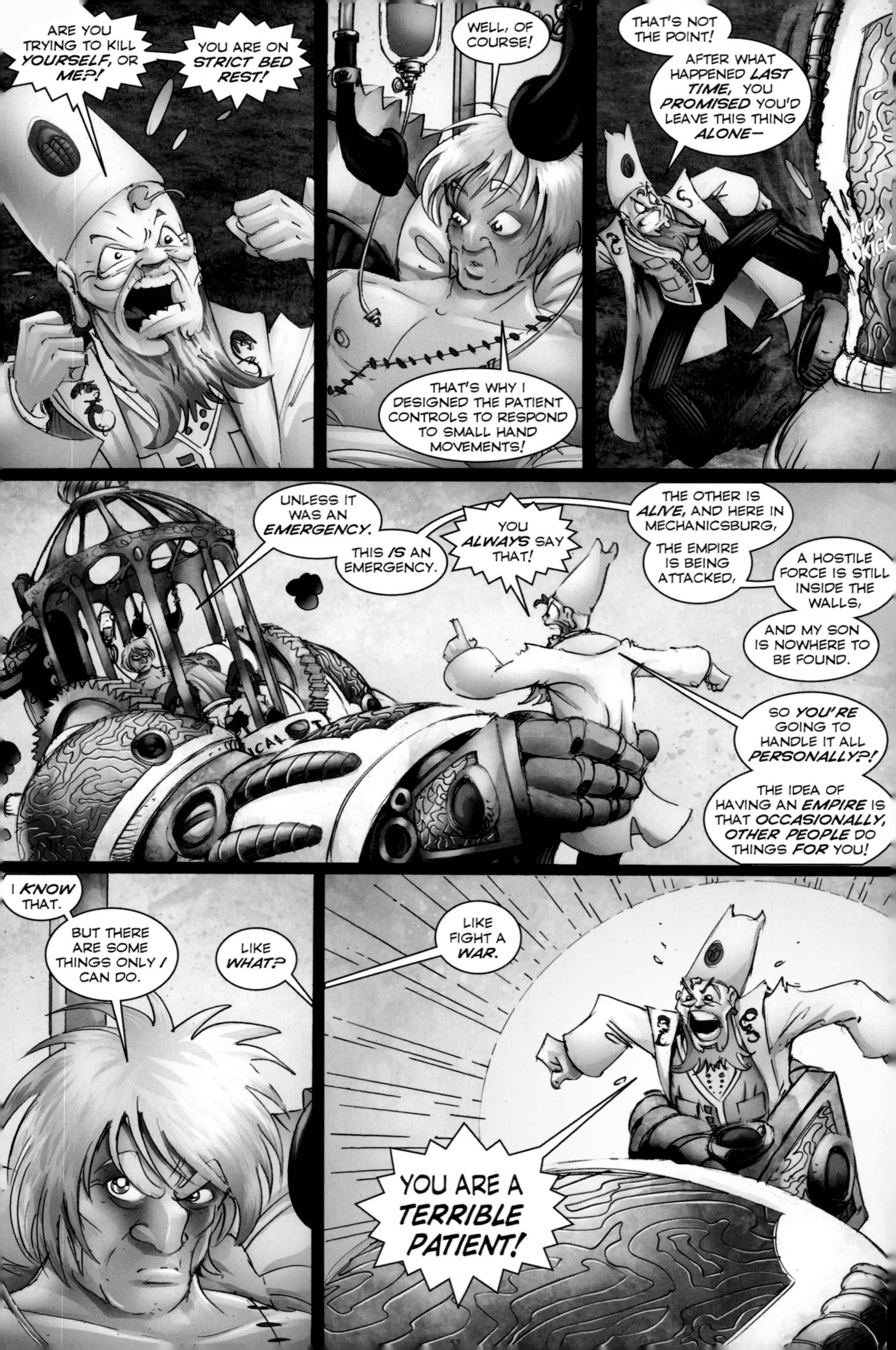

ARE YOU TRYING TO KILL YOURSELF, OR ME?!
YOU ARE ON STRICT BED REST!
WELL, OF COURSE!
THAT'S WHY I DESIGNED THE PATIENT CONTROLS TO RESPOND TO SMALL HAND MOVEMENTS!
THAT'S NOT THE POINT!
AFTER WHAT HAPPENED LAST TIME, YOU PROMISED YOU'D LEAVE THIS THING ALONE—
KICK KICK
UNLESS IT WAS AN EMERGENCY.
THIS IS AN EMERGENCY.
YOU ALWAYS SAY THAT!
THE OTHER IS ALIVE, AND HERE IN MECHANICSBURG,
THE EMPIRE IS BEING ATTACKED,
A HOSTILE FORCE IS STILL INSIDE THE WALLS,
AND MY SON IS NOWHERE TO BE FOUND.
SO YOU'RE GOING TO HANDLE IT ALL PERSONALLY?!
THE IDEA OF HAVING AN EMPIRE IS THAT OCCASIONALLY, OTHER PEOPLE DO THINGS FOR YOU!
I KNOW THAT.
BUT THERE ARE SOME THINGS ONLY I CAN DO.
LIKE WHAT?
LIKE FIGHT A WAR.
YOU ARE A TERRIBLE PATIENT!

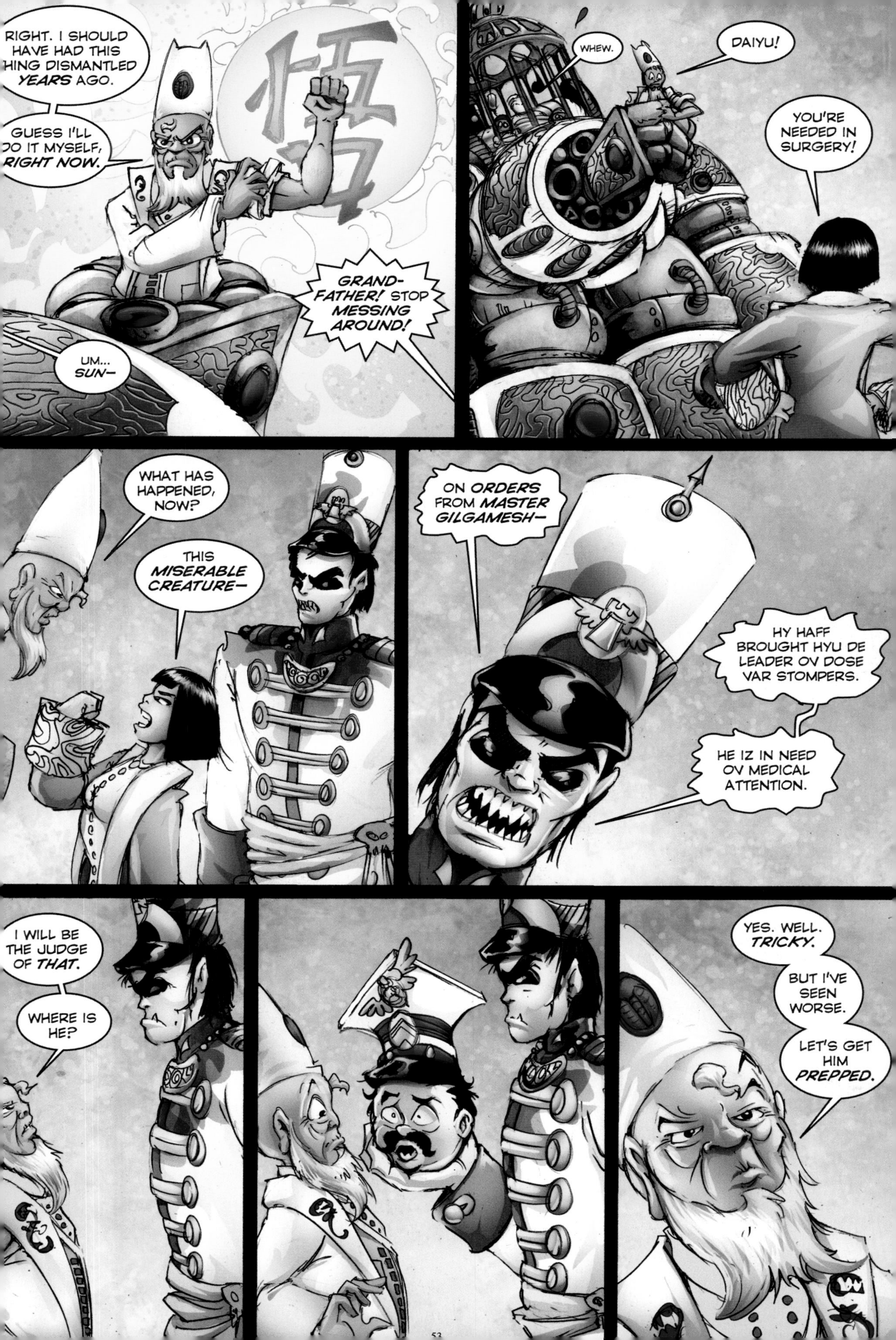

RIGHT. I SHOULD HAVE HAD THIS THING DISMANTLED YEARS AGO.
GUESS I'LL DO IT MYSELF, RIGHT NOW.
UM... SUN—
GRAND-FATHER! STOP MESSING AROUND!
WHEW.
DAIYU!
YOU'RE NEEDED IN SURGERY!
WHAT HAS HAPPENED, NOW?
THIS MISERABLE CREATURE—
ON ORDERS FROM MASTER GILGAMESH—
HY HAFF BROUGHT HYU DE LEADER OV DOSE VAR STOMPERS.
HE IZ IN NEED OV MEDICAL ATTENTION.
I WILL BE THE JUDGE OF THAT.
WHERE IS HE?
YES. WELL. TRICKY.
BUT I'VE SEEN WORSE.
LET'S GET HIM PREPPED.

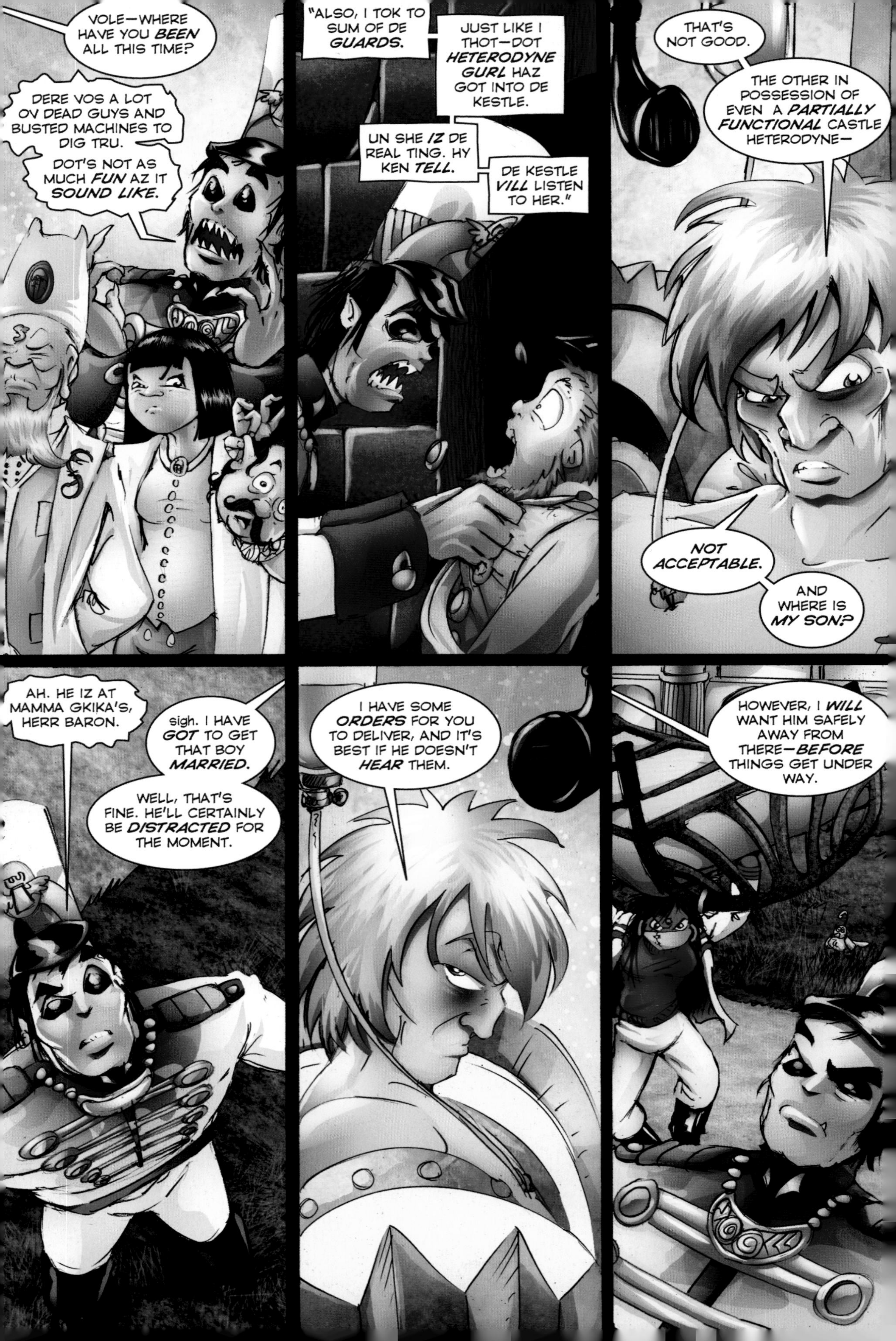
VOLE—WHERE HAVE YOU BEEN ALL THIS TIME?
DERE VOS A LOT OV DEAD GUYS AND BUSTED MACHINES TO DIG TRU.
DOT'S NOT AS MUCH FUN AZ IT SOUND LIKE.
"ALSO, I TOK TO SUM OF DE GUARDS.
JUST LIKE I THOT—DOT HETERODYNE GURL HAZ GOT INTO DE KESTLE.
UN SHE IZ DE REAL TING. HY KEN TELL.
DE KESTLE VILL LISTEN TO HER."
THAT'S NOT GOOD.
THE OTHER IN POSSESSION OF EVEN A PARTIALLY FUNCTIONAL CASTLE HETERODYNE—
NOT ACCEPTABLE.
AND WHERE IS MY SON?
AH. HE IZ AT MAMMA GKIKA'S, HERR BARON.
sigh. I HAVE GOT TO GET THAT BOY MARRIED.
WELL, THAT'S FINE. HE'LL CERTAINLY BE DISTRACTED FOR THE MOMENT.
I HAVE SOME ORDERS FOR YOU TO DELIVER, AND IT'S BEST IF HE DOESN'T HEAR THEM.
HOWEVER, I WILL WANT HIM SAFELY AWAY FROM THERE—BEFORE THINGS GET UNDER WAY.

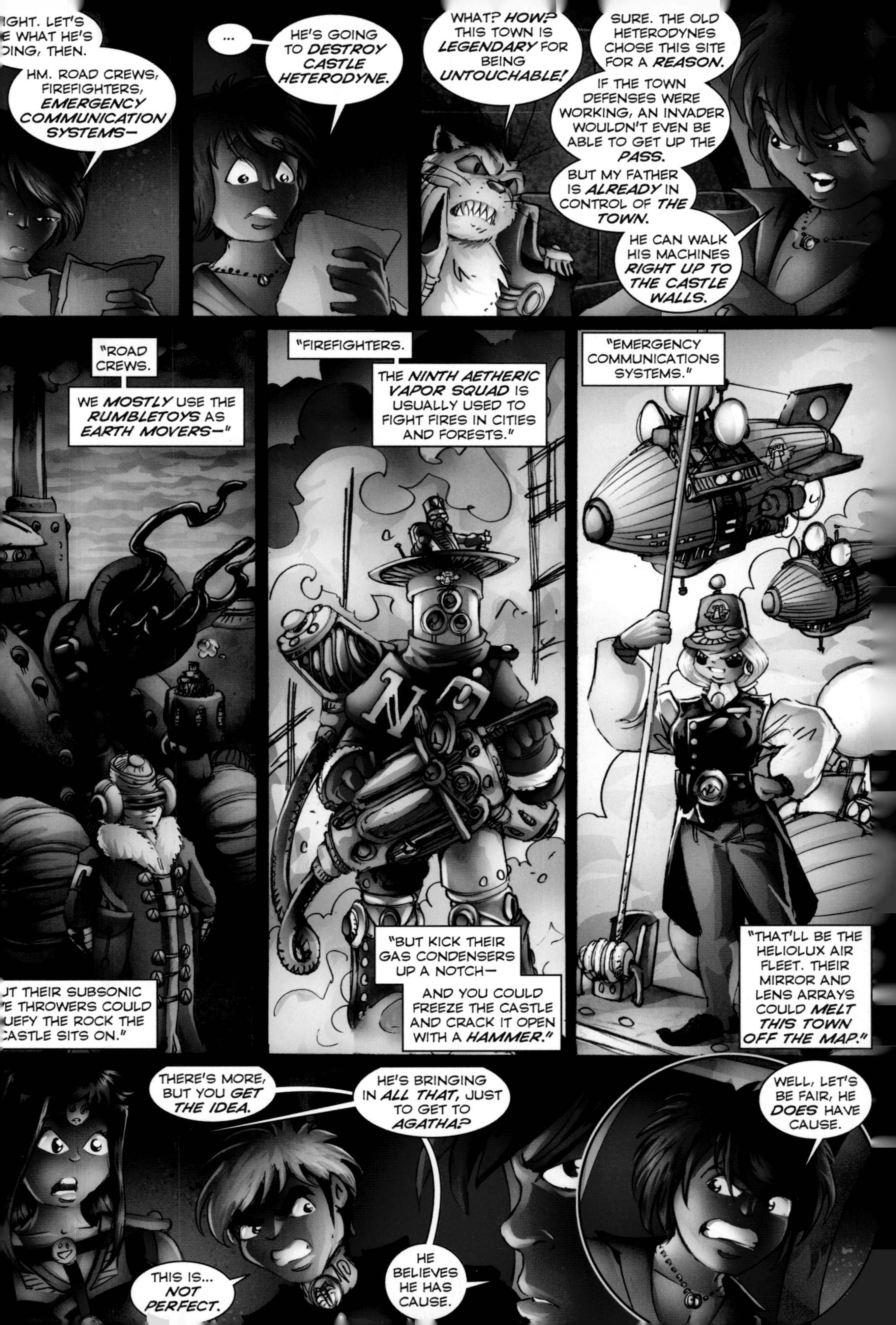
IGHT. LET'S
E WHAT HE'S
OING, THEN.
HM. ROAD CREWS, FIREFIGHTERS, EMERGENCY COMMUNICATION SYSTEMS—
...
HE'S GOING TO DESTROY CASTLE HETERODYNE.
WHAT? HOW? THIS TOWN IS LEGENDARY FOR BEING UNTOUCHABLE!
SURE. THE OLD HETERODYNES CHOSE THIS SITE FOR A REASON.
IF THE TOWN DEFENSES WERE WORKING, AN INVADER WOULDN'T EVEN BE ABLE TO GET UP THE PASS.
BUT MY FATHER IS ALREADY IN CONTROL OF THE TOWN.
HE CAN WALK HIS MACHINES RIGHT UP TO THE CASTLE WALLS.
"ROAD CREWS.
WE MOSTLY USE THE RUMBLETOYS AS EARTH MOVERS—"
JT THEIR SUBSONIC
'E THROWERS COULD
UEFY THE ROCK THE
CASTLE SITS ON."
"FIREFIGHTERS.
THE NINTH AETHERIC VAPOR SQUAD IS USUALLY USED TO FIGHT FIRES IN CITIES AND FORESTS."
"BUT KICK THEIR GAS CONDENSERS UP A NOTCH—
AND YOU COULD FREEZE THE CASTLE AND CRACK IT OPEN WITH A HAMMER."
"EMERGENCY COMMUNICATIONS SYSTEMS."
"THAT'LL BE THE HELIOLUX AIR FLEET. THEIR MIRROR AND LENS ARRAYS COULD MELT THIS TOWN OFF THE MAP."
THERE'S MORE, BUT YOU GET THE IDEA.
HE'S BRINGING IN ALL THAT, JUST TO GET TO AGATHA?
THIS IS... NOT PERFECT.
HE BELIEVES HE HAS CAUSE.
WELL, LET'S BE FAIR, HE DOES HAVE CAUSE.

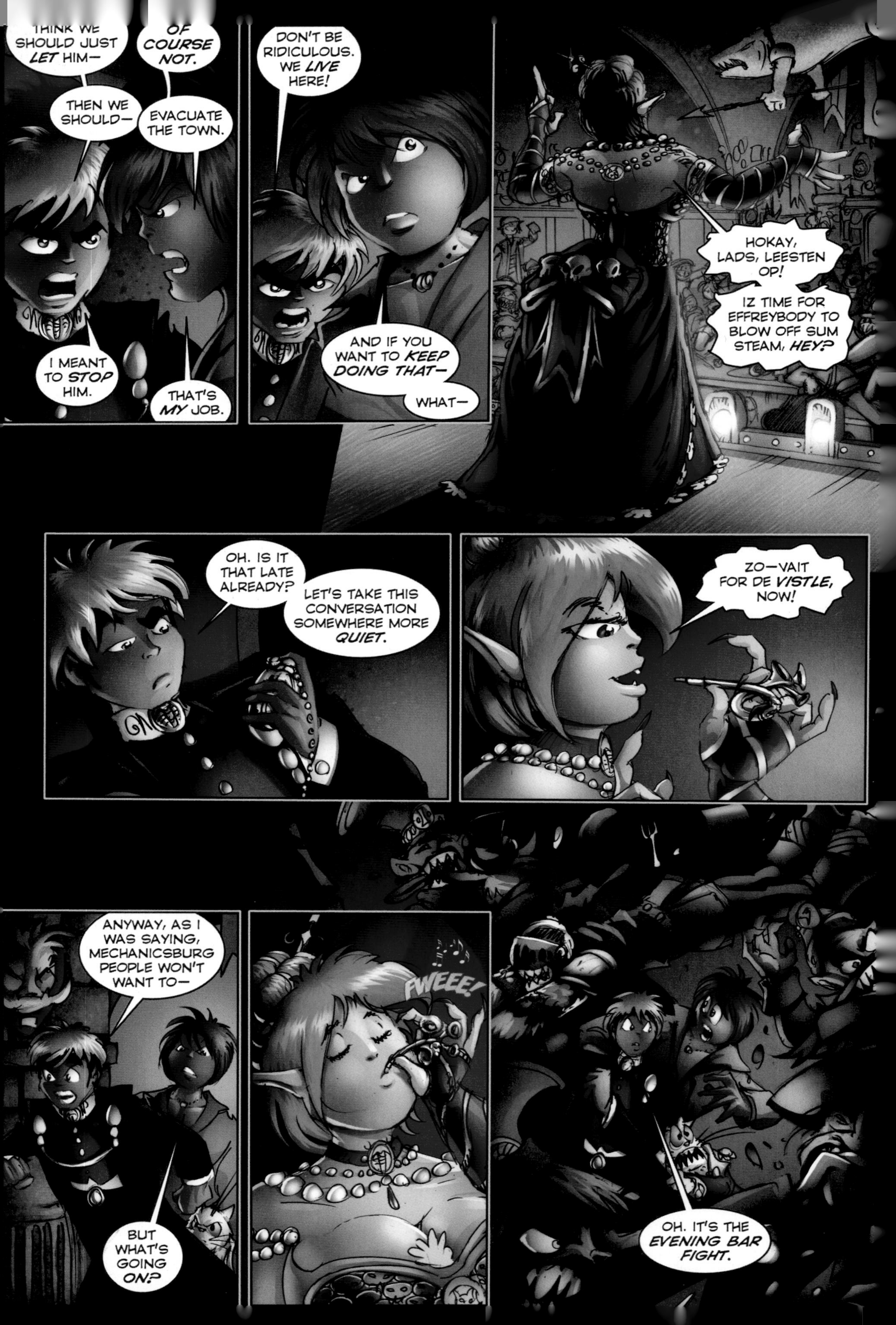
THINK WE SHOULD JUST LET HIM—
OF COURSE NOT.
THEN WE SHOULD—
EVACUATE THE TOWN.
I MEANT TO STOP HIM.
THAT'S MY JOB.
DON'T BE RIDICULOUS. WE LIVE HERE!
AND IF YOU WANT TO KEEP DOING THAT—
WHAT—
HOKAY, LADS, LEESTEN OP!
IZ TIME FOR EFFREYBODY TO BLOW OFF SUM STEAM, HEY?
OH. IS IT THAT LATE ALREADY?
LET'S TAKE THIS CONVERSATION SOMEWHERE MORE QUIET.
ZO—VAIT FOR DE VISTLE, NOW!
ANYWAY, AS I WAS SAYING, MECHANICSBURG PEOPLE WON'T WANT TO—
BUT WHAT'S GOING ON?
FWEEE!
OH. IT'S THE EVENING BAR FIGHT.

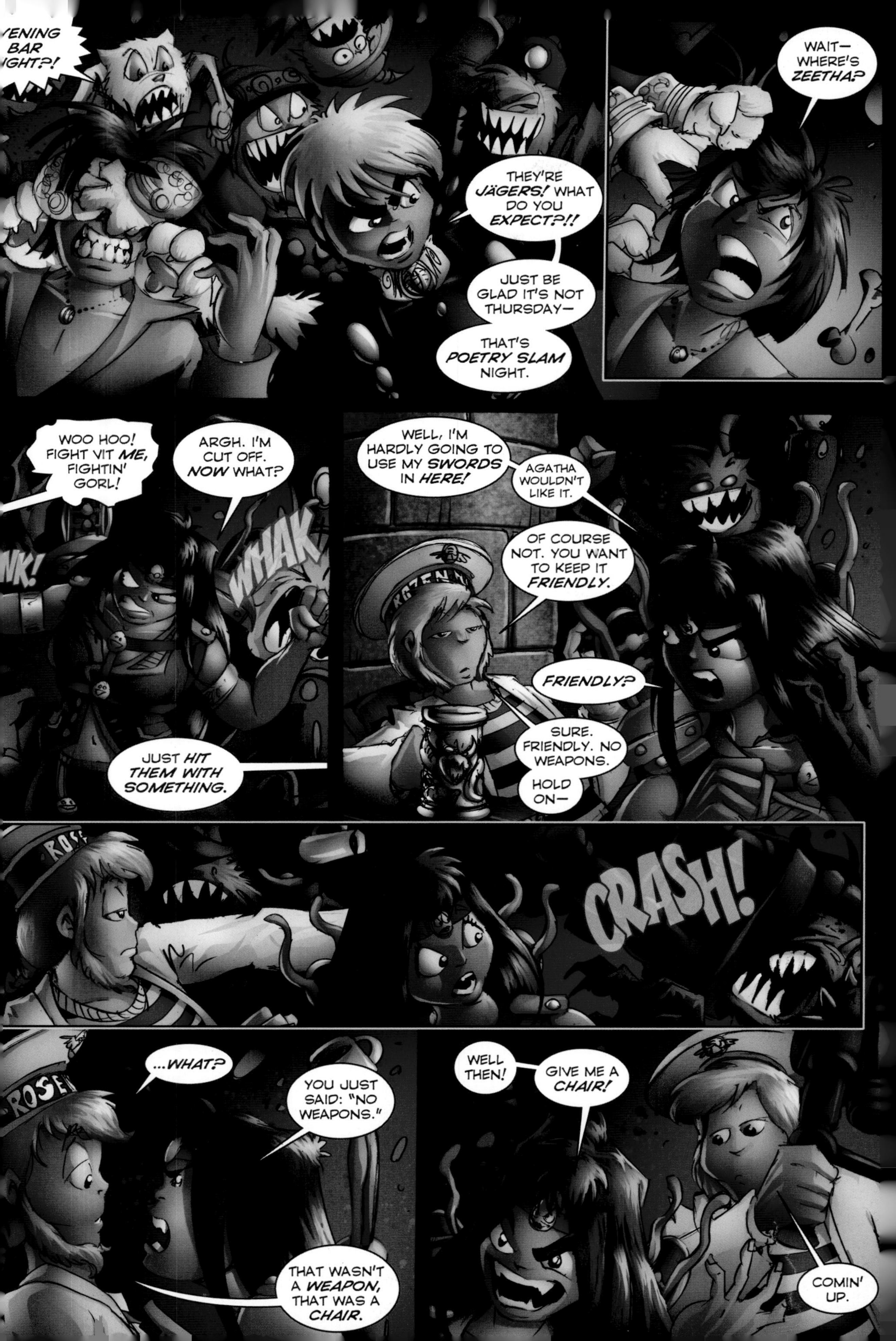

VENING BAR IGHT?!
THEY'RE JÄGERS! WHAT DO YOU EXPECT?!!
JUST BE GLAD IT'S NOT THURSDAY—
THAT'S POETRY SLAM NIGHT.
WAIT—WHERE'S ZEETHA?
WOO HOO! FIGHT VIT ME, FIGHTIN' GORL!
ARGH. I'M CUT OFF. NOW WHAT?
WHAK
NK!
JUST HIT THEM WITH SOMETHING.
WELL, I'M HARDLY GOING TO USE MY SWORDS IN HERE!
AGATHA WOULDN'T LIKE IT.
OF COURSE NOT. YOU WANT TO KEEP IT FRIENDLY.
FRIENDLY?
SURE. FRIENDLY. NO WEAPONS.
HOLD ON—
CRASH!
...WHAT?
YOU JUST SAID: "NO WEAPONS."
THAT WASN'T A WEAPON, THAT WAS A CHAIR.
WELL THEN!
GIVE ME A CHAIR!
COMIN' UP.

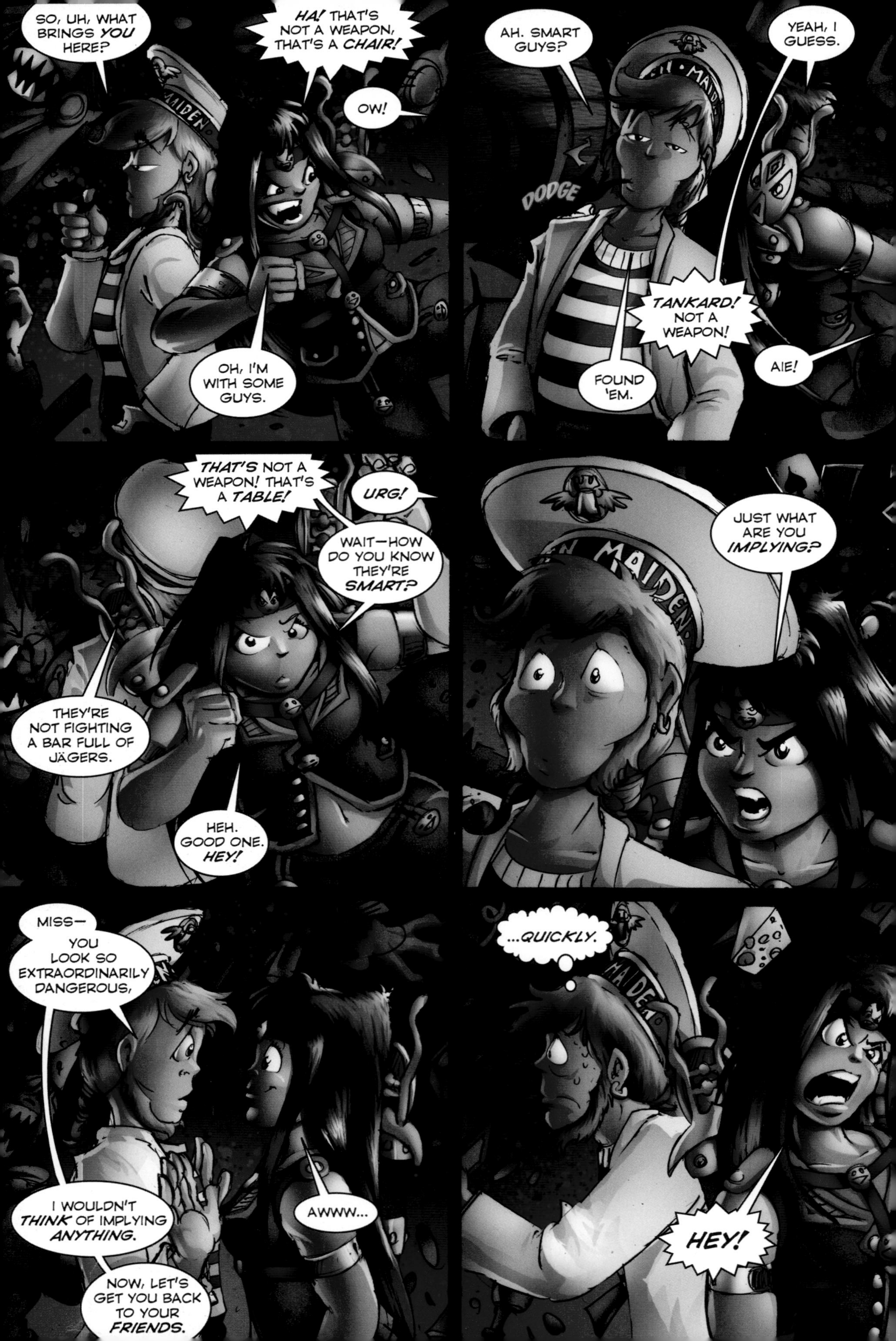
SO, UH, WHAT BRINGS YOU HERE?
HA! THAT'S NOT A WEAPON, THAT'S A CHAIR!
OW!
OH, I'M WITH SOME GUYS.
AH. SMART GUYS?
YEAH, I GUESS.
DODGE
TANKARD! NOT A WEAPON!
FOUND 'EM.
AIE!
THAT'S NOT A WEAPON! THAT'S A TABLE!
URG!
WAIT—HOW DO YOU KNOW THEY'RE SMART?
THEY'RE NOT FIGHTING A BAR FULL OF JÄGERS.
HEH. GOOD ONE. HEY!
JUST WHAT ARE YOU IMPLYING?
MISS—
YOU LOOK SO EXTRAORDINARILY DANGEROUS,
I WOULDN'T THINK OF IMPLYING ANYTHING.
AWWW...
NOW, LET'S GET YOU BACK TO YOUR FRIENDS.
...QUICKLY.
HEY!

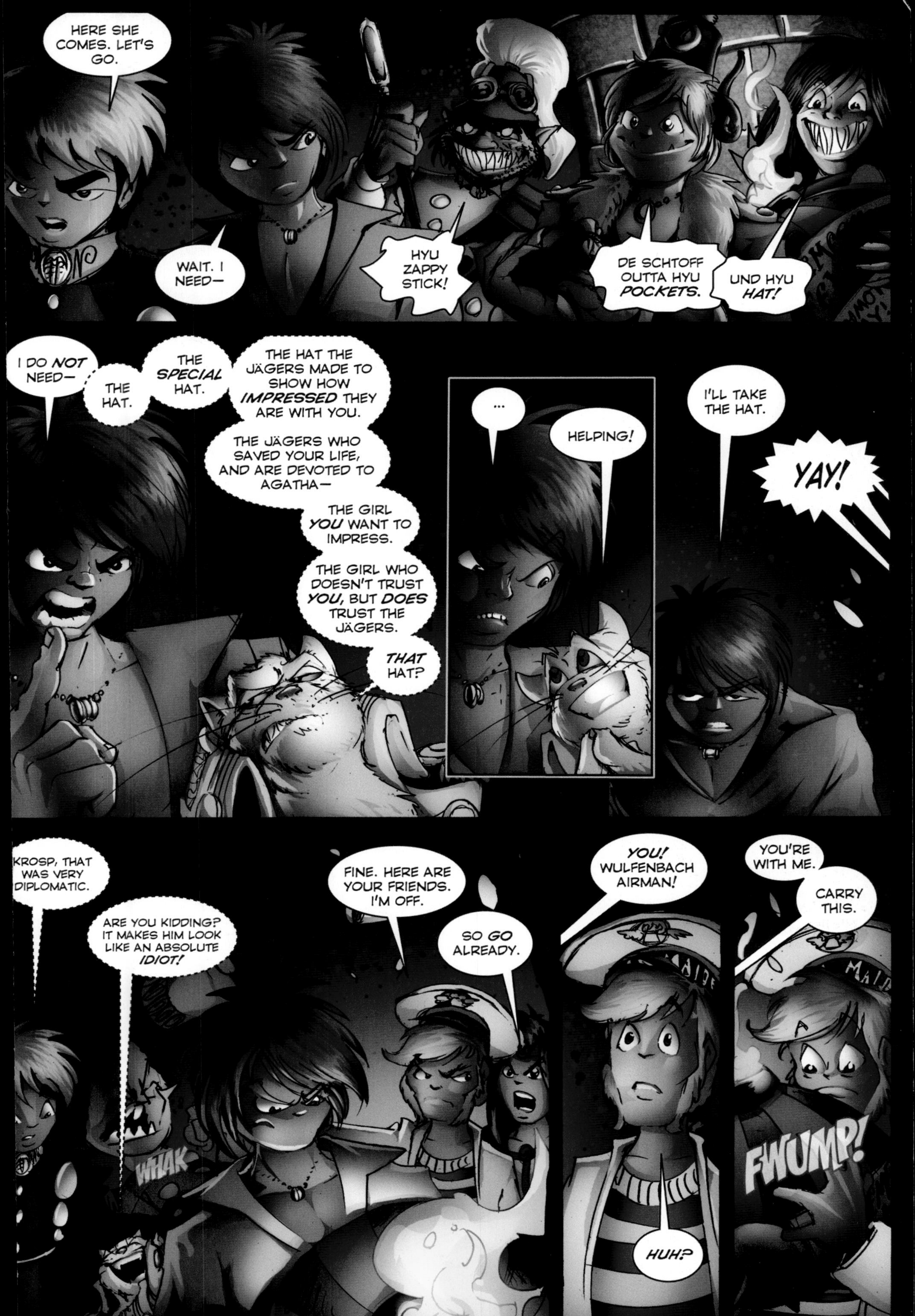

HERE SHE COMES. LET'S GO.
WAIT. I NEED—
HYU ZAPPY STICK!
DE SCHTOFF OUTTA HYU POCKETS.
UND HYU HAT!
I DO NOT NEED—
THE HAT.
THE SPECIAL HAT.
THE HAT THE JÄGERS MADE TO SHOW HOW IMPRESSED THEY ARE WITH YOU.
THE JÄGERS WHO SAVED YOUR LIFE, AND ARE DEVOTED TO AGATHA—
THE GIRL YOU WANT TO IMPRESS.
THE GIRL WHO DOESN'T TRUST YOU, BUT DOES TRUST THE JÄGERS.
THAT HAT?
...
HELPING!
I'LL TAKE THE HAT.
YAY!
KROSP, THAT WAS VERY DIPLOMATIC.
ARE YOU KIDDING? IT MAKES HIM LOOK LIKE AN ABSOLUTE IDIOT!
WHAK
FINE. HERE ARE YOUR FRIENDS. I'M OFF.
SO GO ALREADY.
YOU! WULFENBACH AIRMAN!
HUH?
YOU'RE WITH ME.
CARRY THIS.
FWUMP!

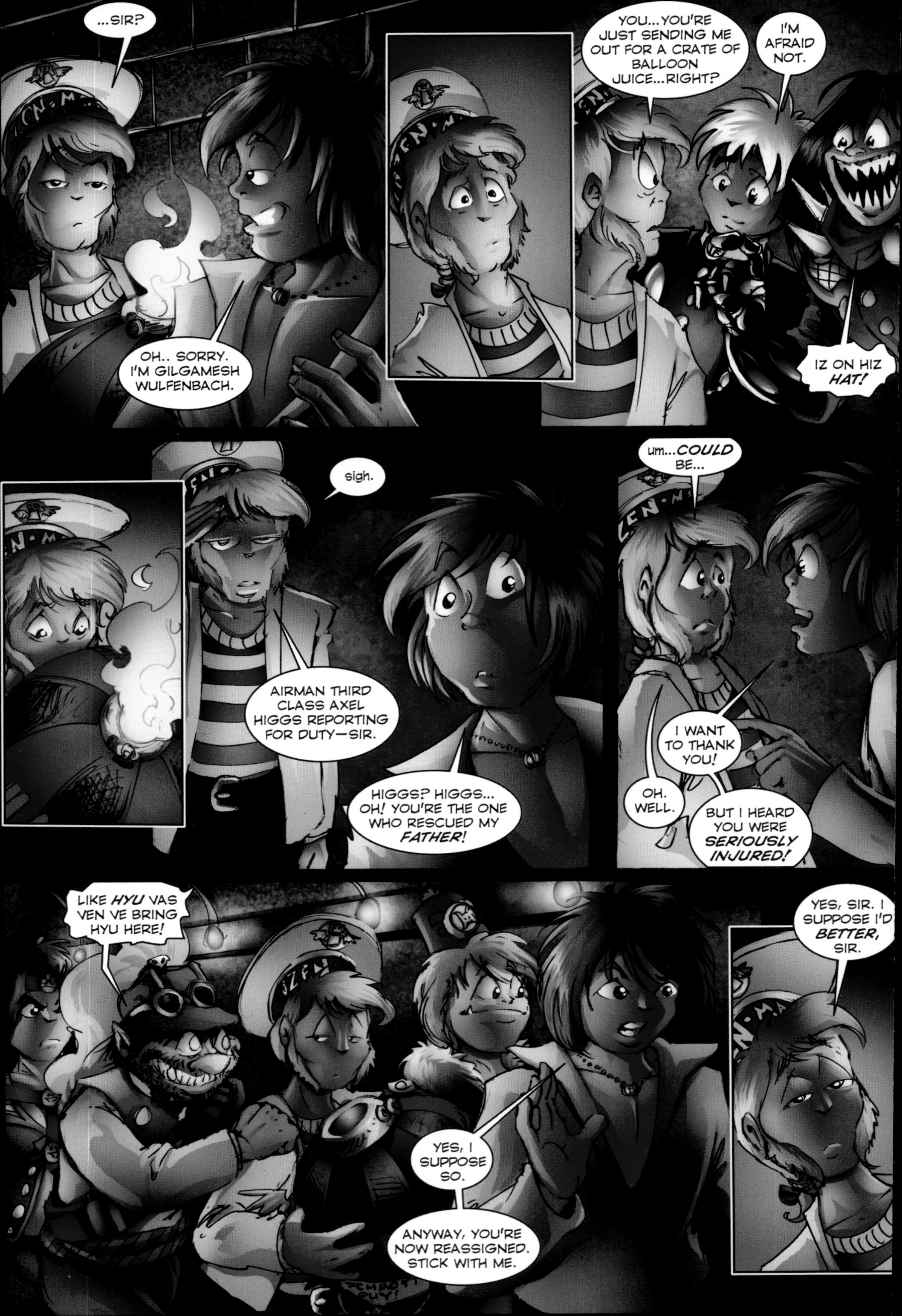
...SIR?
OH.. SORRY. I'M GILGAMESH WULFENBACH.
YOU...YOU'RE JUST SENDING ME OUT FOR A CRATE OF BALLOON JUICE...RIGHT?
I'M AFRAID NOT.
IZ ON HIZ *HAT!*
sigh.
AIRMAN THIRD CLASS AXEL HIGGS REPORTING FOR DUTY—SIR.
HIGGS? HIGGS... OH! YOU'RE THE ONE WHO RESCUED MY *FATHER!*
um...*COULD* BE...
I WANT TO THANK YOU!
OH. WELL.
BUT I HEARD YOU WERE *SERIOUSLY INJURED!*
LIKE *HYU* VAS VEN VE BRING HYU HERE!
YES, I SUPPOSE SO.
ANYWAY, YOU'RE NOW REASSIGNED. STICK WITH ME.
YES, SIR. I SUPPOSE I'D *BETTER,* SIR.

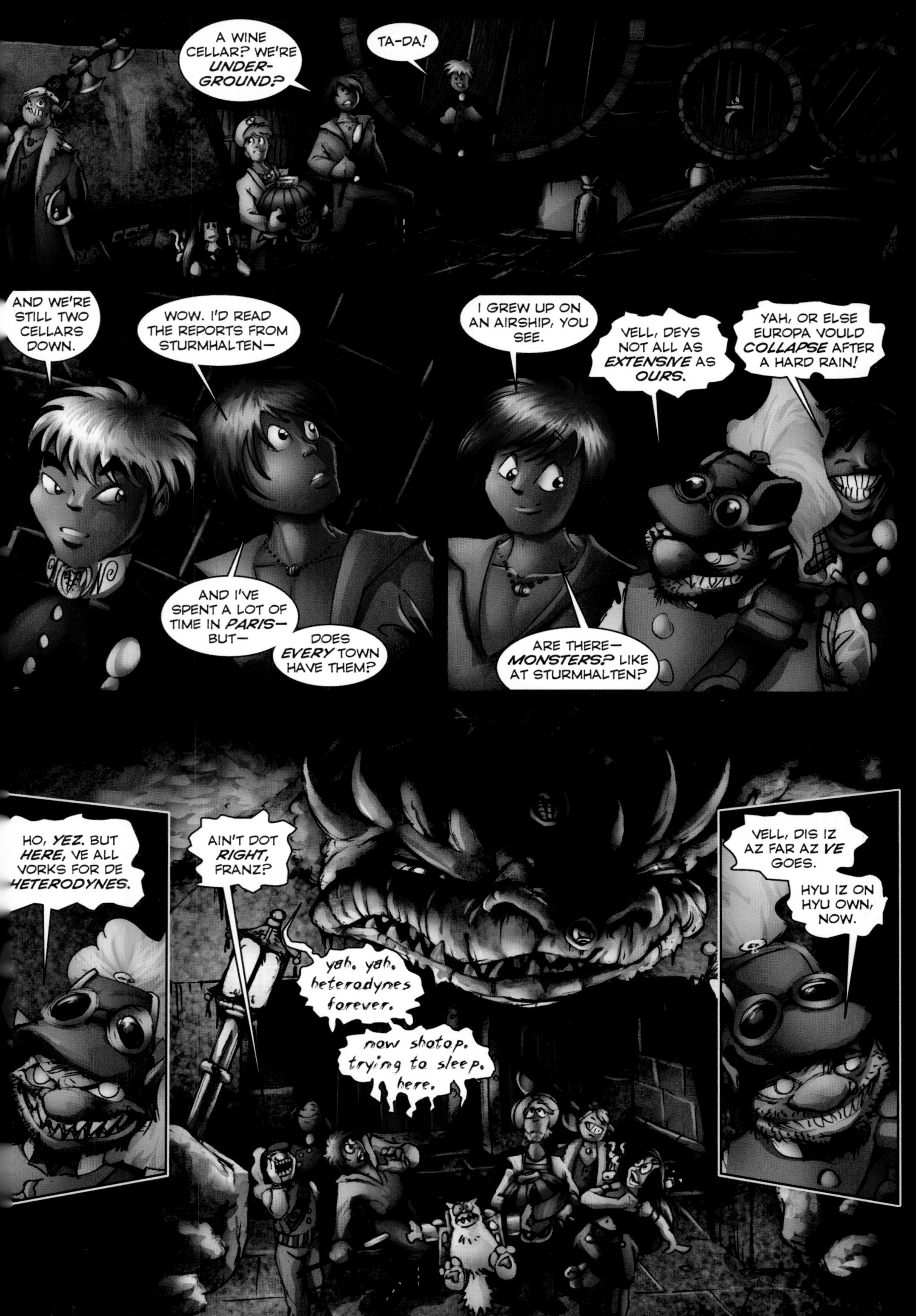
A WINE CELLAR? WE'RE UNDER-GROUND?
TA-DA!
AND WE'RE STILL TWO CELLARS DOWN.
WOW. I'D READ THE REPORTS FROM STURMHALTEN—
AND I'VE SPENT A LOT OF TIME IN PARIS— BUT—
DOES EVERY TOWN HAVE THEM?
I GREW UP ON AN AIRSHIP, YOU SEE.
VELL, DEYS NOT ALL AS EXTENSIVE AS OURS.
YAH, OR ELSE EUROPA VOULD COLLAPSE AFTER A HARD RAIN!
ARE THERE— MONSTERS? LIKE AT STURMHALTEN?
HO, YEZ. BUT HERE, VE ALL VORKS FOR DE HETERODYNES.
AIN'T DOT RIGHT, FRANZ?
yah. yah. heterodynes forever.
now shotop. trying to sleep. here.
VELL, DIS IZ AZ FAR AZ VE GOES.
HYU IZ ON HYU OWN, NOW.

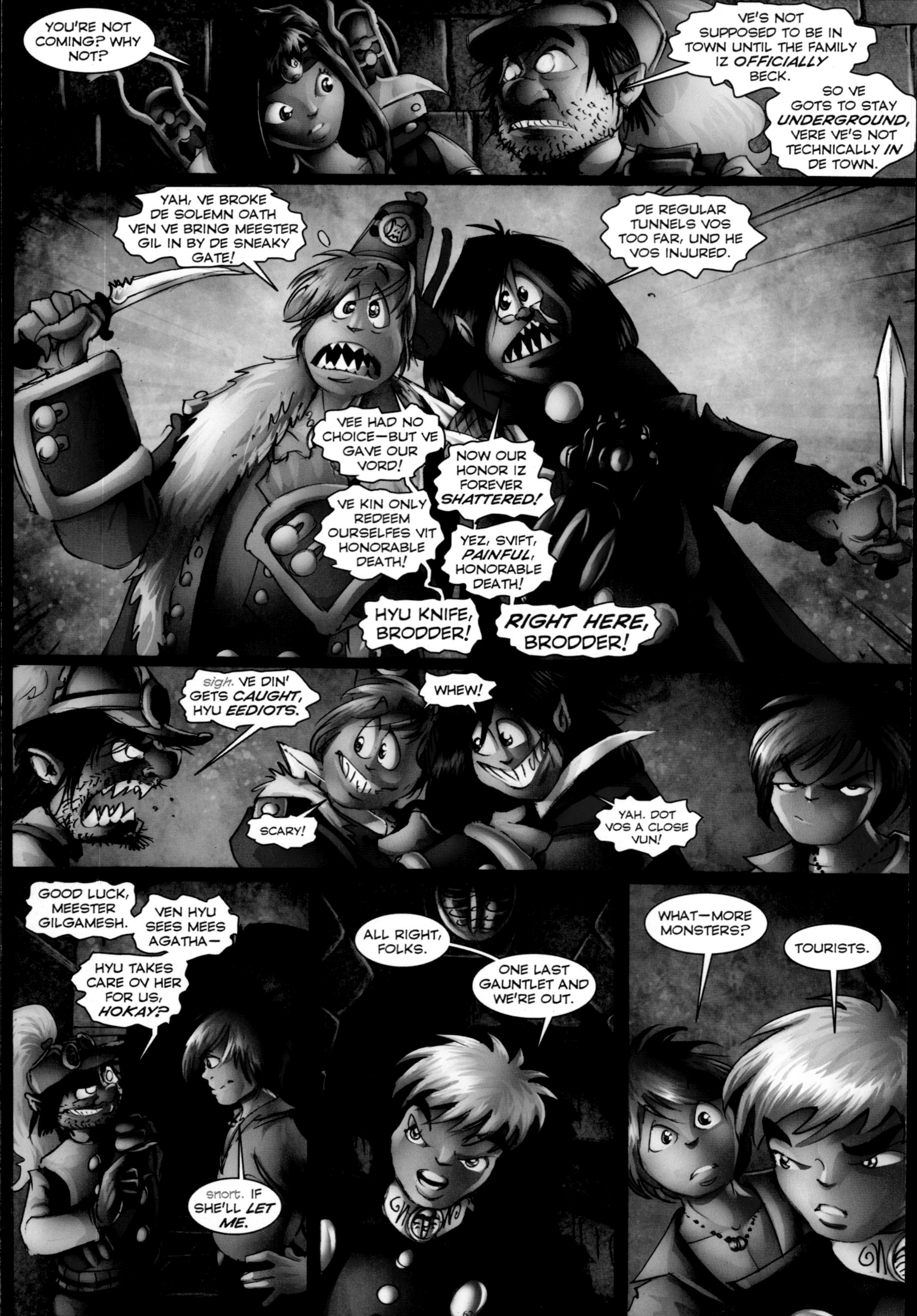
YOU'RE NOT COMING? WHY NOT?
VE'S NOT SUPPOSED TO BE IN TOWN UNTIL THE FAMILY IZ OFFICIALLY BECK.
SO VE GOTS TO STAY UNDERGROUND, VERE VE'S NOT TECHNICALLY IN DE TOWN.
YAH, VE BROKE DE SOLEMN OATH VEN VE BRING MEESTER GIL IN BY DE SNEAKY GATE!
DE REGULAR TUNNELS VOS TOO FAR, UND HE VOS INJURED.
VEE HAD NO CHOICE—BUT VE GAVE OUR VORD!
NOW OUR HONOR IZ FOREVER SHATTERED!
VE KIN ONLY REDEEM OURSELFES VIT HONORABLE DEATH!
YEZ, SVIFT, PAINFUL, HONORABLE DEATH!
HYU KNIFE, BRODDER!
RIGHT HERE, BRODDER!
sigh. VE DIN' GETS CAUGHT, HYU EEDIOTS.
WHEW!
SCARY!
YAH. DOT VOS A CLOSE VUN!
GOOD LUCK, MEESTER GILGAMESH.
VEN HYU SEES MEES AGATHA—
HYU TAKES CARE OV HER FOR US, HOKAY?
snort. IF SHE'LL LET ME.
ALL RIGHT, FOLKS.
ONE LAST GAUNTLET AND WE'RE OUT.
WHAT—MORE MONSTERS?
TOURISTS.

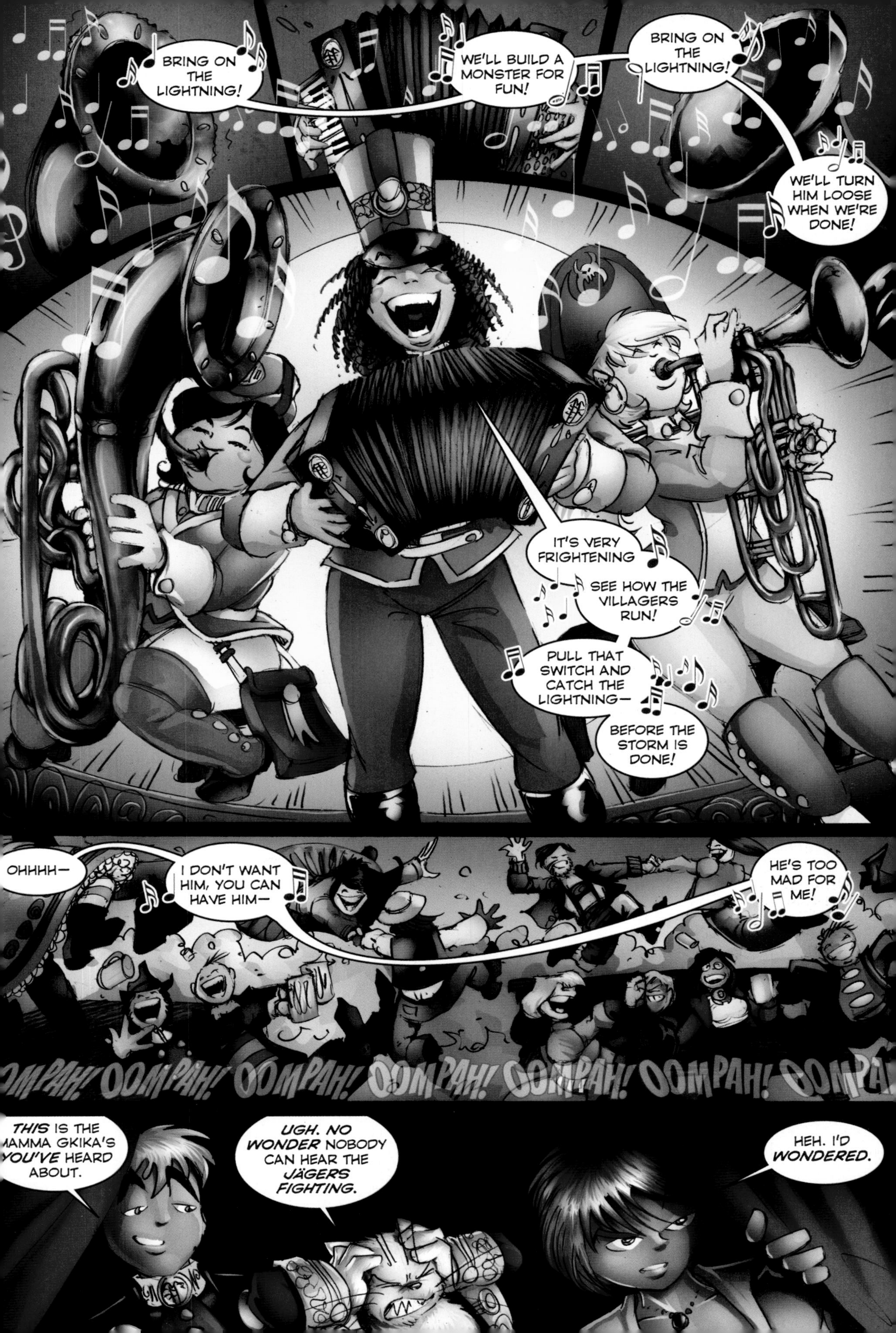
BRING ON THE LIGHTNING!
WE'LL BUILD A MONSTER FOR FUN!
BRING ON THE LIGHTNING!
WE'LL TURN HIM LOOSE WHEN WE'RE DONE!
IT'S VERY FRIGHTENING
SEE HOW THE VILLAGERS RUN!
PULL THAT SWITCH AND CATCH THE LIGHTNING—
BEFORE THE STORM IS DONE!
OHHHH—
I DON'T WANT HIM, YOU CAN HAVE HIM—
HE'S TOO MAD FOR ME!
OOMPAH! OOMPAH! OOMPAH! OOMPAH! OOMPAH!
THIS IS THE MAMMA GKIKA'S YOU'VE HEARD ABOUT.
UGH. NO WONDER NOBODY CAN HEAR THE JÄGERS FIGHTING.
HEH. I'D WONDERED.

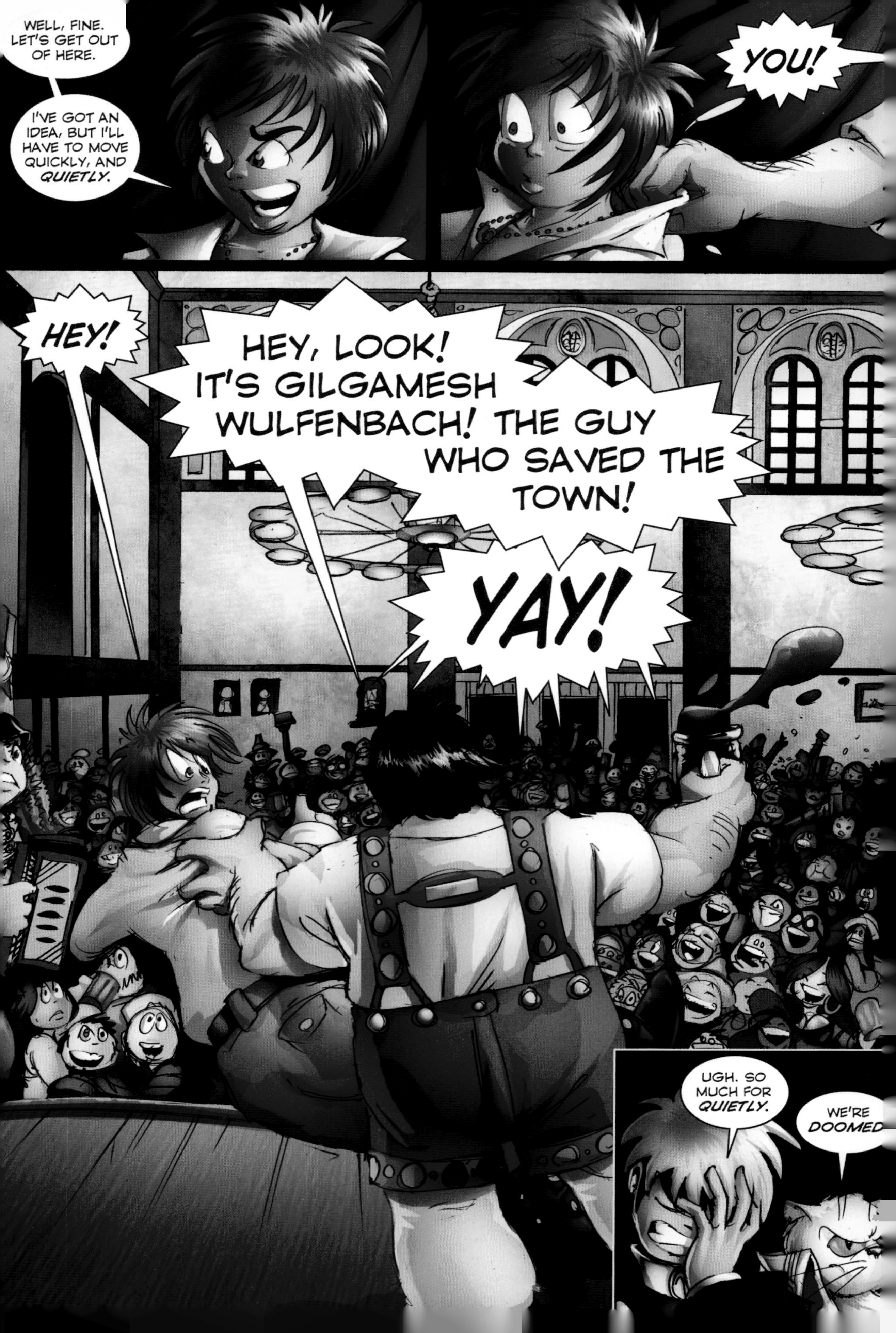
WELL, FINE. LET'S GET OUT OF HERE.
I'VE GOT AN IDEA, BUT I'LL HAVE TO MOVE QUICKLY, AND *QUIETLY*.
YOU!
HEY!
HEY, LOOK! IT'S GILGAMESH WULFENBACH! THE GUY WHO SAVED THE TOWN!
YAY!
UGH. SO MUCH FOR *QUIETLY*.
WE'RE *DOOMED*

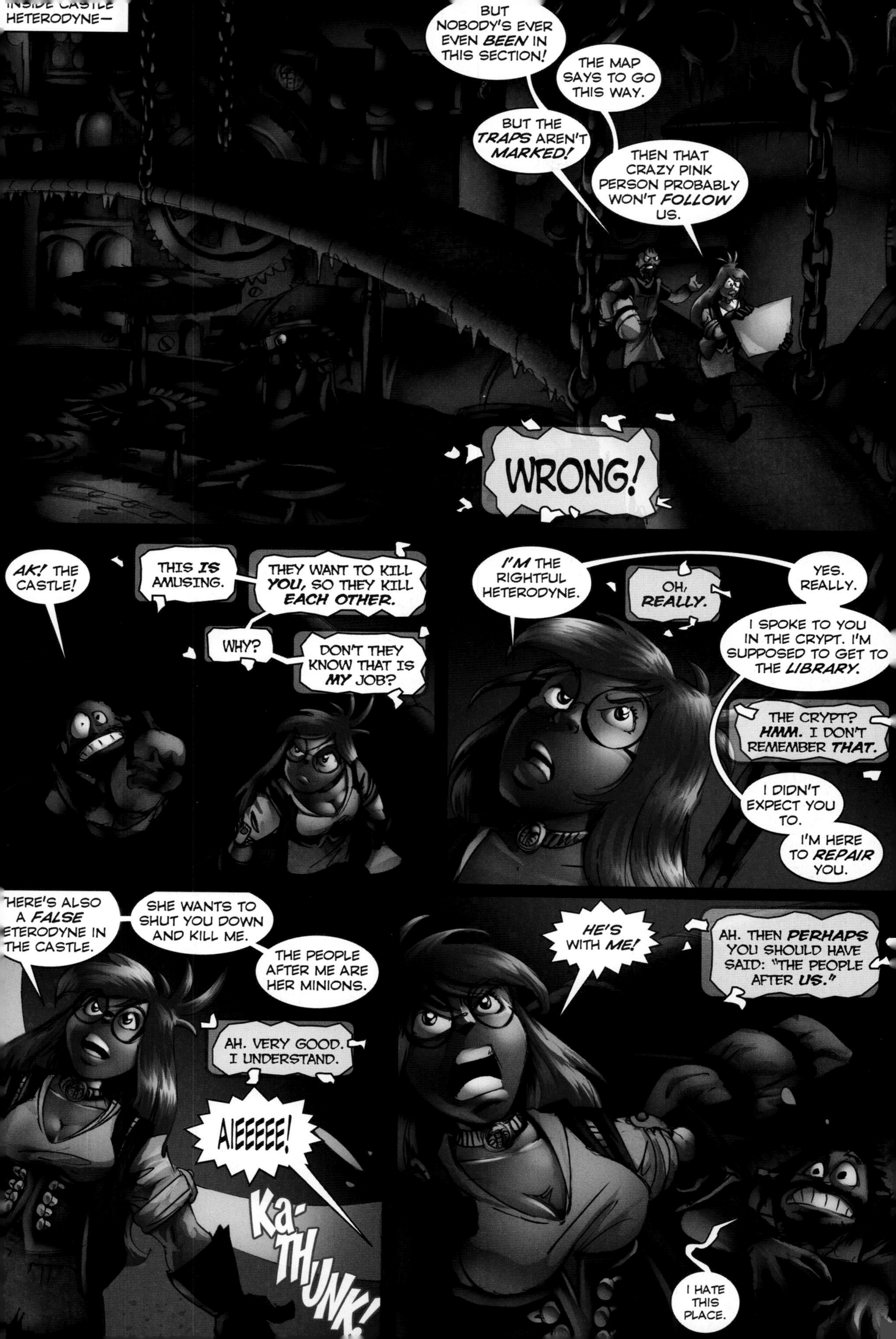
INSIDE CASTLE HETERODYNE—
BUT NOBODY'S EVER EVEN BEEN IN THIS SECTION!
THE MAP SAYS TO GO THIS WAY.
BUT THE TRAPS AREN'T MARKED!
THEN THAT CRAZY PINK PERSON PROBABLY WON'T FOLLOW US.
WRONG!
AK! THE CASTLE!
THIS IS AMUSING.
THEY WANT TO KILL YOU, SO THEY KILL EACH OTHER.
WHY?
DON'T THEY KNOW THAT IS MY JOB?
I'M THE RIGHTFUL HETERODYNE.
OH, REALLY.
YES. REALLY.
I SPOKE TO YOU IN THE CRYPT. I'M SUPPOSED TO GET TO THE LIBRARY.
THE CRYPT? HMM. I DON'T REMEMBER THAT.
I DIDN'T EXPECT YOU TO.
I'M HERE TO REPAIR YOU.
HERE'S ALSO A FALSE ETERODYNE IN THE CASTLE.
SHE WANTS TO SHUT YOU DOWN AND KILL ME.
THE PEOPLE AFTER ME ARE HER MINIONS.
AH. VERY GOOD. I UNDERSTAND.
AIEEEEE!
KA-THUNK!
HE'S WITH ME!
AH. THEN PERHAPS YOU SHOULD HAVE SAID: "THE PEOPLE AFTER US."
I HATE THIS PLACE.

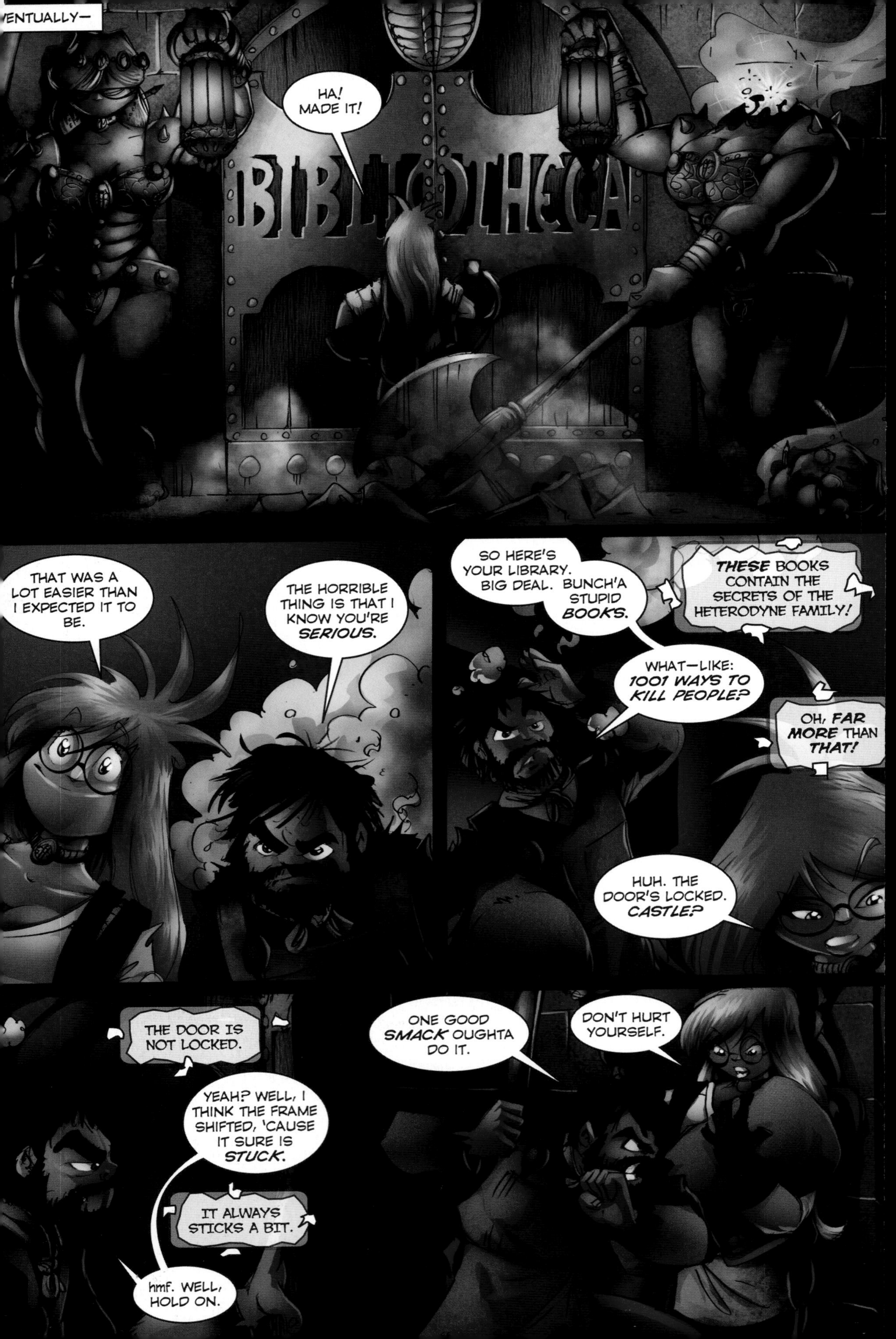
ENTUALLY—
HA! MADE IT!
BIBLIOTHECA
THAT WAS A LOT EASIER THAN I EXPECTED IT TO BE.
THE HORRIBLE THING IS THAT I KNOW YOU'RE SERIOUS.
SO HERE'S YOUR LIBRARY. BIG DEAL. BUNCH'A STUPID BOOKS.
THESE BOOKS CONTAIN THE SECRETS OF THE HETERODYNE FAMILY!
WHAT—LIKE: 1001 WAYS TO KILL PEOPLE?
OH, FAR MORE THAN THAT!
HUH. THE DOOR'S LOCKED. CASTLE?
THE DOOR IS NOT LOCKED.
YEAH? WELL, I THINK THE FRAME SHIFTED, 'CAUSE IT SURE IS STUCK.
IT ALWAYS STICKS A BIT.
hmf. WELL, HOLD ON.
ONE GOOD SMACK OUGHTA DO IT.
DON'T HURT YOURSELF.

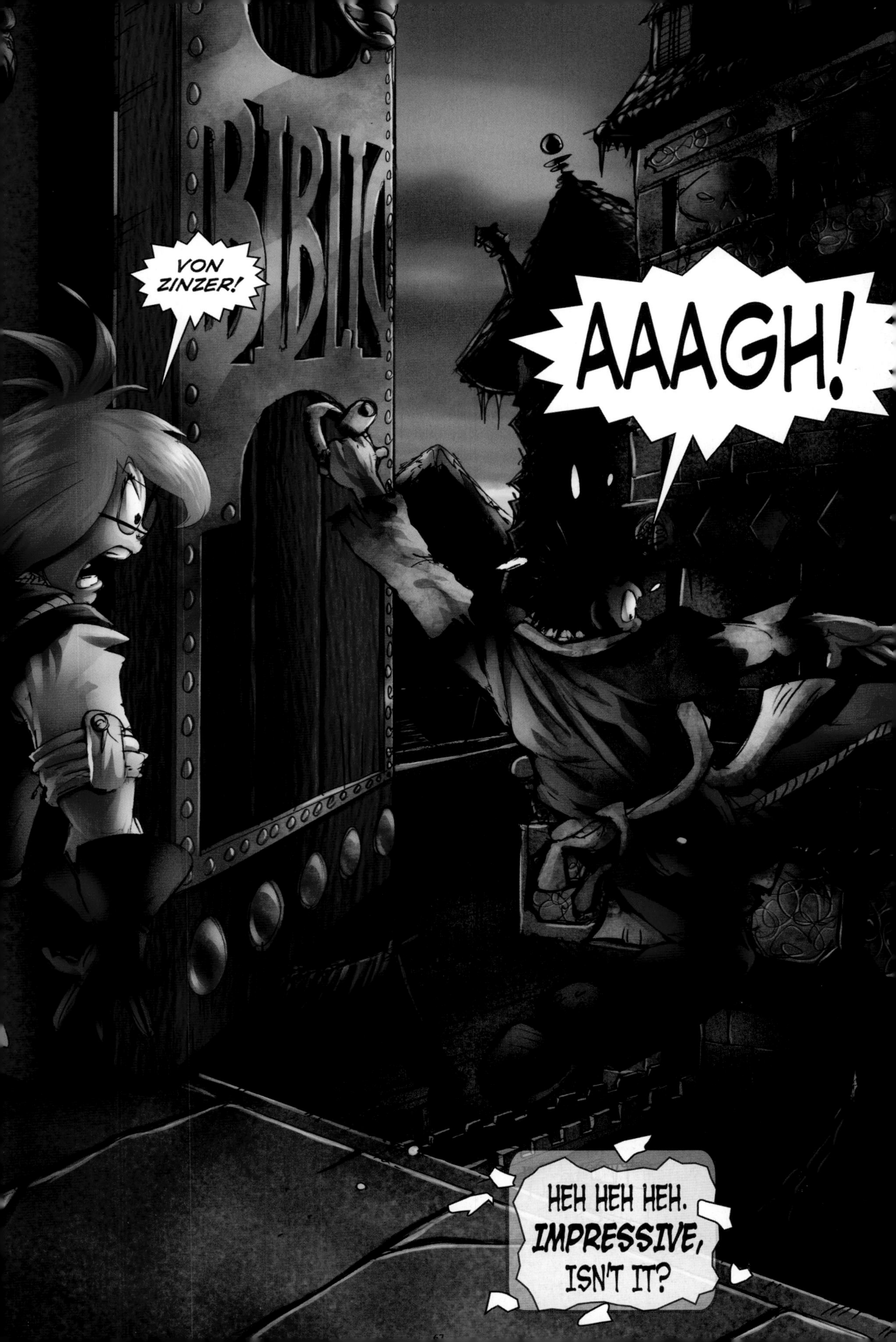
VON ZINZER!
AAAGH!
HEH HEH HEH. IMPRESSIVE, ISN'T IT?

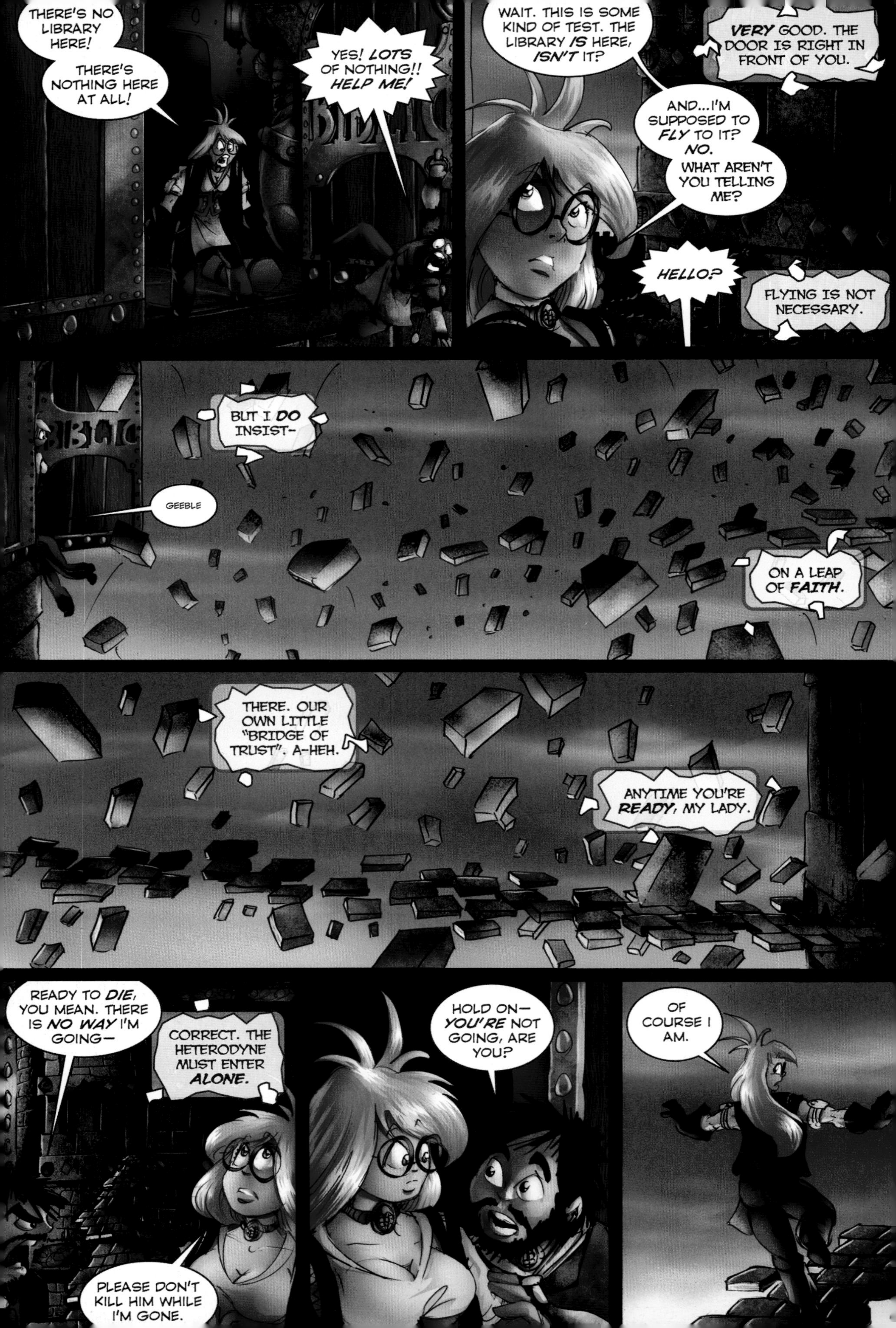
THERE'S NO LIBRARY HERE!
THERE'S NOTHING HERE AT ALL!
YES! LOTS OF NOTHING!! HELP ME!
WAIT. THIS IS SOME KIND OF TEST. THE LIBRARY IS HERE, ISN'T IT?
VERY GOOD. THE DOOR IS RIGHT IN FRONT OF YOU.
AND...I'M SUPPOSED TO FLY TO IT? NO.
WHAT AREN'T YOU TELLING ME?
HELLO?
FLYING IS NOT NECESSARY.
BUT I DO INSIST-
GEEBLE
ON A LEAP OF FAITH.
THERE. OUR OWN LITTLE "BRIDGE OF TRUST". A-HEH.
ANYTIME YOU'RE READY, MY LADY.
READY TO DIE, YOU MEAN. THERE IS NO WAY I'M GOING—
CORRECT. THE HETERODYNE MUST ENTER ALONE.
PLEASE DON'T KILL HIM WHILE I'M GONE.
HOLD ON— YOU'RE NOT GOING, ARE YOU?
OF COURSE I AM.

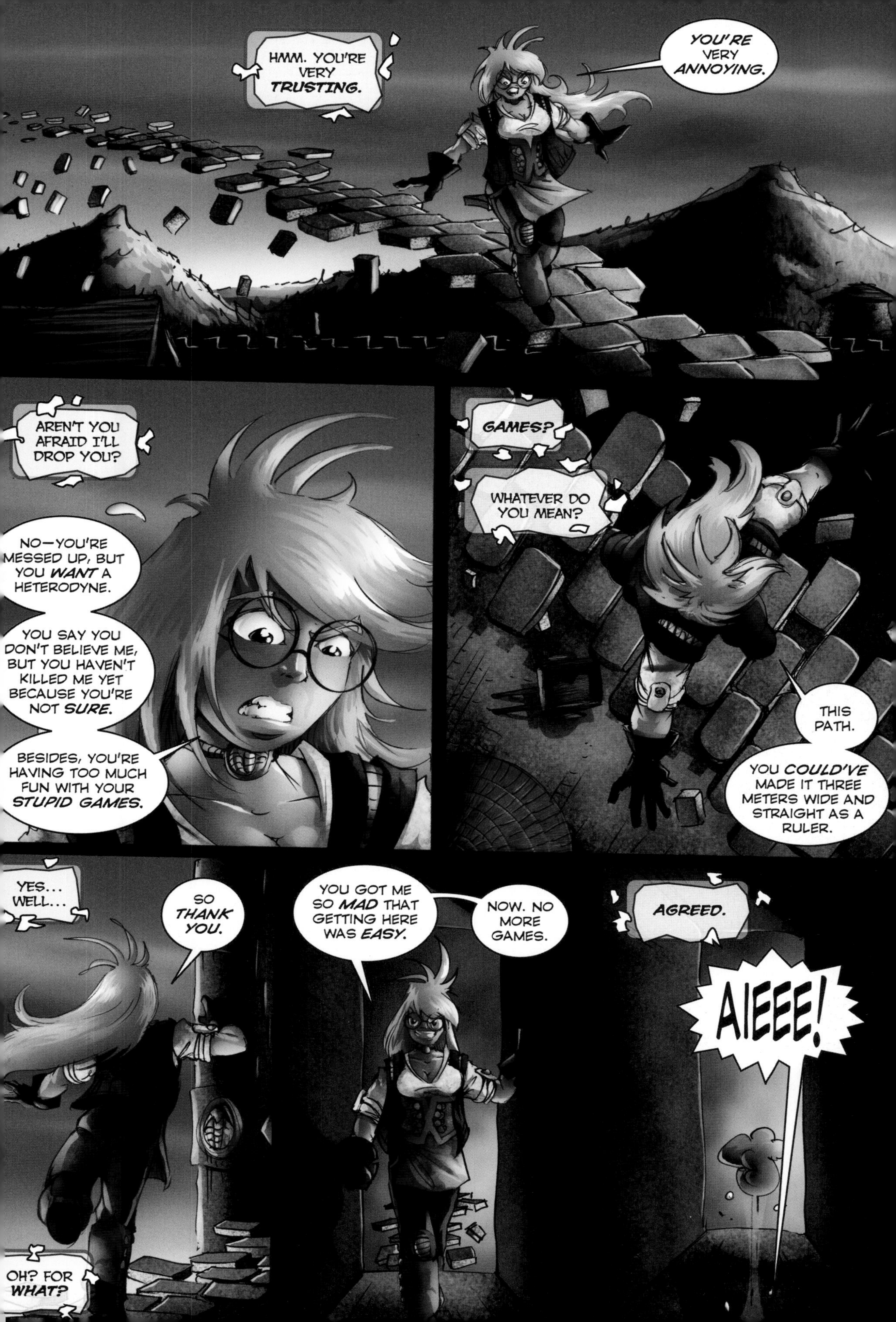
HMM. YOU'RE VERY TRUSTING.
YOU'RE VERY ANNOYING.
AREN'T YOU AFRAID I'LL DROP YOU?
NO—YOU'RE MESSED UP, BUT YOU WANT A HETERODYNE.
YOU SAY YOU DON'T BELIEVE ME, BUT YOU HAVEN'T KILLED ME YET BECAUSE YOU'RE NOT SURE.
BESIDES, YOU'RE HAVING TOO MUCH FUN WITH YOUR STUPID GAMES.
GAMES?
WHATEVER DO YOU MEAN?
THIS PATH.
YOU COULD'VE MADE IT THREE METERS WIDE AND STRAIGHT AS A RULER.
YES... WELL...
SO THANK YOU.
OH? FOR WHAT?
YOU GOT ME SO MAD THAT GETTING HERE WAS EASY.
NOW. NO MORE GAMES.
AGREED.
AIEEE!

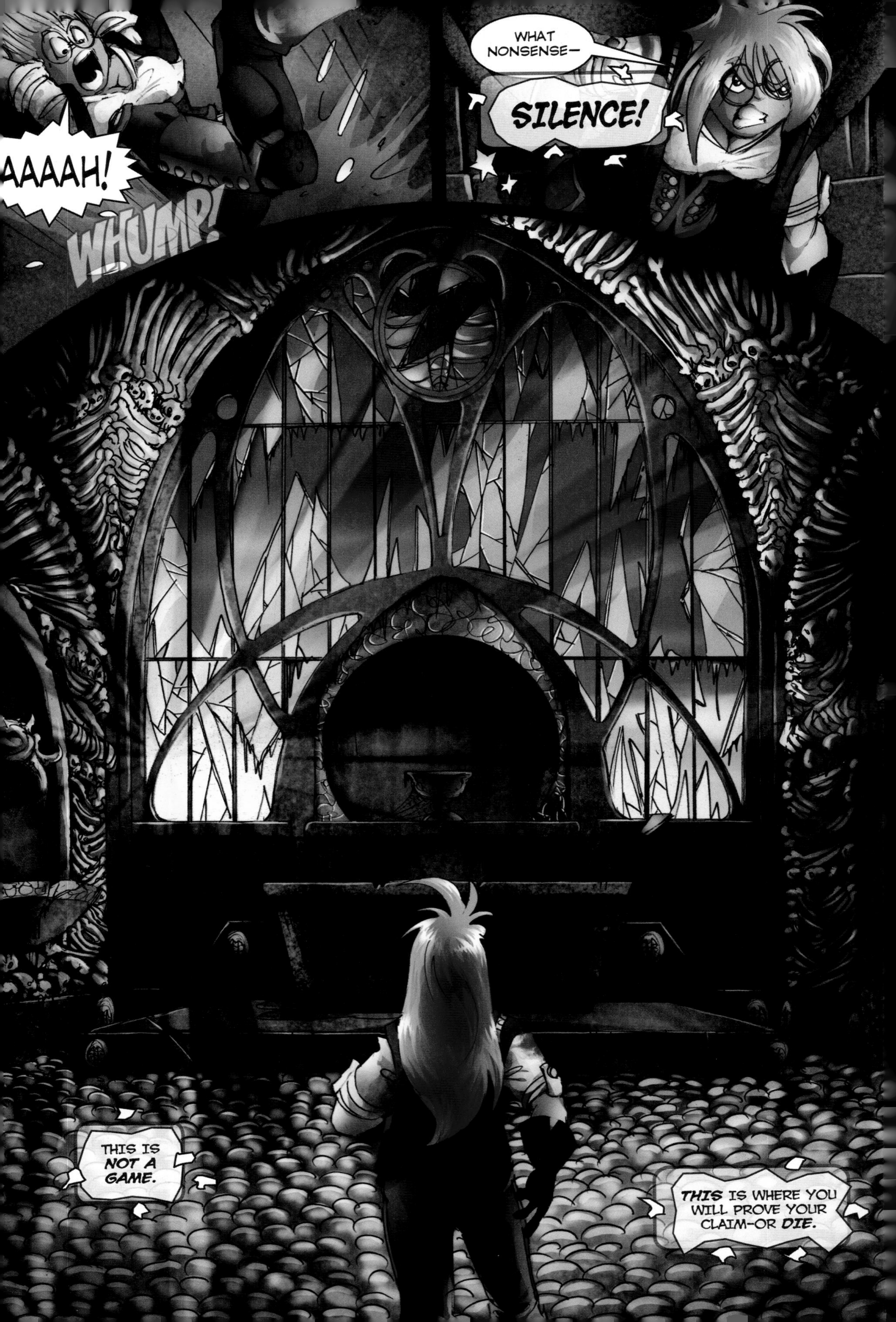

AAAAH!
WHUMP!
WHAT NONSENSE—
SILENCE!
THIS IS NOT A GAME.
THIS IS WHERE YOU WILL PROVE YOUR CLAIM—OR DIE.

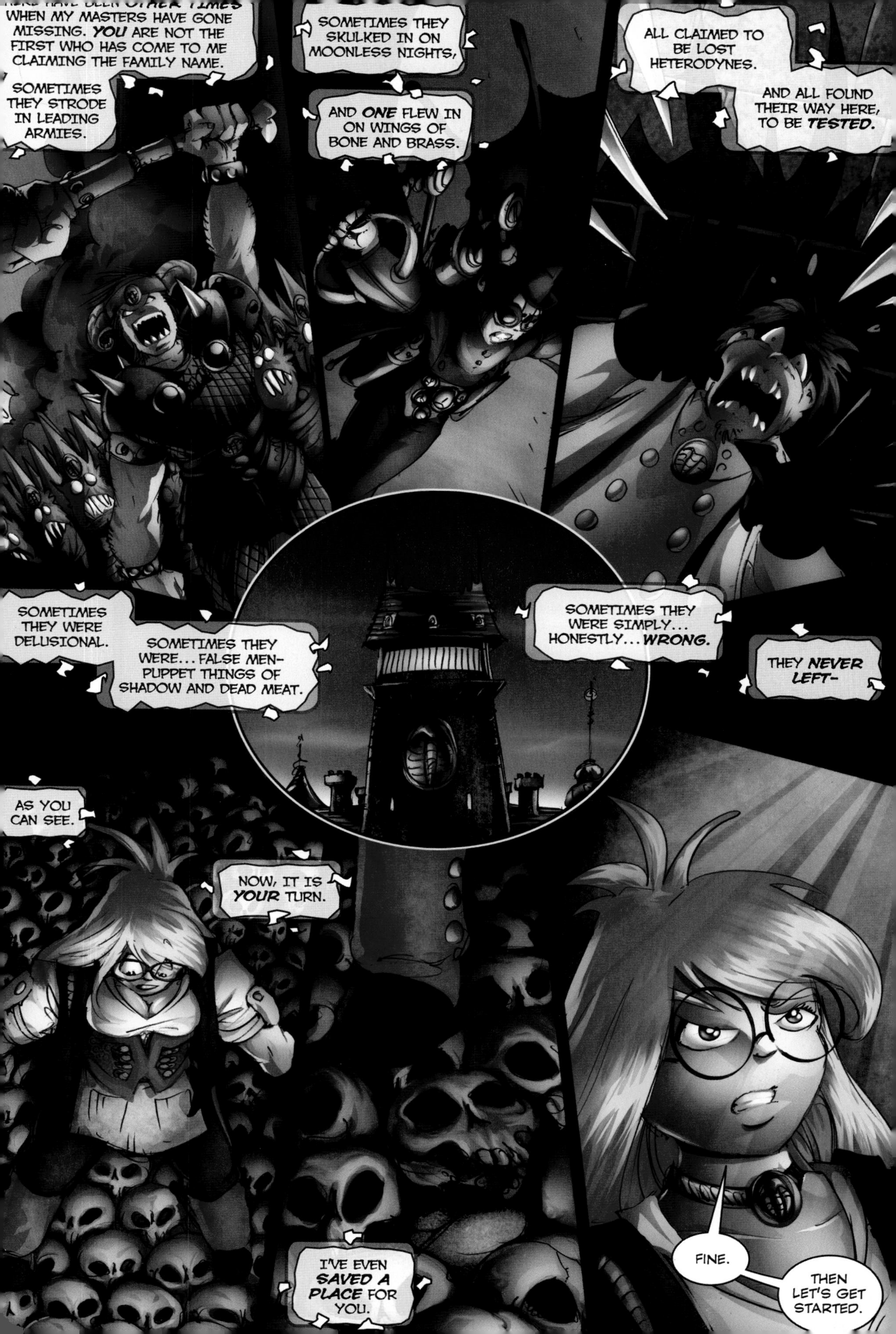
WHEN MY MASTERS HAVE GONE MISSING. YOU ARE NOT THE FIRST WHO HAS COME TO ME CLAIMING THE FAMILY NAME.
SOMETIMES THEY STRODE IN LEADING ARMIES.
SOMETIMES THEY SKULKED IN ON MOONLESS NIGHTS,
AND ONE FLEW IN ON WINGS OF BONE AND BRASS.
ALL CLAIMED TO BE LOST HETERODYNES.
AND ALL FOUND THEIR WAY HERE, TO BE TESTED.
SOMETIMES THEY WERE DELUSIONAL.
SOMETIMES THEY WERE... FALSE MEN- PUPPET THINGS OF SHADOW AND DEAD MEAT.
SOMETIMES THEY WERE SIMPLY... HONESTLY... WRONG.
THEY NEVER LEFT-
AS YOU CAN SEE.
NOW, IT IS YOUR TURN.
I'VE EVEN SAVED A PLACE FOR YOU.
FINE.
THEN LET'S GET STARTED.

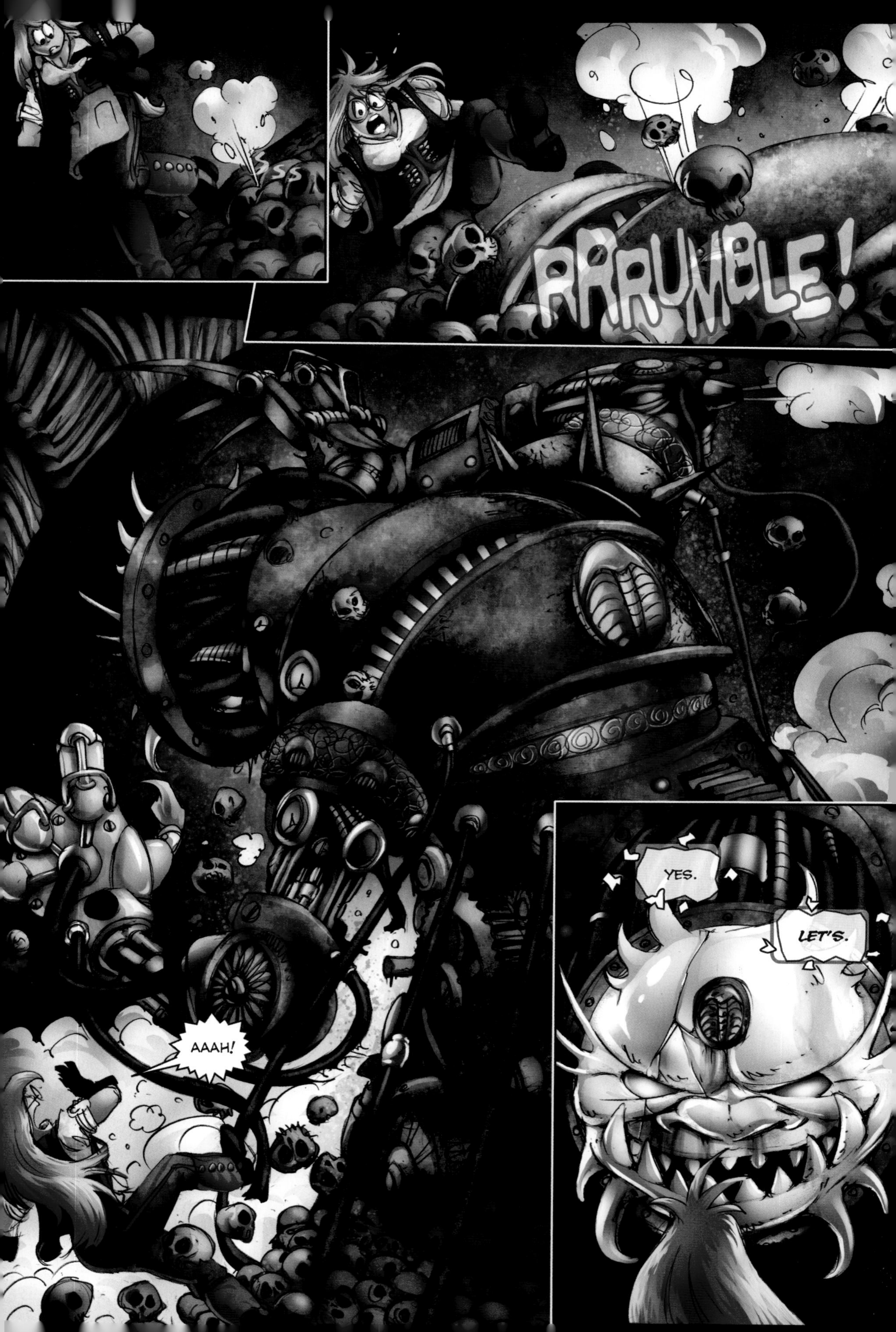
SSS
RRRUMBLE!
AAAH!
YES.
LET'S.

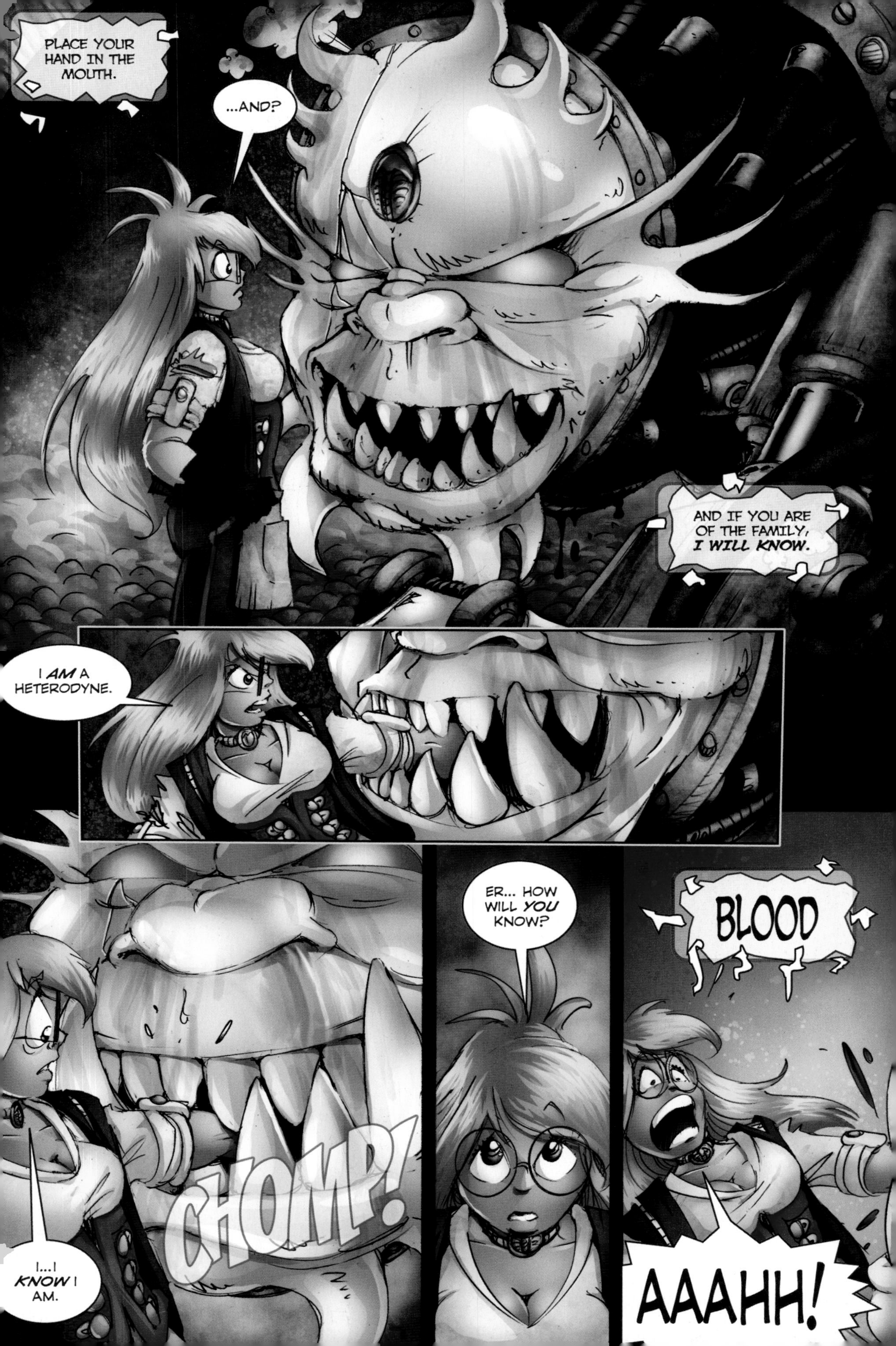
PLACE YOUR HAND IN THE MOUTH.
...AND?
AND IF YOU ARE OF THE FAMILY, I WILL KNOW.
I AM A HETERODYNE.
CHOMP!
I...I KNOW I AM.
ER... HOW WILL YOU KNOW?
BLOOD
AAAHH!

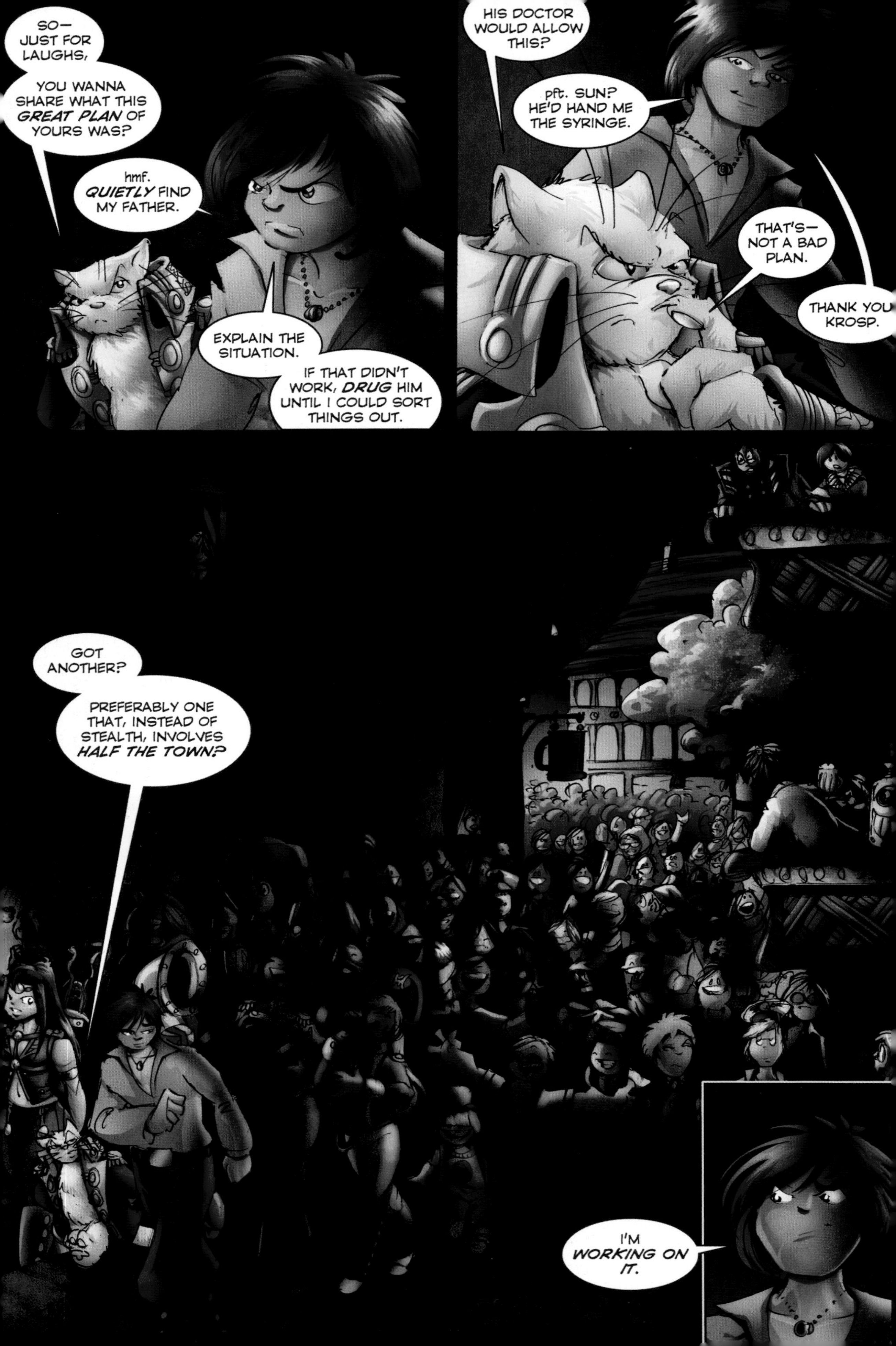
SO— JUST FOR LAUGHS,
YOU WANNA SHARE WHAT THIS *GREAT PLAN* OF YOURS WAS?
hmf. *QUIETLY* FIND MY FATHER.
EXPLAIN THE SITUATION.
IF THAT DIDN'T WORK, *DRUG* HIM UNTIL I COULD SORT THINGS OUT.
HIS DOCTOR WOULD ALLOW THIS?
pft. SUN? HE'D HAND ME THE SYRINGE.
THAT'S— NOT A BAD PLAN.
THANK YOU KROSP.
GOT ANOTHER?
PREFERABLY ONE THAT, INSTEAD OF STEALTH, INVOLVES *HALF THE TOWN?*
I'M *WORKING ON IT.*

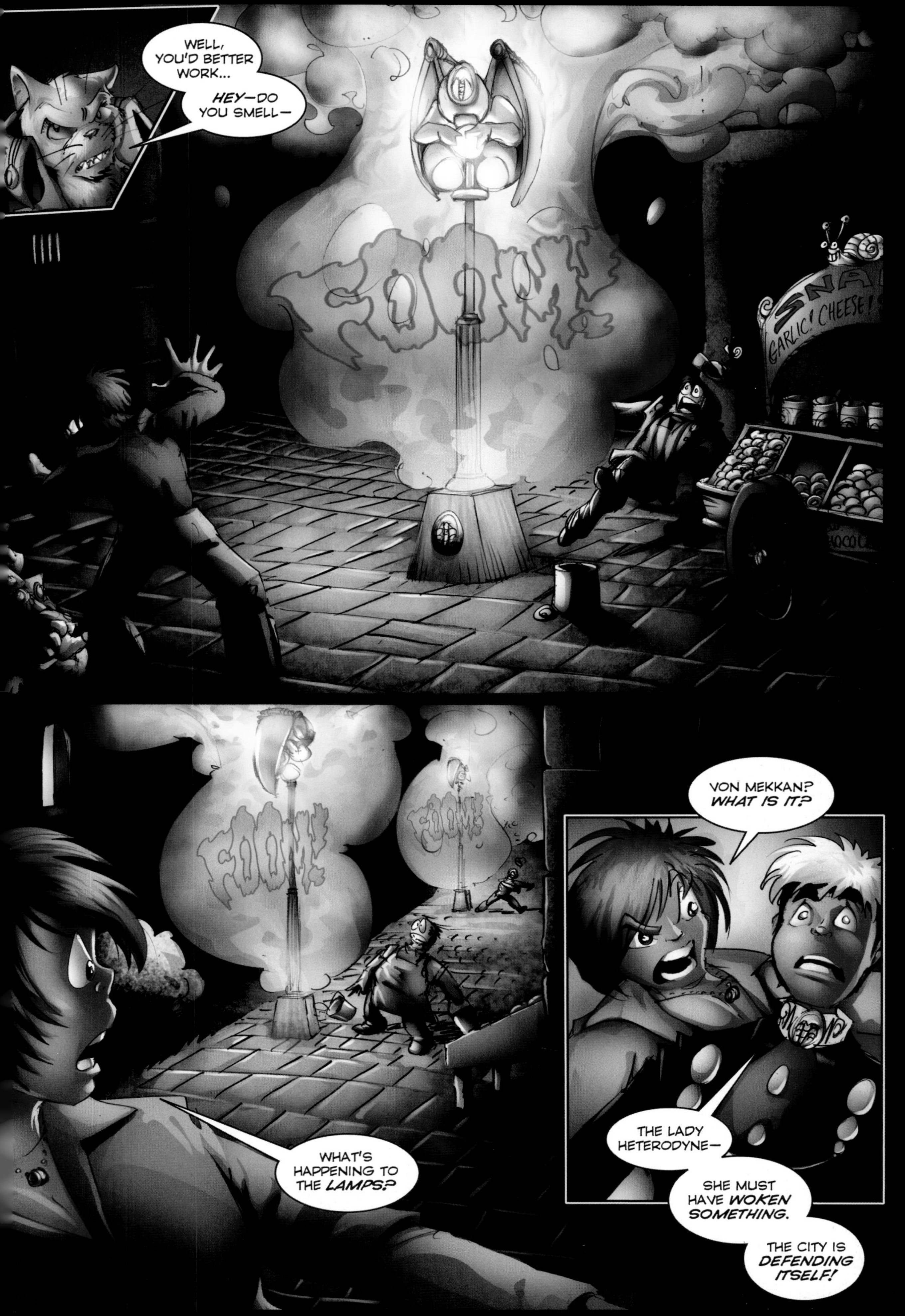
WELL, YOU'D BETTER WORK...
HEY—DO YOU SMELL—
FOOM!
SNA
GARLIC! CHEESE!
FOOM!
FOOM!
VON MEKKAN? WHAT IS IT?
WHAT'S HAPPENING TO THE LAMPS?
THE LADY HETERODYNE—
SHE MUST HAVE WOKEN SOMETHING.
THE CITY IS DEFENDING ITSELF!

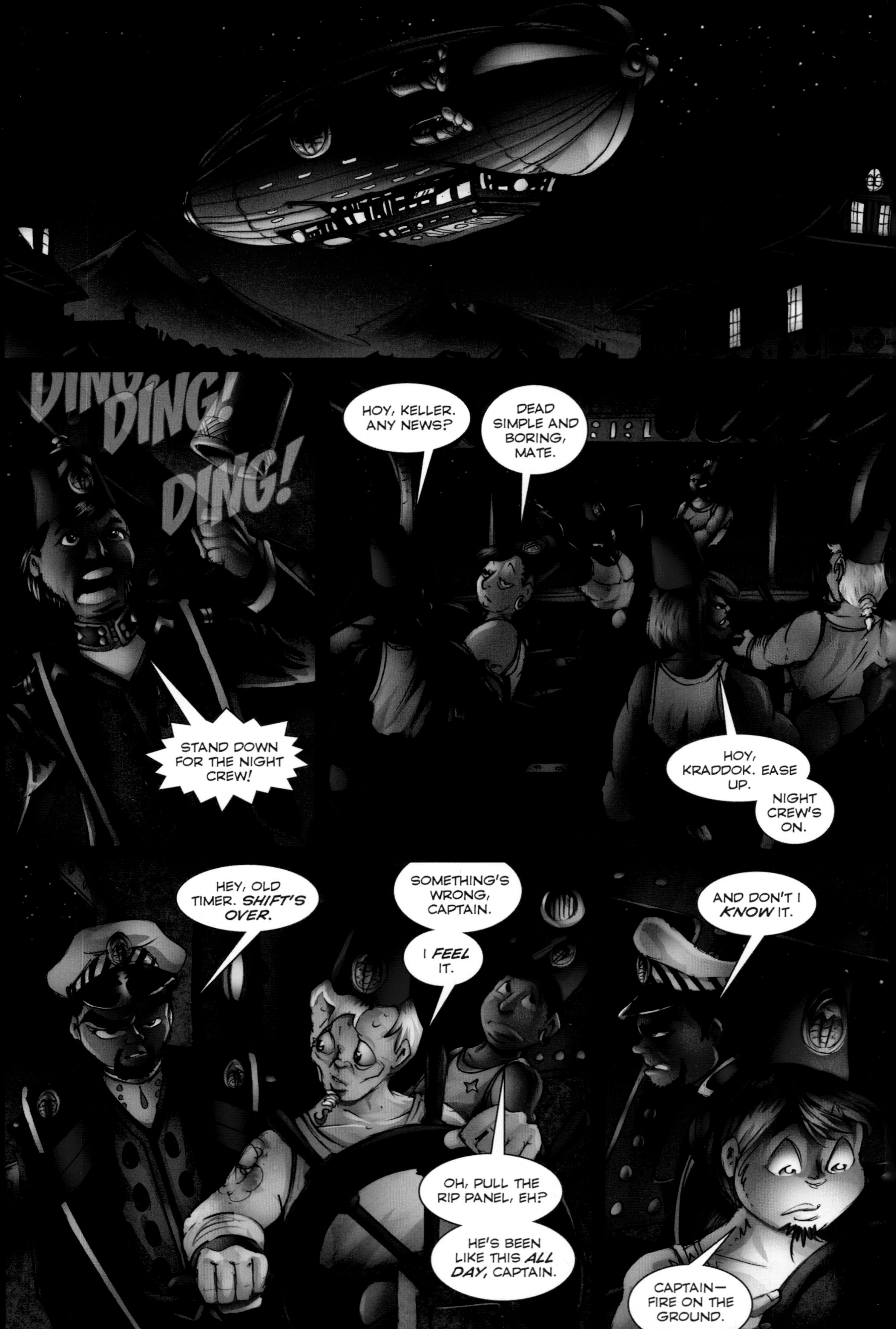
DING! DING!
DING!
STAND DOWN FOR THE NIGHT CREW!
HOY, KELLER. ANY NEWS?
DEAD SIMPLE AND BORING, MATE.
HOY, KRADDOK. EASE UP.
NIGHT CREW'S ON.
HEY, OLD TIMER. SHIFT'S OVER.
SOMETHING'S WRONG, CAPTAIN.
I FEEL IT.
OH, PULL THE RIP PANEL, EH?
HE'S BEEN LIKE THIS ALL DAY, CAPTAIN.
AND DON'T I KNOW IT.
CAPTAIN— FIRE ON THE GROUND.

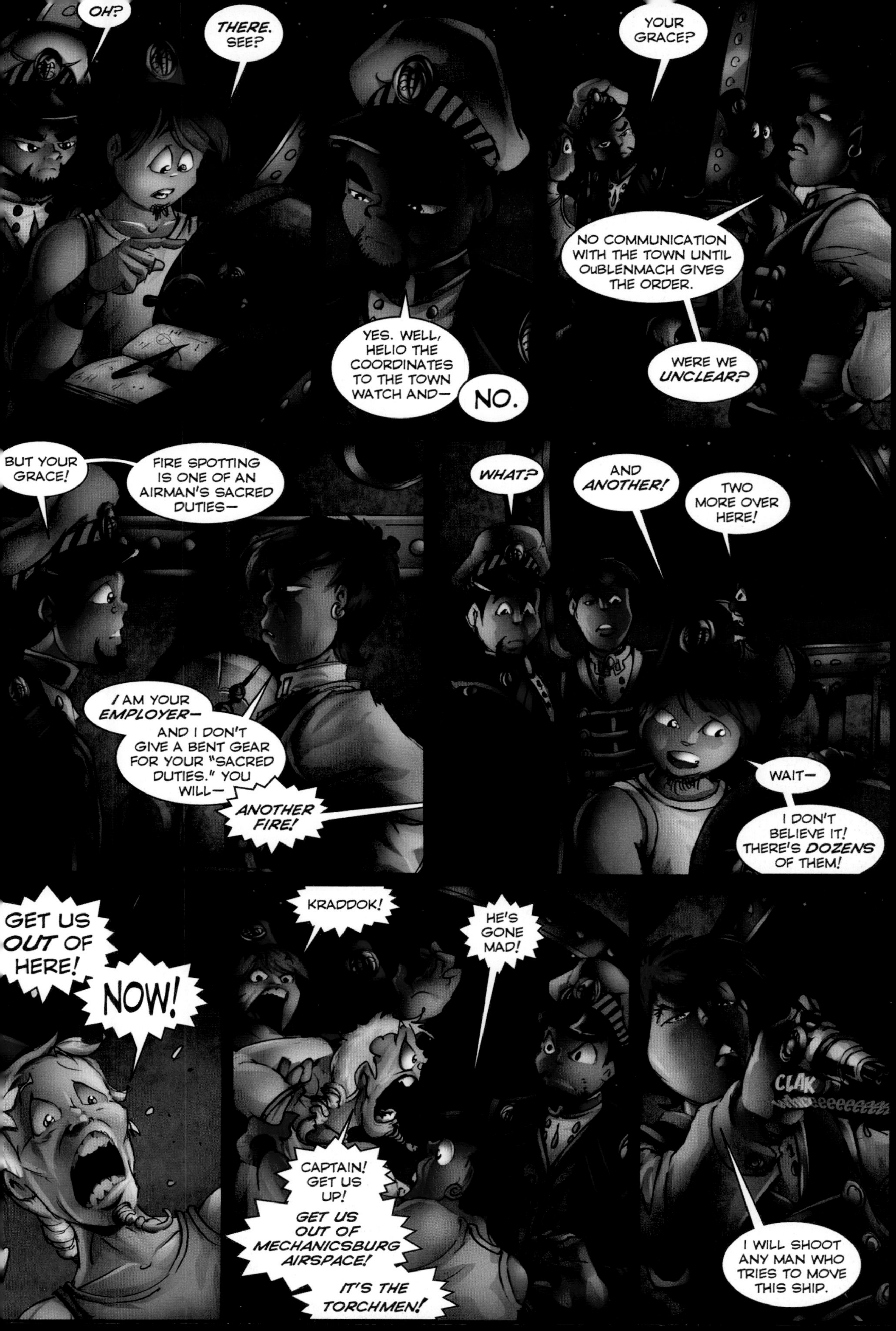
OH?
THERE. SEE?
YES. WELL, HELIO THE COORDINATES TO THE TOWN WATCH AND—
NO.
YOUR GRACE?
NO COMMUNICATION WITH THE TOWN UNTIL OUBLENMACH GIVES THE ORDER.
WERE WE UNCLEAR?
BUT YOUR GRACE!
FIRE SPOTTING IS ONE OF AN AIRMAN'S SACRED DUTIES—
I AM YOUR EMPLOYER—
AND I DON'T GIVE A BENT GEAR FOR YOUR "SACRED DUTIES." YOU WILL—
ANOTHER FIRE!
WHAT?
AND ANOTHER!
TWO MORE OVER HERE!
WAIT—
I DON'T BELIEVE IT! THERE'S DOZENS OF THEM!
GET US OUT OF HERE!
NOW!
KRADDOK!
HE'S GONE MAD!
CAPTAIN! GET US UP!
GET US OUT OF MECHANICSBURG AIRSPACE!
IT'S THE TORCHMEN!
CLAK
I WILL SHOOT ANY MAN WHO TRIES TO MOVE THIS SHIP.

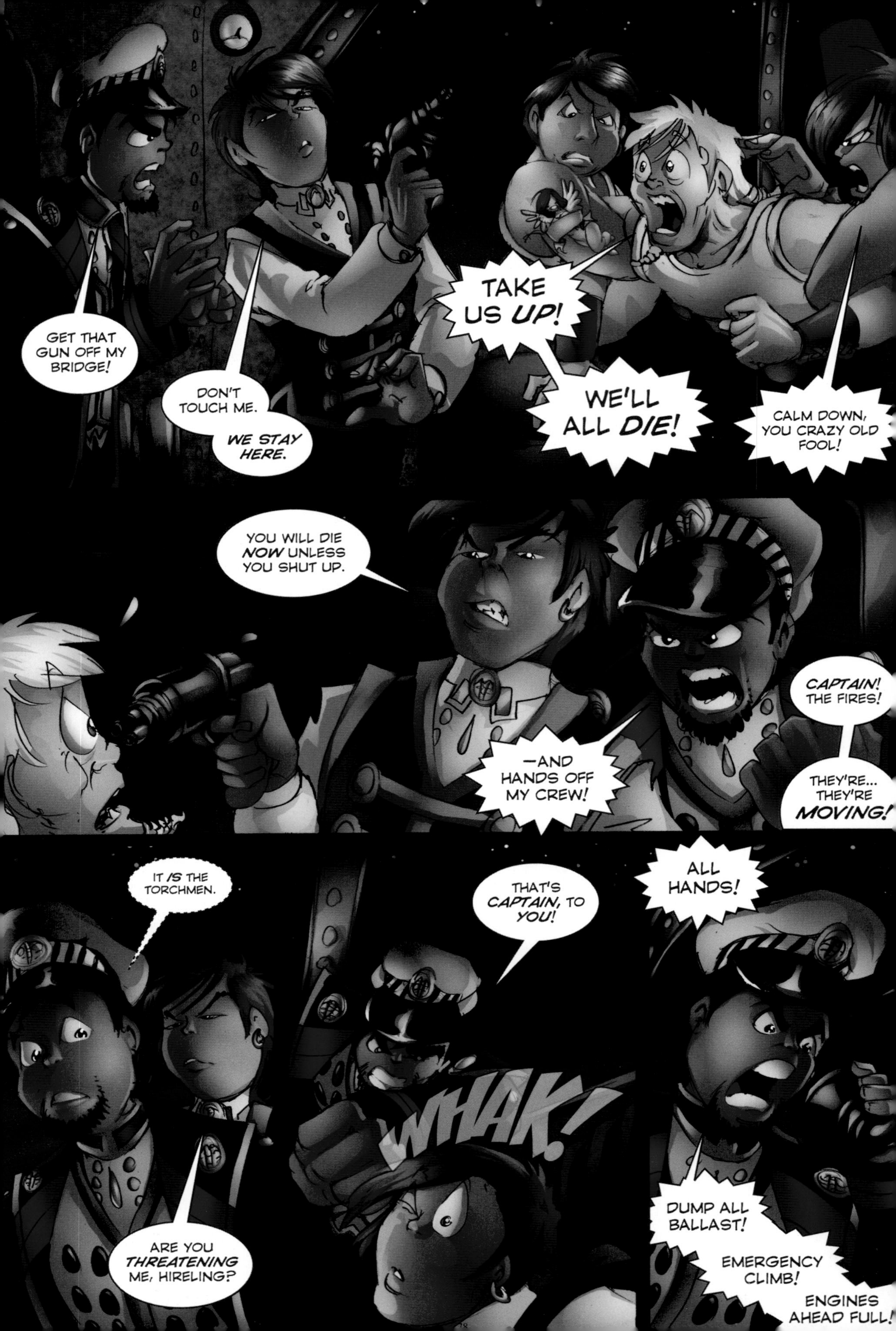
GET THAT GUN OFF MY BRIDGE!
DON'T TOUCH ME.
WE STAY HERE.
TAKE US UP!
WE'LL ALL DIE!
CALM DOWN, YOU CRAZY OLD FOOL!
YOU WILL DIE NOW UNLESS YOU SHUT UP.
—AND HANDS OFF MY CREW!
CAPTAIN! THE FIRES!
THEY'RE... THEY'RE MOVING!
IT IS THE TORCHMEN.
ARE YOU THREATENING ME, HIRELING?
THAT'S CAPTAIN, TO YOU!
WHAK!
ALL HANDS!
DUMP ALL BALLAST!
EMERGENCY CLIMB!
ENGINES AHEAD FULL!

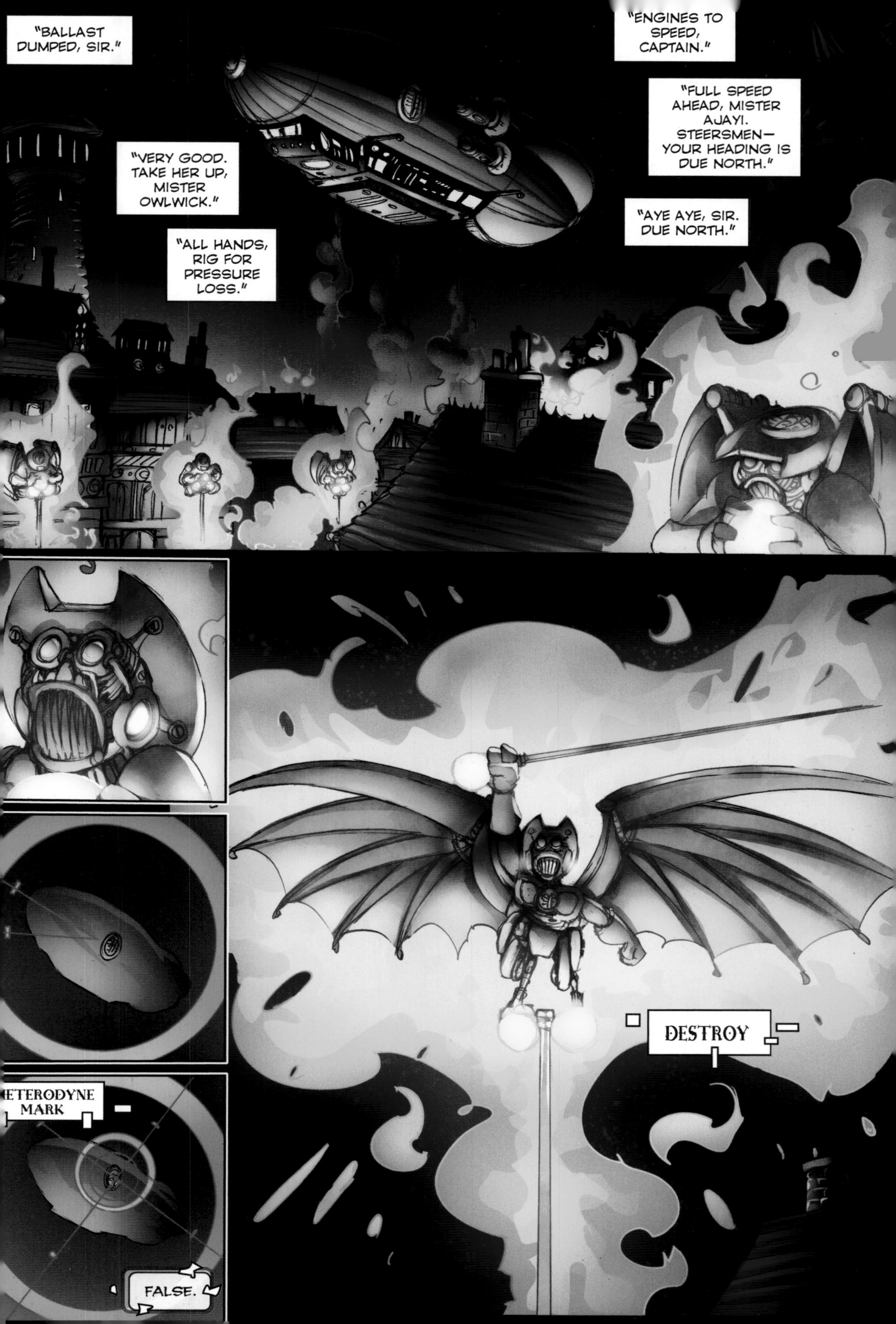
"BALLAST DUMPED, SIR."
"VERY GOOD. TAKE HER UP, MISTER OWLWICK."
"ALL HANDS, RIG FOR PRESSURE LOSS."
"ENGINES TO SPEED, CAPTAIN."
"FULL SPEED AHEAD, MISTER AJAYI. STEERSMEN— YOUR HEADING IS DUE NORTH."
"AYE AYE, SIR. DUE NORTH."
ETERODYNE MARK
FALSE.
DESTROY

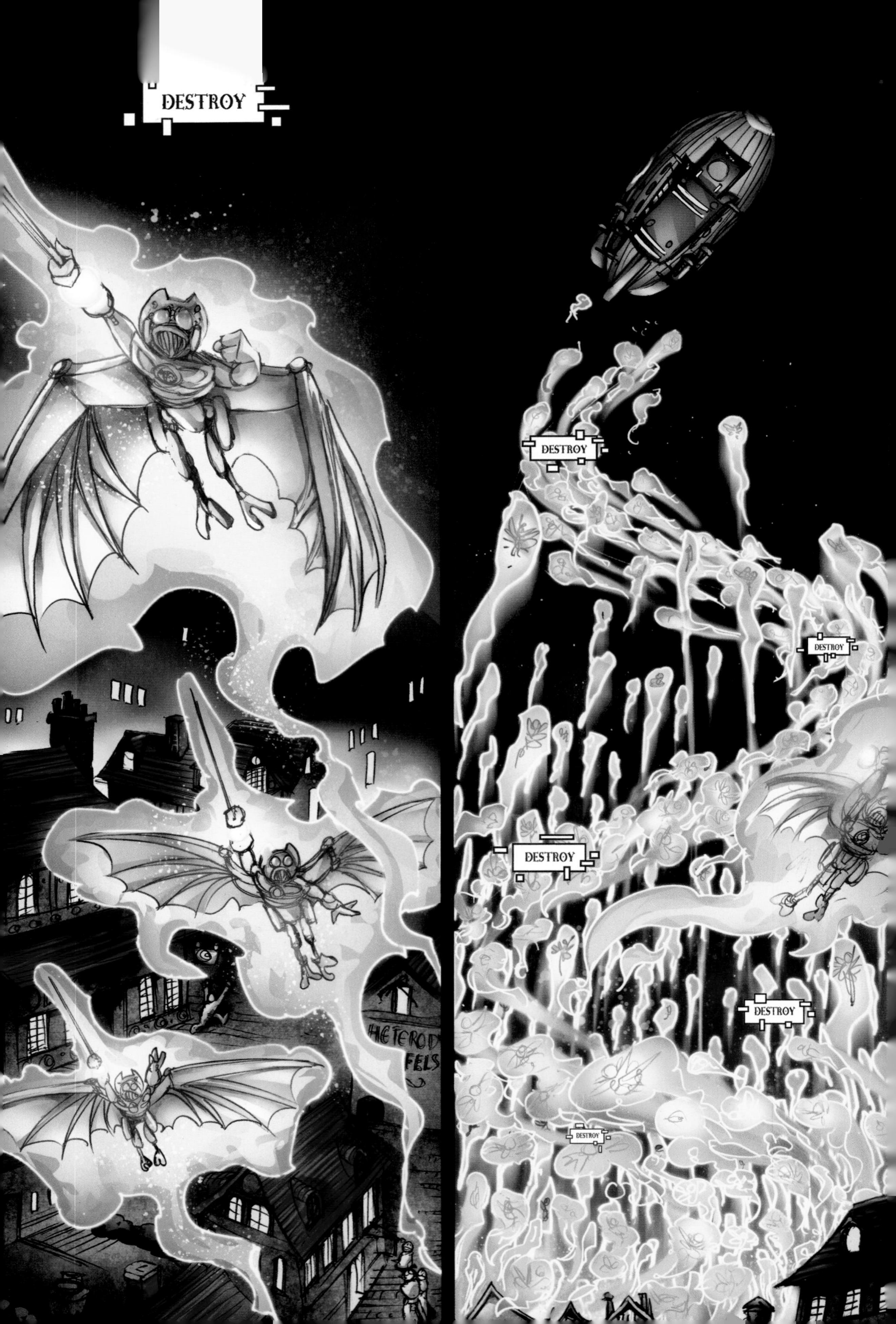
DESTROY
DESTROY
DESTROY
DESTROY
DESTROY
DESTROY

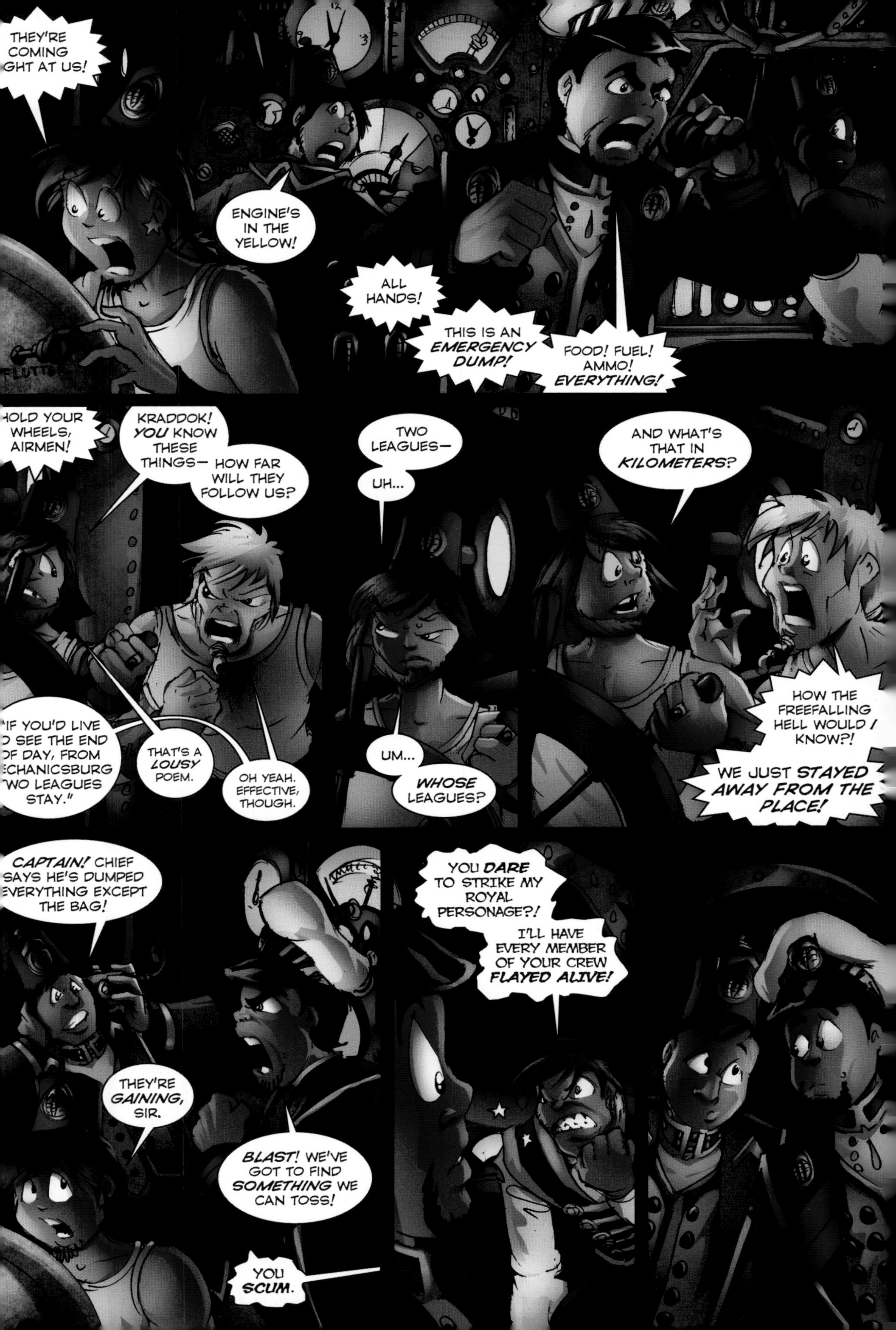
THEY'RE COMING GHT AT US!
ENGINE'S IN THE YELLOW!
ALL HANDS!
THIS IS AN EMERGENCY DUMP!
FOOD! FUEL! AMMO! EVERYTHING!
HOLD YOUR WHEELS, AIRMEN!
KRADDOK! YOU KNOW THESE THINGS— HOW FAR WILL THEY FOLLOW US?
"IF YOU'D LIVE O SEE THE END OF DAY, FROM ECHANICSBURG TWO LEAGUES STAY."
THAT'S A LOUSY POEM.
OH YEAH. EFFECTIVE, THOUGH.
TWO LEAGUES—
UH...
UM...
WHOSE LEAGUES?
AND WHAT'S THAT IN KILOMETERS?
HOW THE FREEFALLING HELL WOULD I KNOW?!
WE JUST STAYED AWAY FROM THE PLACE!
CAPTAIN! CHIEF SAYS HE'S DUMPED EVERYTHING EXCEPT THE BAG!
THEY'RE GAINING, SIR.
BLAST! WE'VE GOT TO FIND SOMETHING WE CAN TOSS!
YOU SCUM.
YOU DARE TO STRIKE MY ROYAL PERSONAGE?!
I'LL HAVE EVERY MEMBER OF YOUR CREW FLAYED ALIVE!

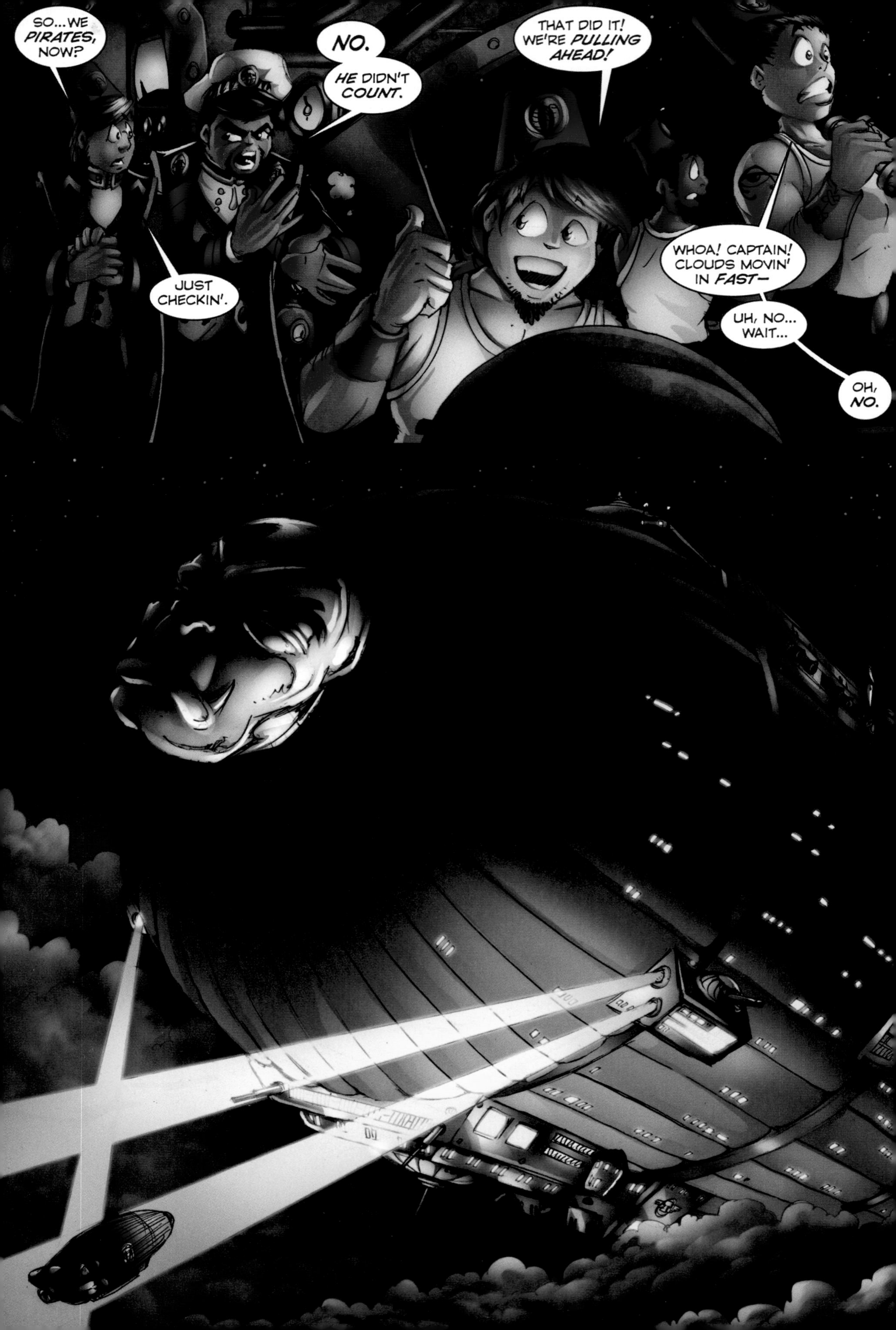
SO...WE PIRATES, NOW?
NO.
HE DIDN'T COUNT.
JUST CHECKIN'.
THAT DID IT! WE'RE PULLING AHEAD!
WHOA! CAPTAIN! CLOUDS MOVIN' IN FAST—
UH, NO... WAIT...
OH, NO.

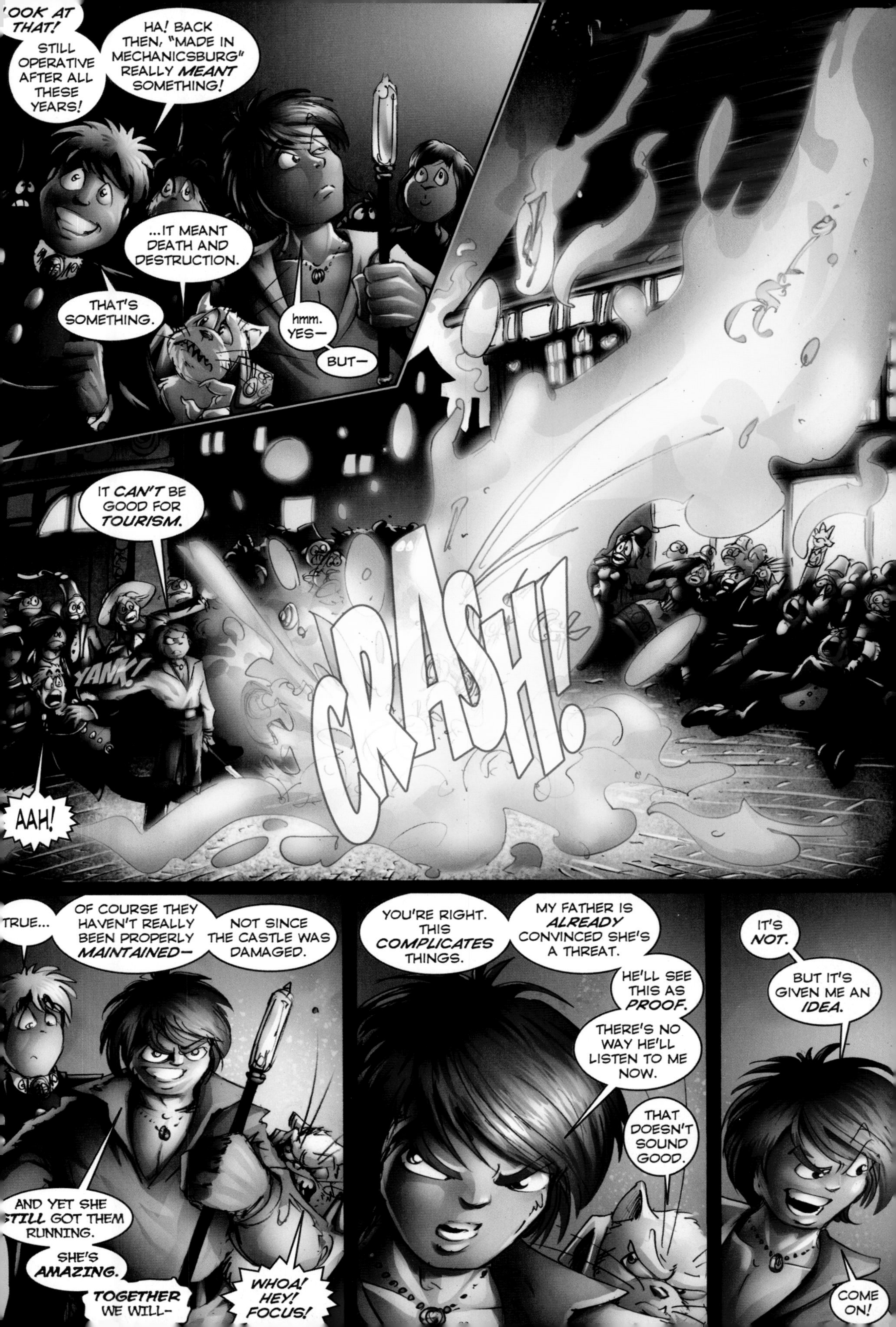

OOK AT THAT!
STILL OPERATIVE AFTER ALL THESE YEARS!
HA! BACK THEN, "MADE IN MECHANICSBURG" REALLY MEANT SOMETHING!
...IT MEANT DEATH AND DESTRUCTION.
THAT'S SOMETHING.
hmm. YES—
BUT—
IT CAN'T BE GOOD FOR TOURISM.
YANK!
CRASH!
AAH!
TRUE...
OF COURSE THEY HAVEN'T REALLY BEEN PROPERLY MAINTAINED—
NOT SINCE THE CASTLE WAS DAMAGED.
AND YET SHE STILL GOT THEM RUNNING.
SHE'S AMAZING.
TOGETHER WE WILL-
WHOA! HEY! FOCUS!
YOU'RE RIGHT. THIS COMPLICATES THINGS.
MY FATHER IS ALREADY CONVINCED SHE'S A THREAT.
HE'LL SEE THIS AS PROOF.
THERE'S NO WAY HE'LL LISTEN TO ME NOW.
THAT DOESN'T SOUND GOOD.
IT'S NOT.
BUT IT'S GIVEN ME AN IDEA.
COME ON!

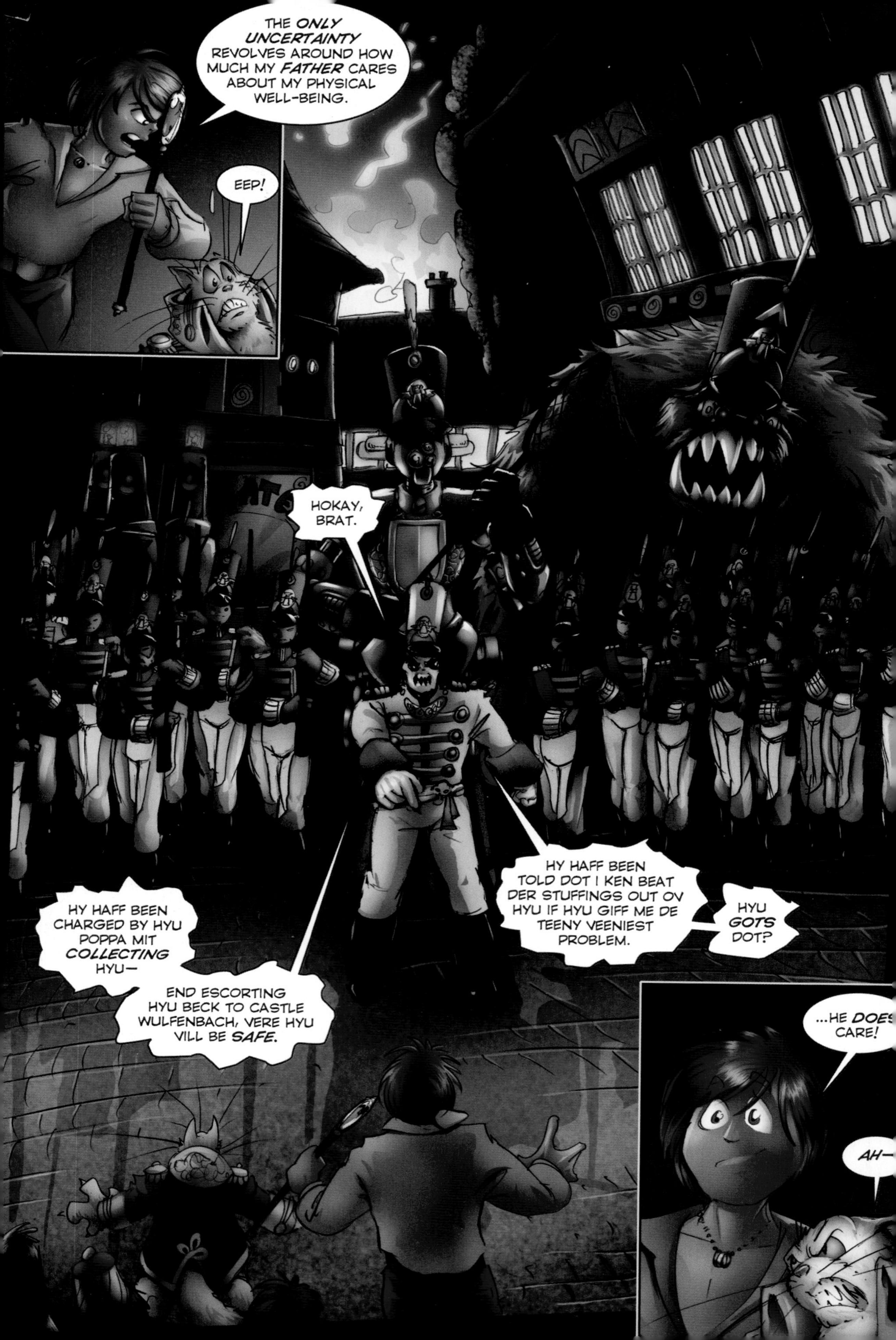
THE ONLY UNCERTAINTY REVOLVES AROUND HOW MUCH MY FATHER CARES ABOUT MY PHYSICAL WELL-BEING.
EEP!
HOKAY, BRAT.
HY HAFF BEEN CHARGED BY HYU POPPA MIT COLLECTING HYU—
END ESCORTING HYU BECK TO CASTLE WULFENBACH, VERE HYU VILL BE SAFE.
HY HAFF BEEN TOLD DOT I KEN BEAT DER STUFFINGS OUT OV HYU IF HYU GIFF ME DE TEENY VEENIEST PROBLEM.
HYU GOTS DOT?
...HE DOES CARE!
AH—

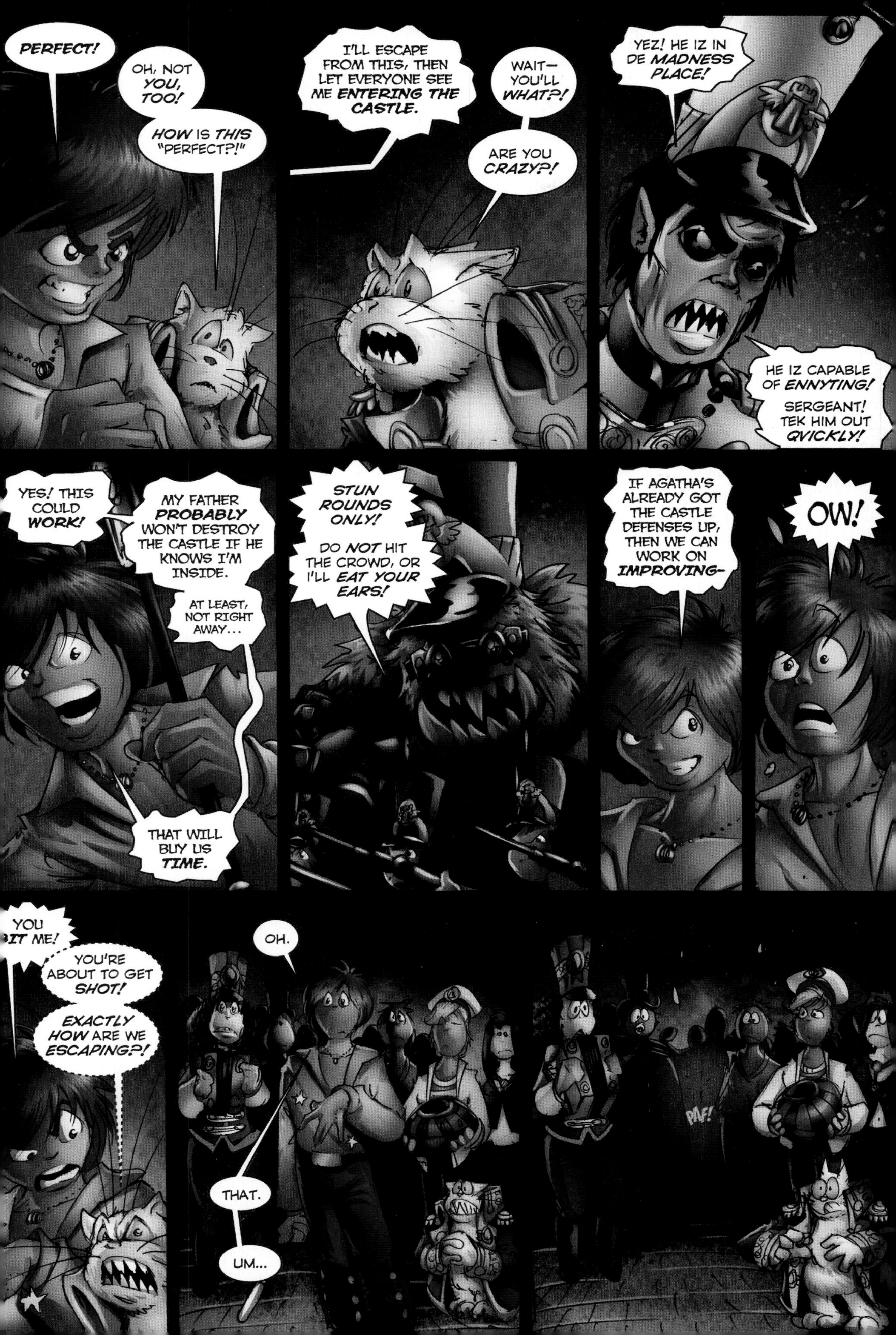
PERFECT!
OH, NOT YOU, TOO!
HOW IS THIS "PERFECT?!"
I'LL ESCAPE FROM THIS, THEN LET EVERYONE SEE ME ENTERING THE CASTLE.
WAIT— YOU'LL WHAT?!
ARE YOU CRAZY?!
YEZ! HE IZ IN DE MADNESS PLACE!
HE IZ CAPABLE OF ENNYTING!
SERGEANT! TEK HIM OUT QVICKLY!
YES! THIS COULD WORK!
MY FATHER PROBABLY WON'T DESTROY THE CASTLE IF HE KNOWS I'M INSIDE.
AT LEAST, NOT RIGHT AWAY...
THAT WILL BUY US TIME.
STUN ROUNDS ONLY!
DO NOT HIT THE CROWD, OR I'LL EAT YOUR EARS!
IF AGATHA'S ALREADY GOT THE CASTLE DEFENSES UP, THEN WE CAN WORK ON IMPROVING-
OW!
YOU BIT ME!
YOU'RE ABOUT TO GET SHOT!
EXACTLY HOW ARE WE ESCAPING?!
OH.
THAT.
UM...
PAF!

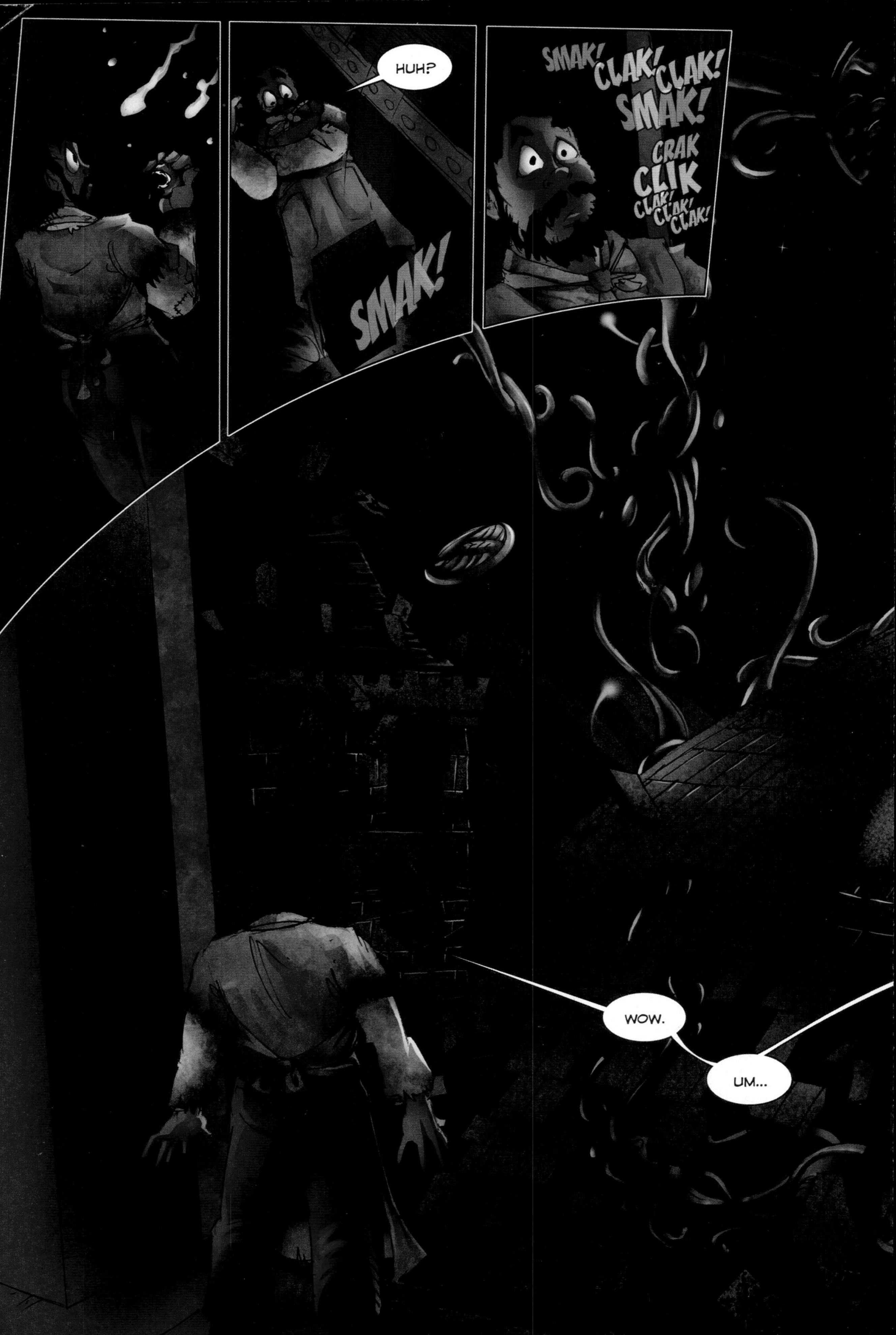
HUH?
SMAK!
SMAK! CLAK! CLAK!
SMAK!
CRAK
CLIK
CLAK! CLAK! CLAK!
WOW.
UM...

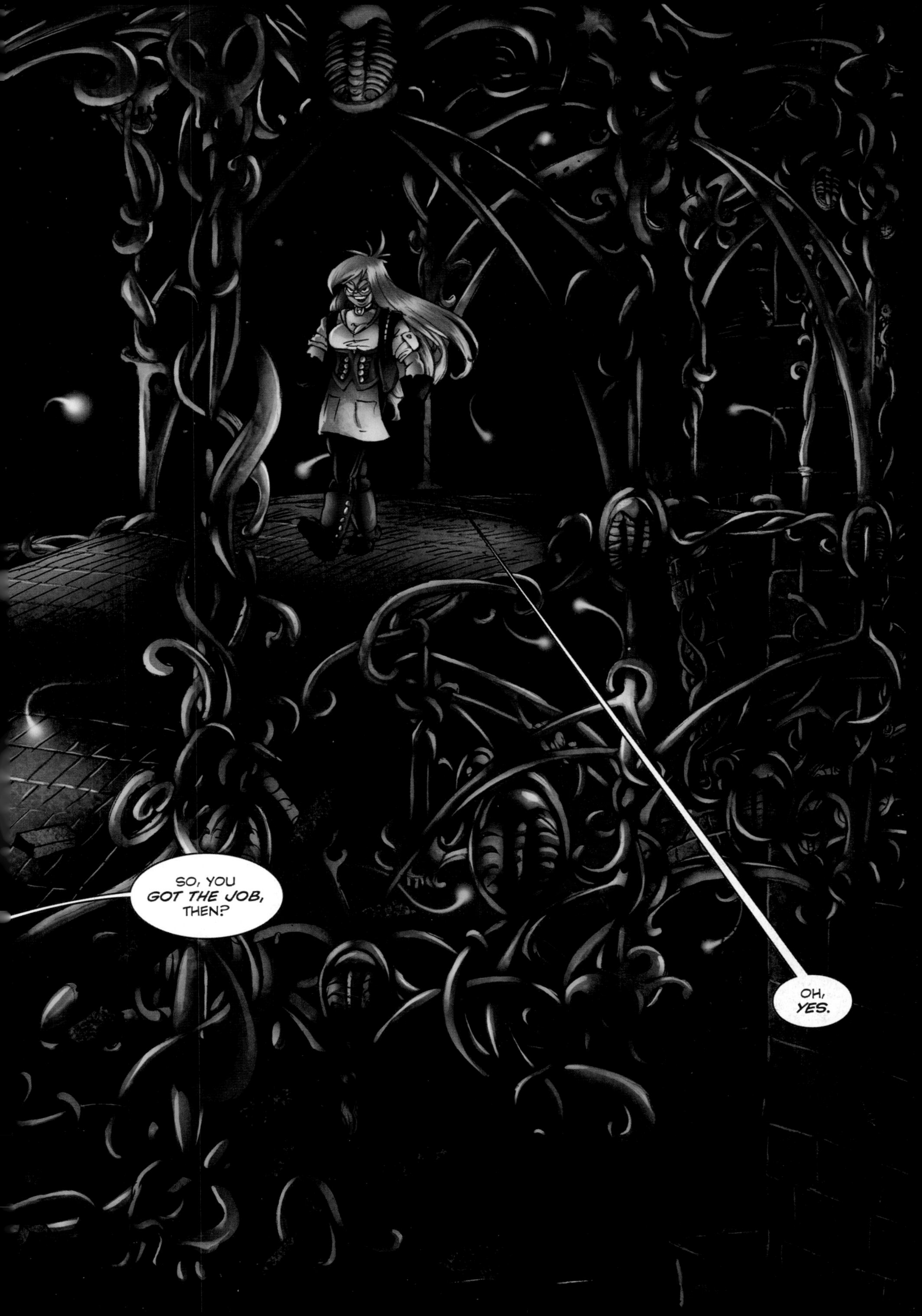
SO, YOU *GOT THE JOB,* THEN?
OH, *YES.*

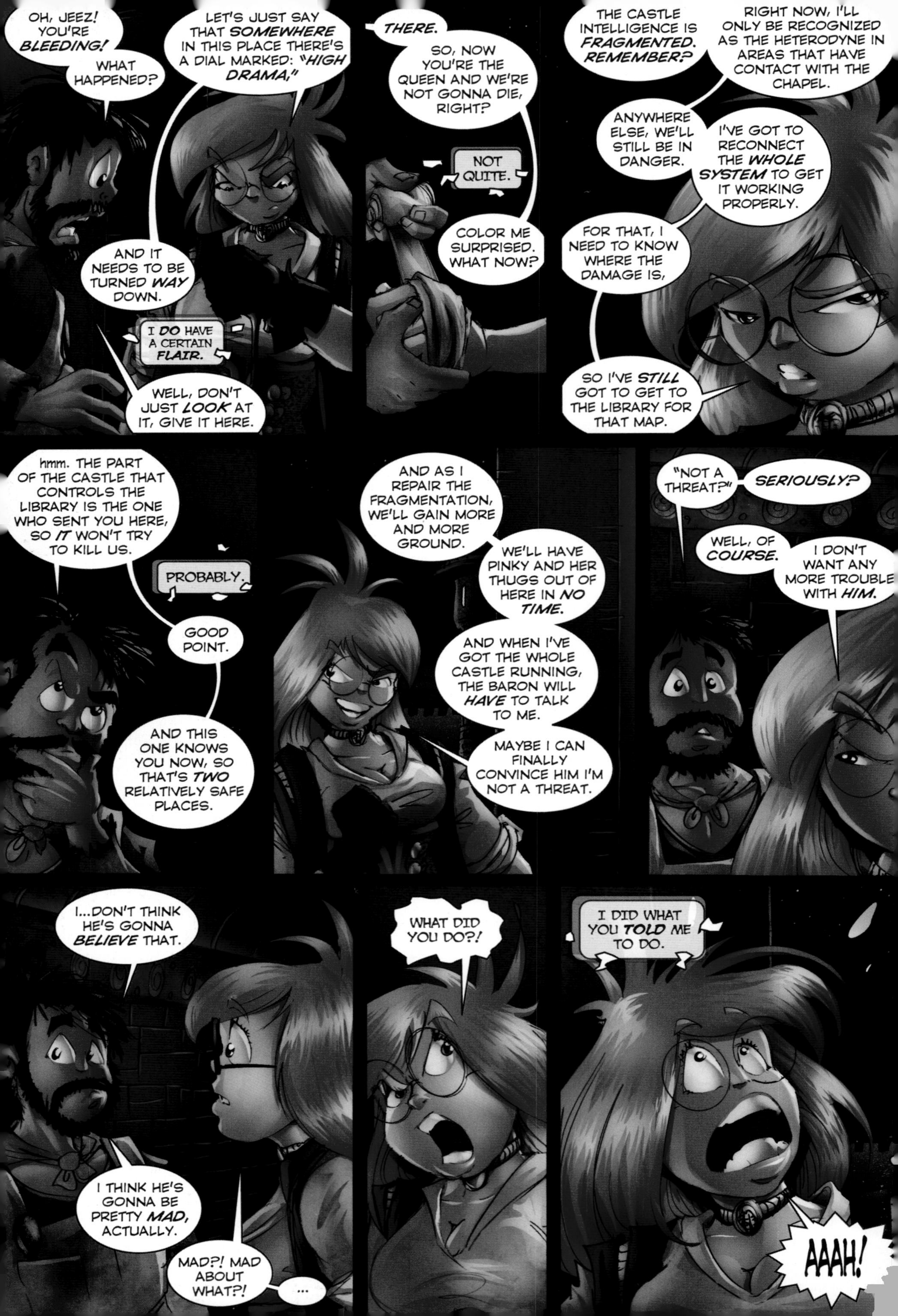

OH, JEEZ! YOU'RE *BLEEDING!*
WHAT HAPPENED?
LET'S JUST SAY THAT *SOMEWHERE* IN THIS PLACE THERE'S A DIAL MARKED: *"HIGH DRAMA,"*
AND IT NEEDS TO BE TURNED *WAY* DOWN.
I *DO* HAVE A CERTAIN *FLAIR.*
WELL, DON'T JUST *LOOK* AT IT, GIVE IT HERE.
THERE.
SO, NOW YOU'RE THE QUEEN AND WE'RE NOT GONNA DIE, RIGHT?
NOT QUITE.
COLOR ME SURPRISED. WHAT NOW?
THE CASTLE INTELLIGENCE IS *FRAGMENTED. REMEMBER?*
RIGHT NOW, I'LL ONLY BE RECOGNIZED AS THE HETERODYNE IN AREAS THAT HAVE CONTACT WITH THE CHAPEL.
ANYWHERE ELSE, WE'LL STILL BE IN DANGER.
I'VE GOT TO RECONNECT THE *WHOLE SYSTEM* TO GET IT WORKING PROPERLY.
FOR THAT, I NEED TO KNOW WHERE THE DAMAGE IS,
SO I'VE *STILL* GOT TO GET TO THE LIBRARY FOR THAT MAP.
hmm. THE PART OF THE CASTLE THAT CONTROLS THE LIBRARY IS THE ONE WHO SENT YOU HERE, SO *IT* WON'T TRY TO KILL US.
PROBABLY.
GOOD POINT.
AND THIS ONE KNOWS YOU NOW, SO THAT'S *TWO* RELATIVELY SAFE PLACES.
AND AS I REPAIR THE FRAGMENTATION, WE'LL GAIN MORE AND MORE GROUND.
WE'LL HAVE PINKY AND HER THUGS OUT OF HERE IN *NO TIME.*
AND WHEN I'VE GOT THE WHOLE CASTLE RUNNING, THE BARON WILL *HAVE* TO TALK TO ME.
MAYBE I CAN FINALLY CONVINCE HIM I'M NOT A THREAT.
"NOT A THREAT?"
SERIOUSLY?
WELL, OF *COURSE.*
I DON'T WANT ANY MORE TROUBLE WITH *HIM.*
I...DON'T THINK HE'S GONNA *BELIEVE* THAT.
I THINK HE'S GONNA BE PRETTY *MAD,* ACTUALLY.
MAD?! MAD ABOUT WHAT?!
...
WHAT DID YOU DO?!
I DID WHAT YOU *TOLD* ME TO DO.
AAAH!

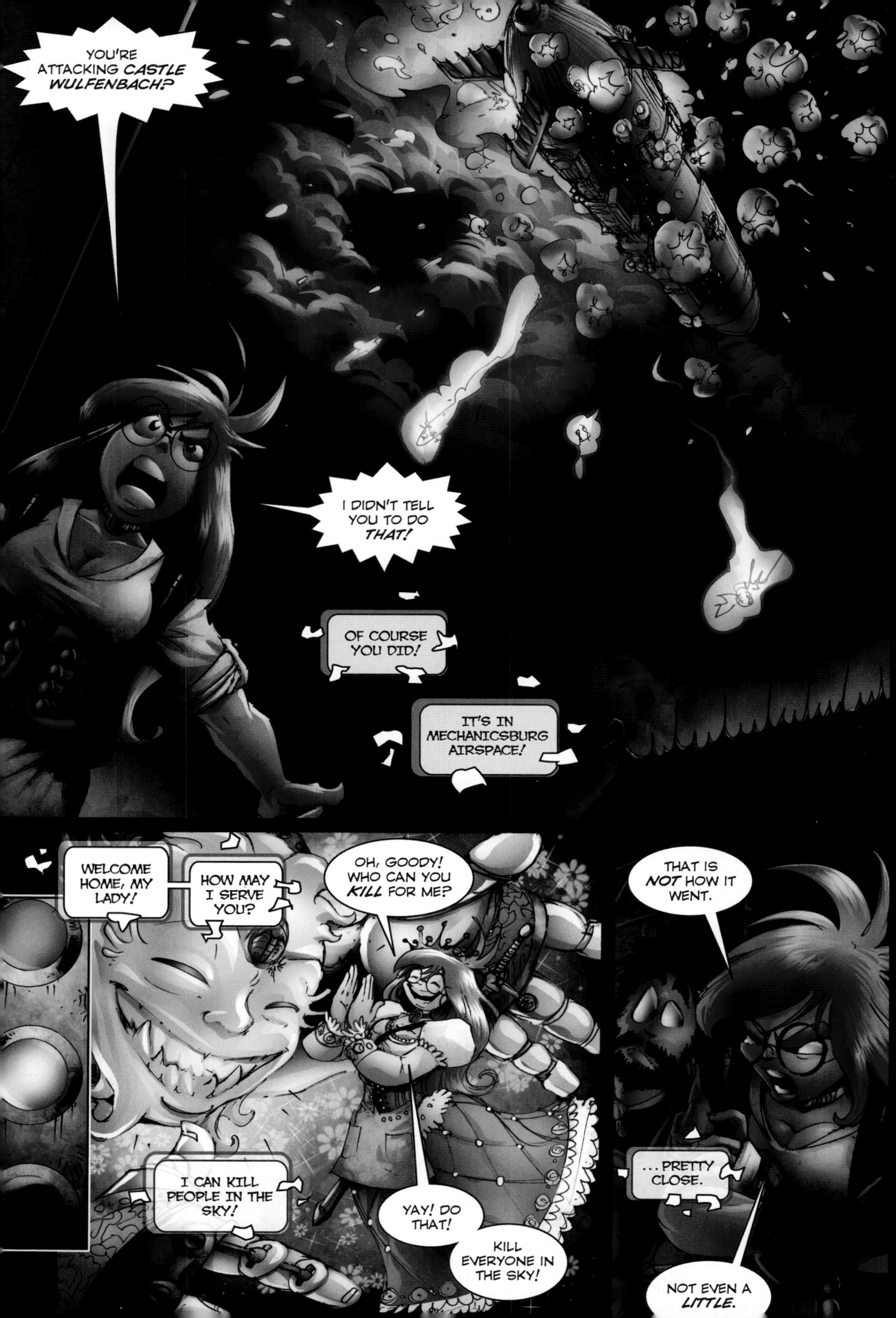
YOU'RE ATTACKING *CASTLE WULFENBACH?*
I DIDN'T TELL YOU TO DO *THAT!*
OF COURSE YOU DID!
IT'S IN MECHANICSBURG AIRSPACE!
WELCOME HOME, MY LADY!
HOW MAY I SERVE YOU?
OH, GOODY! WHO CAN YOU *KILL* FOR ME?
I CAN KILL PEOPLE IN THE SKY!
YAY! DO THAT!
KILL EVERYONE IN THE SKY!
THAT IS *NOT* HOW IT WENT.
...PRETTY CLOSE.
NOT EVEN A *LITTLE.*

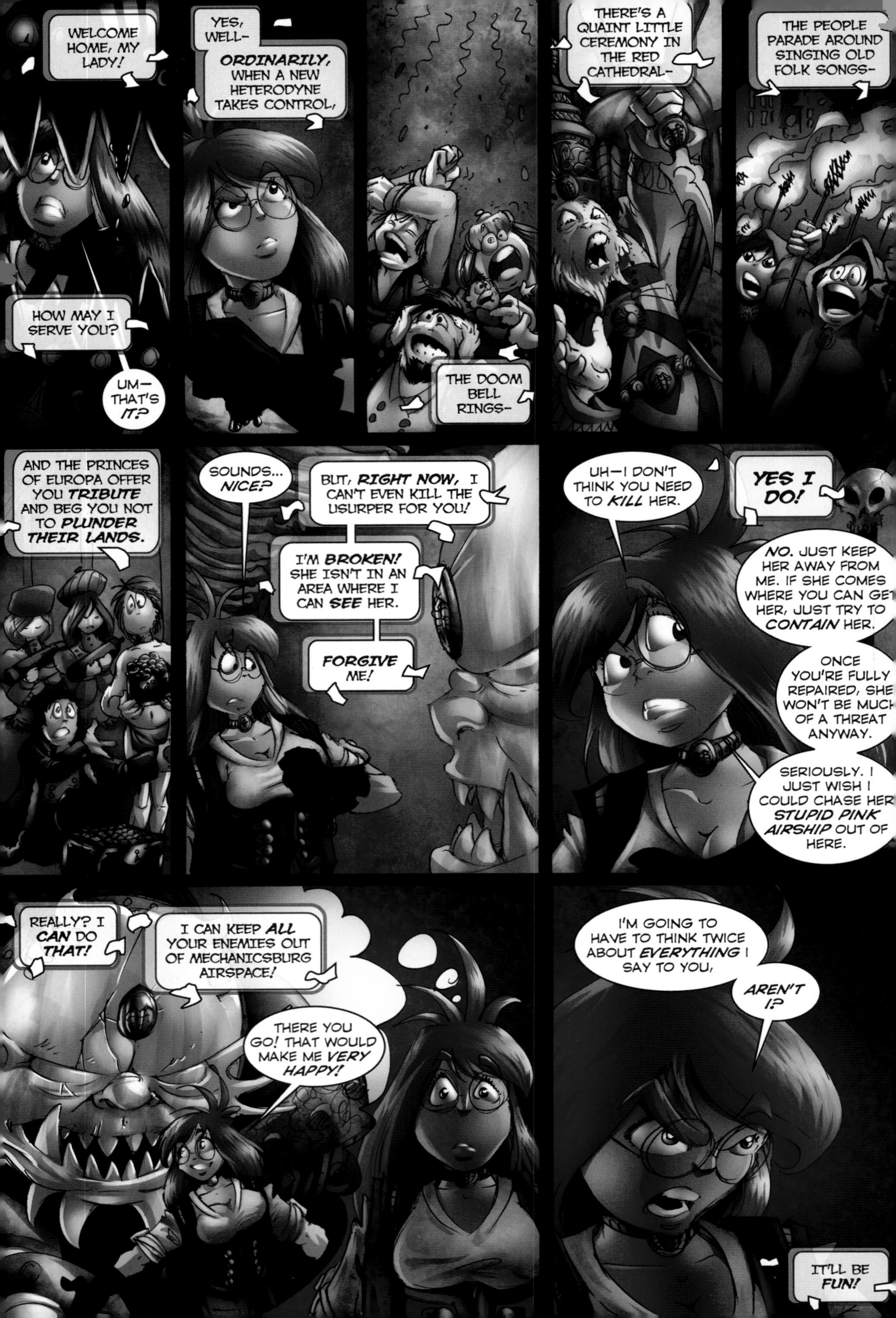
WELCOME HOME, MY LADY!
HOW MAY I SERVE YOU?
UM—THAT'S IT?
YES, WELL-
ORDINARILY, WHEN A NEW HETERODYNE TAKES CONTROL,
THE DOOM BELL RINGS-
THERE'S A QUAINT LITTLE CEREMONY IN THE RED CATHEDRAL-
THE PEOPLE PARADE AROUND SINGING OLD FOLK SONGS-
AND THE PRINCES OF EUROPA OFFER YOU TRIBUTE AND BEG YOU NOT TO PLUNDER THEIR LANDS.
SOUNDS... NICE?
BUT, RIGHT NOW, I CAN'T EVEN KILL THE USURPER FOR YOU!
I'M BROKEN! SHE ISN'T IN AN AREA WHERE I CAN SEE HER.
FORGIVE ME!
UH—I DON'T THINK YOU NEED TO KILL HER.
YES I DO!
NO. JUST KEEP HER AWAY FROM ME. IF SHE COMES WHERE YOU CAN GET HER, JUST TRY TO CONTAIN HER.
ONCE YOU'RE FULLY REPAIRED, SHE WON'T BE MUCH OF A THREAT ANYWAY.
SERIOUSLY. I JUST WISH I COULD CHASE HER STUPID PINK AIRSHIP OUT OF HERE.
REALLY? I CAN DO THAT!
I CAN KEEP ALL YOUR ENEMIES OUT OF MECHANICSBURG AIRSPACE!
THERE YOU GO! THAT WOULD MAKE ME VERY HAPPY!
I'M GOING TO HAVE TO THINK TWICE ABOUT EVERYTHING I SAY TO YOU,
AREN'T I?
IT'LL BE FUN!

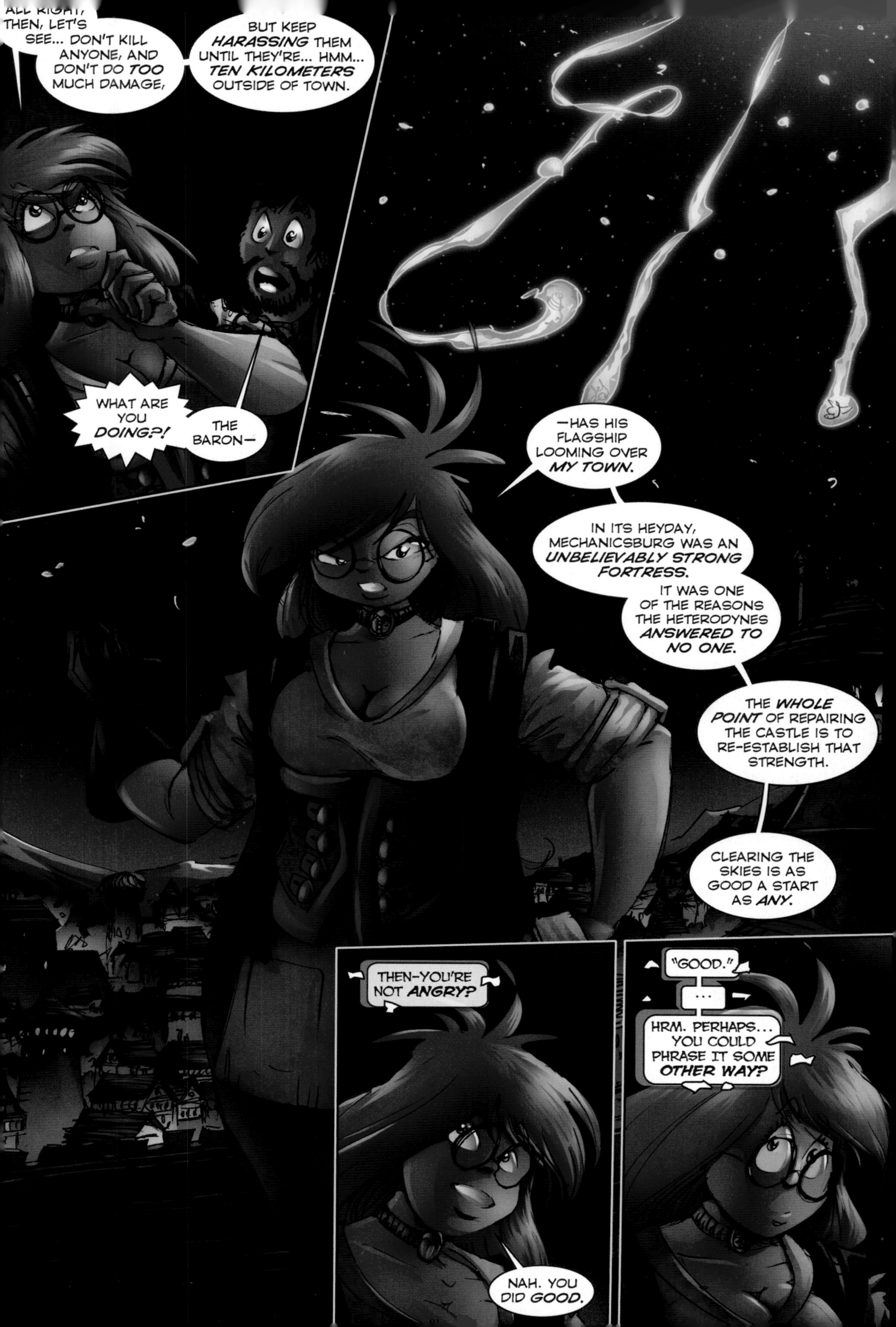

ALL RIGHT, THEN, LET'S SEE... DON'T KILL ANYONE, AND DON'T DO *TOO* MUCH DAMAGE,
BUT KEEP *HARASSING* THEM UNTIL THEY'RE... HMM... *TEN KILOMETERS* OUTSIDE OF TOWN.
WHAT ARE YOU *DOING?!*
THE BARON—
—HAS HIS FLAGSHIP LOOMING OVER *MY TOWN.*
IN ITS HEYDAY, MECHANICSBURG WAS AN *UNBELIEVABLY STRONG FORTRESS.*
IT WAS ONE OF THE REASONS THE HETERODYNES *ANSWERED TO NO ONE.*
THE *WHOLE POINT* OF REPAIRING THE CASTLE IS TO RE-ESTABLISH THAT STRENGTH.
CLEARING THE SKIES IS AS GOOD A START AS *ANY.*
THEN—YOU'RE NOT *ANGRY?*
NAH. YOU DID *GOOD.*
"GOOD."
...
HRM. PERHAPS... YOU COULD PHRASE IT SOME *OTHER WAY?*

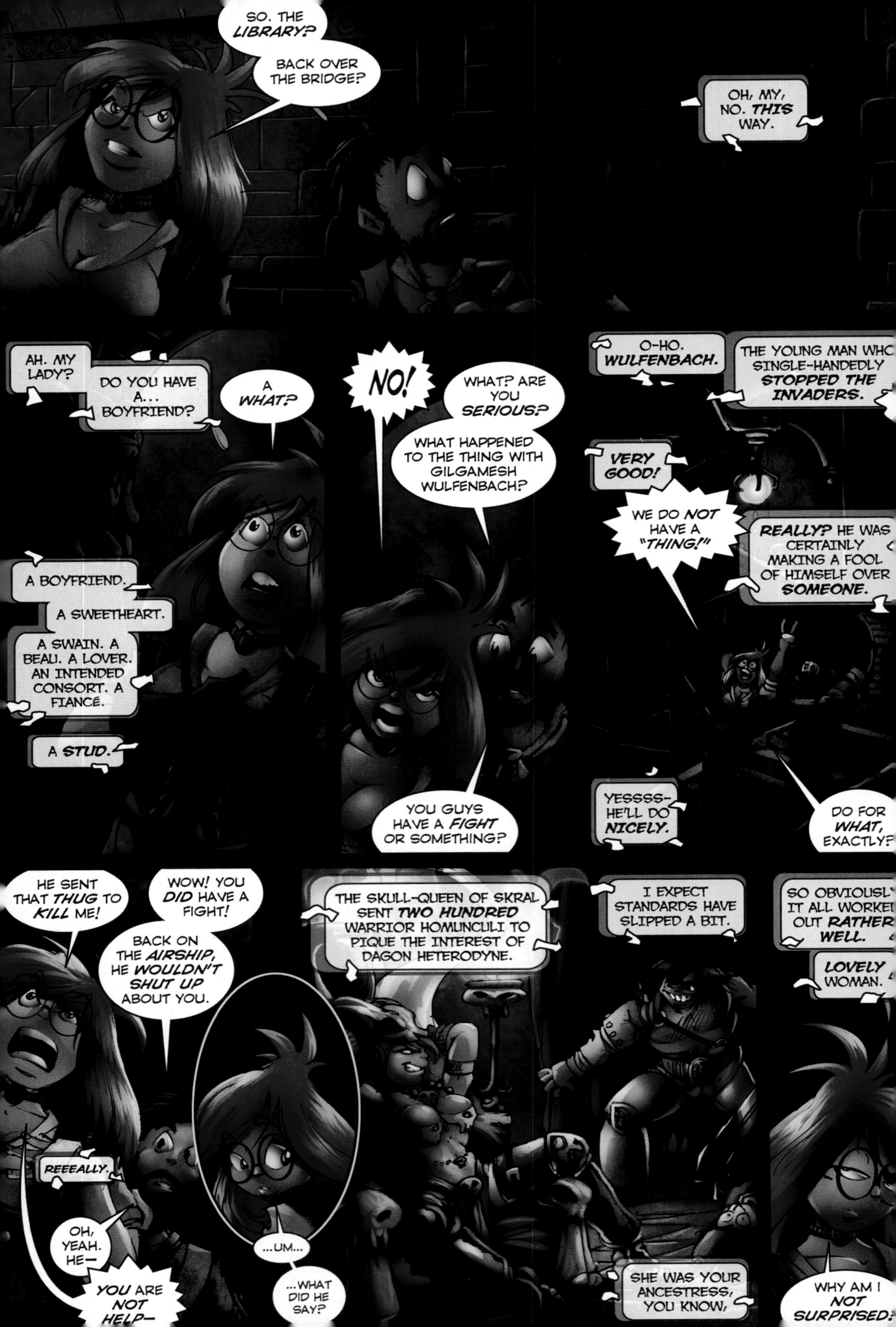

SO. THE LIBRARY?
BACK OVER THE BRIDGE?
OH, MY, NO. THIS WAY.
AH. MY LADY?
DO YOU HAVE A... BOYFRIEND?
A WHAT?
A BOYFRIEND.
A SWEETHEART.
A SWAIN. A BEAU. A LOVER. AN INTENDED CONSORT. A FIANCÉ.
A STUD.
NO!
WHAT? ARE YOU SERIOUS?
WHAT HAPPENED TO THE THING WITH GILGAMESH WULFENBACH?
YOU GUYS HAVE A FIGHT OR SOMETHING?
O-HO. WULFENBACH.
THE YOUNG MAN WHO SINGLE-HANDEDLY STOPPED THE INVADERS.
VERY GOOD!
WE DO NOT HAVE A "THING!"
REALLY? HE WAS CERTAINLY MAKING A FOOL OF HIMSELF OVER SOMEONE.
YESSSS- HE'LL DO NICELY.
DO FOR WHAT, EXACTLY?
HE SENT THAT THUG TO KILL ME!
WOW! YOU DID HAVE A FIGHT!
BACK ON THE AIRSHIP, HE WOULDN'T SHUT UP ABOUT YOU.
REEEALLY.
OH, YEAH. HE—
YOU ARE NOT HELP—
...UM...
...WHAT DID HE SAY?
THE SKULL-QUEEN OF SKRAL SENT TWO HUNDRED WARRIOR HOMUNCULI TO PIQUE THE INTEREST OF DAGON HETERODYNE.
I EXPECT STANDARDS HAVE SLIPPED A BIT.
SHE WAS YOUR ANCESTRESS, YOU KNOW,
SO OBVIOUSLY IT ALL WORKED OUT RATHER WELL.
LOVELY WOMAN.
WHY AM I NOT SURPRISED?

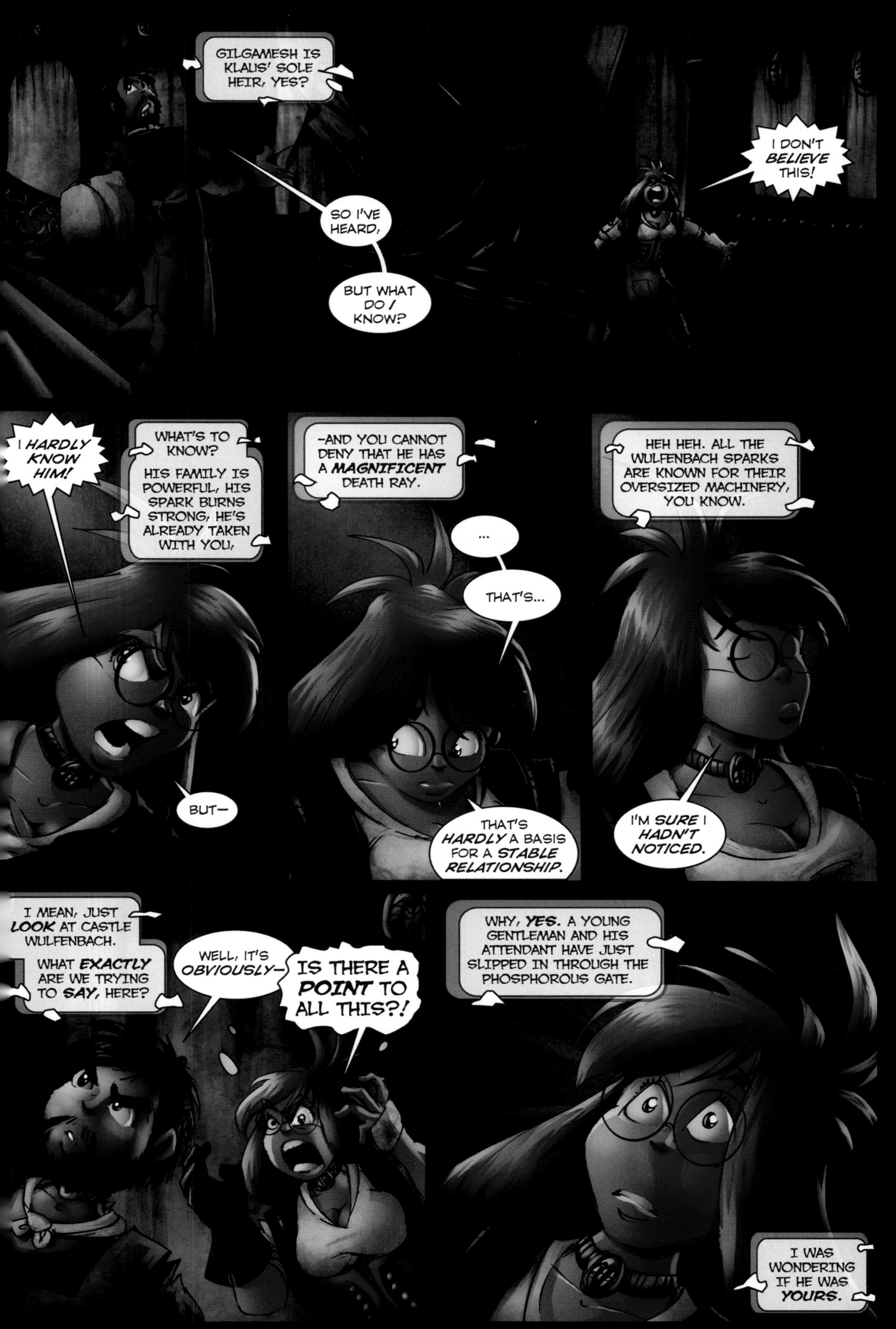
GILGAMESH IS KLAUS' SOLE HEIR, YES?
SO I'VE HEARD,
BUT WHAT DO I KNOW?
I DON'T BELIEVE THIS!
I HARDLY KNOW HIM!
WHAT'S TO KNOW?
HIS FAMILY IS POWERFUL, HIS SPARK BURNS STRONG, HE'S ALREADY TAKEN WITH YOU,
BUT—
-AND YOU CANNOT DENY THAT HE HAS A MAGNIFICENT DEATH RAY.
...
THAT'S...
THAT'S HARDLY A BASIS FOR A STABLE RELATIONSHIP.
HEH HEH. ALL THE WULFENBACH SPARKS ARE KNOWN FOR THEIR OVERSIZED MACHINERY, YOU KNOW.
I'M SURE I HADN'T NOTICED.
I MEAN, JUST LOOK AT CASTLE WULFENBACH.
WHAT EXACTLY ARE WE TRYING TO SAY, HERE?
WELL, IT'S OBVIOUSLY—
IS THERE A POINT TO ALL THIS?!
WHY, YES. A YOUNG GENTLEMAN AND HIS ATTENDANT HAVE JUST SLIPPED IN THROUGH THE PHOSPHOROUS GATE.
I WAS WONDERING IF HE WAS YOURS.

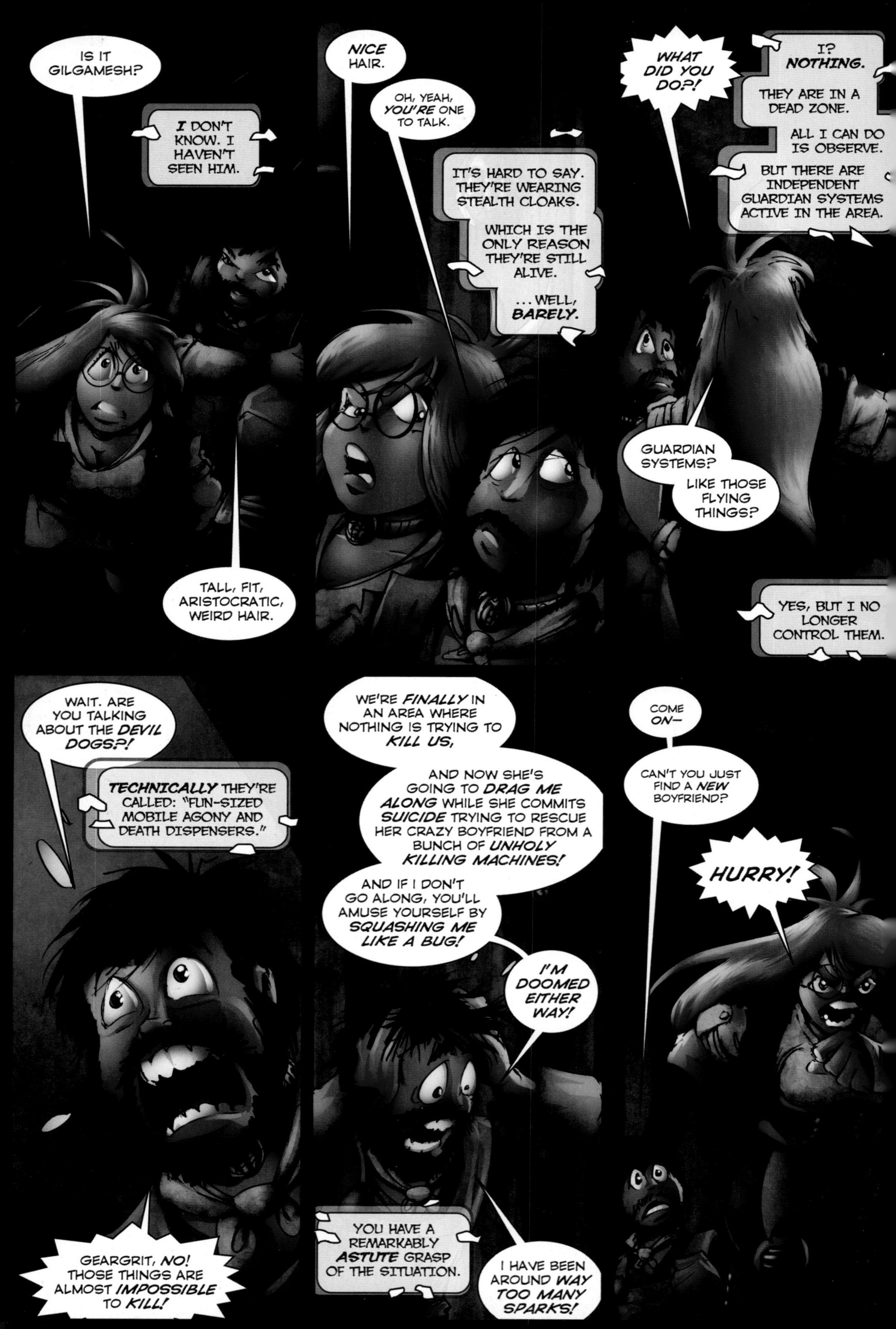

IS IT GILGAMESH?
I DON'T KNOW. I HAVEN'T SEEN HIM.
TALL, FIT, ARISTOCRATIC, WEIRD HAIR.
NICE HAIR.
OH, YEAH, YOU'RE ONE TO TALK.
IT'S HARD TO SAY. THEY'RE WEARING STEALTH CLOAKS.
WHICH IS THE ONLY REASON THEY'RE STILL ALIVE.
...WELL, BARELY.
WHAT DID YOU DO?!
I? NOTHING.
THEY ARE IN A DEAD ZONE.
ALL I CAN DO IS OBSERVE.
BUT THERE ARE INDEPENDENT GUARDIAN SYSTEMS ACTIVE IN THE AREA.
GUARDIAN SYSTEMS?
LIKE THOSE FLYING THINGS?
YES, BUT I NO LONGER CONTROL THEM.
WAIT. ARE YOU TALKING ABOUT THE DEVIL DOGS?!
TECHNICALLY THEY'RE CALLED: "FUN-SIZED MOBILE AGONY AND DEATH DISPENSERS."
GEARGRIT, NO! THOSE THINGS ARE ALMOST IMPOSSIBLE TO KILL!
WE'RE FINALLY IN AN AREA WHERE NOTHING IS TRYING TO KILL US,
AND NOW SHE'S GOING TO DRAG ME ALONG WHILE SHE COMMITS SUICIDE TRYING TO RESCUE HER CRAZY BOYFRIEND FROM A BUNCH OF UNHOLY KILLING MACHINES!
AND IF I DON'T GO ALONG, YOU'LL AMUSE YOURSELF BY SQUASHING ME LIKE A BUG!
I'M DOOMED EITHER WAY!
YOU HAVE A REMARKABLY ASTUTE GRASP OF THE SITUATION.
I HAVE BEEN AROUND WAY TOO MANY SPARKS!
COME ON—
CAN'T YOU JUST FIND A NEW BOYFRIEND?
HURRY!

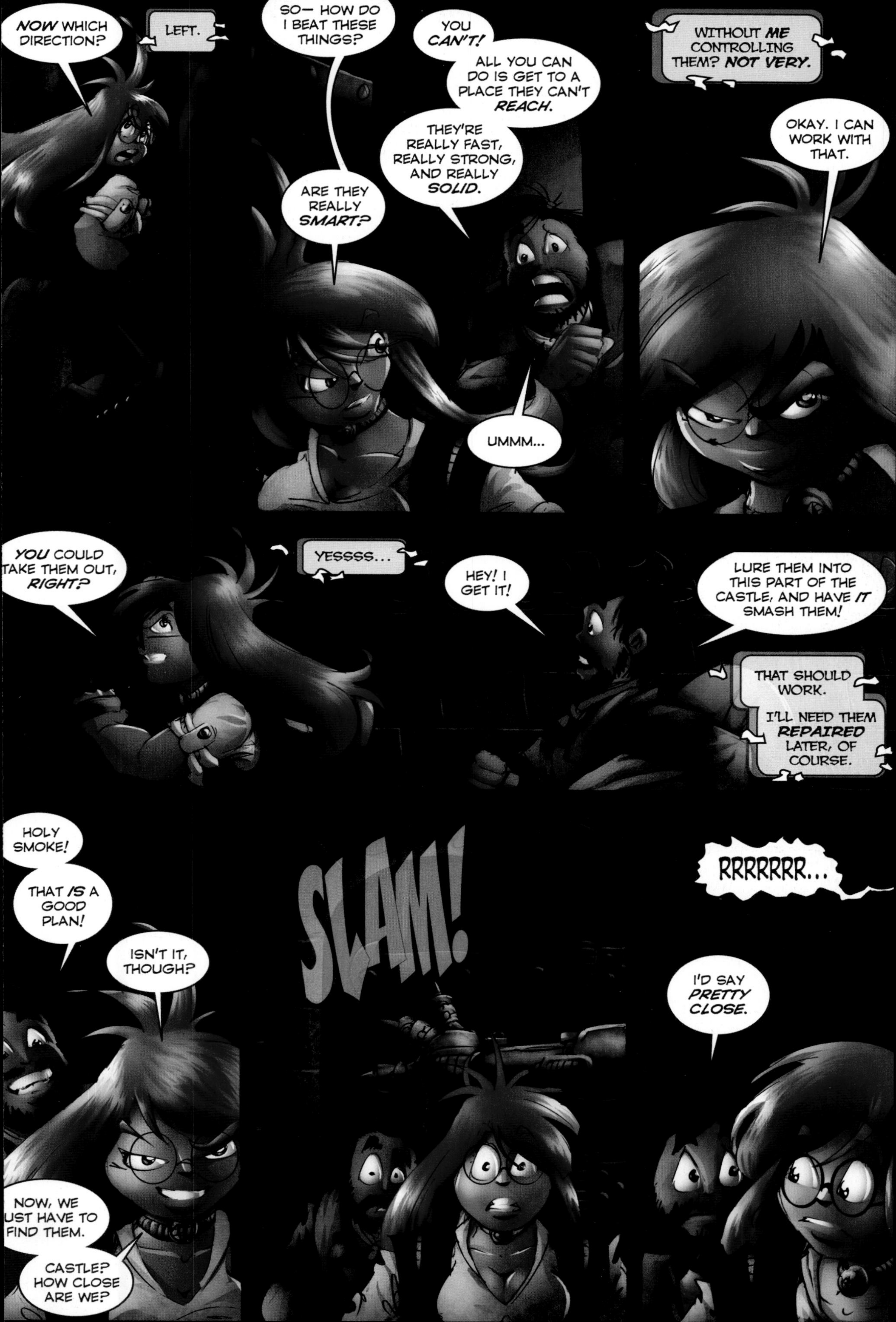
NOW WHICH DIRECTION?
LEFT.
SO— HOW DO I BEAT THESE THINGS?
ARE THEY REALLY SMART?
YOU CAN'T!
ALL YOU CAN DO IS GET TO A PLACE THEY CAN'T REACH.
THEY'RE REALLY FAST, REALLY STRONG, AND REALLY SOLID.
UMMM...
WITHOUT ME CONTROLLING THEM? NOT VERY.
OKAY. I CAN WORK WITH THAT.
YOU COULD TAKE THEM OUT, RIGHT?
YESSSS...
HEY! I GET IT!
LURE THEM INTO THIS PART OF THE CASTLE, AND HAVE IT SMASH THEM!
THAT SHOULD WORK.
I'LL NEED THEM REPAIRED LATER, OF COURSE.
HOLY SMOKE!
THAT IS A GOOD PLAN!
ISN'T IT, THOUGH?
NOW, WE UST HAVE TO FIND THEM.
CASTLE? HOW CLOSE ARE WE?
SLAM!
RRRRRRR...
I'D SAY PRETTY CLOSE.

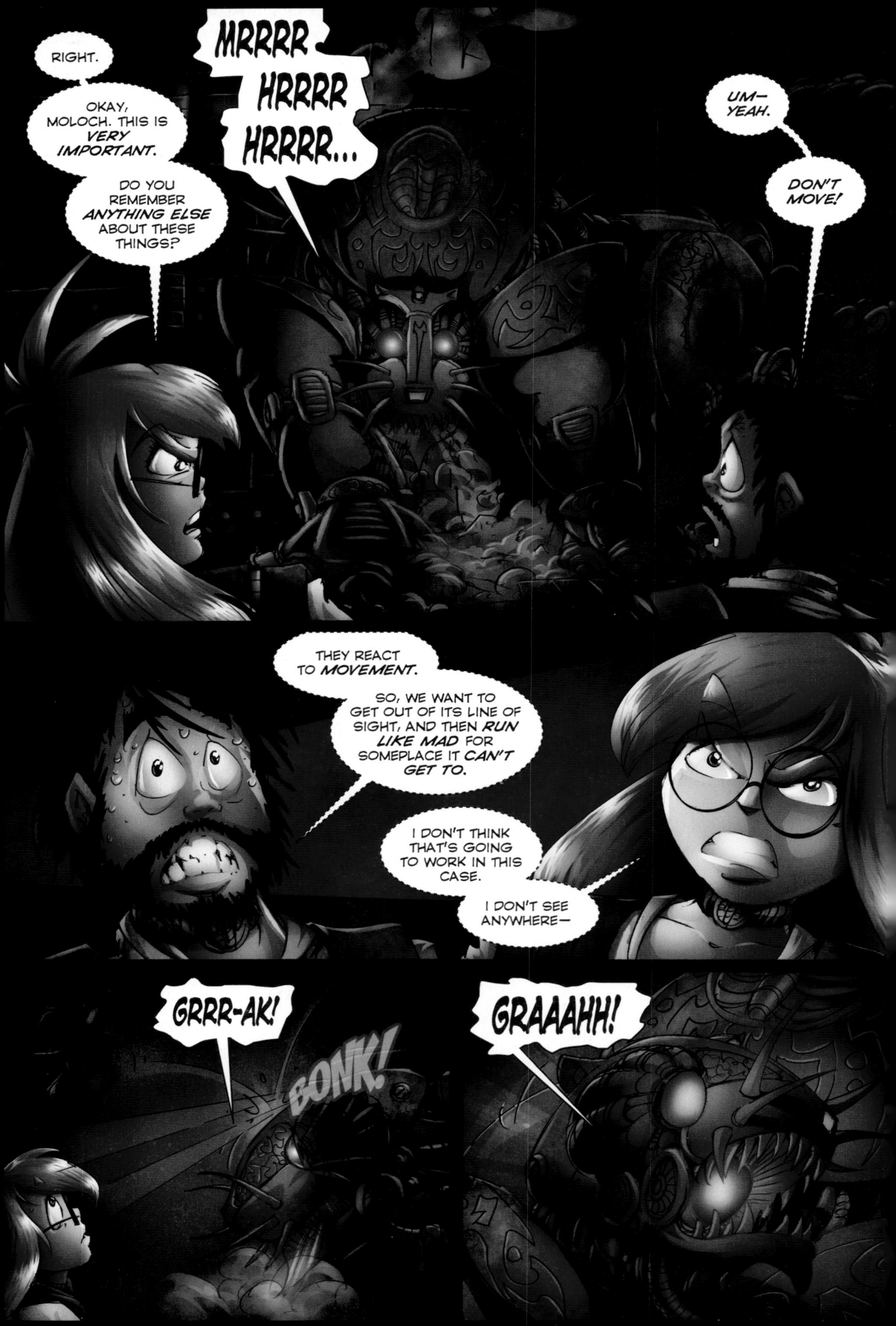
RIGHT.
OKAY, MOLOCH. THIS IS VERY IMPORTANT.
DO YOU REMEMBER ANYTHING ELSE ABOUT THESE THINGS?
MRRRR HRRRR HRRRR...
UM— YEAH.
DON'T MOVE!
THEY REACT TO MOVEMENT.
SO, WE WANT TO GET OUT OF ITS LINE OF SIGHT, AND THEN RUN LIKE MAD FOR SOMEPLACE IT CAN'T GET TO.
I DON'T THINK THAT'S GOING TO WORK IN THIS CASE.
I DON'T SEE ANYWHERE—
GRRR-AK!
BONK!
GRAAAHH!

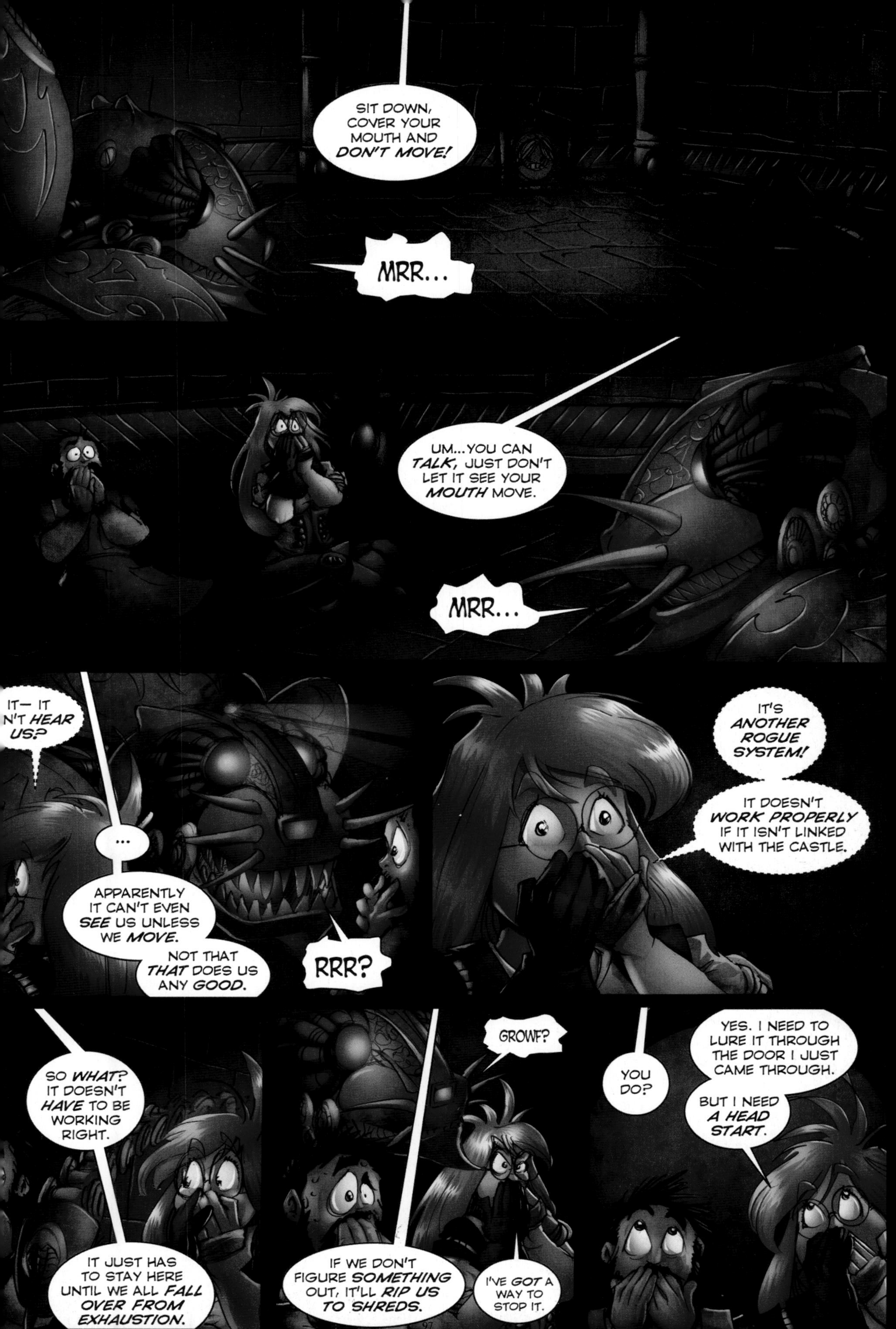
SIT DOWN, COVER YOUR MOUTH AND DON'T MOVE!
MRR...
UM...YOU CAN TALK, JUST DON'T LET IT SEE YOUR MOUTH MOVE.
MRR...
IT— IT N'T HEAR US?
...
APPARENTLY IT CAN'T EVEN SEE US UNLESS WE MOVE.
NOT THAT THAT DOES US ANY GOOD.
RRR?
IT'S ANOTHER ROGUE SYSTEM!
IT DOESN'T WORK PROPERLY IF IT ISN'T LINKED WITH THE CASTLE.
SO WHAT? IT DOESN'T HAVE TO BE WORKING RIGHT.
IT JUST HAS TO STAY HERE UNTIL WE ALL FALL OVER FROM EXHAUSTION.
GROWF?
IF WE DON'T FIGURE SOMETHING OUT, IT'LL RIP US TO SHREDS.
I'VE GOT A WAY TO STOP IT.
YOU DO?
YES. I NEED TO LURE IT THROUGH THE DOOR I JUST CAME THROUGH.
BUT I NEED A HEAD START.

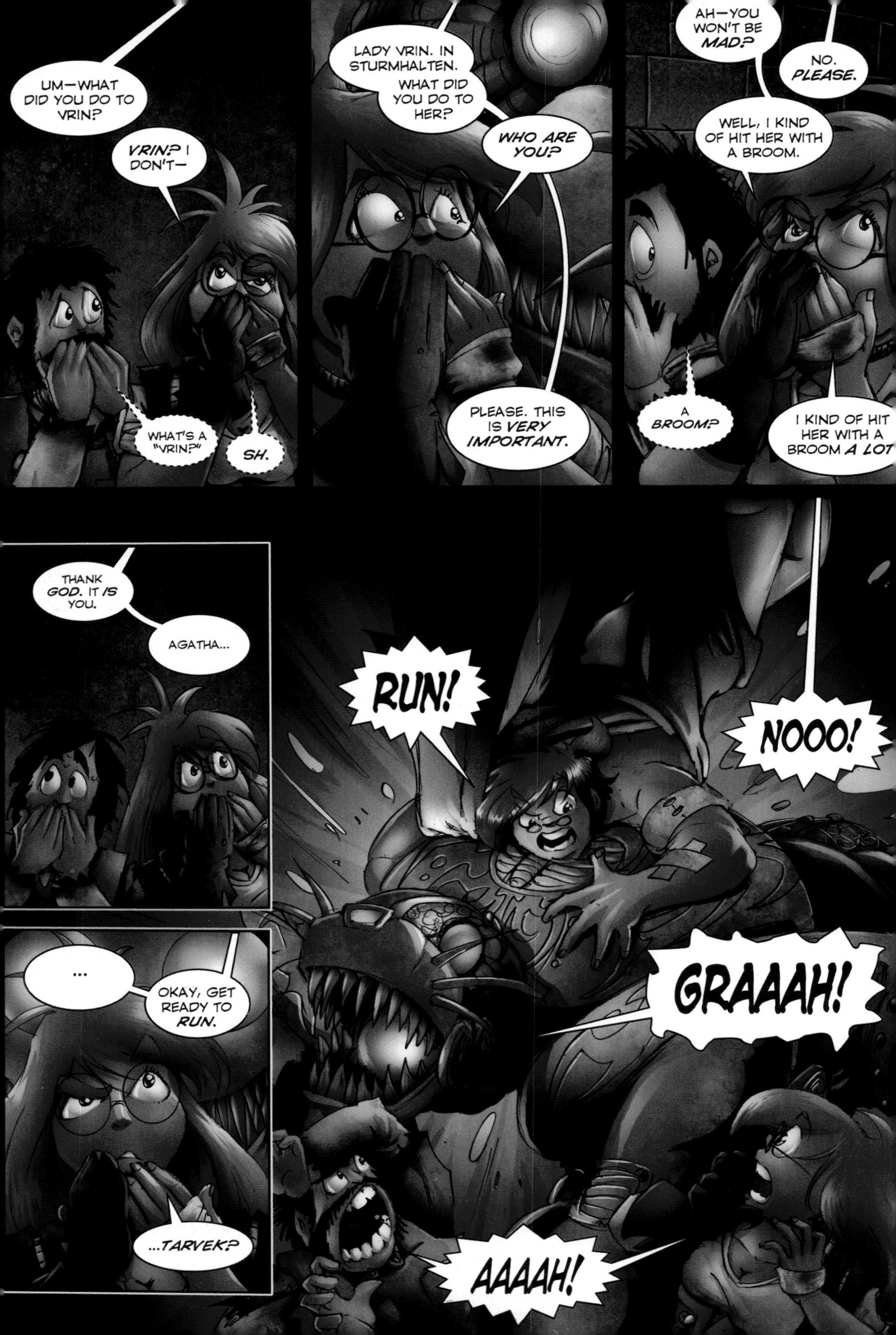
UM—WHAT DID YOU DO TO VRIN?
VRIN? I DON'T—
WHAT'S A "VRIN?"
SH.
LADY VRIN. IN STURMHALTEN.
WHAT DID YOU DO TO HER?
WHO ARE YOU?
PLEASE. THIS IS VERY IMPORTANT.
AH—YOU WON'T BE MAD?
NO. PLEASE.
WELL, I KIND OF HIT HER WITH A BROOM.
A BROOM?
I KIND OF HIT HER WITH A BROOM A LOT
THANK GOD. IT IS YOU.
AGATHA...
...
OKAY, GET READY TO RUN.
...TARVEK?
RUN!
NOOO!
GRAAAH!
AAAAH!

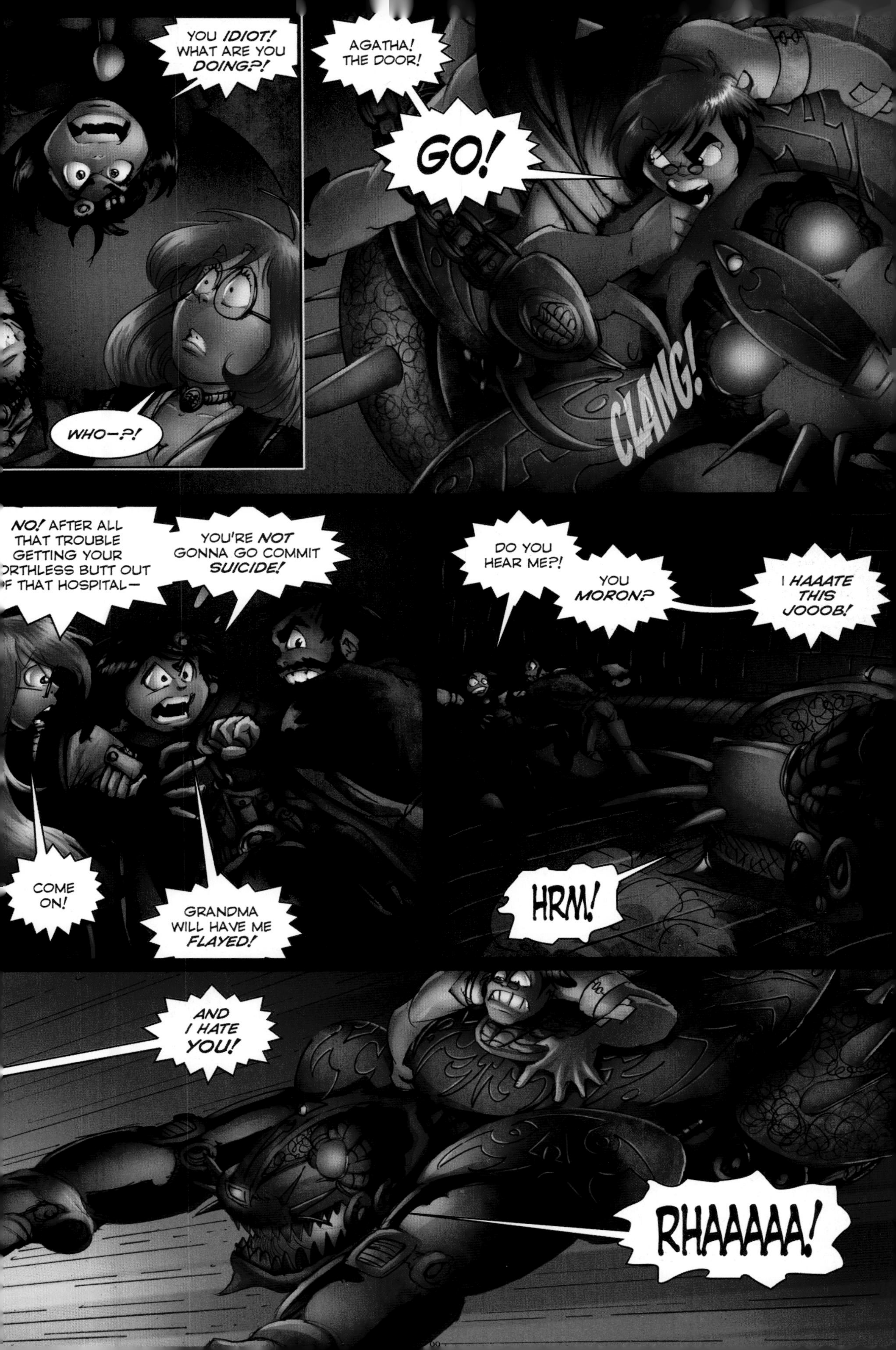
YOU IDIOT! WHAT ARE YOU DOING?!
WHO-?!
AGATHA! THE DOOR!
GO!
CLANG!
NO! AFTER ALL THAT TROUBLE GETTING YOUR ORTHLESS BUTT OUT OF THAT HOSPITAL—
YOU'RE NOT GONNA GO COMMIT SUICIDE!
COME ON!
GRANDMA WILL HAVE ME FLAYED!
DO YOU HEAR ME?!
YOU MORON?
I HAAATE THIS JOOOB!
HRM!
AND I HATE YOU!
RHAAAAA!

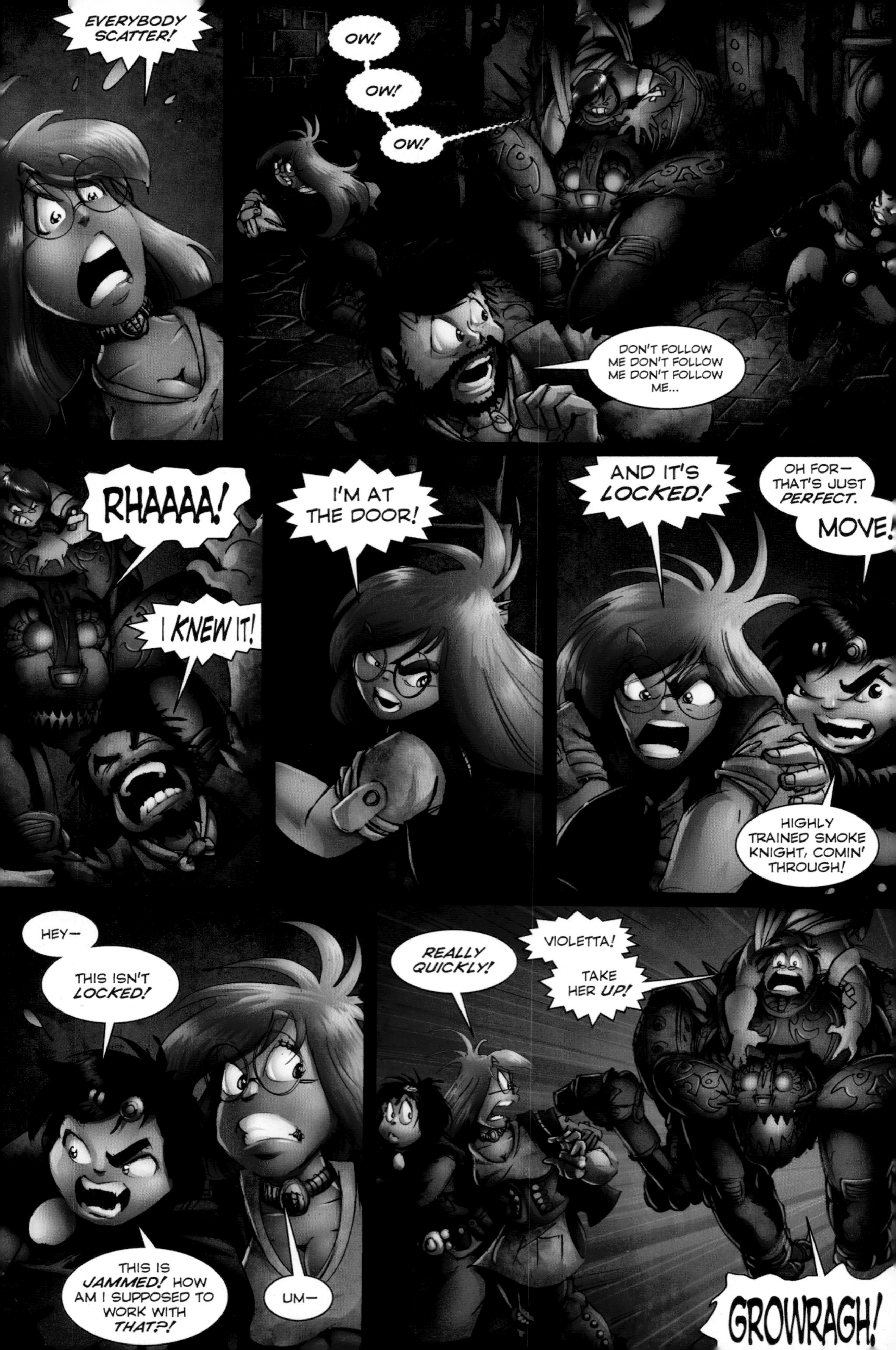
EVERYBODY SCATTER!
OW!
OW!
OW!
DON'T FOLLOW ME DON'T FOLLOW ME DON'T FOLLOW ME...
RHAAAA!
I KNEW IT!
I'M AT THE DOOR!
AND IT'S LOCKED!
OH FOR— THAT'S JUST PERFECT.
MOVE!
HIGHLY TRAINED SMOKE KNIGHT, COMIN' THROUGH!
HEY—
THIS ISN'T LOCKED!
THIS IS JAMMED! HOW AM I SUPPOSED TO WORK WITH THAT?!
UM—
REALLY QUICKLY!
VIOLETTA!
TAKE HER UP!
GROWRAGH!

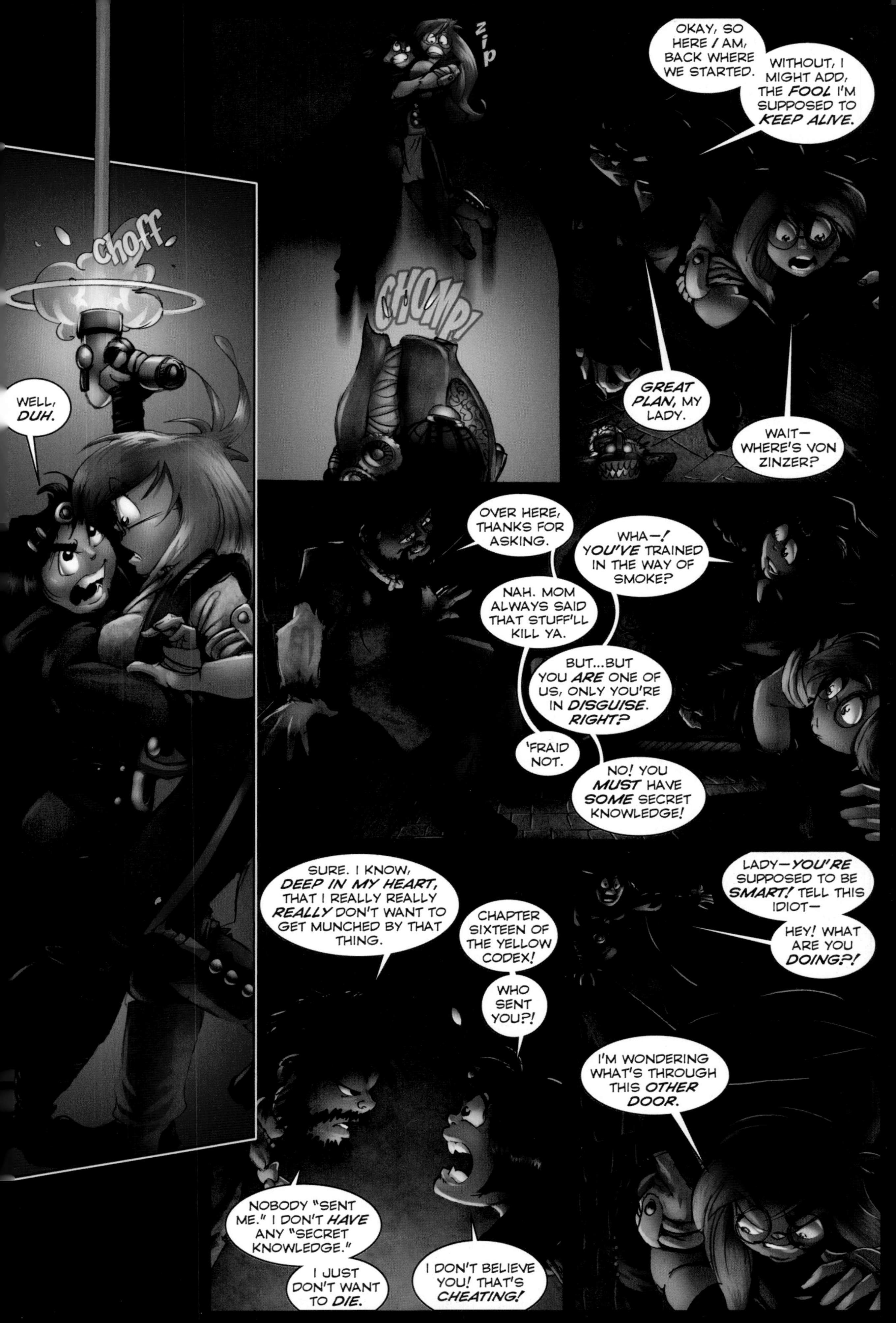
choff
WELL, DUH.
zip
CHOMP!
OKAY, SO HERE I AM, BACK WHERE WE STARTED.
WITHOUT, I MIGHT ADD, THE FOOL I'M SUPPOSED TO KEEP ALIVE.
GREAT PLAN, MY LADY.
WAIT— WHERE'S VON ZINZER?
OVER HERE, THANKS FOR ASKING.
WHA—! YOU'VE TRAINED IN THE WAY OF SMOKE?
NAH. MOM ALWAYS SAID THAT STUFF'LL KILL YA.
BUT...BUT YOU ARE ONE OF US, ONLY YOU'RE IN DISGUISE. RIGHT?
'FRAID NOT.
NO! YOU MUST HAVE SOME SECRET KNOWLEDGE!
SURE. I KNOW, DEEP IN MY HEART, THAT I REALLY REALLY REALLY DON'T WANT TO GET MUNCHED BY THAT THING.
CHAPTER SIXTEEN OF THE YELLOW CODEX!
WHO SENT YOU?!
NOBODY "SENT ME." I DON'T HAVE ANY "SECRET KNOWLEDGE."
I JUST DON'T WANT TO DIE.
I DON'T BELIEVE YOU! THAT'S CHEATING!
LADY—YOU'RE SUPPOSED TO BE SMART! TELL THIS IDIOT—
HEY! WHAT ARE YOU DOING?!
I'M WONDERING WHAT'S THROUGH THIS OTHER DOOR.

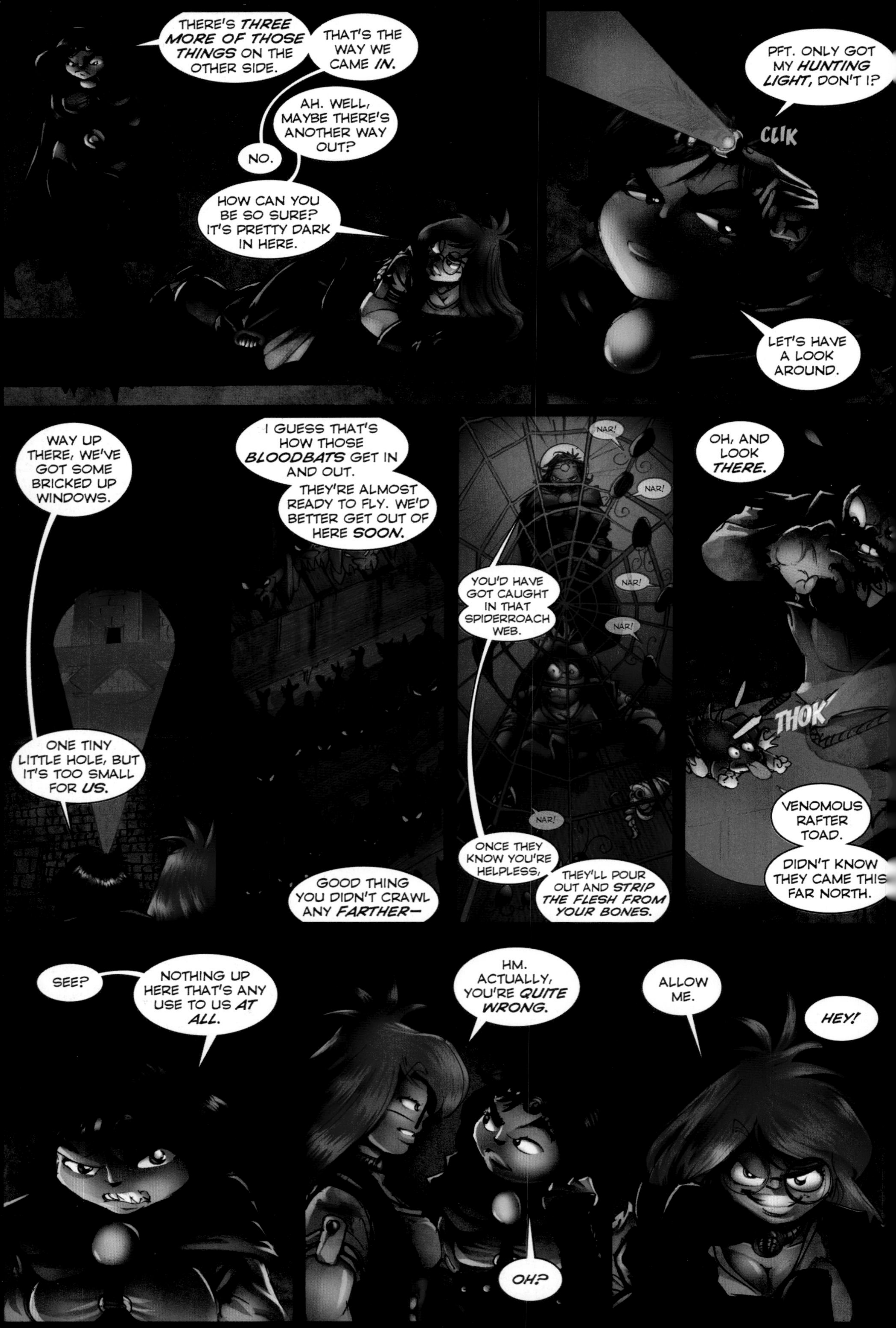
THERE'S THREE MORE OF THOSE THINGS ON THE OTHER SIDE.
THAT'S THE WAY WE CAME IN.
AH. WELL, MAYBE THERE'S ANOTHER WAY OUT?
NO.
HOW CAN YOU BE SO SURE? IT'S PRETTY DARK IN HERE.
PFT. ONLY GOT MY HUNTING LIGHT, DON'T I?
CLIK
LET'S HAVE A LOOK AROUND.
WAY UP THERE, WE'VE GOT SOME BRICKED UP WINDOWS.
ONE TINY LITTLE HOLE, BUT IT'S TOO SMALL FOR US.
I GUESS THAT'S HOW THOSE BLOODBATS GET IN AND OUT.
THEY'RE ALMOST READY TO FLY. WE'D BETTER GET OUT OF HERE SOON.
GOOD THING YOU DIDN'T CRAWL ANY FARTHER—
NAR!
NAR!
NAR!
NAR!
NAR!
YOU'D HAVE GOT CAUGHT IN THAT SPIDERROACH WEB.
ONCE THEY KNOW YOU'RE HELPLESS,
THEY'LL POUR OUT AND STRIP THE FLESH FROM YOUR BONES.
OH, AND LOOK THERE.
THOK
VENOMOUS RAFTER TOAD.
DIDN'T KNOW THEY CAME THIS FAR NORTH.
SEE?
NOTHING UP HERE THAT'S ANY USE TO US AT ALL.
HM. ACTUALLY, YOU'RE QUITE WRONG.
OH?
ALLOW ME.
HEY!

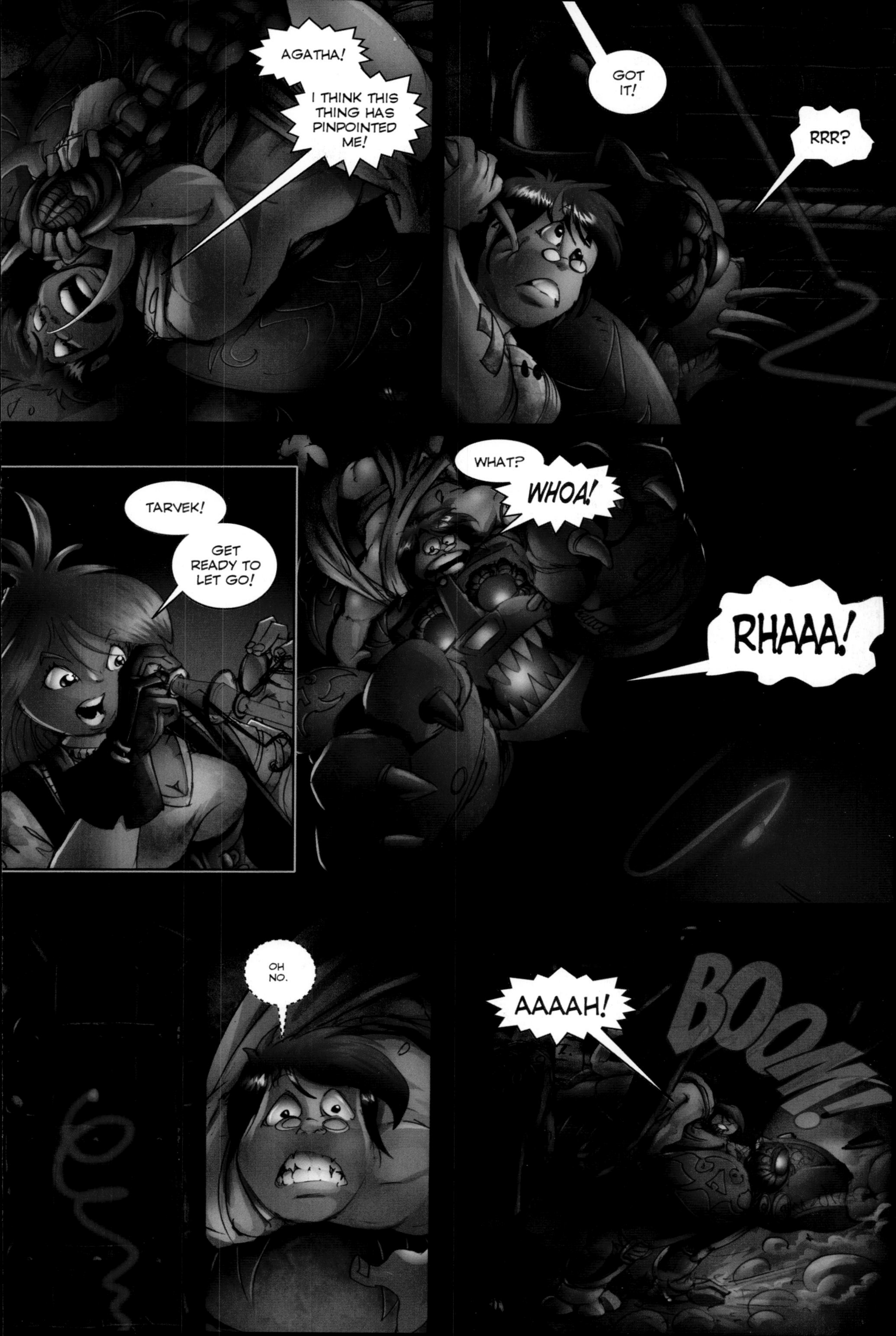
AGATHA!
I THINK THIS THING HAS PINPOINTED ME!
GOT IT!
RRR?
TARVEK!
GET READY TO LET GO!
WHAT?
WHOA!
RHAAA!
OH NO.
AAAAH!
BOOM!

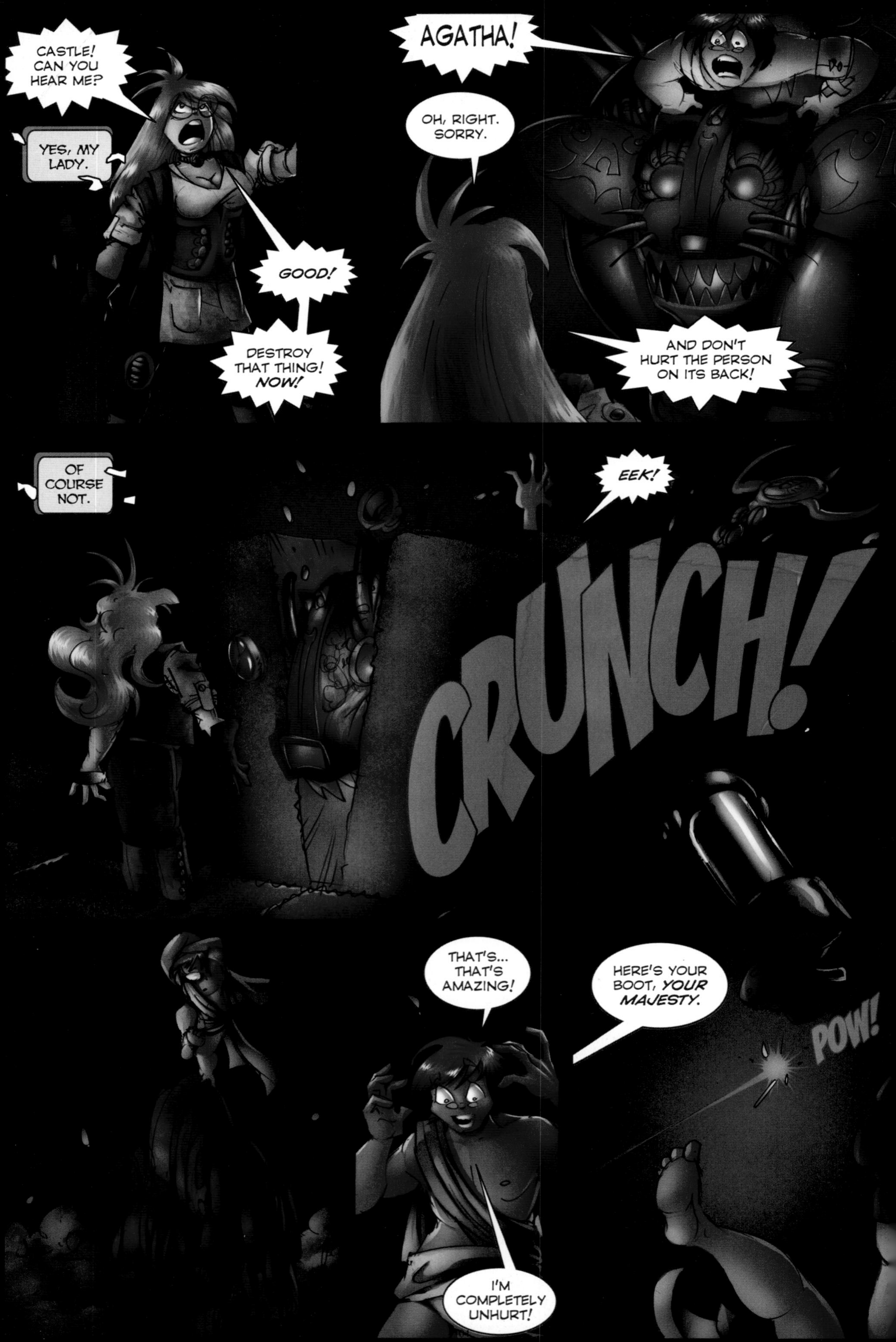
CASTLE! CAN YOU HEAR ME?
YES, MY LADY.
GOOD!
DESTROY THAT THING! NOW!
AGATHA!
OH, RIGHT. SORRY.
AND DON'T HURT THE PERSON ON ITS BACK!
OF COURSE NOT.
EEK!
CRUNCH!
THAT'S... THAT'S AMAZING!
I'M COMPLETELY UNHURT!
HERE'S YOUR BOOT, YOUR MAJESTY.
POW!

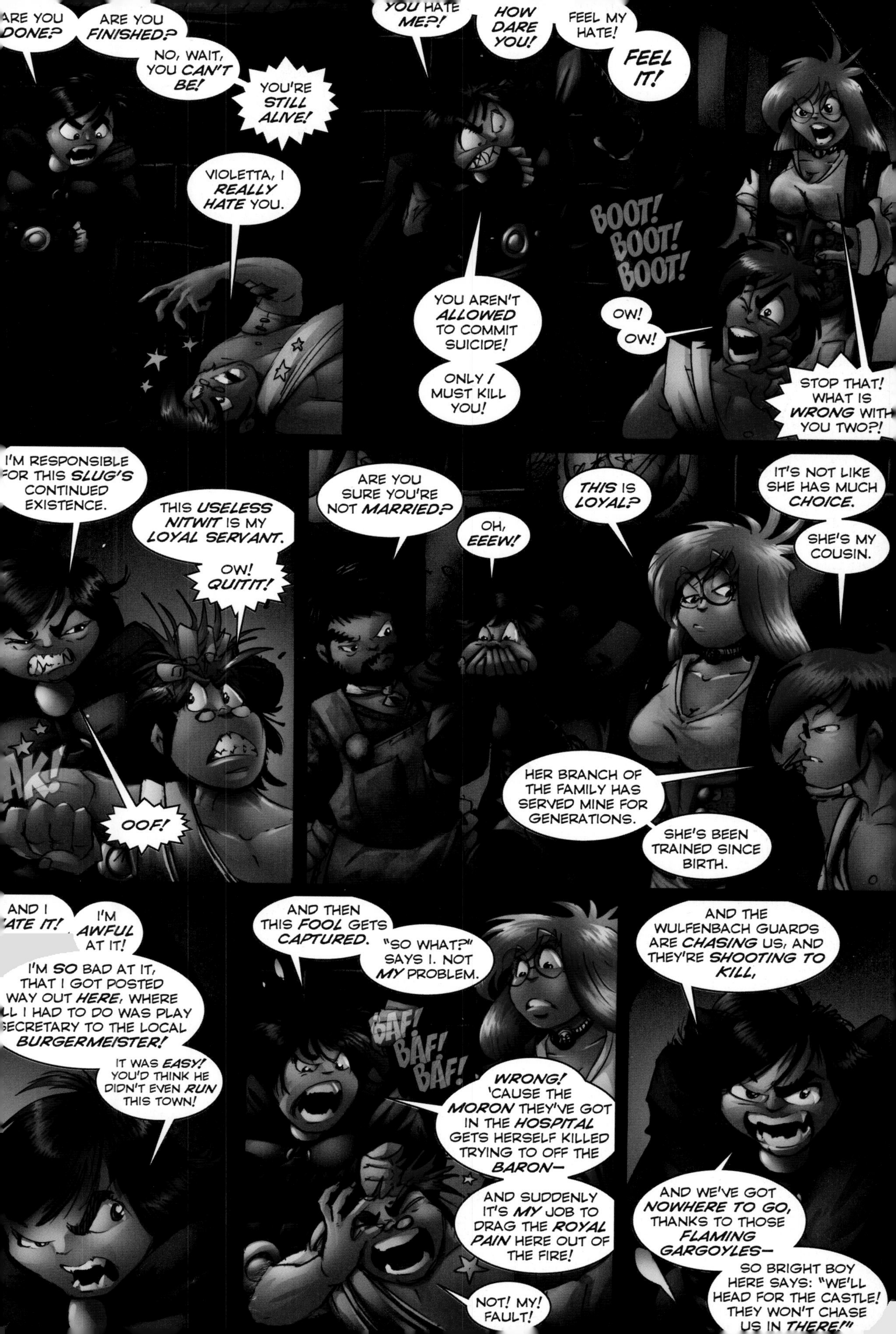
ARE YOU DONE?
ARE YOU FINISHED?
NO, WAIT, YOU CAN'T BE!
YOU'RE STILL ALIVE!
VIOLETTA, I REALLY HATE YOU.
YOU HATE ME?!
HOW DARE YOU!
FEEL MY HATE!
FEEL IT!
YOU AREN'T ALLOWED TO COMMIT SUICIDE!
ONLY I MUST KILL YOU!
BOOT! BOOT! BOOT!
OW!
OW!
STOP THAT! WHAT IS WRONG WITH YOU TWO?!
I'M RESPONSIBLE FOR THIS SLUG'S CONTINUED EXISTENCE.
THIS USELESS NITWIT IS MY LOYAL SERVANT.
OW! QUITIT!
OOF!
ARE YOU SURE YOU'RE NOT MARRIED?
OH, EEEW!
THIS IS LOYAL?
IT'S NOT LIKE SHE HAS MUCH CHOICE.
SHE'S MY COUSIN.
HER BRANCH OF THE FAMILY HAS SERVED MINE FOR GENERATIONS.
SHE'S BEEN TRAINED SINCE BIRTH.
AND I ATE IT!
I'M AWFUL AT IT!
I'M SO BAD AT IT, THAT I GOT POSTED WAY OUT HERE, WHERE LL I HAD TO DO WAS PLAY ECRETARY TO THE LOCAL BURGERMEISTER!
IT WAS EASY! YOU'D THINK HE DIDN'T EVEN RUN THIS TOWN!
AND THEN THIS FOOL GETS CAPTURED.
"SO WHAT?" SAYS I. NOT MY PROBLEM.
BAF! BAF! BAF!
WRONG! 'CAUSE THE MORON THEY'VE GOT IN THE HOSPITAL GETS HERSELF KILLED TRYING TO OFF THE BARON—
AND SUDDENLY IT'S MY JOB TO DRAG THE ROYAL PAIN HERE OUT OF THE FIRE!
NOT! MY! FAULT!
AND THE WULFENBACH GUARDS ARE CHASING US, AND THEY'RE SHOOTING TO KILL,
AND WE'VE GOT NOWHERE TO GO, THANKS TO THOSE FLAMING GARGOYLES—
SO BRIGHT BOY HERE SAYS: "WE'LL HEAD FOR THE CASTLE! THEY WON'T CHASE US IN THERE!"

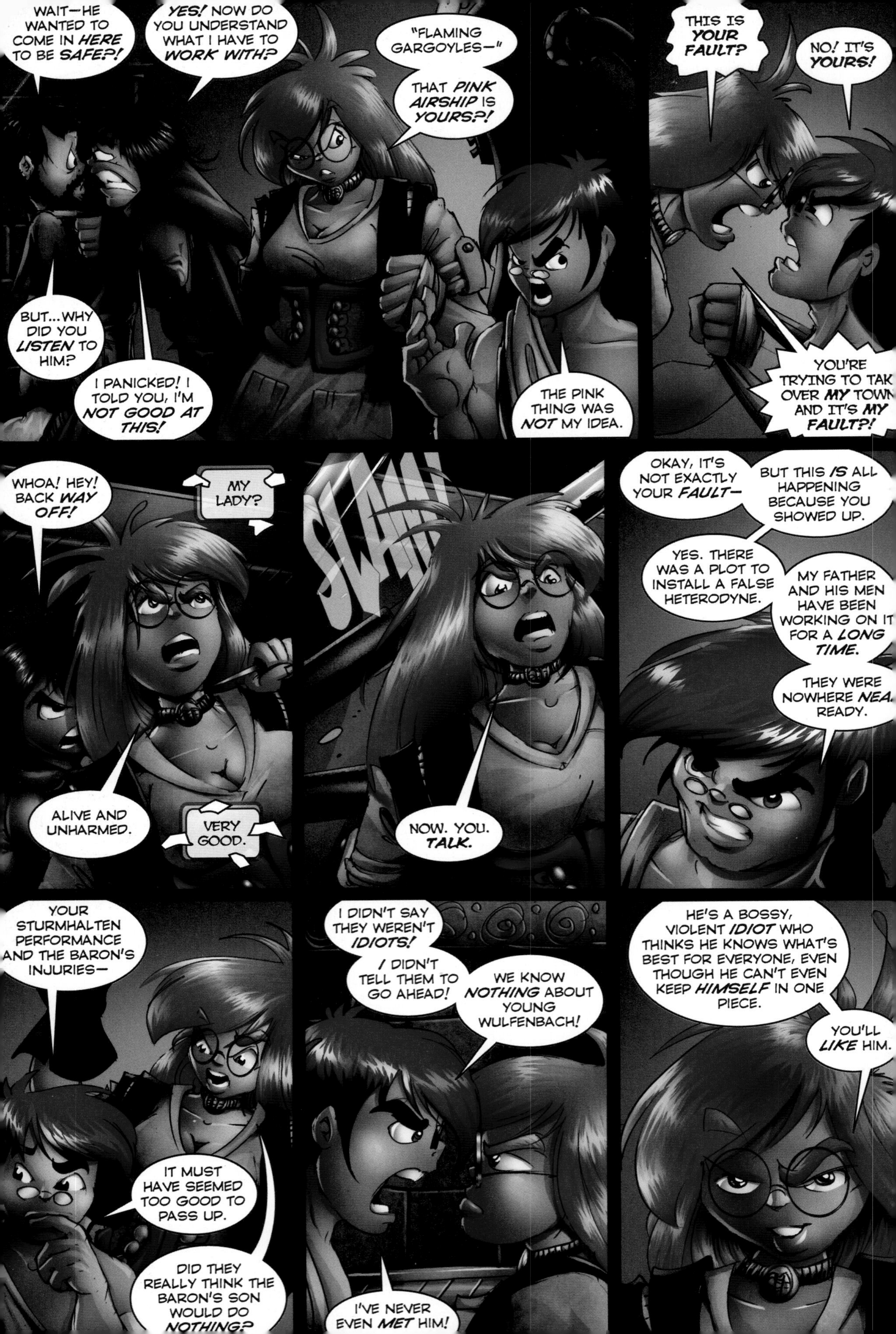
WAIT—HE WANTED TO COME IN *HERE* TO BE *SAFE?!*
YES! NOW DO YOU UNDERSTAND WHAT I HAVE TO *WORK WITH?*
BUT...WHY DID YOU *LISTEN* TO HIM?
I PANICKED! I TOLD YOU, I'M *NOT GOOD AT THIS!*
"FLAMING GARGOYLES—"
THAT *PINK AIRSHIP* IS *YOURS?!*
THE PINK THING WAS *NOT* MY IDEA.
THIS IS *YOUR FAULT?*
NO! IT'S *YOURS!*
YOU'RE TRYING TO TAK OVER *MY* TOWN AND IT'S *MY FAULT?!*
WHOA! HEY! BACK *WAY OFF!*
MY LADY?
ALIVE AND UNHARMED.
VERY GOOD.
SLAM
NOW. YOU. *TALK.*
OKAY, IT'S NOT EXACTLY YOUR *FAULT—*
BUT THIS *IS* ALL HAPPENING BECAUSE YOU SHOWED UP.
YES. THERE WAS A PLOT TO INSTALL A FALSE HETERODYNE.
MY FATHER AND HIS MEN HAVE BEEN WORKING ON IT FOR A *LONG TIME.*
THEY WERE NOWHERE *NEA* READY.
YOUR STURMHALTEN PERFORMANCE AND THE BARON'S INJURIES—
IT MUST HAVE SEEMED TOO GOOD TO PASS UP.
DID THEY REALLY THINK THE BARON'S SON WOULD DO *NOTHING?*
I DIDN'T SAY THEY WEREN'T *IDIOTS!*
I DIDN'T TELL THEM TO GO AHEAD!
WE KNOW *NOTHING* ABOUT YOUNG WULFENBACH!
I'VE NEVER EVEN *MET* HIM!
HE'S A BOSSY, VIOLENT *IDIOT* WHO THINKS HE KNOWS WHAT'S BEST FOR EVERYONE, EVEN THOUGH HE CAN'T EVEN KEEP *HIMSELF* IN ONE PIECE.
YOU'LL *LIKE* HIM.

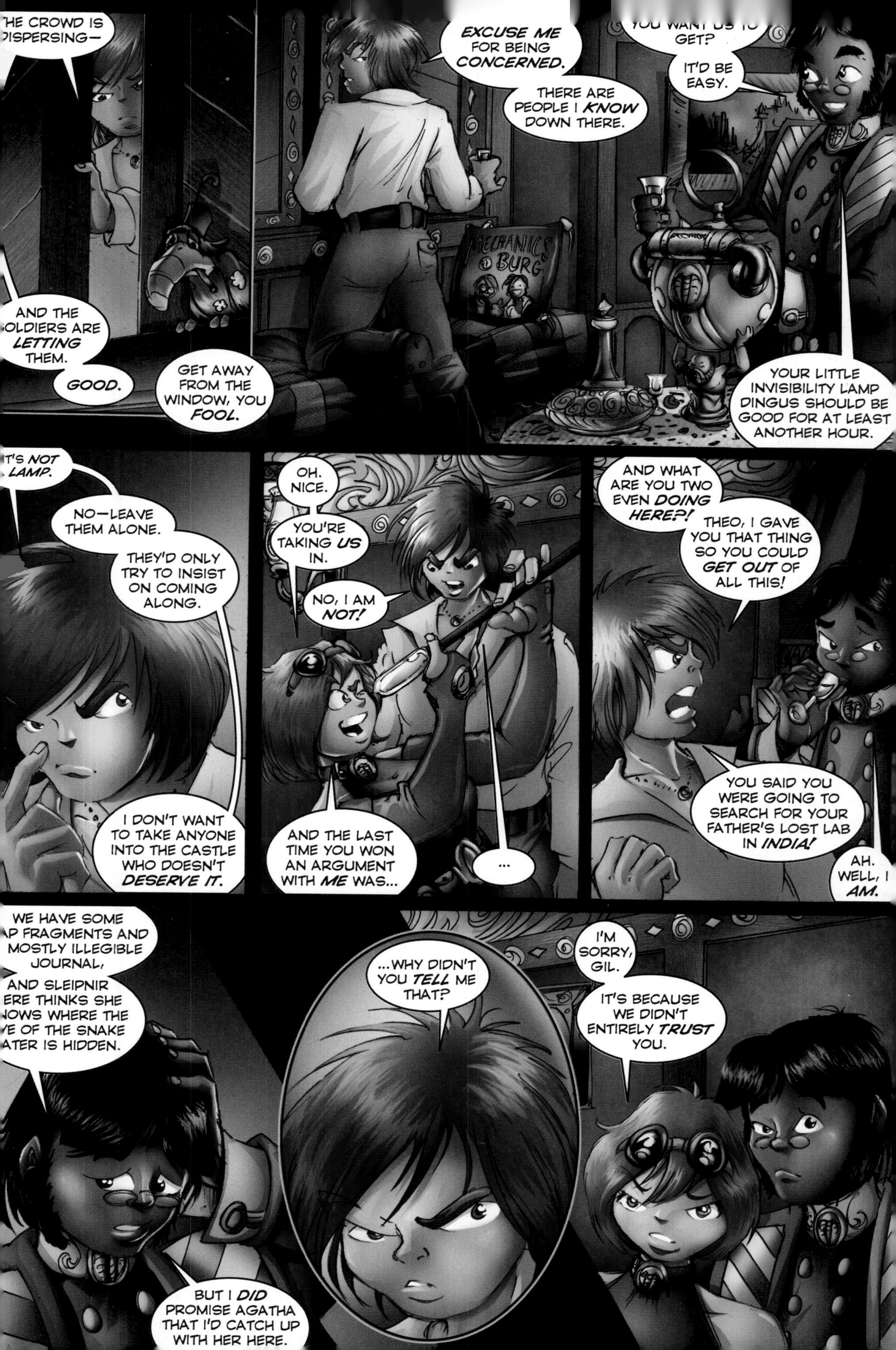
HE CROWD IS
DISPERSING—
EXCUSE ME FOR BEING CONCERNED.
THERE ARE PEOPLE I KNOW DOWN THERE.
YOU WANT US TO GET?
IT'D BE EASY.
MECHANICSBURG
AND THE OLDIERS ARE LETTING THEM.
GOOD.
GET AWAY FROM THE WINDOW, YOU FOOL.
YOUR LITTLE INVISIBILITY LAMP DINGUS SHOULD BE GOOD FOR AT LEAST ANOTHER HOUR.
IT'S NOT LAMP.
NO—LEAVE THEM ALONE.
THEY'D ONLY TRY TO INSIST ON COMING ALONG.
I DON'T WANT TO TAKE ANYONE INTO THE CASTLE WHO DOESN'T DESERVE IT.
OH. NICE.
YOU'RE TAKING US IN.
NO, I AM NOT!
AND THE LAST TIME YOU WON AN ARGUMENT WITH ME WAS...
...
AND WHAT ARE YOU TWO EVEN DOING HERE?!
THEO, I GAVE YOU THAT THING SO YOU COULD GET OUT OF ALL THIS!
YOU SAID YOU WERE GOING TO SEARCH FOR YOUR FATHER'S LOST LAB IN INDIA!
AH. WELL, I AM.
WE HAVE SOME AP FRAGMENTS AND MOSTLY ILLEGIBLE JOURNAL,
AND SLEIPNIR ERE THINKS SHE NOWS WHERE THE VE OF THE SNAKE ATER IS HIDDEN.
BUT I DID PROMISE AGATHA THAT I'D CATCH UP WITH HER HERE.
...WHY DIDN'T YOU TELL ME THAT?
I'M SORRY, GIL.
IT'S BECAUSE WE DIDN'T ENTIRELY TRUST YOU.

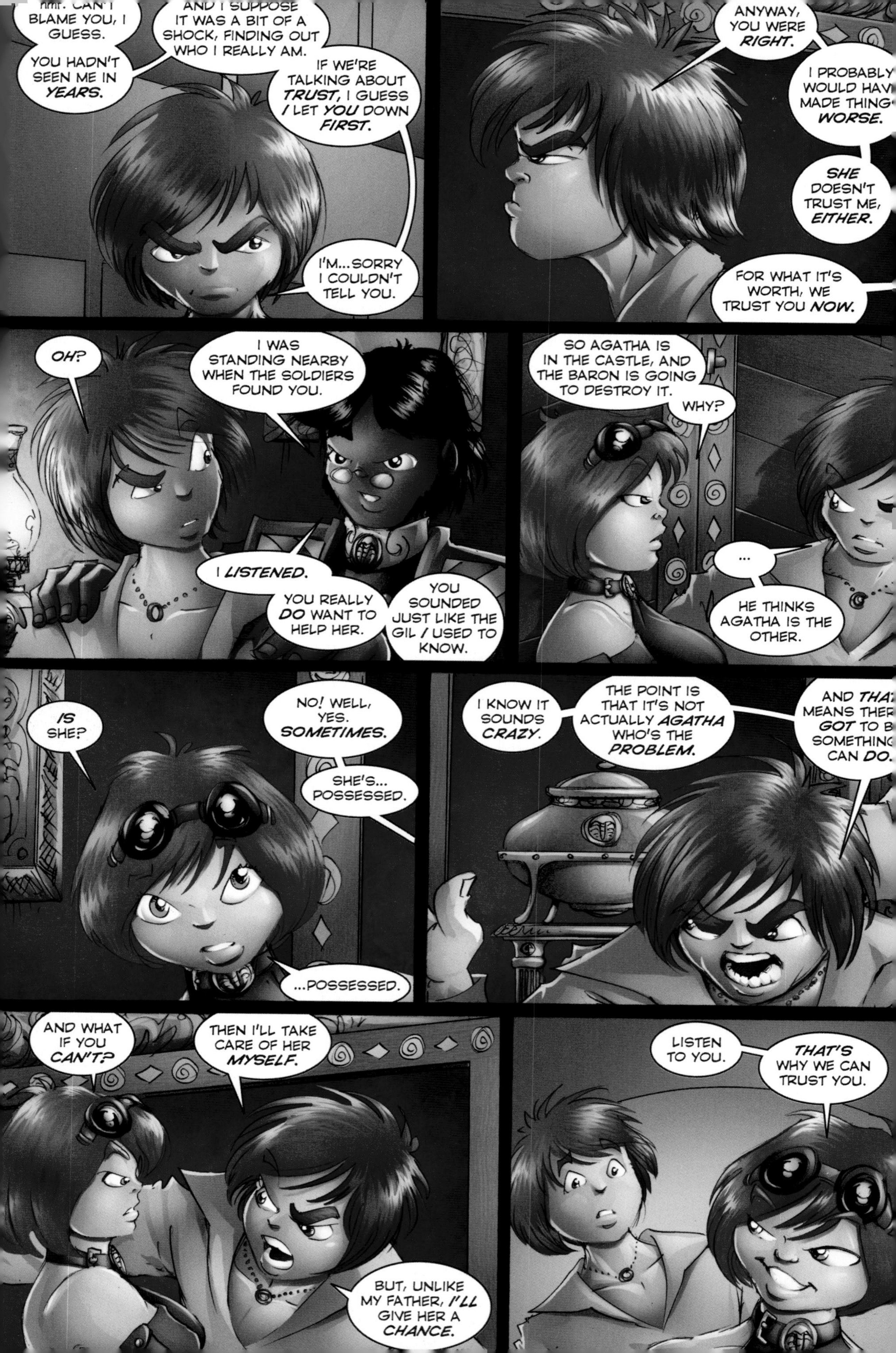
HMF. CAN'T BLAME YOU, I GUESS.
YOU HADN'T SEEN ME IN YEARS.
AND I SUPPOSE IT WAS A BIT OF A SHOCK, FINDING OUT WHO I REALLY AM.
IF WE'RE TALKING ABOUT TRUST, I GUESS I LET YOU DOWN FIRST.
I'M...SORRY I COULDN'T TELL YOU.
ANYWAY, YOU WERE RIGHT.
I PROBABLY WOULD HAV MADE THING WORSE.
SHE DOESN'T TRUST ME, EITHER.
FOR WHAT IT'S WORTH, WE TRUST YOU NOW.
OH?
I WAS STANDING NEARBY WHEN THE SOLDIERS FOUND YOU.
I LISTENED.
YOU REALLY DO WANT TO HELP HER.
YOU SOUNDED JUST LIKE THE GIL I USED TO KNOW.
SO AGATHA IS IN THE CASTLE, AND THE BARON IS GOING TO DESTROY IT.
WHY?
...
HE THINKS AGATHA IS THE OTHER.
IS SHE?
NO! WELL, YES. SOMETIMES.
SHE'S... POSSESSED.
...POSSESSED.
I KNOW IT SOUNDS CRAZY.
THE POINT IS THAT IT'S NOT ACTUALLY AGATHA WHO'S THE PROBLEM.
AND THA MEANS THER GOT TO B SOMETHING CAN DO.
AND WHAT IF YOU CAN'T?
THEN I'LL TAKE CARE OF HER MYSELF.
BUT, UNLIKE MY FATHER, I'LL GIVE HER A CHANCE.
LISTEN TO YOU.
THAT'S WHY WE CAN TRUST YOU.

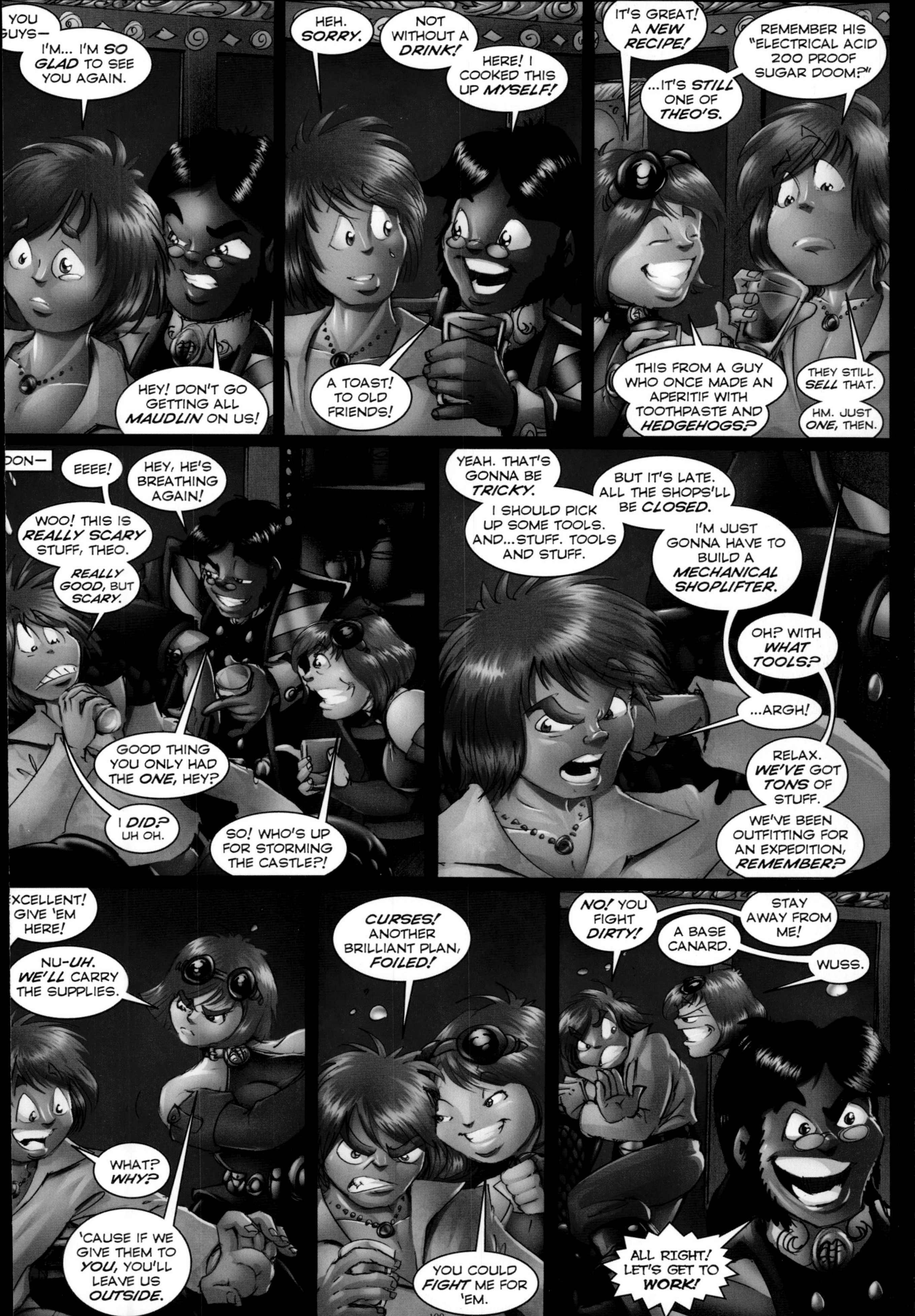
YOU GUYS—
I'M... I'M SO GLAD TO SEE YOU AGAIN.
HEY! DON'T GO GETTING ALL MAUDLIN ON US!
HEH. SORRY.
NOT WITHOUT A DRINK!
HERE! I COOKED THIS UP MYSELF!
A TOAST! TO OLD FRIENDS!
IT'S GREAT! A NEW RECIPE!
...IT'S STILL ONE OF THEO'S.
REMEMBER HIS "ELECTRICAL ACID 200 PROOF SUGAR DOOM?"
THIS FROM A GUY WHO ONCE MADE AN APERITIF WITH TOOTHPASTE AND HEDGEHOGS?
THEY STILL SELL THAT.
HM. JUST ONE, THEN.
DON—
EEEE!
HEY, HE'S BREATHING AGAIN!
WOO! THIS IS REALLY SCARY STUFF, THEO.
REALLY GOOD, BUT SCARY.
GOOD THING YOU ONLY HAD THE ONE, HEY?
I DID? UH OH.
SO! WHO'S UP FOR STORMING THE CASTLE?!
YEAH. THAT'S GONNA BE TRICKY.
I SHOULD PICK UP SOME TOOLS. AND...STUFF. TOOLS AND STUFF.
BUT IT'S LATE. ALL THE SHOPS'LL BE CLOSED.
I'M JUST GONNA HAVE TO BUILD A MECHANICAL SHOPLIFTER.
OH? WITH WHAT TOOLS?
...ARGH!
RELAX. WE'VE GOT TONS OF STUFF.
WE'VE BEEN OUTFITTING FOR AN EXPEDITION, REMEMBER?
XCELLENT! GIVE 'EM HERE!
NU-UH. WE'LL CARRY THE SUPPLIES.
WHAT? WHY?
'CAUSE IF WE GIVE THEM TO YOU, YOU'LL LEAVE US OUTSIDE.
CURSES! ANOTHER BRILLIANT PLAN, FOILED!
YOU COULD FIGHT ME FOR 'EM.
NO! YOU FIGHT DIRTY!
STAY AWAY FROM ME!
A BASE CANARD.
WUSS.
ALL RIGHT! LET'S GET TO WORK!

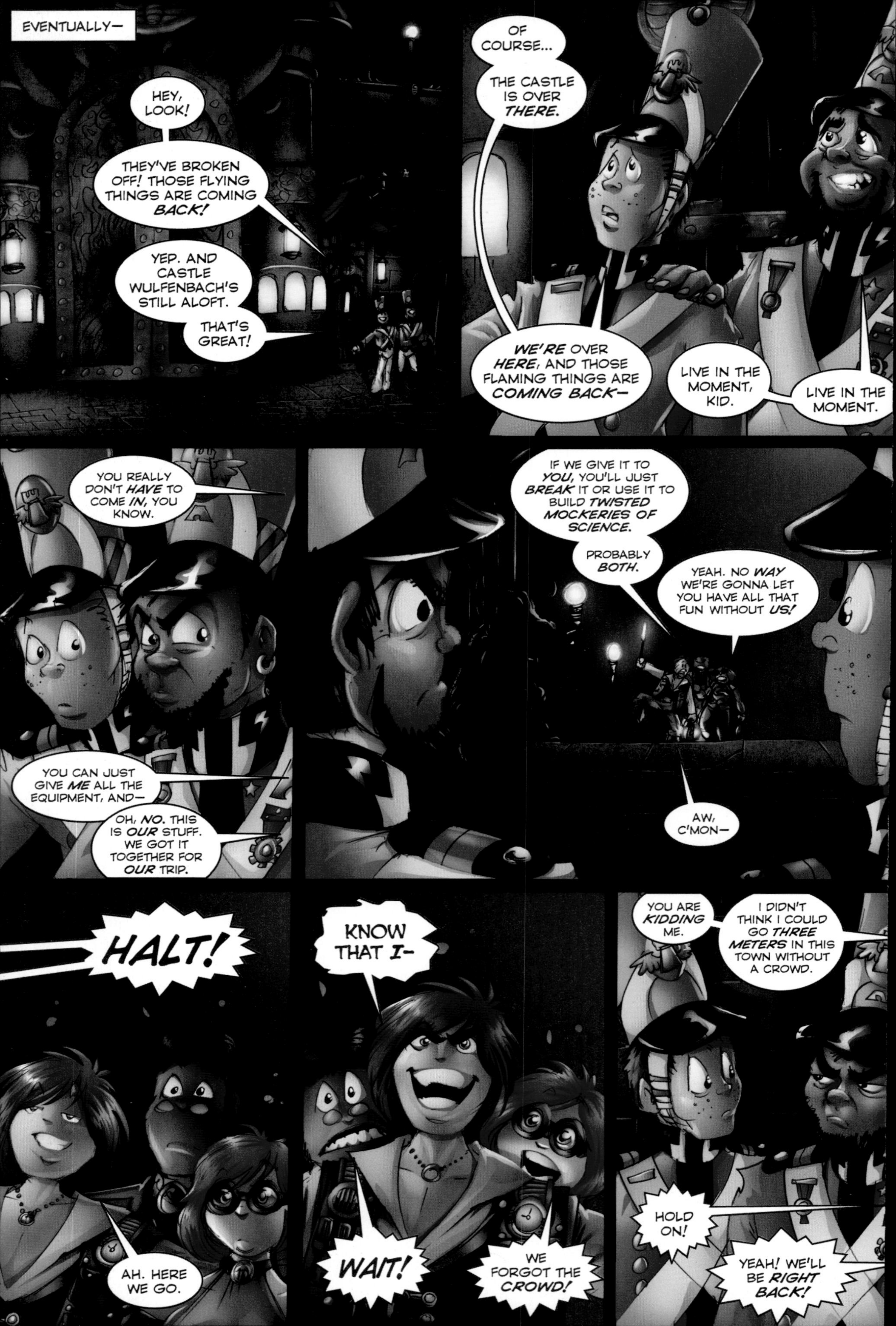
EVENTUALLY—
HEY, LOOK!
THEY'VE BROKEN OFF! THOSE FLYING THINGS ARE COMING BACK!
YEP. AND CASTLE WULFENBACH'S STILL ALOFT.
THAT'S GREAT!
OF COURSE...
THE CASTLE IS OVER THERE.
WE'RE OVER HERE; AND THOSE FLAMING THINGS ARE COMING BACK—
LIVE IN THE MOMENT, KID.
LIVE IN THE MOMENT.
YOU REALLY DON'T HAVE TO COME IN, YOU KNOW.
YOU CAN JUST GIVE ME ALL THE EQUIPMENT, AND—
OH, NO. THIS IS OUR STUFF. WE GOT IT TOGETHER FOR OUR TRIP.
IF WE GIVE IT TO YOU, YOU'LL JUST BREAK IT OR USE IT TO BUILD TWISTED MOCKERIES OF SCIENCE.
PROBABLY BOTH.
YEAH. NO WAY WE'RE GONNA LET YOU HAVE ALL THAT FUN WITHOUT US!
AW, C'MON—
HALT!
AH. HERE WE GO.
KNOW THAT I-
WAIT!
WE FORGOT THE CROWD!
YOU ARE KIDDING ME.
I DIDN'T THINK I COULD GO THREE METERS IN THIS TOWN WITHOUT A CROWD.
HOLD ON!
YEAH! WE'LL BE RIGHT BACK!

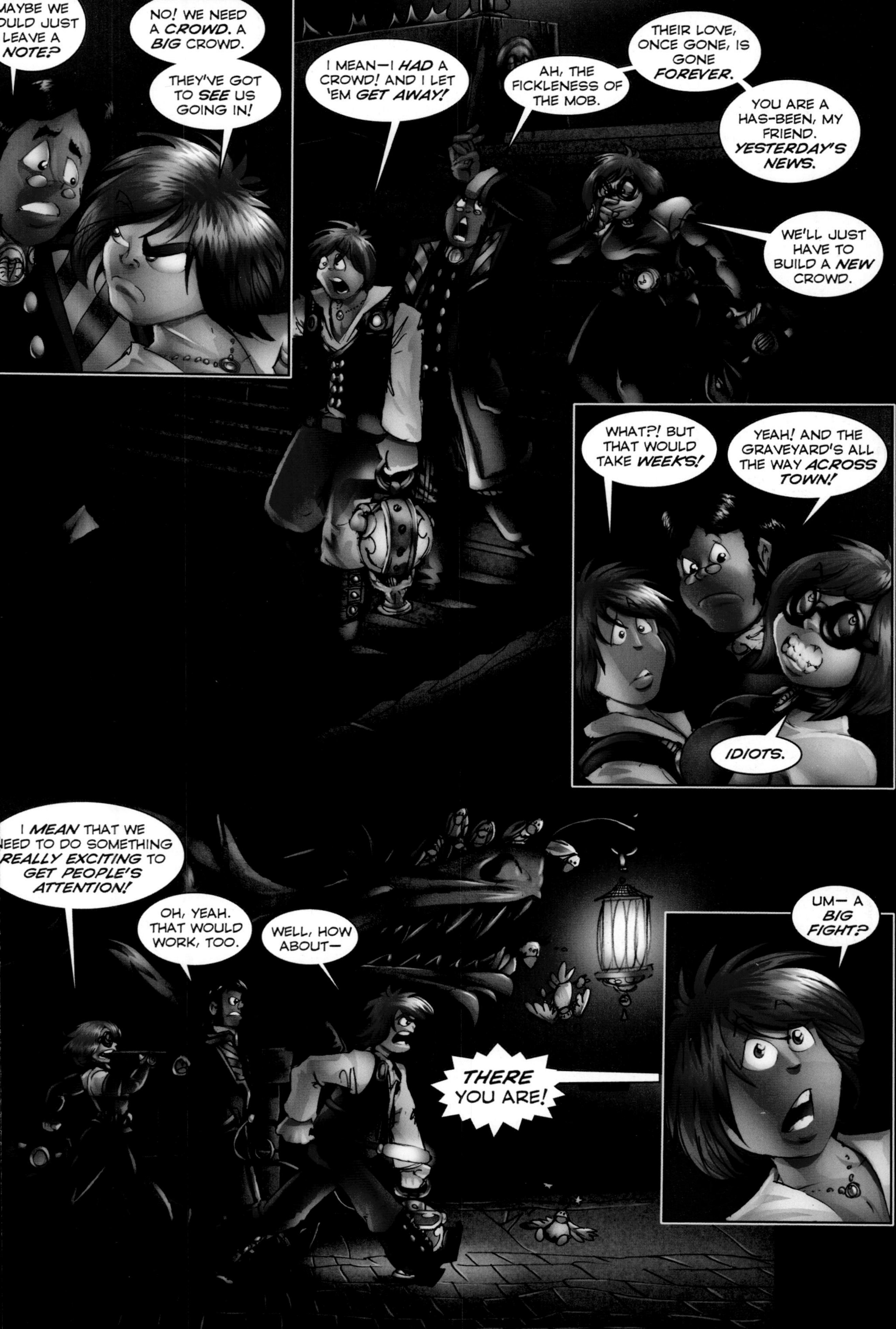
MAYBE WE OULD JUST LEAVE A NOTE?
NO! WE NEED A CROWD. A BIG CROWD.
THEY'VE GOT TO SEE US GOING IN!
I MEAN—I HAD A CROWD! AND I LET 'EM GET AWAY!
AH, THE FICKLENESS OF THE MOB.
THEIR LOVE, ONCE GONE, IS GONE FOREVER.
YOU ARE A HAS-BEEN, MY FRIEND. YESTERDAY'S NEWS.
WE'LL JUST HAVE TO BUILD A NEW CROWD.
WHAT?! BUT THAT WOULD TAKE WEEKS!
YEAH! AND THE GRAVEYARD'S ALL THE WAY ACROSS TOWN!
IDIOTS.
I MEAN THAT WE EED TO DO SOMETHING REALLY EXCITING TO GET PEOPLE'S ATTENTION!
OH, YEAH. THAT WOULD WORK, TOO.
WELL, HOW ABOUT—
UM— A BIG FIGHT?
THERE YOU ARE!

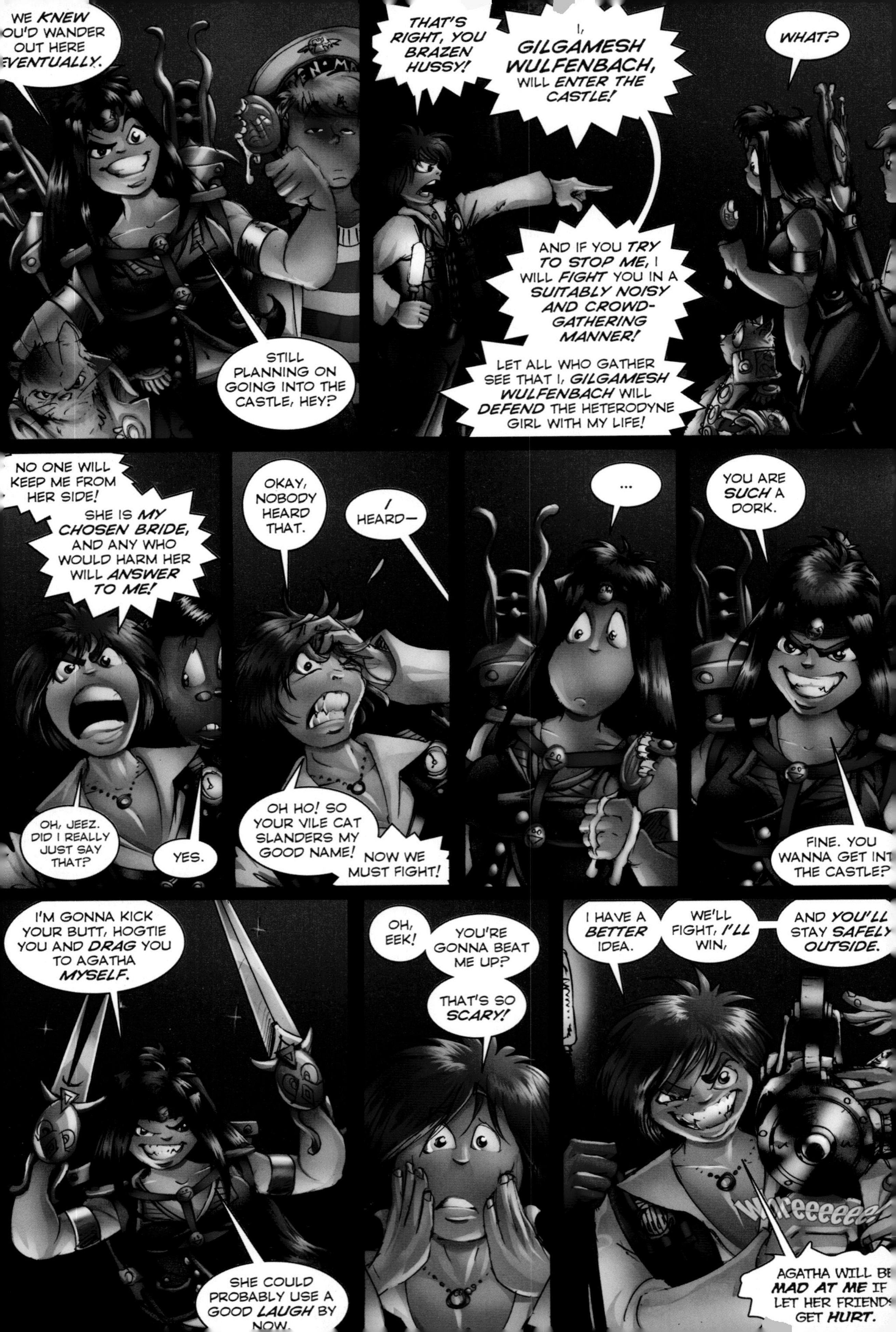
WE KNEW
OU'D WANDER OUT HERE
EVENTUALLY.
STILL PLANNING ON GOING INTO THE CASTLE, HEY?
THAT'S RIGHT, YOU BRAZEN HUSSY!
I, GILGAMESH WULFENBACH, WILL ENTER THE CASTLE!
AND IF YOU TRY TO STOP ME, I WILL FIGHT YOU IN A SUITABLY NOISY AND CROWD-GATHERING MANNER!
LET ALL WHO GATHER SEE THAT I, GILGAMESH WULFENBACH WILL DEFEND THE HETERODYNE GIRL WITH MY LIFE!
WHAT?
NO ONE WILL KEEP ME FROM HER SIDE!
SHE IS MY CHOSEN BRIDE, AND ANY WHO WOULD HARM HER WILL ANSWER TO ME!
OH, JEEZ. DID I REALLY JUST SAY THAT?
YES.
OKAY, NOBODY HEARD THAT.
I HEARD—
OH HO! SO YOUR VILE CAT SLANDERS MY GOOD NAME!
NOW WE MUST FIGHT!
...
YOU ARE SUCH A DORK.
FINE. YOU WANNA GET INT
THE CASTLE?
I'M GONNA KICK YOUR BUTT, HOGTIE YOU AND DRAG YOU TO AGATHA MYSELF.
SHE COULD PROBABLY USE A GOOD LAUGH BY NOW.
OH, EEK!
YOU'RE GONNA BEAT ME UP?
THAT'S SO SCARY!
I HAVE A BETTER IDEA.
WE'LL FIGHT, I'LL WIN,
AND YOU'LL STAY SAFELY OUTSIDE.
AGATHA WILL BE MAD AT ME IF LET HER FRIENDS GET HURT.

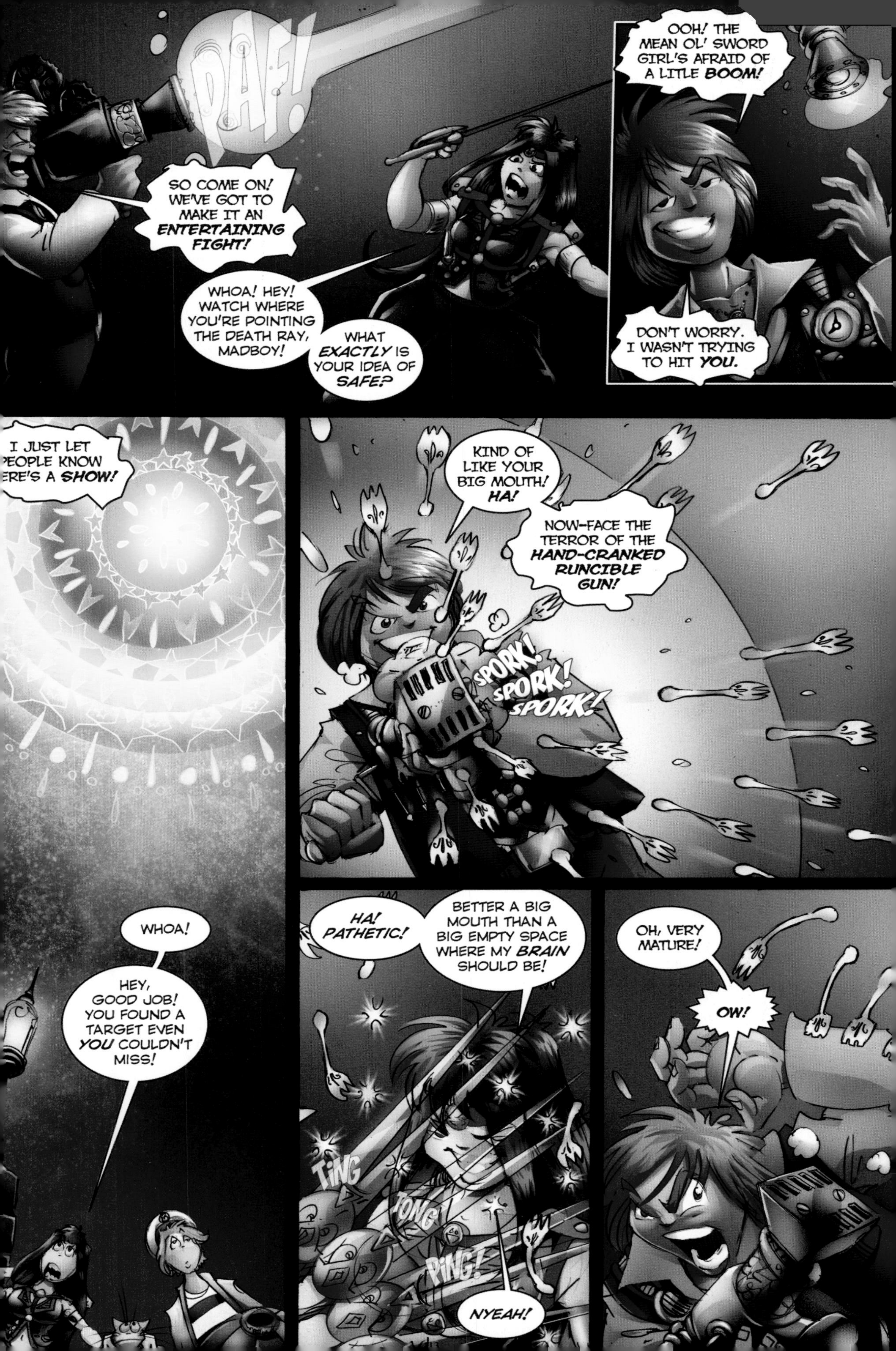
PAF!
SO COME ON! WE'VE GOT TO MAKE IT AN ENTERTAINING FIGHT!
WHOA! HEY! WATCH WHERE YOU'RE POINTING THE DEATH RAY, MADBOY!
WHAT EXACTLY IS YOUR IDEA OF SAFE?
OOH! THE MEAN OL' SWORD GIRL'S AFRAID OF A LITLE BOOM!
DON'T WORRY. I WASN'T TRYING TO HIT YOU.
I JUST LET PEOPLE KNOW ERE'S A SHOW!
KIND OF LIKE YOUR BIG MOUTH! HA!
NOW-FACE THE TERROR OF THE HAND-CRANKED RUNCIBLE GUN!
SPORK! SPORK! SPORK!
WHOA!
HEY, GOOD JOB! YOU FOUND A TARGET EVEN YOU COULDN'T MISS!
HA! PATHETIC!
BETTER A BIG MOUTH THAN A BIG EMPTY SPACE WHERE MY BRAIN SHOULD BE!
TING
TONG
PING!
NYEAH!
OH, VERY MATURE!
OW!

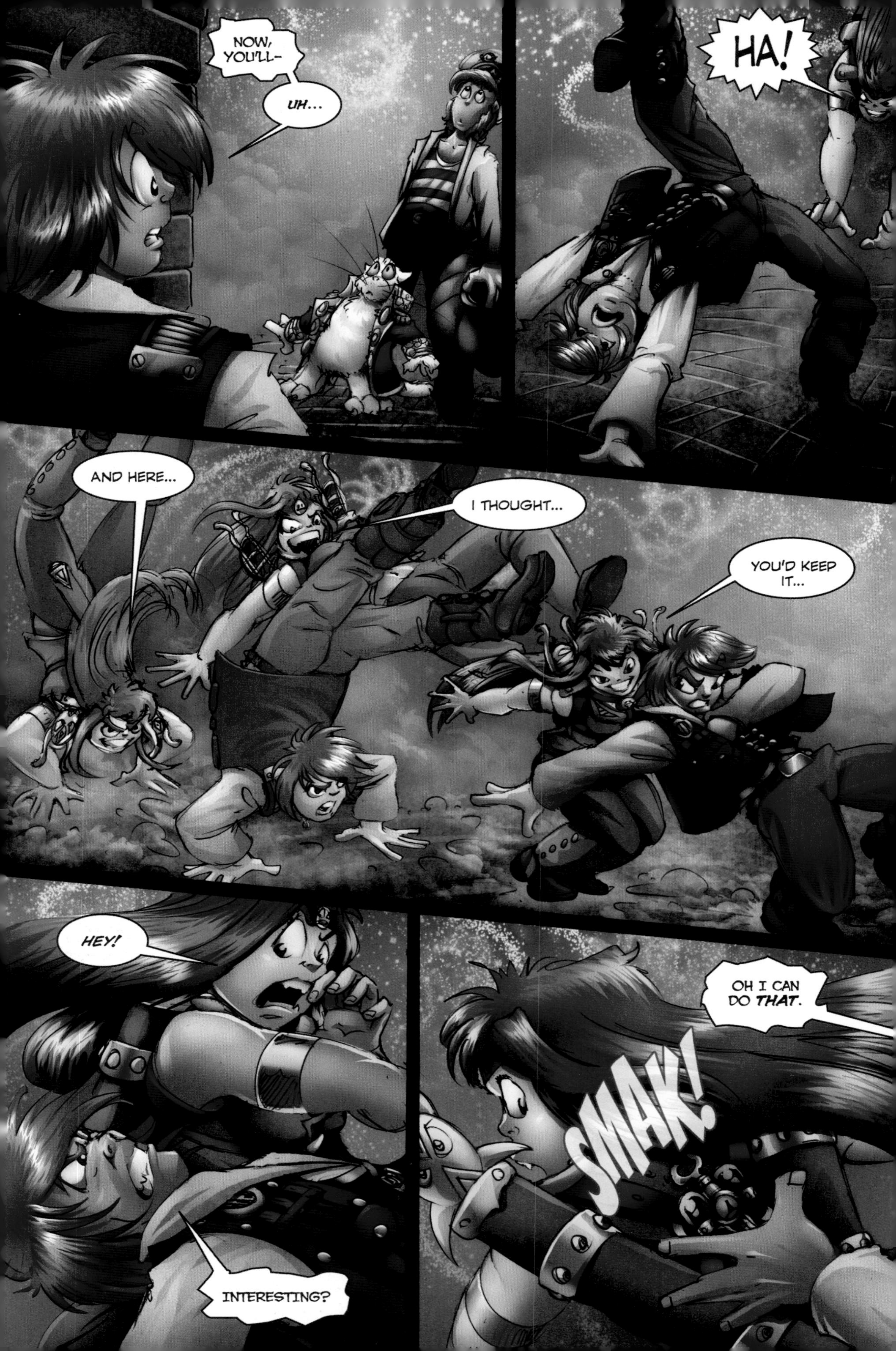
NOW, YOU'LL-
UH...
HA!
AND HERE...
I THOUGHT...
YOU'D KEEP IT...
HEY!
INTERESTING?
OH I CAN DO *THAT*.
SMAK!

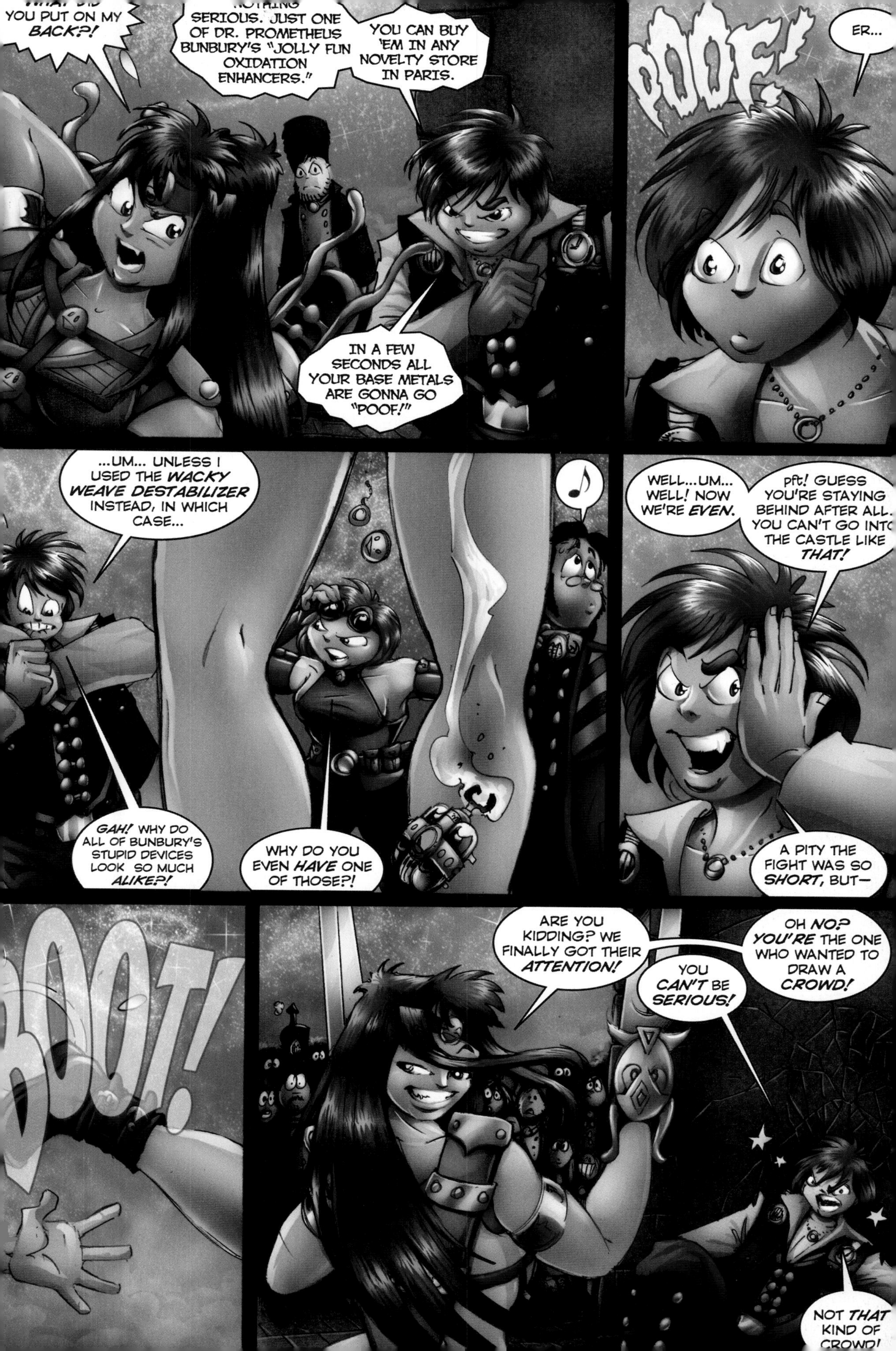
YOU PUT ON MY BACK?!
SERIOUS. JUST ONE OF DR. PROMETHEUS BUNBURY'S "JOLLY FUN OXIDATION ENHANCERS."
YOU CAN BUY 'EM IN ANY NOVELTY STORE IN PARIS.
IN A FEW SECONDS ALL YOUR BASE METALS ARE GONNA GO "POOF!"
POOF!
ER...
...UM... UNLESS I USED THE WACKY WEAVE DESTABILIZER INSTEAD, IN WHICH CASE...
GAH! WHY DO ALL OF BUNBURY'S STUPID DEVICES LOOK SO MUCH ALIKE?!
WHY DO YOU EVEN HAVE ONE OF THOSE?!
♪
WELL...UM... WELL! NOW WE'RE EVEN.
pft! GUESS YOU'RE STAYING BEHIND AFTER ALL. YOU CAN'T GO INTO THE CASTLE LIKE THAT!
A PITY THE FIGHT WAS SO SHORT, BUT—
BOOT!
ARE YOU KIDDING? WE FINALLY GOT THEIR ATTENTION!
YOU CAN'T BE SERIOUS!
OH NO? YOU'RE THE ONE WHO WANTED TO DRAW A CROWD!
NOT THAT KIND OF CROWD!

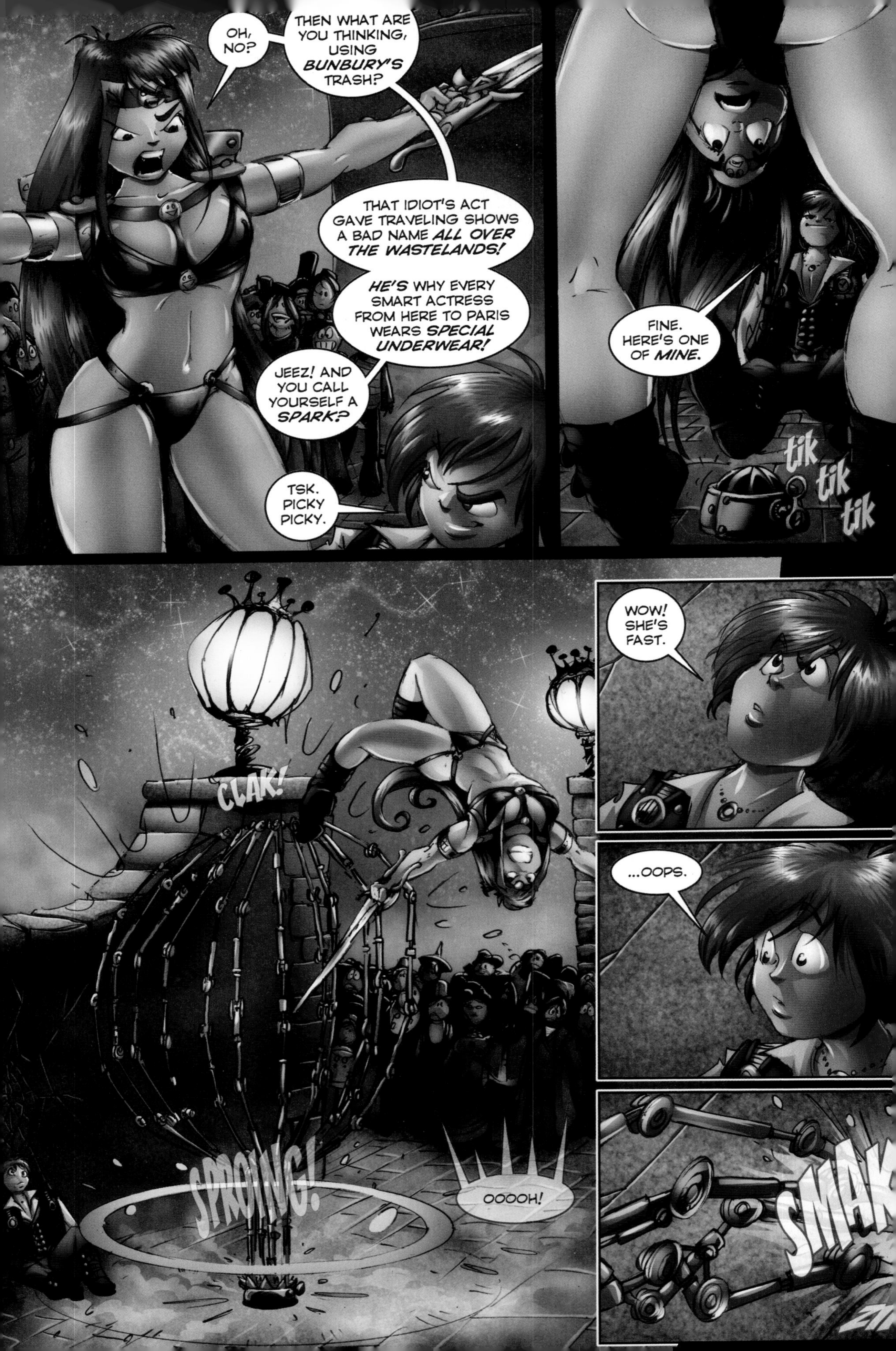
OH, NO?
THEN WHAT ARE YOU THINKING, USING BUNBURY'S TRASH?
THAT IDIOT'S ACT GAVE TRAVELING SHOWS A BAD NAME ALL OVER THE WASTELANDS!
HE'S WHY EVERY SMART ACTRESS FROM HERE TO PARIS WEARS SPECIAL UNDERWEAR!
JEEZ! AND YOU CALL YOURSELF A SPARK?
TSK. PICKY PICKY.
FINE. HERE'S ONE OF MINE.
tik tik tik
CLAK!
SPROING!
OOOOH!
WOW! SHE'S FAST.
...OOPS.
SMAK

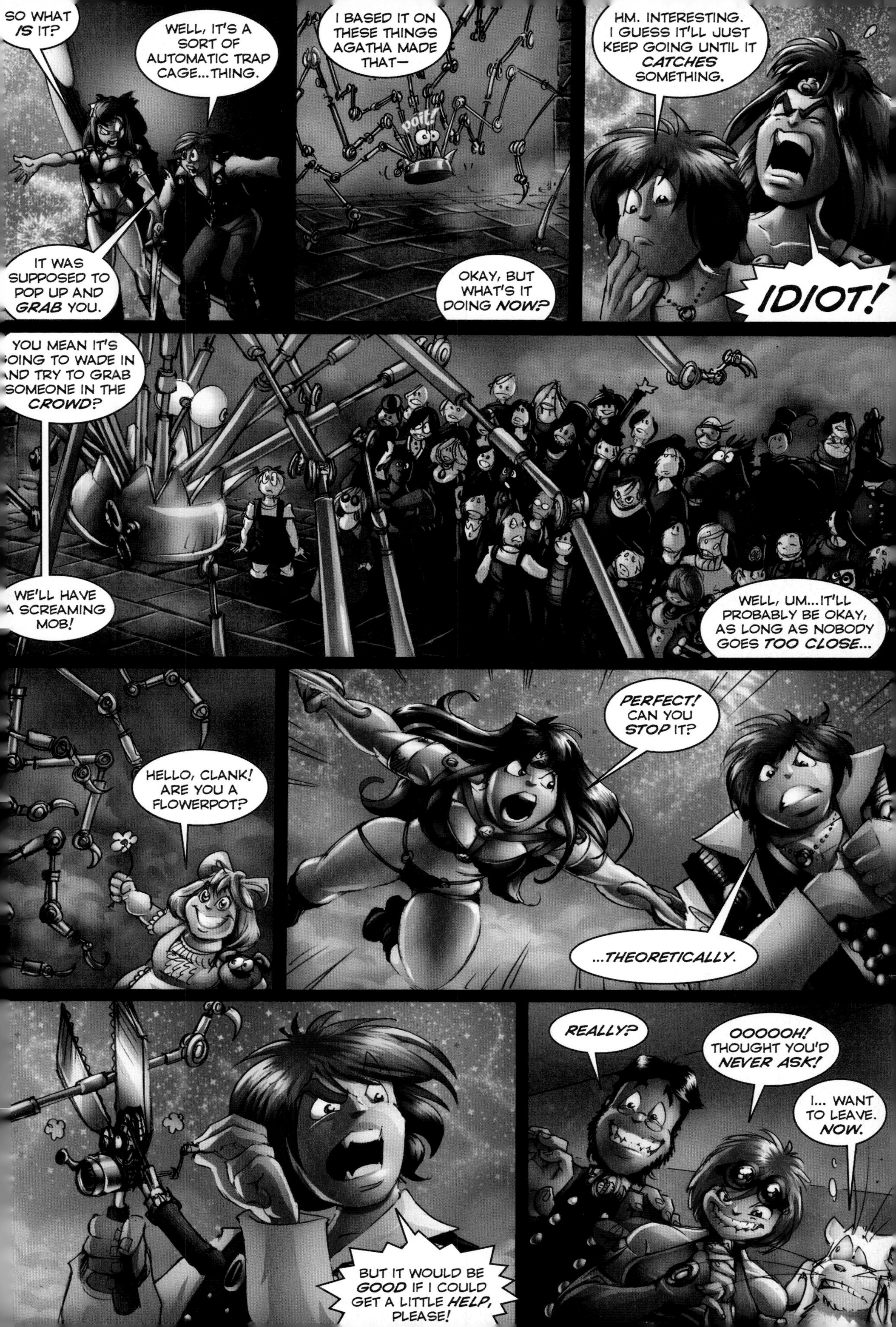

SO WHAT *IS* IT?
WELL, IT'S A SORT OF AUTOMATIC TRAP CAGE...THING.
IT WAS SUPPOSED TO POP UP AND *GRAB* YOU.
I BASED IT ON THESE THINGS AGATHA MADE THAT—
poit!
OKAY, BUT WHAT'S IT DOING *NOW?*
HM. INTERESTING. I GUESS IT'LL JUST KEEP GOING UNTIL IT *CATCHES* SOMETHING.
IDIOT!
YOU MEAN IT'S GOING TO WADE IN AND TRY TO GRAB SOMEONE IN THE *CROWD?*
WE'LL HAVE A SCREAMING MOB!
WELL, UM...IT'LL PROBABLY BE OKAY, AS LONG AS NOBODY GOES *TOO CLOSE...*
HELLO, CLANK! ARE YOU A FLOWERPOT?
PERFECT! CAN YOU *STOP* IT?
...*THEORETICALLY.*
BUT IT WOULD BE *GOOD* IF I COULD GET A LITTLE *HELP,* PLEASE!
REALLY?
OOOOOH! THOUGHT YOU'D *NEVER ASK!*
I... WANT TO LEAVE. *NOW.*

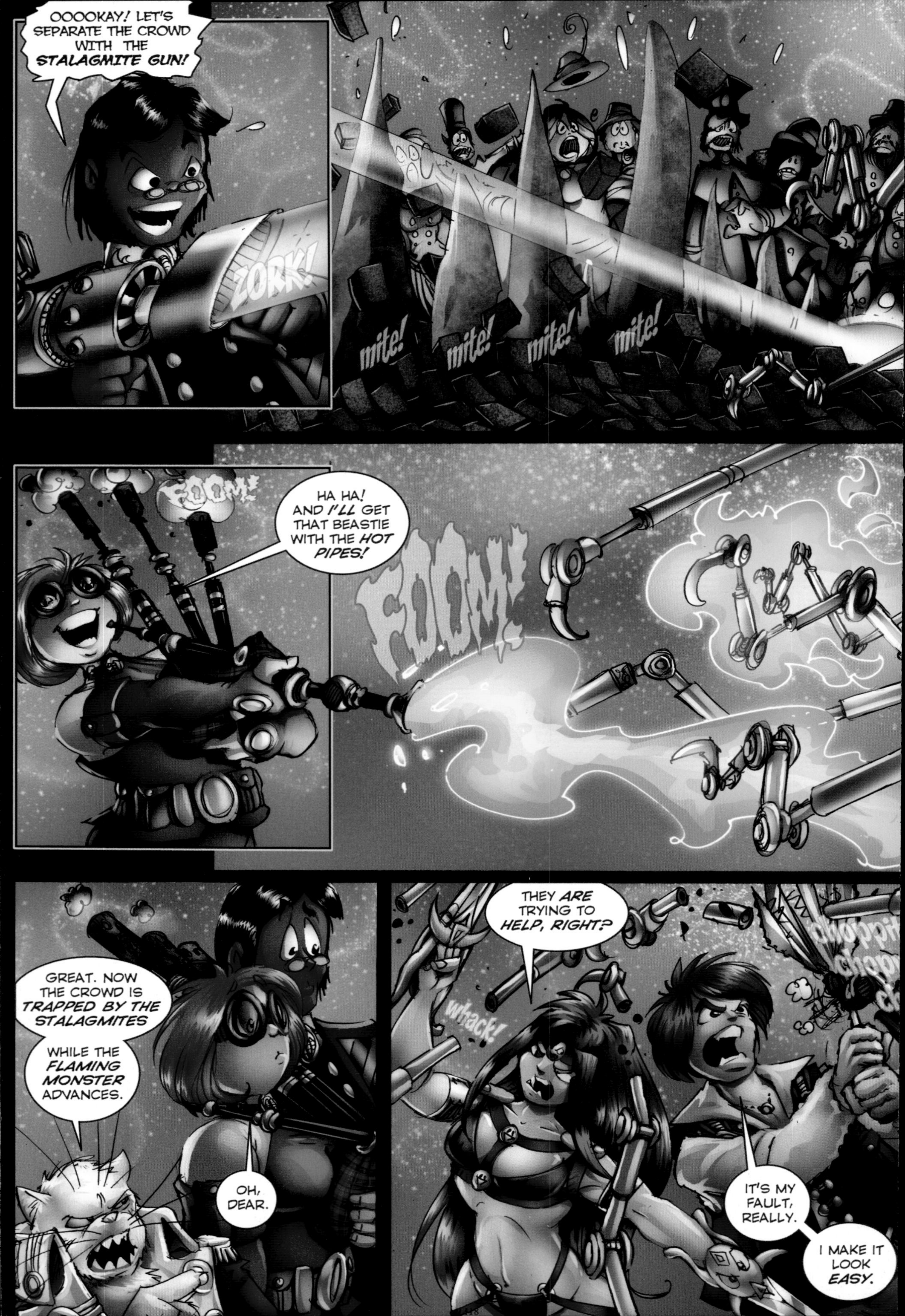

OOOOKAY! LET'S SEPARATE THE CROWD WITH THE STALAGMITE GUN!
ZORK!
mite! mite! mite! mite!
FOOM!
HA HA! AND I'LL GET THAT BEASTIE WITH THE HOT PIPES!
FOOM!
GREAT. NOW THE CROWD IS TRAPPED BY THE STALAGMITES
WHILE THE FLAMING MONSTER ADVANCES.
OH, DEAR.
THEY ARE TRYING TO HELP, RIGHT?
whack!
IT'S MY FAULT, REALLY.
I MAKE IT LOOK EASY.

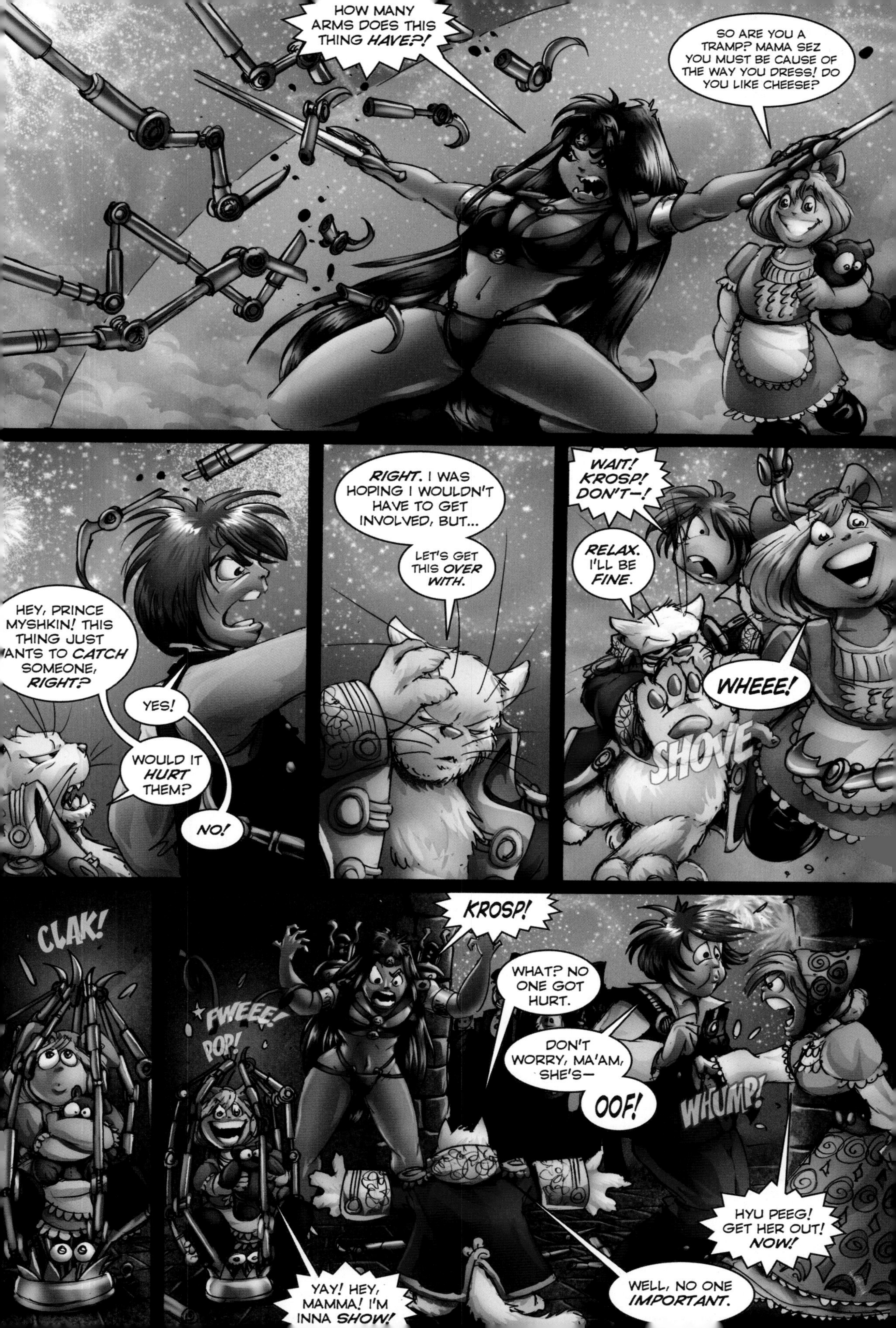
HOW MANY ARMS DOES THIS THING *HAVE?!*
SO ARE YOU A TRAMP? MAMA SEZ YOU MUST BE CAUSE OF THE WAY YOU DRESS! DO YOU LIKE CHEESE?
HEY, PRINCE MYSHKIN! THIS THING JUST ANTS TO *CATCH* SOMEONE, *RIGHT?*
YES!
WOULD IT *HURT* THEM?
NO!
RIGHT. I WAS HOPING I WOULDN'T HAVE TO GET INVOLVED, BUT...
LET'S GET THIS *OVER* WITH.
WAIT! KROSP! DON'T—!
RELAX. I'LL BE *FINE.*
WHEEE!
SHOVE
CLAK!
KROSP!
FWEEE!
POP!
WHAT? NO ONE GOT HURT.
DON'T WORRY, MA'AM, SHE'S—
OOF!
WHUMP!
HYU PEEG! GET HER OUT! *NOW!*
YAY! HEY, MAMMA! I'M INNA *SHOW!*
WELL, NO ONE *IMPORTANT.*

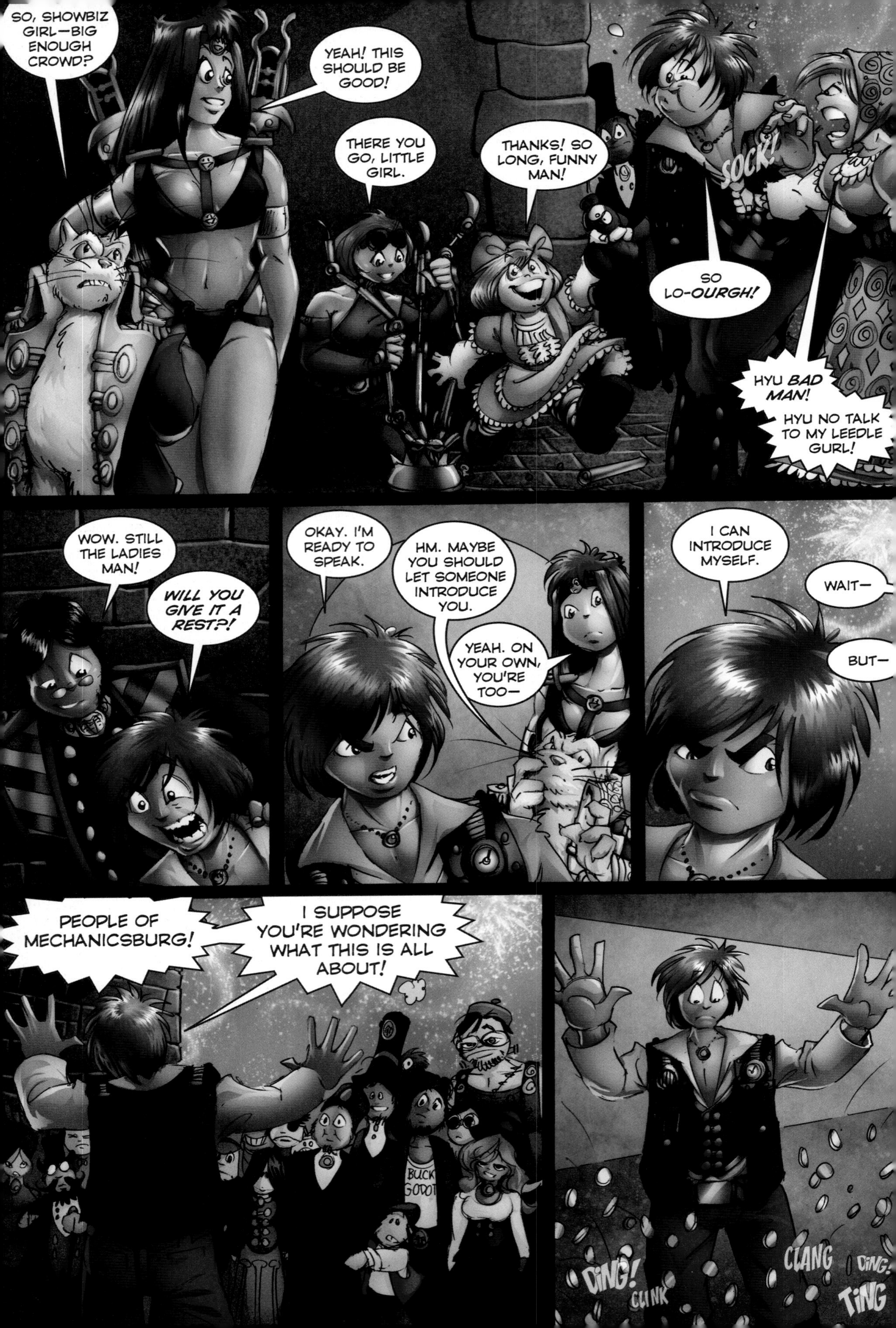
SO, SHOWBIZ GIRL—BIG ENOUGH CROWD?
YEAH! THIS SHOULD BE GOOD!
THERE YOU GO, LITTLE GIRL.
THANKS! SO LONG, FUNNY MAN!
SOCK!
SO LO-OURGH!
HYU BAD MAN!
HYU NO TALK TO MY LEEDLE GURL!
WOW. STILL THE LADIES MAN!
WILL YOU GIVE IT A REST?!
OKAY. I'M READY TO SPEAK.
HM. MAYBE YOU SHOULD LET SOMEONE INTRODUCE YOU.
YEAH. ON YOUR OWN, YOU'RE TOO—
I CAN INTRODUCE MYSELF.
WAIT—
BUT—
PEOPLE OF MECHANICSBURG!
I SUPPOSE YOU'RE WONDERING WHAT THIS IS ALL ABOUT!
BUCK GODOT
DING!
CLINK
CLANG
DING!
TING

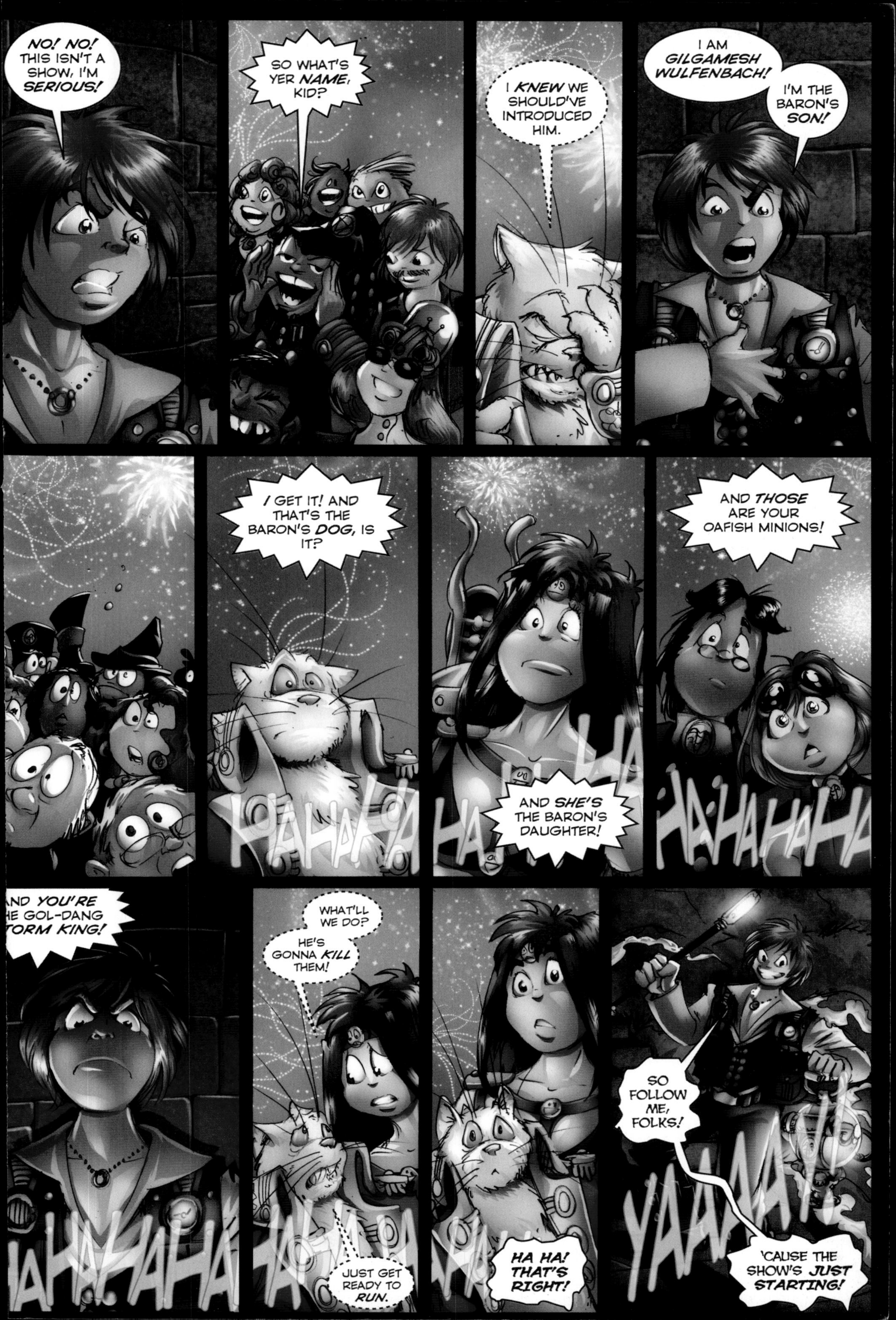
NO! NO! THIS ISN'T A SHOW, I'M SERIOUS!
SO WHAT'S YER NAME, KID?
I KNEW WE SHOULD'VE INTRODUCED HIM.
I AM GILGAMESH WULFENBACH!
I'M THE BARON'S SON!
I GET IT! AND THAT'S THE BARON'S DOG, IS IT?
HAHAHA
AND SHE'S THE BARON'S DAUGHTER!
HA HA
AND THOSE ARE YOUR OAFISH MINIONS!
HAHAHAHA
AND YOU'RE THE GOL-DANG STORM KING!
HAHAHAHA
WHAT'LL WE DO?
HE'S GONNA KILL THEM!
JUST GET READY TO RUN.
HA HA! THAT'S RIGHT!
SO FOLLOW ME, FOLKS!
YAAAAY!
'CAUSE THE SHOW'S JUST STARTING!

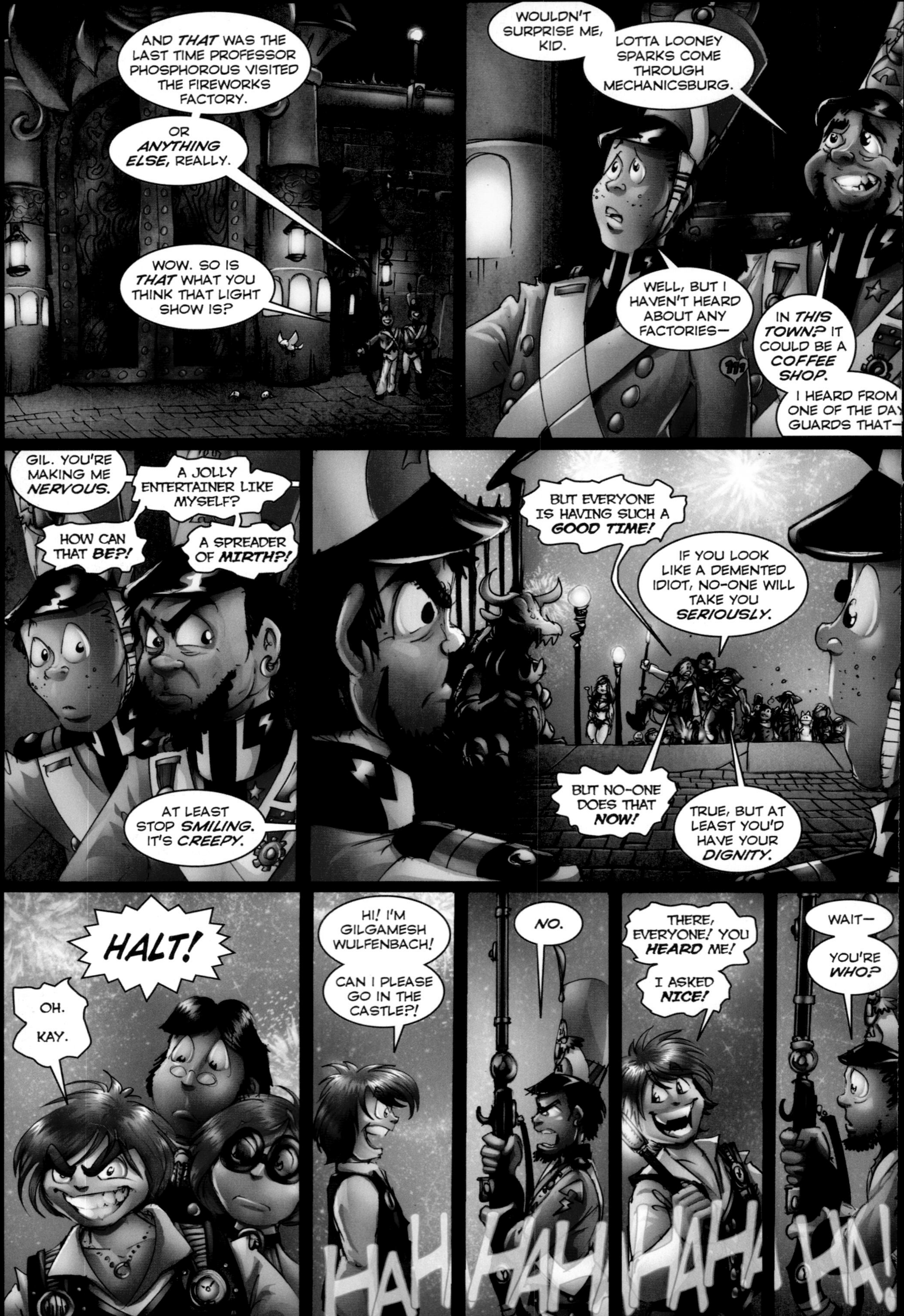
AND THAT WAS THE LAST TIME PROFESSOR PHOSPHOROUS VISITED THE FIREWORKS FACTORY.
OR ANYTHING ELSE, REALLY.
WOW. SO IS THAT WHAT YOU THINK THAT LIGHT SHOW IS?
WOULDN'T SURPRISE ME, KID.
LOTTA LOONEY SPARKS COME THROUGH MECHANICSBURG.
WELL, BUT I HAVEN'T HEARD ABOUT ANY FACTORIES—
IN THIS TOWN? IT COULD BE A COFFEE SHOP.
I HEARD FROM ONE OF THE DAY GUARDS THAT—
GIL. YOU'RE MAKING ME NERVOUS.
A JOLLY ENTERTAINER LIKE MYSELF?
HOW CAN THAT BE?!
A SPREADER OF MIRTH?!
AT LEAST STOP SMILING. IT'S CREEPY.
BUT EVERYONE IS HAVING SUCH A GOOD TIME!
IF YOU LOOK LIKE A DEMENTED IDIOT, NO-ONE WILL TAKE YOU SERIOUSLY.
BUT NO-ONE DOES THAT NOW!
TRUE, BUT AT LEAST YOU'D HAVE YOUR DIGNITY.
HALT!
OH.
KAY.
HI! I'M GILGAMESH WULFENBACH!
CAN I PLEASE GO IN THE CASTLE?!
NO.
THERE, EVERYONE! YOU HEARD ME!
I ASKED NICE!
WAIT—
YOU'RE WHO?
HAH HAH HAH HA!

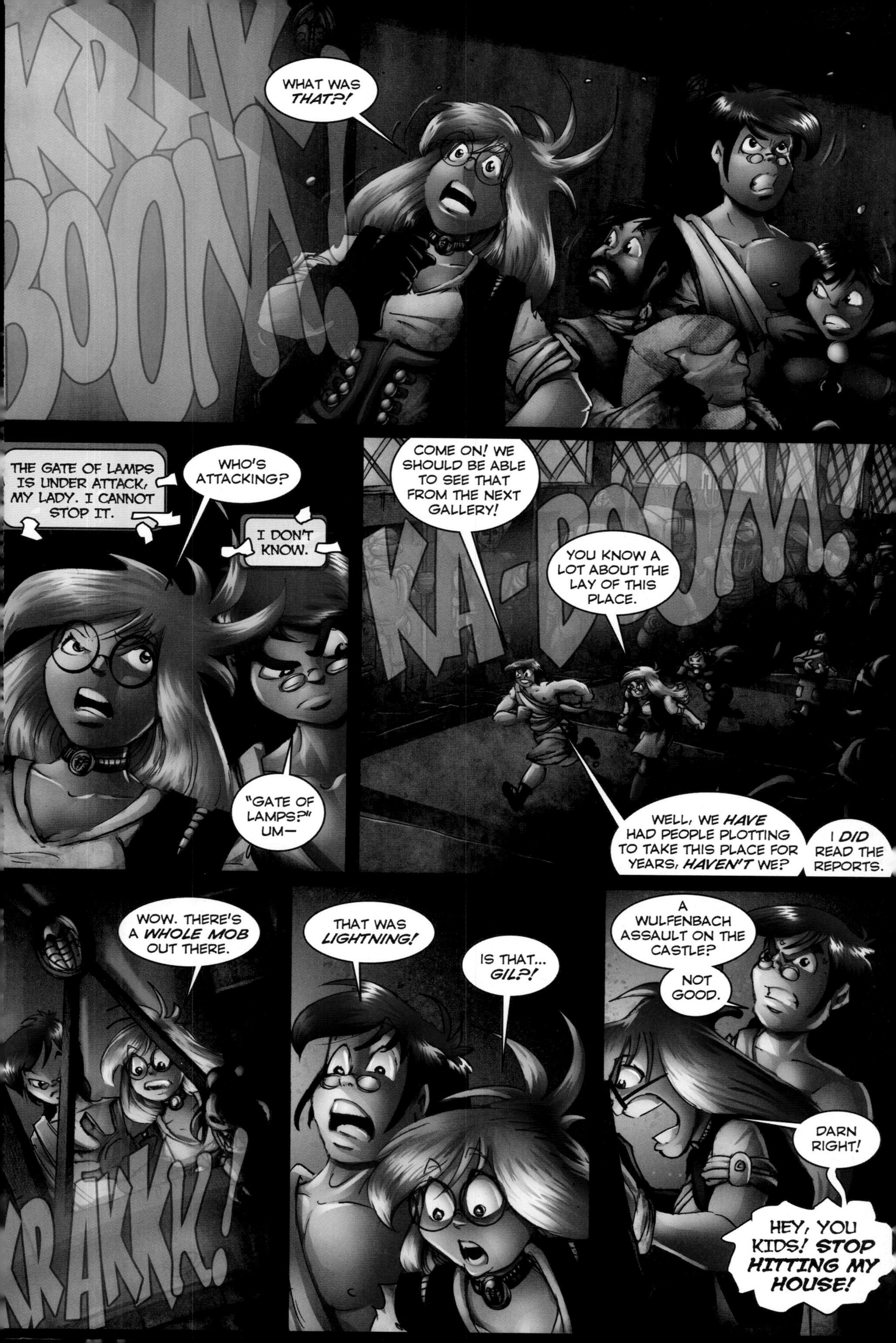
KRAK-BOOM!!
WHAT WAS THAT?!
THE GATE OF LAMPS IS UNDER ATTACK, MY LADY. I CANNOT STOP IT.
WHO'S ATTACKING?
I DON'T KNOW.
"GATE OF LAMPS?" UM—
COME ON! WE SHOULD BE ABLE TO SEE THAT FROM THE NEXT GALLERY!
KA-BOOM!!
YOU KNOW A LOT ABOUT THE LAY OF THIS PLACE.
WELL, WE HAVE HAD PEOPLE PLOTTING TO TAKE THIS PLACE FOR YEARS, HAVEN'T WE?
I DID READ THE REPORTS.
WOW. THERE'S A WHOLE MOB OUT THERE.
KRAKKK!
THAT WAS LIGHTNING!
IS THAT... GIL?!
A WULFENBACH ASSAULT ON THE CASTLE?
NOT GOOD.
DARN RIGHT!
HEY, YOU KIDS! STOP HITTING MY HOUSE!

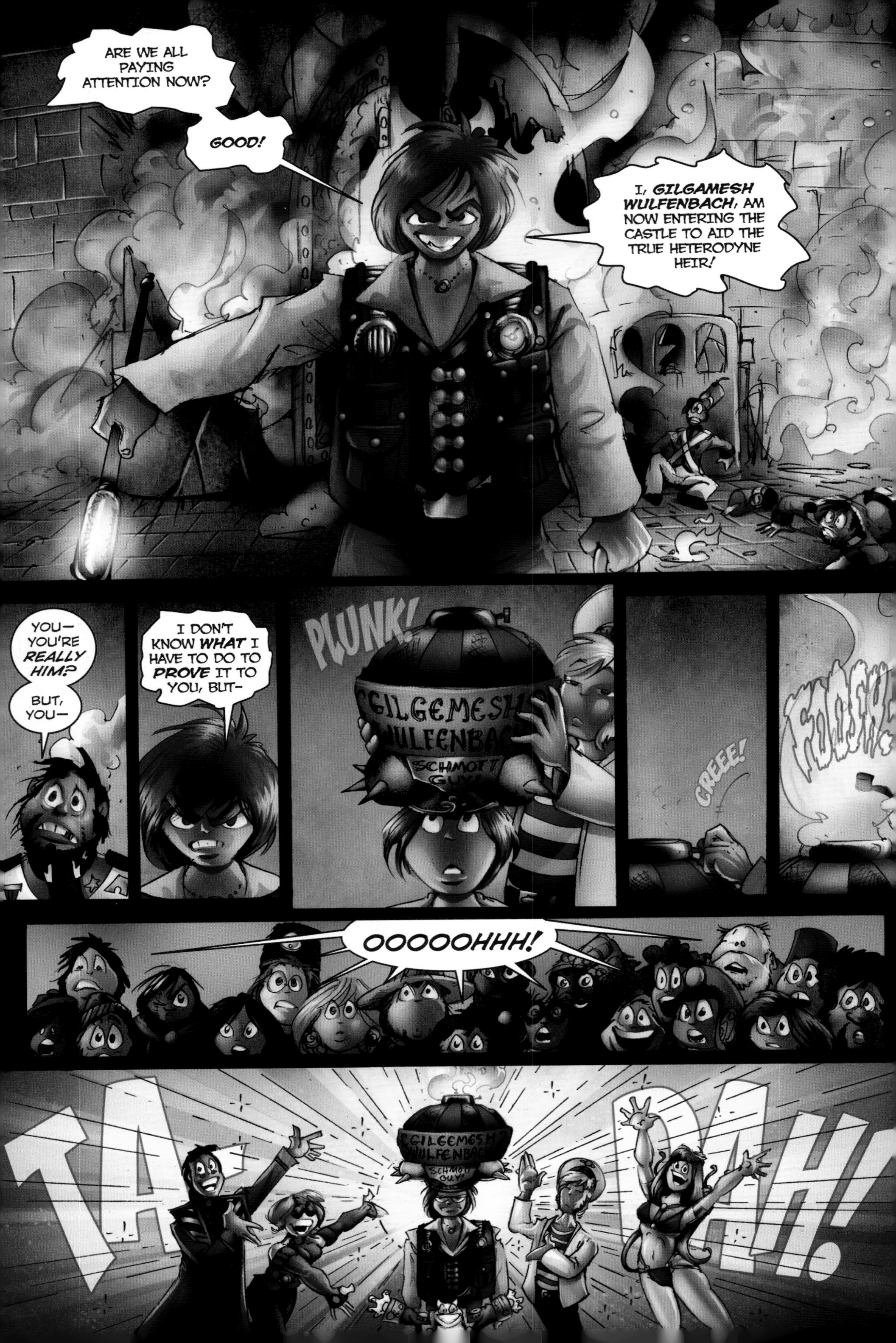

ARE WE ALL PAYING ATTENTION NOW?
GOOD!
I, GILGAMESH WULFENBACH, AM NOW ENTERING THE CASTLE TO AID THE TRUE HETERODYNE HEIR!
YOU— YOU'RE REALLY HIM?
BUT, YOU—
I DON'T KNOW WHAT I HAVE TO DO TO PROVE IT TO YOU, BUT-
PLUNK!
GILGEMESH WULFENBACH
SCHMOTT GUY!
CREEE!
OOOOOHHH!
TA DAH!

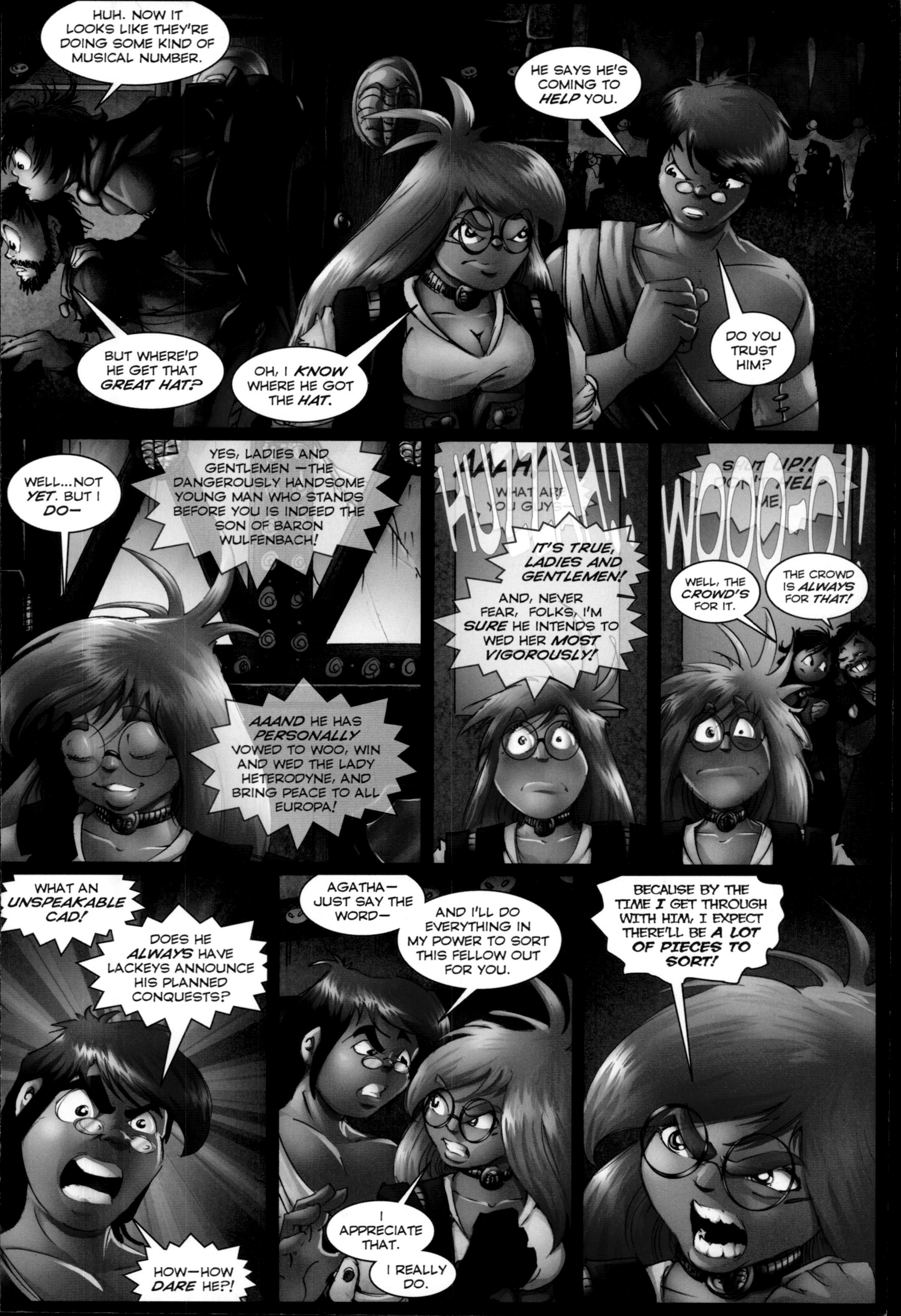
HUH. NOW IT LOOKS LIKE THEY'RE DOING SOME KIND OF MUSICAL NUMBER.
BUT WHERE'D HE GET THAT GREAT HAT?
OH, I KNOW WHERE HE GOT THE HAT.
HE SAYS HE'S COMING TO HELP YOU.
DO YOU TRUST HIM?
WELL...NOT YET. BUT I DO—
YES, LADIES AND GENTLEMEN —THE DANGEROUSLY HANDSOME YOUNG MAN WHO STANDS BEFORE YOU IS INDEED THE SON OF BARON WULFENBACH!
AAAND HE HAS PERSONALLY VOWED TO WOO, WIN AND WED THE LADY HETERODYNE, AND BRING PEACE TO ALL EUROPA!
IT'S TRUE, LADIES AND GENTLEMEN!
AND, NEVER FEAR, FOLKS, I'M SURE HE INTENDS TO WED HER MOST VIGOROUSLY!
WELL, THE CROWD'S FOR IT.
THE CROWD IS ALWAYS FOR THAT!
WHAT AN UNSPEAKABLE CAD!
DOES HE ALWAYS HAVE LACKEYS ANNOUNCE HIS PLANNED CONQUESTS?
HOW—HOW DARE HE?!
AGATHA— JUST SAY THE WORD—
AND I'LL DO EVERYTHING IN MY POWER TO SORT THIS FELLOW OUT FOR YOU.
I APPRECIATE THAT.
I REALLY DO.
BECAUSE BY THE TIME I GET THROUGH WITH HIM, I EXPECT THERE'LL BE A LOT OF PIECES TO SORT!

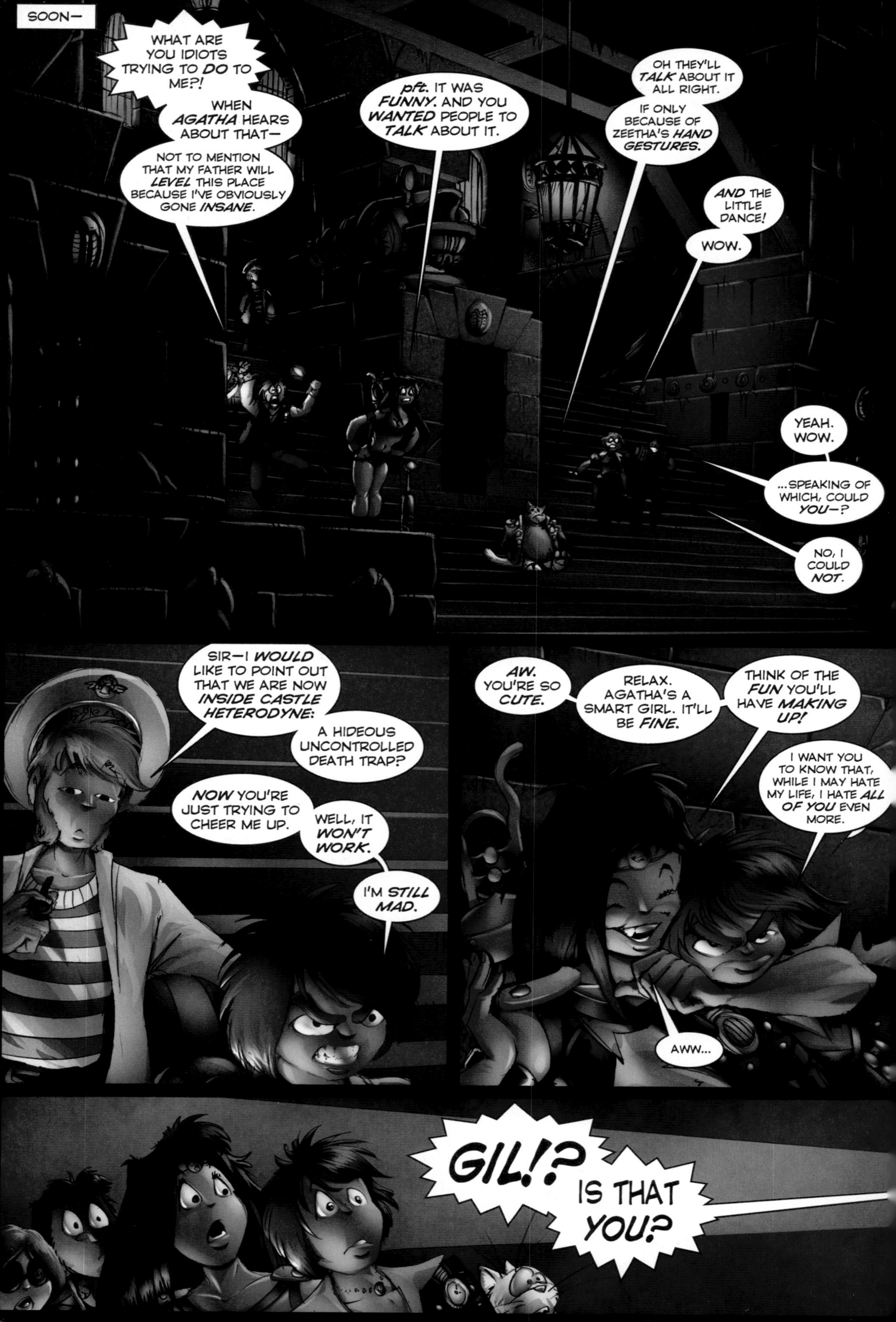
SOON—
WHAT ARE YOU IDIOTS TRYING TO DO TO ME?!
WHEN AGATHA HEARS ABOUT THAT—
NOT TO MENTION THAT MY FATHER WILL LEVEL THIS PLACE BECAUSE I'VE OBVIOUSLY GONE INSANE.
pft. IT WAS FUNNY. AND YOU WANTED PEOPLE TO TALK ABOUT IT.
OH THEY'LL TALK ABOUT IT ALL RIGHT.
IF ONLY BECAUSE OF ZEETHA'S HAND GESTURES.
AND THE LITTLE DANCE!
WOW.
YEAH. WOW.
...SPEAKING OF WHICH, COULD YOU—?
NO, I COULD NOT.
SIR—I WOULD LIKE TO POINT OUT THAT WE ARE NOW INSIDE CASTLE HETERODYNE:
A HIDEOUS UNCONTROLLED DEATH TRAP?
NOW YOU'RE JUST TRYING TO CHEER ME UP.
WELL, IT WON'T WORK.
I'M STILL MAD.
AW. YOU'RE SO CUTE.
RELAX. AGATHA'S A SMART GIRL. IT'LL BE FINE.
THINK OF THE FUN YOU'LL HAVE MAKING UP!
I WANT YOU TO KNOW THAT, WHILE I MAY HATE MY LIFE, I HATE ALL OF YOU EVEN MORE.
AWW...
GIL!?
IS THAT YOU?

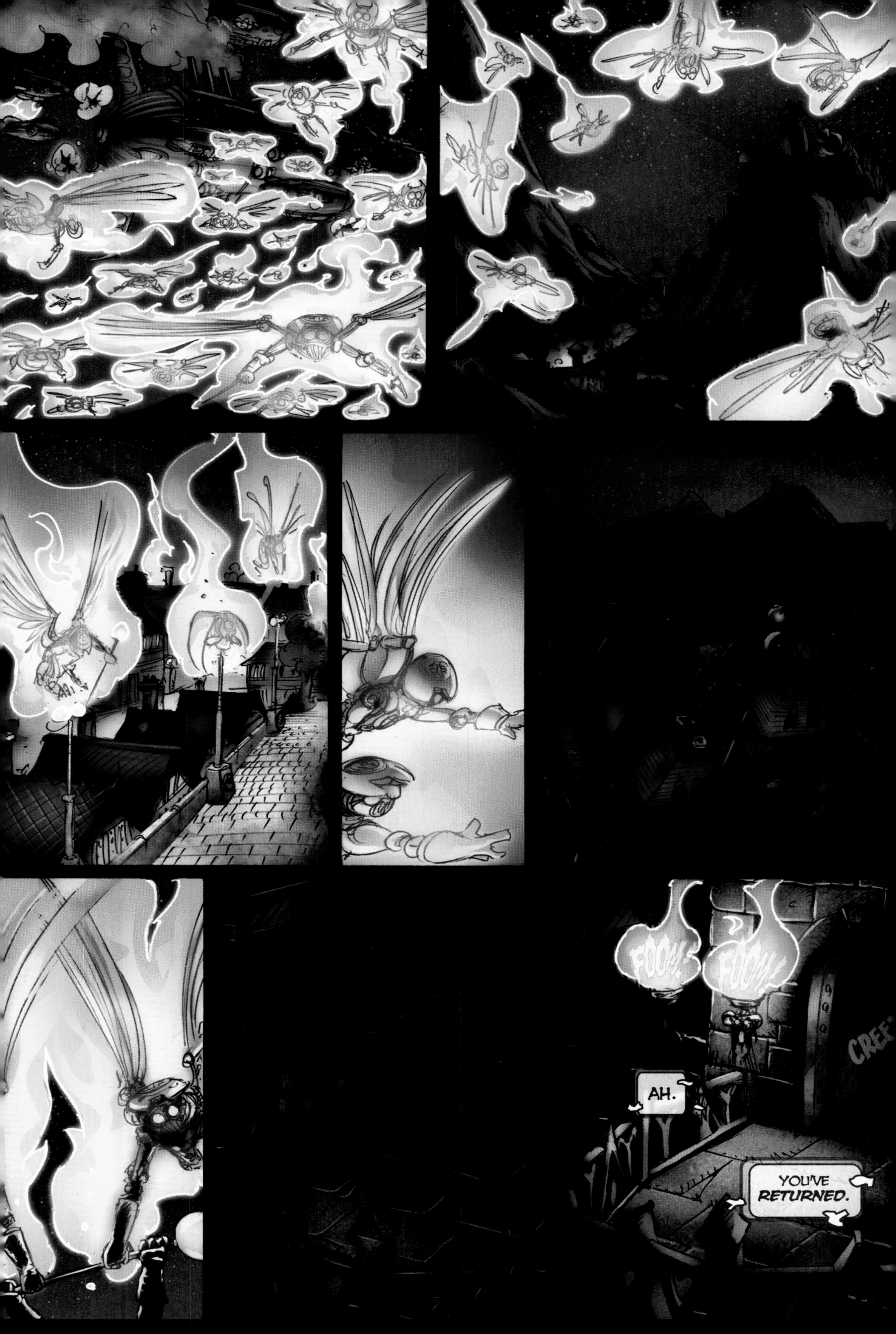
FOOM!
FOOM!
AH.
YOU'VE RETURNED.

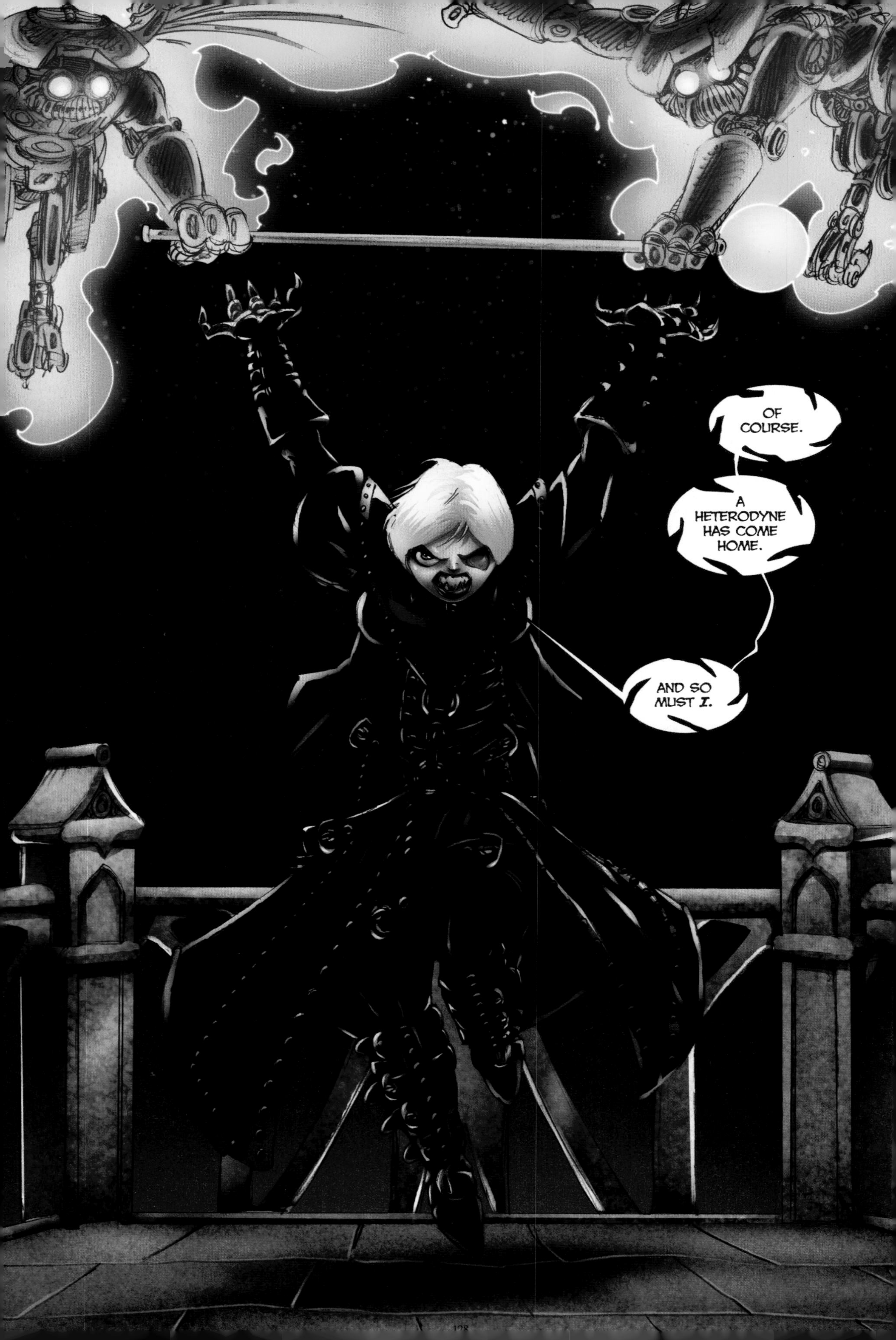
OF COURSE.
A HETERODYNE HAS COME HOME.
AND SO MUST I.

TO BE CONTINUED IN:

GIRL GENIUS® Book NINE

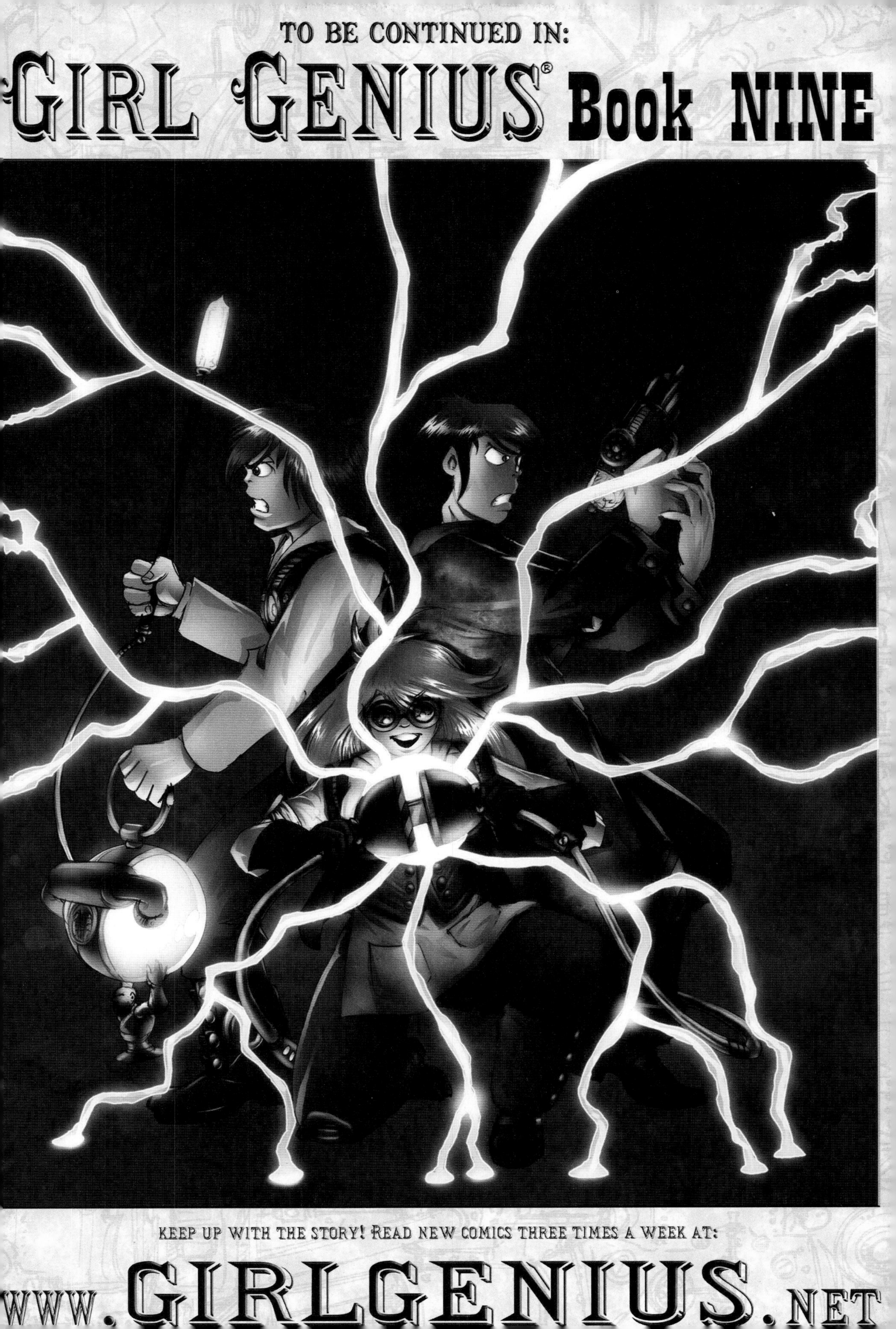

KEEP UP WITH THE STORY! READ NEW COMICS THREE TIMES A WEEK AT:

WWW.GIRLGENIUS.NET

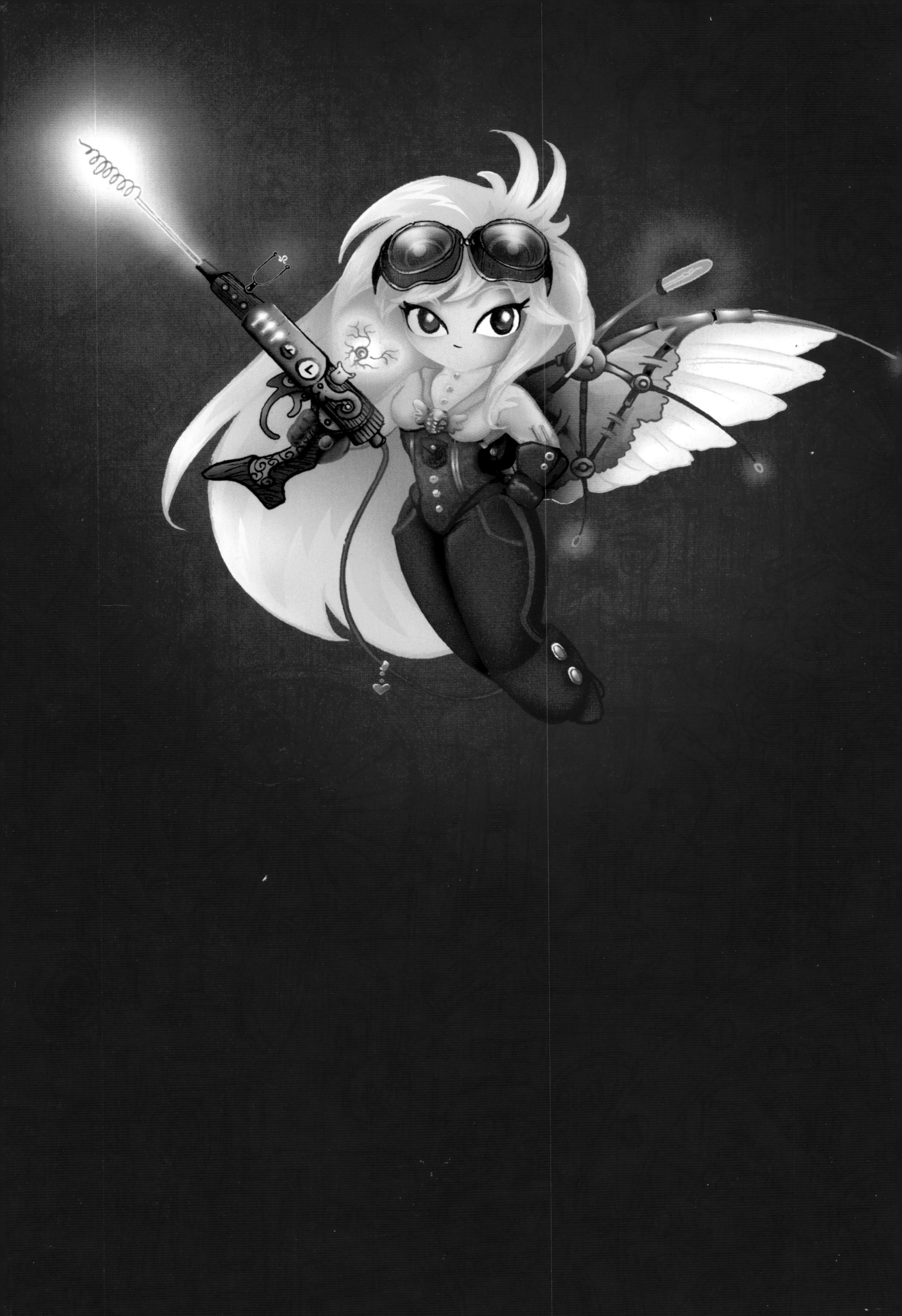

ART BY KAJA FOGLIO

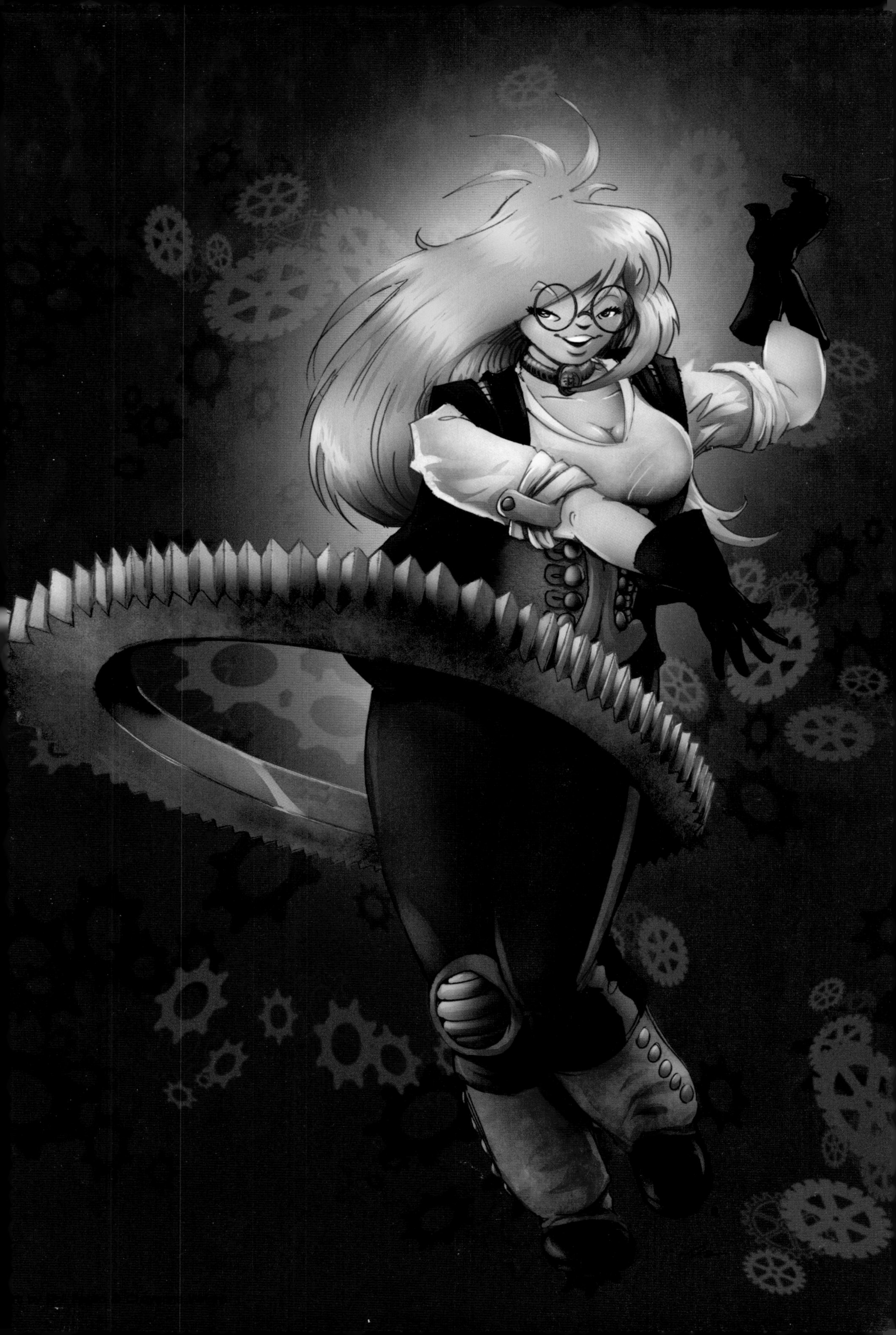

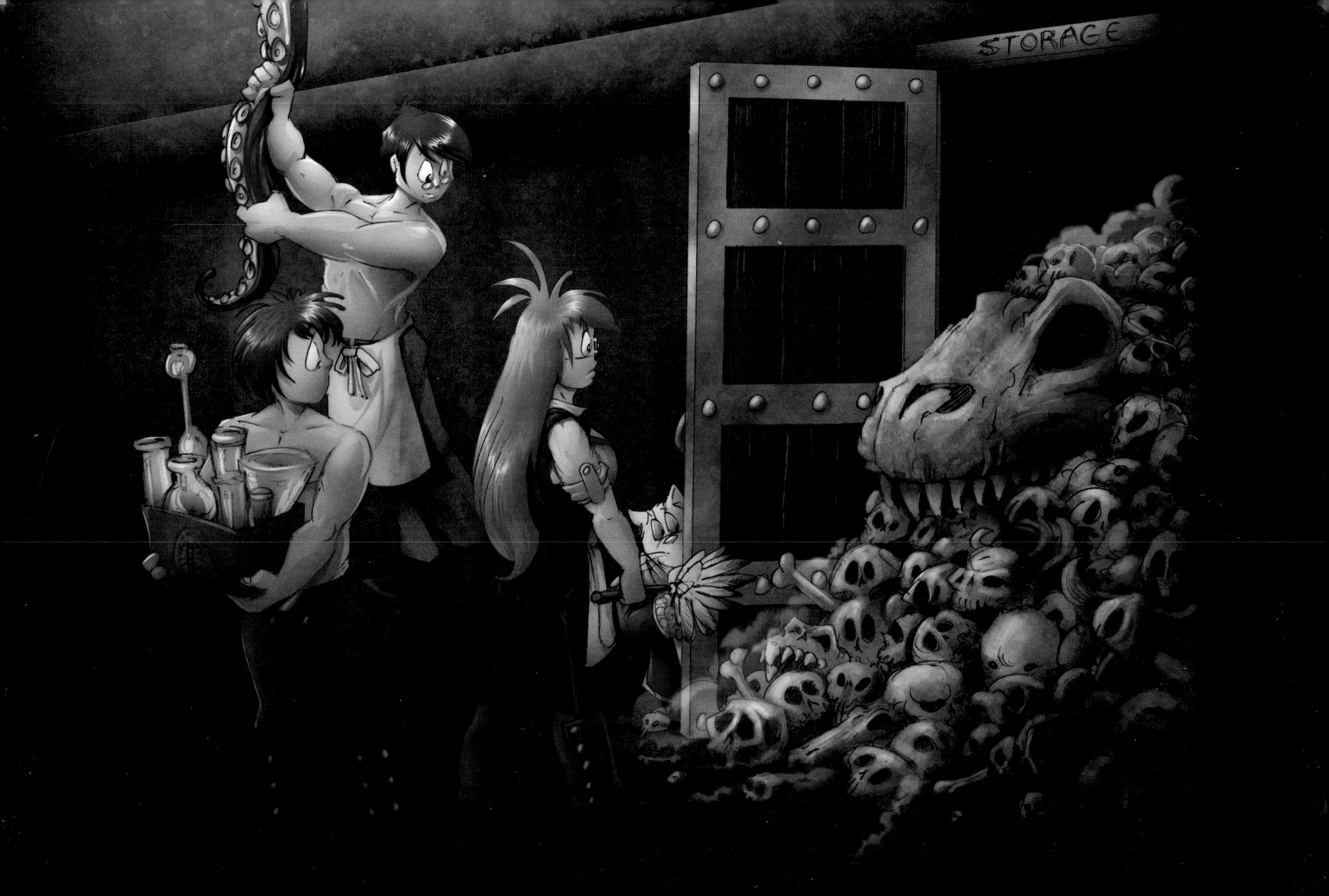
STORAGE

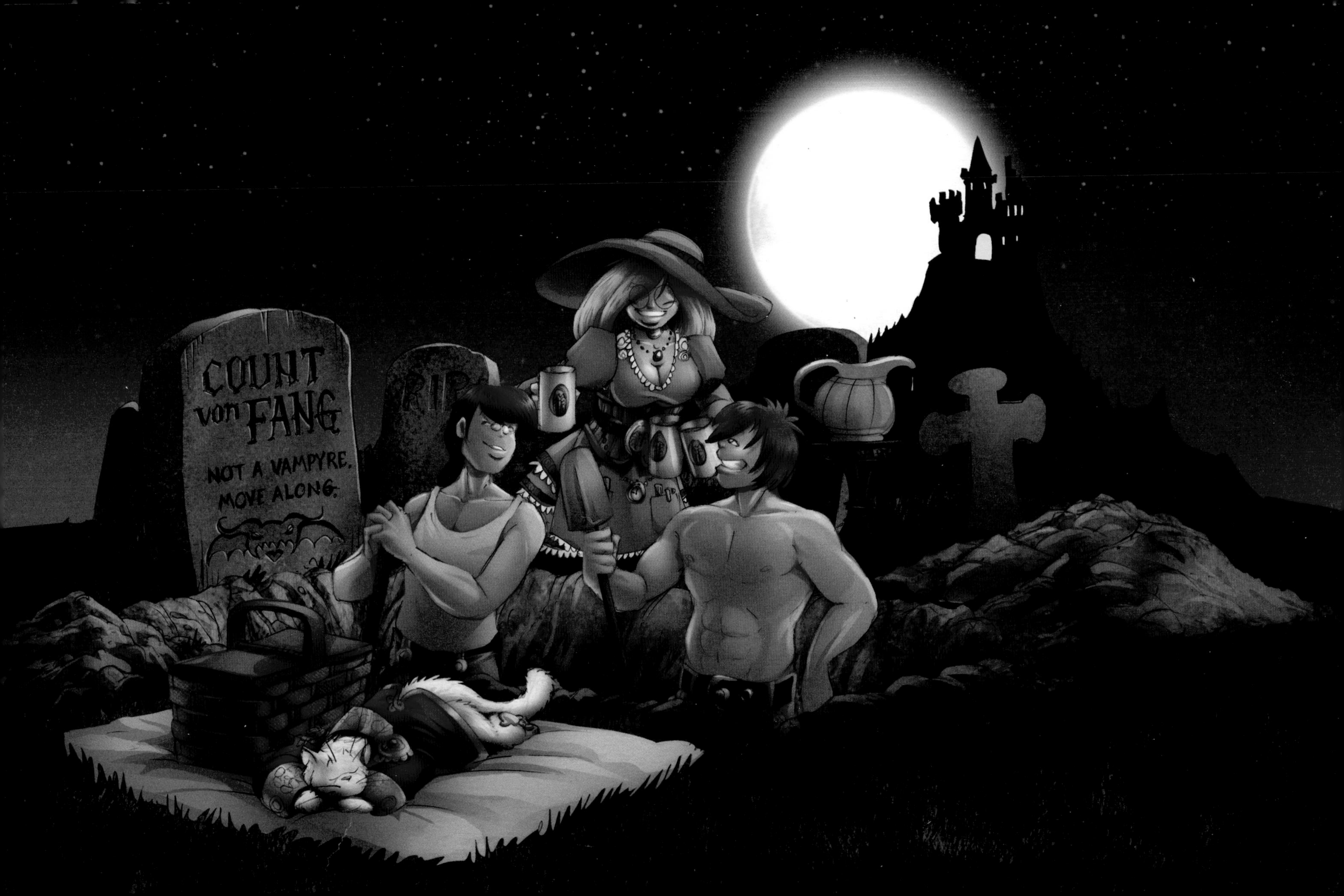
COUNT von FANG
NOT A VAMPYRE. MOVE ALONG.
RIP

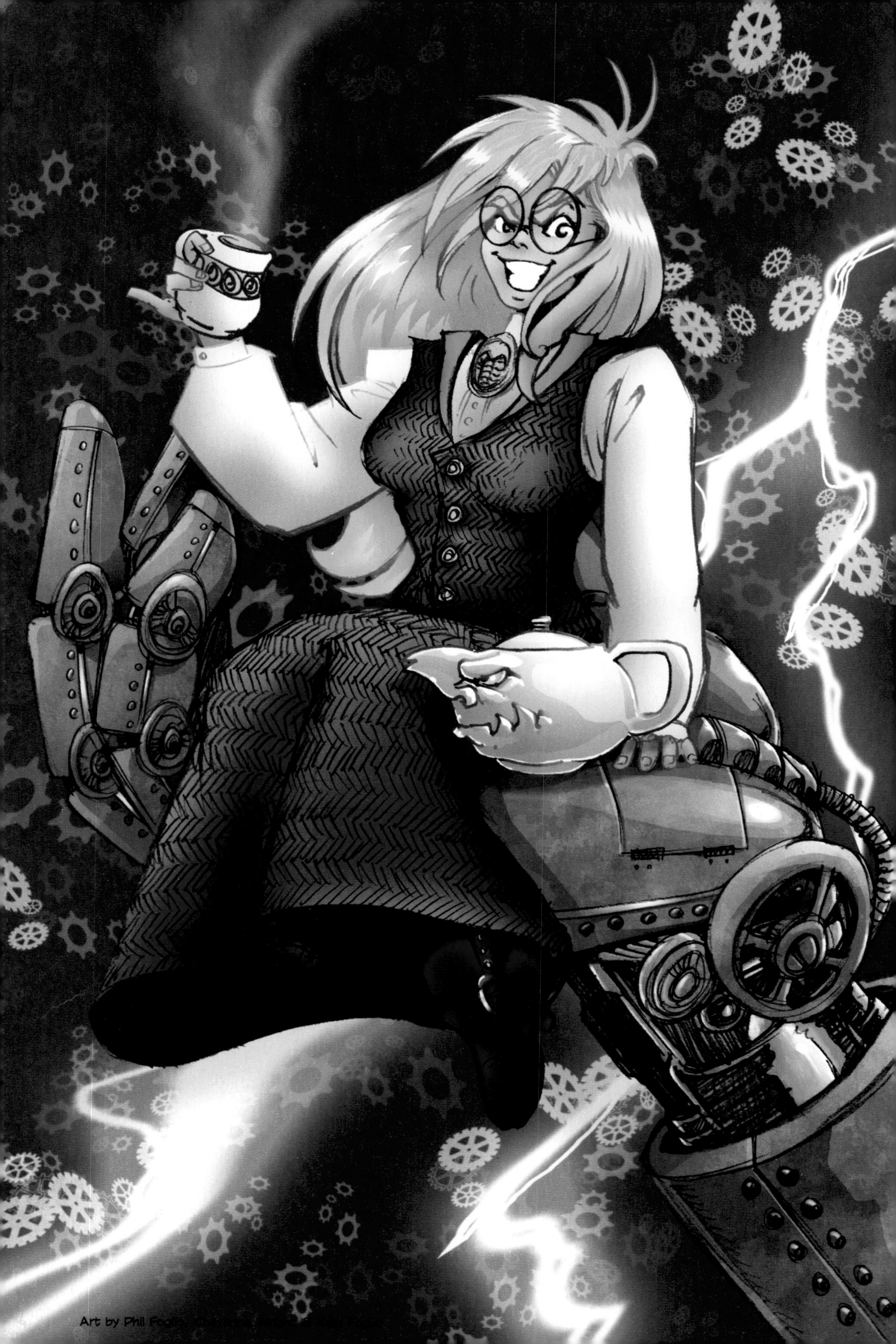

Art by Phil

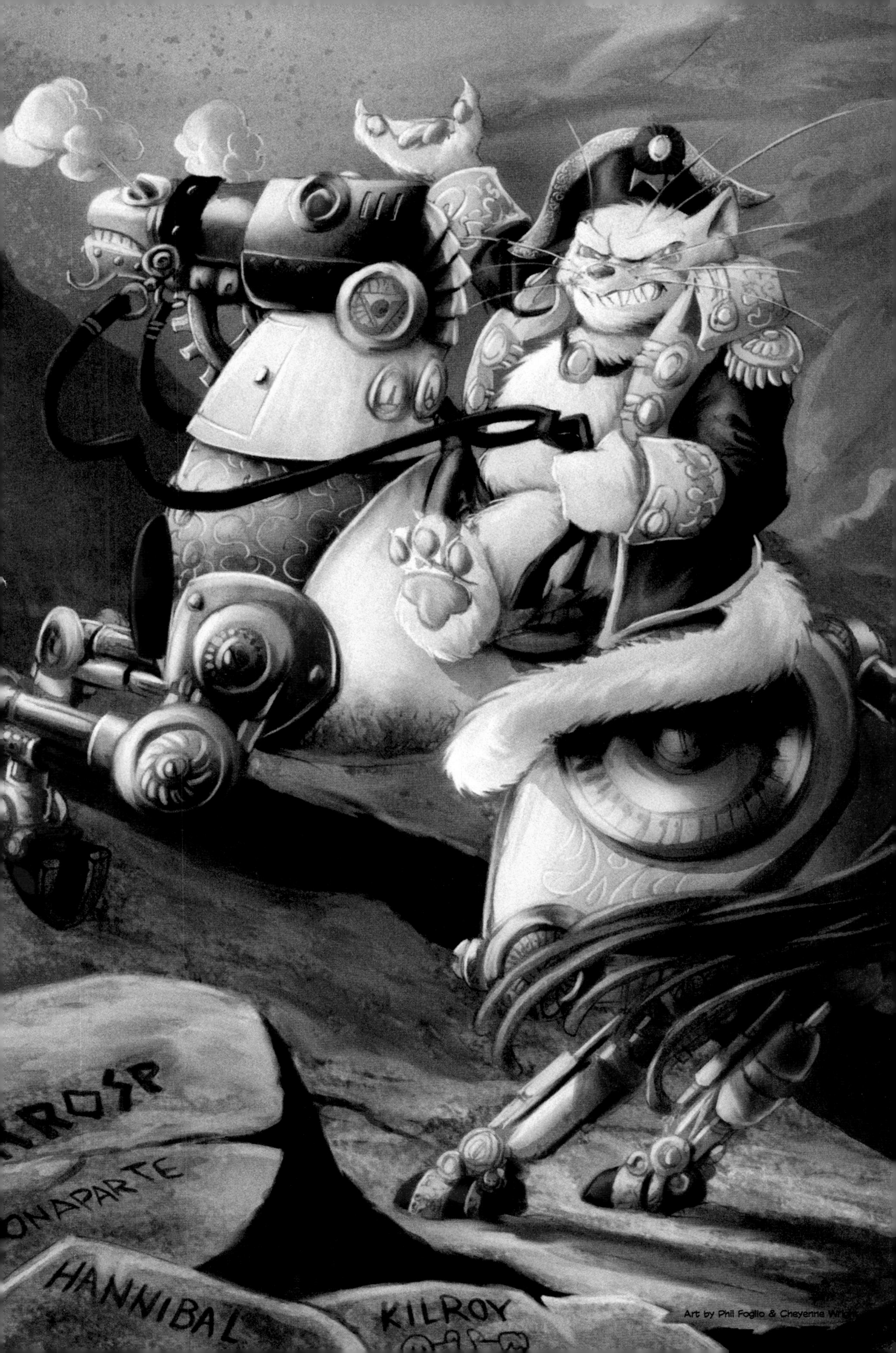
ROSP
ONAPARTE
HANNIBAL
KILROY
Art by Phil Foglio & Cheyenne Wri

READ MORE COMICS ONLINE AT:

WWW.GIRLGENIUS.NET

MONDAY • WEDNESDAY • FRIDAY

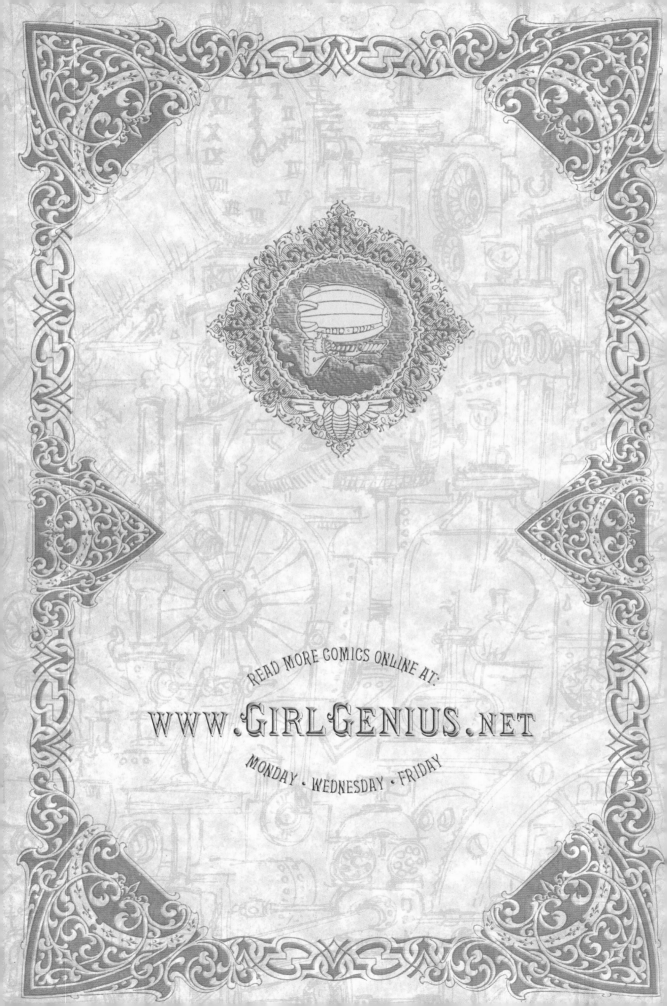